Asian Business Groups

CHANDOS
ASIAN STUDIES SERIES:
CONTEMPORARY ISSUES AND TRENDS

Series Editor: Professor Chris Rowley,
Cass Business School, City University, UK
(email: c.rowley@city.ac.uk)

Chandos Publishing is pleased to publish this major Series of books entitled *Asian Studies: Contemporary Issues and Trends*. The Series Editor is Professor Chris Rowley, Cass Business School, City University, UK.

Asia has clearly undergone some major transformations in recent years and books in the Series examine this transformation from a number of perspectives: economic, management, social, political and cultural. We seek authors from a broad range of areas and disciplinary interests: covering, for example, business/management, political science, social science, history, sociology, gender studies, ethnography, economics and international relations, etc.

Importantly, the Series examines both current developments and possible future trends. The Series is aimed at an international market of academics and professionals working in the area. The books have been specially commissioned from leading authors. The objective is to provide the reader with an authoritative view of current thinking.

New authors: we would be delighted to hear from you if you have an idea for a book. We are interested in both shorter, practically orientated publications (45,000+ words) and longer, theoretical monographs (75,000–100,000 words). Our books can be single, joint or multi-author volumes. If you have an idea for a book, please contact the publishers or Professor Chris Rowley, the Series Editor.

Dr Glyn Jones
Chandos Publishing (Oxford) Ltd
Email: gjones@chandospublishing.com
www.chandospublishing.com

Professor Chris Rowley
Cass Business School, City University
Email: c.rowley@city.ac.uk
www.cass.city.ac.uk/faculty/c.rowley

Chandos Publishing: is a privately owned and wholly independent publisher based in Oxford, UK. The aim of Chandos Publishing is to publish books of the highest possible standard: books that are both intellectually stimulating and innovative.

We are delighted and proud to count our authors from such well known international organisations as the Asian Institute of Technology, Tsinghua University, Kookmin University, Kobe University, Kyoto Sangyo University, London School of Economics, University of Oxford, Michigan State University, Getty Research Library, University of Texas at Austin, University of South Australia, University of Newcastle, Australia, University of Melbourne, ILO, Max-Planck Institute, Duke University and the leading law firm Clifford Chance.

A key feature of Chandos Publishing's activities is the service it offers its authors and customers. Chandos Publishing recognises that its authors are at the core of its publishing ethos, and authors are treated in a friendly, efficient and timely manner. Chandos Publishing's books are marketed on an international basis, via its range of overseas agents and representatives.

Professor Chris Rowley: Dr Rowley, BA, MA (Warwick), DPhil (Nuffield College, Oxford) is Subject Group leader and the inaugural Professor of Human Resource Management at Cass Business School, City University, London, UK. He is the founding Director of the new, multi-disciplinary and internationally networked *Centre for Research on Asian Management*, Editor of the leading journal *Asia Pacific Business Review* (www.tandf.co.uk/journals/titles/13602381.asp). He is well known and highly regarded in the area, with visiting appointments at leading Asian universities and top journal Editorial Boards in the US and UK. He has given a range of talks and lectures to universities and companies internationally with research and consultancy experience with unions, business and government and his previous employment includes varied work in both the public and private sectors. Professor Rowley researches in a range of areas, including international and comparative human resource management and Asia Pacific management and business. He has been awarded grants from the British Academy, an ESRC AIM International Study Fellowship and gained a 5-year RCUK Fellowship in Asian Business and Management. He acts as a reviewer for many funding bodies, as well as for numerous journals and publishers. Professor Rowley publishes very widely, including in leading US and UK journals, with over 100 articles, 80 book chapters and other contributions and 20 edited and sole authored books.

Bulk orders: some organisations buy a number of copies of our books. If you are interested in doing this, we would be pleased to discuss a discount. Please contact Hannah Grace-Williams on email info@chandospublishing.com or telephone number +44 (0) 1993 848726.

Textbook adoptions: inspection copies are available to lecturers considering adopting a Chandos Publishing book as a textbook. Please email Hannah Grace-Williams on email info@chandospublishing.com or telephone number +44 (0) 1993 848726.

Asian Business Groups

Context, governance and performance

MICHAEL CARNEY

Chandos Publishing

Oxford · England

Chandos Publishing (Oxford) Limited
TBAC Business Centre
Avenue 4
Station Lane
Witney
Oxford OX28 4BN
UK
Tel: +44 (0) 1993 848726 Fax: +44 (0) 1865 884448
Email: info@chandospublishing.com
www.chandospublishing.com

First published in Great Britain in 2008

ISBN:
978 1 84334 244 1 (hardback)
1 84334 244 8 (hardback)

© M. Carney, 2008

British Library Cataloguing-in-Publication Data.
A catalogue record for this book is available from the British Library.

Typeset by Domex e-Data Pvt.Ltd.
Printed in the UK and USA.

100 6 323 63 x

For Ana Cappelluto

Contents

List of figures and tables

Figures

Tables

About the author

Dr Michael Carney is a professor in the Department of Management, John Molson School of Business, Montréal, Québec, Canada, where he teaches strategic management and international business. His research focuses upon the corporate governance, competitiveness, and strategies of ethnic Chinese family business groups and the development of large family firms in East and Southeast Asia. His current work focuses upon general corporations in Vietnam and the emergence of privately owned conglomerates in mainland China. His research is published in journals such as *Asia Pacific Journal of Management, Asia Pacific Business Review, Entrepreneurship: Theory and Practice, Journal of Management Studies, Organizations Studies,* and *Strategic Management Journal.* Professor Carney is a senior editor of the *Asia Pacific Journal of Management* and has taught at Hong Kong Polytechnic University and Tianjin University, China.

The author may be contacted at:

E-mail: *mcarney@jmsb.concordia.ca*

Preface

A business group is 'a collection of firms bound together in some formal and informal ways' (Granovetter, 1994: 454). Business groups are the dominant form of organisation in Asian economies but there are significant differences between them and they are known under a variety of designations: the *keiretsu* and *zaibatsu* of Japan, *chaebol* of Korea, *business houses* of India, the *hongs* of Hong Kong, the *national team* and *qiye jituan* of China, *government-led enterprise groups* of Singapore, *ethnic Chinese business groups* in Thailand, Malaysia, Indonesia and the Philippines, and the *bumiputera* groups of Malaysia and Indonesia. Business groups are also particularly prevalent in transitional and emerging market economies beyond Asia. For example, in Russia and the Ukraine, we have seen the emergence of *oligarchic financial-industrial* groups. In Latin America, family-owned *grupos economicas* have long been part of the industrial landscape. In Turkey and Pakistan, major firms are affiliated with business groups. Business groups are also found in more advanced economies such as Belgium, France, Italy, Germany, Spain and Sweden. It is in Asian countries, however, that business groups dominate their domestic economies. In this volume, we will survey the extent of this dominance. Subsequent chapters will examine the origins, establishment and growth of business groups in each of Asia's major economies. We describe their structure and functioning as well as their financial and economic performance. This preface considers why the business group is such a special form of organisation and how it differs from the way we typically think about the organisation and structure of an economy's largest and most important firms.

Business groups in comparative perspective

One of the most widely accepted explanations of the organisation of firms is transaction cost theory. This theory suggests that exchanges between independent agents may be organised by means of market transactions or 'internalised' and governed within a hierarchical system called a 'firm' (Williamson, 1975). Market transactions between suppliers, distributors and other partners tend to be conducted by simple contracts (Williamson, 1985). These contracts also tend to be discrete and pertain to clearly defined activities over a specified period. MacNeil (1974: 738) describes such relations as 'sharp-in by clear agreement, sharp-out by clear performance'. As transactions become more uncertain and risky, agents will craft intricate intermediate arrangements such as equity-joint ventures, licences, franchises, strategic alliances and so forth. On close inspection, these arrangements are revealed to be very complex contracts: they are governed by clearly designed partnership agreements, carefully allocated property rights, value appropriation rules and clear exit options that account for a variety of possible contingencies. Under conditions of very high market uncertainty, agents discover that contractual forms of organisation are inadequate because they cannot provide enough credible safeguards for the governance of exchange. Consequently, transactions must be brought inside the firm where they will be governed by a bureaucratic system that we think of as the vertically-integrated, hierarchically-coordinated firm. This is at least how many scholars view the organisation of western firms operating in mature and well-developed economies.

In contrast, many scholars of Asian organisation argue that transaction costs cannot account for the structure of Asia's highly networked and interdependent economy (Biggart and Hamilton, 1992). Due to deep differences in history, culture, society and institutions, Asian firms have developed different business systems and divergent forms of capitalism (Hamilton and Biggart, 1988; Redding, 1990; Whitley, 1999). Instead, studies of Asian business organisation frequently focus upon diverse ways of organising exchange. Many point to the importance of informal and personal business relationships, sometimes called *guanxi* (Chen, 1995). Others draw attention to the role of extensive networks that are characterised as clans (Ouchi, 1980) or fiefs (Boisot and Child, 1996) that reflect historical and cultural differences. Increasingly, scholars recognise that the predominant form of organisation in Asia is the business group. We shall explore several definitions of a business group in some detail below, but at this point we need to see business groups as an intermediate organisational form that is neither market nor hierarchical and which cannot be understood as an intermediate form of a complex contract.

Business group dimensions and definition

Collections of legally independent firms are neither affiliated to one another by full ownership, as we find in the multidivisional firm, nor are they linked by legal contractual means. What is interesting about business groups is the nature of the 'binding' that links them together. On closer inspection, we find a large and rich variation in the types of linkages between group affiliates both within Asia and elsewhere. Appendix A provides an extensive survey of business group definitions culled from the growing literature. The differences in definitions typically pertain to the kinds of linkages between groups. Most scholars agree that linkages will be complex and multidimensional. For example, a comparison between business groups in Japan and China shows that 'Japanese business groups are best defined as clusters of firms linked through overlapping ties of shareholding, debt, interlocking directors, and dispatch of personnel to other levels, shared history, membership in group-wide clubs and councils, and often shared brands' (Ahmadjian, 2006: 30). According to Keister, similar complexity is evident among China's business groups: 'business groups are coalitions of firms from multiple industries that interact over long periods of time and are distinguished by elaborate inter-firm networks of lending, trade, ownership, and social relations' (Keister, 1998: 408). Moreover, the importance of specific types of linkages will vary over time depending on a variety of factors. While each definition differs in some respects, two themes emerge. The first is that a business group is a diverse collection of unrelated and related business units that resembles a multidivisional conglomerate. Most scholars are quick to qualify this resemblance by pointing out that unlike conglomerates, business groups are composed of independent legal entities. However, business groups are more diversified than the 'related-constrained' diversified firm described by Rumelt (1974). A second recurring theme in these definitions is that, despite the absence of legal unity among affiliated business units, some type of governance mechanism exists to permit a central entity to exercise control and/or coordination over the actions of affiliated firms. Economists and finance scholars emphasise the existence of equity mechanisms to achieve control, while sociologists and organisation theorists tend to emphasise informal mechanisms such as trust and commitments. Many studies focus upon the precise instruments used to achieve coordination. For example, studies of Japanese business groups have focused upon presidents' clubs, cross-shareholdings, debt and recurrent trade ties.

Studies of Korean *chaebol* have identified the importance of a centralised planning office, family ownership and state credit ties. In the majority of cases, control and coordination is achieved by multiple overlapping mechanisms, which will vary from group to group and across different institutional settings. In this respect, the essence of the organisational form is captured by Chang's (2006a) definition: 'Business groups pursue unrelated diversification under centralised control'.

To facilitate comparison with Western conglomerates and multidivisional firms, the term 'ownership concentration' emerges as a proxy for the capacity of an agent to exercise control and coordination among group affiliates. Here ownership concentration is used to reflect the probability that ownership provides an identifiable agent with a sufficient concentration of power to be able to set goals, monitor executive performance, and intervene in member firms' affairs if deemed necessary. The identity of that agent-owner may vary. In Southeast Asia, ownership concentration may reside in an individual entrepreneur or family at the peak of a pyramid system, or may be exercised by a state through state ownership, or ownership may be partially diffused with control exercised by a particular class of shareholder, such as a bank or core firm. The specific workings of the governance and control mechanisms will depend upon historical and institutional factors specific to the context.

Because business groups are legally independent firms that are linked together in various ways, they are often considered to be a type of network (Fruin, 1998; Hamilton, Zeile and Kim, 1990; Lincoln and Gerlach, 2004). However, there are many types of networks that are not business groups. In the terms of Chang (2006a: 1), what distinguishes business groups is that they 'pursue unrelated diversification under centralised control'. It is their concentrated ownership and coordination and diversification that captures the essence of the organisational form and distinguishes business groups from other forms of network, as depicted in the figure (Cuervo-Cazurra, 2006).

Finally, Granovetter (2005) also suggests that they vary along six dimensions:

- *Source of solidarity* (the basis of a firm's identification with a group): In much of Asian business, the basis of identity is kinship or family connections, but other factors such as ethnicity, the region of origin, or state enforcement also form the basis of identity.

- *Extent of moral economy*: The degree to which groups act as coherent social systems in which participants have a strong sense of obligation to one another.

Figure P.1   Distinguishing business groups from other networks

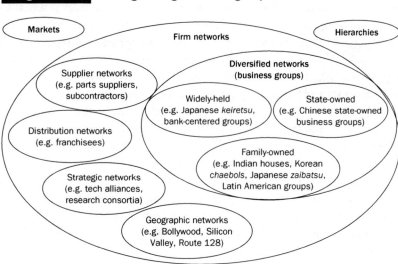

Source: Cuervo-Cazurra (2006).

- *Structure of ownership*: The extent to which ownership is concentrated in the hands of a single individual, or family, or is more widely diffused among other types of owners.

- *Structure of authority*: The degree to which groups are coordinated by a central authority or more loosely coordinated and decentralised.

- *The role of financial associations*: Many groups typically access a main bank on which they rely for credit, while others are self-funding and generate their own capital.

- *Relationship with the state*: This is a more complex dimension which will be discussed at length below. Many business groups are state-created entities, while others have developed independently of or in opposition to the state. In the following chapters, we offer descriptions of the governance, structure and composition of business groups.

The context for business groups

Chapter 2 provides an inventory of the positive and negative attributes of business groups that have recently been identified by researchers. Business groups are complex phenomena with the potential both to promote and to retard a nation's economic development. Whether positive or negative attributes prevail may depend on factors internal to the group or on developments in the business environment. One popular view suggests that primary business group attributes will tend to vary over time. This view is well stated in Strachan's (1976) lifecycle hypothesis, which suggests that during the early stages of economic development and industrialisation, business groups initially enjoy a dynamic growth phase. In this phase, independent firms choose to affiliate with a group to gain access to reduced transactions costs and quasi-capital market benefits. As a result of these benefits, business group affiliates outperform independent firms to become dominant players in the economy. At the later stages of economic maturity, negative attributes begin to prevail. In particular, managers seek to entrench their positions and firms that enjoy a monopoly use their market power to prevent start-up firms who pose a competitive threat from entering the marketplace.

A complementary perspective puts greater emphasis on environmental factors, suggesting that business groups are an emerging market phenomenon formed in response to market failure and missing institutional infrastructure. In this perspective, such institutional infrastructure will begin to develop and transactions costs will tend to be reduced as industrialisation proceeds. As institutional development proceeds, the rationale for the existence of business groups disappears and they will become de-institutionalised, which gradually leads to their dismantling or to their restructuring. For instance, *chaebol* business groups served as a catch-up mechanism during Korea's rapid growth in the period from the 1960s to the 1980s (Amsden, 1989). As Korean firms approached the technology frontier in the 1990s, negative attributes surfaced and it became apparent that dominant family owners had expropriated their minority shareholders (Chang, 2003).

Other analysts, however, recognise that business groups continue to be important even at advanced stages of development and note that business groups are found in more advanced economies such as Germany, Japan, France, Belgium, Italy and Sweden. These analysts argue that business groups can continue to be a positive force in the economy but the specific positive role that they play may change over time. For example, business groups may well have played the role of catch-up mechanism in the development of the Japanese and German economies. However, once firms in these economies began to approach the technology frontier, business groups' capital market and monitoring functions became more important. In an approach referred to as the 'varieties of capitalism' perspective (Whitley, 1999; Hall and Soskice, 2001; Lazonick and O'Sullivan, 2002), firms and institutions interact in a complementary manner to create a self-reinforcing system of regulations and institutions. The effect of this pattern of firm and institutional development is that several distinct and equally productive business systems may develop around the world, each reflecting its own historical circumstances and each following a different development path.

What each of these approaches has in common is the view that history influences the kinds of corporate structures that firms adopt and the quality of performance they will deliver in an economy. In particular, the historical conditions prevailing at the founding of a business group are believed to especially important. Moreover, each of these perspectives suggests that business group functions and performance are likely to be different in a context of early industrialisation characterised by market failures and institutional underdevelopment versus one in the later stages of economic maturity.

The structure of this book

Because our knowledge of business groups is so contradictory and their structure and performance seems to be so much the product of particular historical and institutional conditions, we shall examine business groups in their own unique settings. In Chapter 2, we will examine business groups in their post-Second World War context. Of particular importance here are the European colonial-era business groups from Europe and the *zaibatsu* of Japan. The vestiges of these business groups still linger on in parts of Asia. Chapter 3 contains a survey of the extensive literature on Japan's *keiretsu* business groups. In terms of economic development, the next wave of economies that followed Japan's impressive growth is represented by Vogel's (1991) four little dragons: Korea, Taiwan, Hong Kong and Singapore. Chapters 4 and 5 provide an overview a of business groups in Korea and Taiwan respectively, and Chapter 7 contains an analysis of business groups in Hong Kong.

As the economies of Japan and the four little dragons began to mature, a third wave of economies in Southeast Asia embarked upon a plan of rapid economic development. In the Philippines, Indonesia, Malaysia and Thailand, state-owned and state-led business groups and business groups owned by ethnic overseas Chinese were particularly important. Chapter 9 provides an overview of business groups in these Southeast Asian economies. The huge populations of China and India and their potential economic growth set them apart from other countries in Asia, and therefore, Chapters 6 and 8 provide an overview of the emergence and performance of business groups in those two countries respectively. Chapter 10 concludes this volume by pulling together the various strands in order to provide insight into development path and growth dynamics.

The structure of each chapter

As said by Granovetter (1994: 456), 'a small theoretical literature of business groups does exist, though it is a peripheral subject in the study of industrial organization'. Since Granovetter's comment there has been a blizzard of research on the topic. In this review of the research, each chapter is organised in accordance with Granovetter's proposed three-point agenda for research on the subject. This proposed agenda includes:

- emergence/origins context (origins, contemporary issues);
- governance (corporate and organisational structure);
- performance (financial, market, technological).

We examine the historical and institutional conditions under which business groups were formed and became viable. We consider the circumstances in which federations of firms are viable and will continue to operate rather than merge into a single entity. By understanding the conditions in which business groups are viable, we will attain some insight into why they are founded and how preponderant they are. Second, we need to know more about the nature of business groups and exactly how they function. This necessitates an examination of the empirical literature to determine the main dimensions along which business groups vary. In each chapter, we describe the governance structure and the basic pattern of authority prevailing in the group. Particular attention is given to ownership, organisational structure, the relations between the suppliers of capital, and firm management and the major agency relationships found in business groups. Third, business group performance is examined. Here, we address Granovetter's third question regarding implications for economic and social outcomes. Our main focus is financial and market performance based on large sample empirical studies and anecdotal data from case studies.

The bright and dark sides of Asian business groups

Asian business groups deserve our special attention because they are closely identified with the region's industrialisation and subsequent economic growth. Business groups are identified by various names, such as Japan's *keiretsu*, Korea's *chaebol*, China's *qiye jituan* or national team, India's business houses, and the ethnic Chinese business groups that have played a pivotal role in the economic success of countries throughout East and Southeast Asia. Elsewhere, business groups are economically important forms of organisation. In countries such as the Ukraine, Russia, Pakistan, Mexico, Chile and Nicaragua, many of the largest domestic enterprises are affiliated with business groups. However, they have not always been associated with economic success in these countries (Granovetter, 2005). It is only in Asia that strong claims are made about the economic efficacy of business groups. Developing states in post-colonial societies such as Korea, Singapore, India, Malaysia, Indonesia and transitional economies, such as China and Vietnam, that are intent on catching up with a more economically advanced West, have selected the business group as the chosen instrument of economic development. Politicians, government leaders and business leaders appear to have cooperated in creating large business groups and to have charged them with industrialising their domestic economies. Due to the central role played by business groups, some analysts argue that governments, entrepreneurs and managers in Asia have collectively developed a new organisational form (Biggart and Hamilton, 1992; Granovetter, 2005) and a new style of capitalism (Best, 1990).

In the wake of the Asian financial crisis in 1997/98, business groups have become controversial. Some business group practices were thought to contribute to and worsen the impact of the crisis. After the crisis, analysts began to examine business groups with a more critical eye.

While some studies have found support for the hypothesis that business group affiliation improves firm performance (Chang and Choi, 1988; Keister, 1998; Chang and Hong, 2000; Khanna and Palepu, 2000a, 2000b), other studies offer only mixed support and many suggest a negative effect (Bertrand, Mehta and Mullainathan, 2002; Lins and Servaes, 2002; Chang, 2003). The growing number of studies finding negative attributes has cohered into a 'dark-side' perspective of business group affiliation (Scharfstein and Stein, 2000). In these perspectives, business groups are viewed not as efficient responses to market failures, but instead as organisations formed to expropriate minority shareholders, strip assets and 'loot' affiliates (Johnson, Boone, Breach and Friedman, 2000). Others characterise business groups as rent-seeking instruments of politically connected elites whose dominant owners entrench their management, exploit their control rights and fail to invest and support innovation in their affiliates (Fisman, 2001; Chang, 2003; Morck, Wolfenzon and Yeung, 2005). Because business groups may contain both positive and negative performance tendencies, it is unclear whether they should be cast as 'heroes or villains' (Claessens, Djanov and Lang, 2000a). Recent surveys of business groups around the world have identified this dualism asking whether business groups are an 'anachronism or avatars' (Granovetter, 2005) 'paragons or parasites' (Khanna and Yafeh, 2007), 'Red Barons or robber barons' (Perotti and Gelfer, 2001), or 'tunnellers or proppers' (Friedman, Johnson and Mitton, 2003).

The bright side: what is the good news about business groups?

Many scholars and policy makers believe that, where markets are imperfect and legal/regulatory institutions are of poor quality, affiliation with a business group will enhance a firm's performance. Arguments based on exchange theory (Keister, 2001), transaction cost analysis (Khanna and Palepu, 1997), the resource-based view of the firm (Guillen, 2000) and embeddedness (Granovetter, 1994) suggest that business group affiliation will improve a firm's performance in imperfect markets because it allows firms to internalise market transactions, it provides better access to scarce resources, and introduces firms to networks of value-creating relationships, including those with governments. Some of these arguments overlap and build upon one another as will become evident in the inventory of eight business group performance attributes below.

Business groups lower transactions costs for affiliated firms

In mature industrial economies, managers can take for granted the existence of high-quality regulatory institutions and well-developed factor markets that allow firms to acquire key resources such as finance, human capital and complementary assets by means of market transactions. Khanna and Palepu (1999) describe the institutions that support market transactions as a 'soft market infrastructure' – this consists of a system of contractual enforcement, an autonomous judicial system, arbitration services and accountable, transparent regulatory processes. For markets to operate efficiently decision makers require accurate and timely information, so a soft market infrastructure also includes a variety of agencies that provide credible and reliable information to managers about the people and firms with whom they seek to do business. These agencies include credit rating bureaus, market research firms, executive placement agencies, and an active and independent business press. Mature economies also possess sophisticated capital markets consisting of banks, stock exchanges and specialist private equity providers such as venture capital and leveraged buyout funds. This infrastructure allows managers to construct complex contracts for a wide range of resources with assurance that a matrix of economic and legal institutions will invisibly operate to make the market work. In many cases, these institutional conditions are likely to be more efficient in external markets than internalised transactions, where firms produce their own resources and assets (Williamson, 1985). Because so many resources are available on external markets, firms can focus upon the activities they do best and contract for other resources from other specialists.

In contrast, emerging markets often lack a comparable range and depth of market-supporting institutions. Analysts describe this condition as 'institutional voids' characterised by extensive market imperfections and the absence of intermediary agencies and actors that facilitate transactions (Khanna and Palepu, 1997, 1999). Markets in which legal and regulatory systems are undeveloped or not enforced where they do exist, are particularly problematic. The absence of rule of law and protection for property rights, inefficient judicial systems, risk of state expropriation, risk of contractual repudiation and the inefficiency of the judicial system can make even routine business transactions hazardous (La Porta, Lopez-de-Silanes and Shleifer, 1999). Often governments in emerging markets intervene in the economy and impose cumbersome and restrictive regulations, discriminatory taxation and other procedures that hamper the development of factor markets. At the same time, governments may neglect regulations governing corporate disclosure, accounting standards and protection for minority stockholders, all of which are serious obstacles to the development of capital markets. In the absence of market infrastructure, contract enforcement will be unreliable and transactions costs in open markets will be high for the general population of firms and many beneficial exchanges will go unrealised.

Business groups may however act as 'safe havens' for internalising transactions among member firms. Affiliation with a business group allows for the credible exchange of information about its members and reduces search and screening costs. Because the group can identify and apply binding sanctions on members who behave opportunistically, contracts can be more reliably enforced. Many studies of business groups emphasise their capacity to reduce transactions costs as the basis for their economic importance. In an imperfect market, many intermediary services are not available through local markets and business groups are formed to 'internalise' the production of that service for the benefit of their members. An extension of the basic logic of market failure and the reduction of transactions costs suggests that business groups solve numerous factor market failures, and group membership provides firms with a menu of additional benefits including improved access to information, scarce resources and business opportunities. Larger groups may also benefit from economies of scope with regard to shared assets. A brief enumeration suggests that business groups are formed to internalise the following services: financing, human capital, technology, insurance or risk sharing, and the monitoring and oversight of executives.

Business groups serve as a quasi-internal capital market for their members

Much of the economics and finance literature views the business group as a quasi-internal capital market that can operate as a substitute for external capital markets. The weakness and the scarcity of intermediary financial institutions, such as markets for equity, bonds and venture capital, present considerable difficulties for firms that have many profitable growth opportunities but lack the necessary capital to pursue these opportunities. A firm that is generating more cash than it can profitably reinvest in its own lines of business may be unable to find productive uses for its excess resources. In these circumstances, affiliation with a business group may provide a context for cash-constrained and cash-rich firms to exchange resources. In this respect, the business group resembles a multidivisional firm that houses a portfolio of cash-cow businesses that are able to provide cash for 'star' and 'question mark' businesses. The crucial difference is that the multidivisional firm is organised as a unified hierarchy under common ownership and is able to present a consolidated statement of its assets, while business groups are simply collections of 'legally independent firms who are bound together in some way'. In addition, the multidivisional firm is generally limited to a relatively narrow range of businesses that are related by market or technological similarities, allowing its senior managers to make detailed evaluations of the profit potential for each constituent business. In contrast, business groups typically have much broader scope and contain affiliates that operate in diverse and unrelated businesses. Moreover, senior executives do not normally perform detailed profitability evaluations of affiliated business as a precondition to supplying financial resources. These differences suggest business groups operate their quasi-capital markets according to principles different from those governing the multidivisional firm.

To operate as a quasi-internal capital market, business groups have developed several hybridised arrangements that mimic some of the qualities of both internal and external capital markets, such as equity, banking and venture capitalist functions; this is why they are described as quasi capital markets. Some business groups possess a core firm that makes and receives loans and offers trade credit to affiliated firms, thus performing a role resembling that of a central bank. On occasion, the core firm may also act as a loan guarantor to third-party lenders. In other arrangements, group affiliates may make loans and guarantee third-party loans for one another without recourse to a core firm. In some business groups, trade credit and debt linkages are reinforced and overlaid with equity linkages. These equity linkages may be unidirectional, leading in a pyramid fashion to a single identifiable owner, or bi-directional, producing a series of horizontal cross-linkages. Additionally, some business groups borrow certain elements that are found in leveraged buyout organisations (LBOs) insofar as each affiliate is organised as an independent legal entity, with its own management board of directors and fiduciary responsibilities (Khanna and Yafeh, 2007). Like LBO partnerships that acquire assets through highly leveraged 'junk bonds', so business groups often create new ventures with debt supplied by financial intermediaries, in many cases state banks. For example, such heavy leverage was a distinguishing feature of Korean *chaebol* prior to the Asian financial crisis. Because the group's core firm is able to exercise control through its equity ownership position in the highly-leveraged firm, it may play a disciplinary role similar to the LBO partnership.

Some scholars suggest that some business groups emulate a number of the features of a private equity or venture capital partnership. Both the venture capital partnership and the business group are adept at identifying risky opportunities and locating private investors as a source of seed capital. In addition, like the venture capital firm, the business group performs a monitoring role over the new venture, provides appropriate managerial talent for the venture from its own in-house staff, and plays a lead role in taking the venture public through the initial public offering (IPO) process. For example, Gerlach (1997) argues that the core firms in Japan's pre-Second World War *zaibatsu* groups operated much like a venture capital firm that supports, but does not dominate, the management of subsidiary enterprise. Gerlach notes that these groups were characterised by strategic centralisation and operational decentralisation, and this determined their ability to reallocate resources to firms operating near the technology frontier. The core firm permitted affiliated firms to embark on educational missions in Japan and elsewhere, to purchase foreign technology and product licences and to invest in new plant and equipment. Through processes of operational decentralisation, the most promising firms were spun-off from the head office to create new enterprises in a process Gerlach terms 'satellite formation'. This latter point is a key difference between business groups and 'pure' venture capital firms in that venture capital firms largely sever their linkages with an enterprise following an IPO, whereas business groups play a continuing role in the new firm's affairs. Some business groups perform capital market activities performed elsewhere by multidivisional firms, equity markets, banks, LBOs and venture capital firms, suggesting that business groups are versatile organisations whose adaptations and specific features arise from the comparative absence of diverse capital market institutions found in mature economies.

Business groups are a source of scarce human capital

Beginning with Leff (1978), analysts emphasise imperfections in human capital markets as a source of group advantages. Leff agrees that, in developing economies, capital markets' failures partly explain the emergence of business groups, but he observes that there are also numerous other inter-market failures that create difficulties for independent entrepreneurial activity, leading to a more general problem of insufficient entrepreneurship. Leff argues that business groups internalise the entrepreneurship role, suggesting that 'the group constitutes a pattern of industrial organisation which permits structure rather than gifted individuals to perform the key interactivity function of entrepreneurship' (Leff, 1978: 669). In the context of multiple market failure, business groups can help to relax the entrepreneurial constraint that limits the rate of economic development and they can permit true 'Schumpeterian' entrepreneurship to occur. This is because groups can articulate the necessary combination of financial, technical and managerial resources into production decisions.

Market imperfections are also evident in the supply of executive talent. Leff (1978: 666) notes that it is inherently difficult to efficiently market 'honesty and trustworthy competence on the part of high level managers'. He suggests that a group's internal relations are characterised by interpersonal trust permitting the formation of a larger cadre of top managers than would otherwise be possible. The existence of a pool of skilled managers permits the attainment of economies scale and scope that would be beyond the scope of family-owned and managed firms. Khanna and Palepu (1997) have developed this argument. They suggest that emerging markets are short of institutions with the ability to supply high-quality executive talent. For example, not only is the mobility of executives limited in emerging markets, but such markets also lack business schools, training programmes for senior managers and executive search firms. In the absence of these human capital market institutions, it is very difficult for freestanding firms to find skilled managers who match their needs. Within the business group, however, a pool of specialised management is potentially available for dispatch to firms that might otherwise have difficulty finding specialised talent. A noted feature of Japanese business groups is the dispatch of senior management to assist affiliates in specific projects such as business turnaround, new venture start-up, or foreign market entry (Gerlach, 1992a).

In China's early reform period experienced and skilled managers were practically nonexistent, but business groups were established under strong, charismatic CEOs who had demonstrated their abilities in competitive markets (Hahn and Lee, 2006).

Business group reputation signals quality and helps acquire scarce resources in factor markets

Due to lack of information, it is often difficult for consumers to determine the quality or reliability of a firm's products and services. Buyers face information imperfections due to the absence of market research firms, advertising agencies, consumer protection organisations and credit rating agencies, or because of restrictions on press freedom, which inhibit investigative reporting of firms' malpractice. In these circumstances it is difficult for a firm to establish a brand image or to establish new contractual relationships with unknown suppliers. Khanna and Palepu (1997) suggest that business groups allow firms with a visible and known reputation to enjoy a 'reputation premium' when objective information is difficult to find and evaluate. Businesses with a reputation for fairness and good management practices may command a premium as business partners in such environments. This reputation premium may facilitate the growth of member firms; for example, they may attain economies of scale and more easily enter new markets. The reputation premium arises because business groups operate in many sectors of the economy and are highly visible. Due to their visibility, it is difficult for the group's affiliates to engage in opportunistic acts without being detected and damaging their reputation. As Khanna and Palepu put it:

> because the misdeeds of one company in a group will damage the prospects of the other, all the group companies have credibility when they promise to honor their agreements with any single partner. They (conglomerates) provide a haven where property rights are respected. (Khanna and Palepu, 1997: 17)

The core firm in the business group has an incentive to monitor the behaviour of group affiliate members in order to uphold the group's collective reputation in the same manner as a franchisor monitors and audits the operation of franchisees who license the franchisor's trade marks and businesses processes.

The reputation premium may provide advantages in several factor markets. For example, in bringing new companies to market through the IPO process, a potential investor should be able to put more confidence in a group-sponsored IPO than that of an unknown freestanding firm. These positive reputational attributes are also useful in the acquisition of foreign technologies. In the absence of reliable property rights enforcement, foreign firms may be unwilling to enter into licensing agreements or joint ventures with emerging market firms due to their fear of losing valuable intellectual property. However, their doubts may be allayed if they are dealing with a firm with a reputation for honouring its commitments.

Business groups are a mutual insurance device

The mutual insurance or risk-sharing hypothesis (Khanna and Yafeh, 2005) suggests that affiliation with a business group allows affiliates to share risk by smoothing income flows between firms and by coming to one another's aid in times of crisis, thus reducing the risk of bankruptcy. Income smoothing is achieved by channelling resources from stronger and more profitable firms to underperforming firms or firms in financial distress. In so doing, strong firms 'prop up' their troubled affiliates. Numerous resource-channelling mechanisms are available to attain this end; these include transfer pricing, related party transactions and purchasing goods or services from a group firm at a price higher than that available outside the group. If there is cross-ownership, funds may be transferred by paying dividends, or by spreading liquidity through loans or extending favourable trade credit. The ability to reduce the risk of bankruptcy provides several material benefits to member firms, such as increasing a firm's capacity to take on debt and lowering the firm's cost of capital. Income smoothing can also help firms to reduce their tax, while risk sharing may also encourage firms to undertake projects that two independent firms would pass over in the absence of alternative risk-sharing mechanisms.

Note that the insurance hypothesis does not necessarily imply that resources will be reallocated from cash-rich firms that have few investment opportunities to cash-flow negative firms that have numerous investment opportunities, which is the principle applied in the multidivisional firm. Rather, Aoki (1984) suggests that redistribution occurs because firms maximise the joint profits of group members. The insurance hypothesis therefore implies that income smoothing is a means by which strong firms help weaker firms, and often bail out underperforming and failing firms. Some analysts argue that redistribution might be viewed as a response to transitional uncertainty. For example, Keister (2001) notes a form of income smoothing in China's early reform period. In this period, factor markets were underdeveloped and managers attached greater value to suppliers who were reliable rather than those with the absolute lowest cost. Groups began to form around a principle of paying more to trade with those they knew and could trust (Keister, 2001). Similarly, Poukliakova, Estrin and Shaprio (2006) suggest that group income redistribution is a survival strategy when uncertainty is very high. Redistribution is likely to be particularly important when the long-term goal of profit maximisation is threatened by short-term external shocks such as those that occur in a transitional period. When markets are immature and imperfect, protecting customers, suppliers and other group members may be essential to long-term survival.

Business groups are effective monitors of affiliate management

Agency theory scholars such as Jensen and Meckling (1976) propose that concentrated ownership has attractive corporate governance qualities because it unifies the ownership and control of the firm. Unified ownership and control averts the classic agency problems inherent in widely-held, professionally managed firms because owner-managers have a direct claim on their firm's residual income and so have a strong incentive to monitor their employees, manage costs tightly, and otherwise manage the firm efficiently (Alchian and Demsetz, 1972). Many of Asia's business groups are controlled by a single individual or family and in managing their assets they may bring a parsimonious mentality to the operation of the various subunits by closely monitoring executives to ensure that they do not incur unnecessary costs or engage in practices such as overexpansion and empire building. In emerging markets with imperfect capital markets the top executives are insulated somewhat from capital market pressures; for example, there is often no market for corporate control. In these circumstances, professional managers can disregard stock market pressures and expropriate value from the firm for their own private use. In some cases, corporate governance supplied by a concentrated owner may be an effective means of controlling the potential for this managerial agency problem.

In Japan, capital has historically been supplied by large banks, sometimes called main banks, which have devised various mechanisms to monitor executives, such as president's councils and interlocking directorates. Moreover, these mechanisms have served to dislodge executives whose performance is judged to be unsatisfactory (Kaplan, 1994). In China, where the state retains theoretical ownership of enterprises, reforms have left property rights over assets and operating surpluses ambiguous and ill-defined (Jefferson and Rawski, 1996), and this situation has given rise to 'ownership voids' (Ma, Yao and Xi, 2006) or 'agents without principals' (Clarke, 2003). It is believed that state officials lack either the competence or incentive to perform adequate oversight; consequently, businesses have been bundled into business groups that are managed by powerful CEOs who have proved their mettle in the early days of reform (Lin, 2001). In each of these cases, the underdevelopment of equity markets means that professional managers are inadequately monitored, and the emergence of concentrated ownership represents an alternative to agency monitoring mechanisms.

Business groups are a 'catch-up' mechanism

Some accounts characterise business groups as an amalgam of some of the factors inventoried above. The industrial latecomer theory suggests business groups are a catch-up device that can be used as a policy instrument by the developmental state. Hobday (1995) and Amsden (1997) have described emerging market states as industrial latecomers. Located in countries that are far from centres of science and technology, domestic firms from emerging markets lack their own pioneering or proprietary technologies and are dependent upon technologies controlled by foreign firms. To initiate their growth cycle, such firms usually begin with 'intermediary technology', which may not be state-of-the-art but nevertheless represents a significant improvement over local competitors. Developing states seek to shelter these nascent enterprises from the effects of foreign competition by creating artificial barriers to the entry of foreign multinational enterprises or by providing direct financial support that offers local enterprises the opportunity to develop internationally competitive capabilities and sufficient economies of scale. Amsden's study of the growth of Korean firms shows that managers in firms such as Hyundai and Samsung initially developed project-execution capabilities that served as a basis for entry into mature product markets such as shipbuilding, construction and electrical equipment manufacturing. Through a variety of mechanisms such as technology licensing, joint ventures and subcontracting, these firms were able to imitate the technologies of foreign firms. Many East Asian firms paid particular attention to manufacturing process improvements that helped them to learn rapidly and in some cases leapfrog toward the technology frontier (Hobday, 1994, 1995). Following a product market strategy of diversification, firms became 'generalists' in their relatively protected domestic markets, while venturing into international markets pumping out exports on the basis of their low costs and high-quality products. Hence, in the industrial latecomer perspective, business groups fulfil many roles. They simultaneously fill institutional voids, pool scarce capital, and acquire technology and management expertise that can be utilised to repeatedly enter new industries. Business groups also launch new ventures, which can be subsidised and nurtured until they have attained stability. Meanwhile, the state protects business groups by excluding stronger competitive foreign firms from domestic markets until domestic firms have 'caught up' and can compete without state support.

Powerful business groups make implied contracts with the state

An argument related to the latecomer catch-up thesis suggests that business group leaders must enter into an implied contract with the state that requires them to perform some social good in exchange for the freedom or right to exercise economic power. Granovetter (1994: 467) suggests that business groups are governed by the rules of a moral economy: 'No single firm, however, powerful, is exempt from duties; top financial institutions and industrial firms are bound by role expectations'. In this perspective, some business group leaders are subject to, or willingly accept normative constraints on their behaviour, forgoing profit maximisation and opportunistic behaviour in pursuit of a broader social purpose. In some settings, business groups may exhibit a tendency toward 'inter-temporal income smoothing'; in this phenomenon, powerful economic interests exhibit forbearance in their private interests during difficult economic conditions in expectation of government-mediated reciprocity in more prosperous times. For example, a business group may support a government goal such as employment creation or infrastructure creation in return for favourable contracts later. Alternatively, the state may agree that domestic groups should exert domestic control over important commercial and strategic assets, which might otherwise be acquired by foreign interests; in turn, the group agrees to implement certain government policy goals. Reliable, competent and trustworthy firms will be nominated as national champions and offered state aid and protection in return for their cooperation in implementing industrial policy.

Because business groups may perform some or all of these welfare enhancing activities they are viewed in a positive light. However, successive Asian crises such as the collapse of Japan's bubble economy in 1992 and its subsequent economic inertia along with the Asian financial crisis in 1997 has tempered arguments significantly. There is now much contradictory evidence about business group purpose and performance. The growing number of studies finding negative attributes has cohered into a 'dark-side' perspective on business groups (Scharfstein and Stein 2000). Rather than being an efficient response to imperfect markets, business groups are viewed as a means of expropriating minority shareholders, tunnelling, and looting and plundering the assets of their affiliates (Johnson et al., 2000). Others characterise business groups as rent-seeking instruments of politically-connected elites whose dominant owners entrench their management and exploit their control rights (Fisman, 2001; Chang, 2003; Morck et al., 2005). Below we inventory some of the arguments that point to the darker side of business groups.

What's wrong with business groups?

Business groups are organised as pyramids designed to plunder their affiliates

Business groups are often organised with a controlling minority structure that provides full control rights to a shareholder with only a small fraction of the equity claims on a firm's cash flows. Minority control is achieved using either one or several structural devices that include stock pyramids, dual-class share structures or cross-ownership ties (Morck et al., 2005). Under a pyramid structure, an apex or peak firm controls several other firms, each of which controls yet other firms, which in turn control more firms, and so on. Pyramids let dominant owners magnify their control rights beyond their cash-flow rights in firms located lower down the pyramid. In so doing, they leverage their relatively small personal wealth into control over corporations and assets worth vastly more. This sort of inflated control may cause a variety of corporate governance problems, principally the extraction of value from minority shareholders. When there is a significant deviation of control rights from cash-flow rights, dominant owners can transfer cash from one firm to another in many ways. For example, firms can grant each other high or low-interest rate loans, manipulate transfer prices or sell assets to one another at above or below market prices through related party transactions such as transfer pricing, the provision of capital at artificially high prices, or inflated charges for intangibles such as corporate services or consulting fees. Analysts describe this using various colourful terms, such as 'expropriation', 'tunnelling', 'looting' and 'plundering', but all refer to the act of transferring value from one firm in the pyramid to another. The use of such mechanisms allows value to percolate up the pyramid from where cash-flow rights are low, into peak firms, often a private family firm, where a dominant owner has full or greater rights over cash flows accruing there.

Consider Figure 1.1; a private apex firm owns a 51 per cent stake in firm A, entitling it to 51 per cent of firm A's profits. In each case the residual cash-flow rights are owned by public or outside shareholders. Continuing down the left-hand side of the pyramid, firm A has a 51 per cent stake in firm B, which has a 51 per cent stake in firm C, which has a 30 per cent stake in firm D. Along the right-hand side of the pyramid, the apex firm has a 100 per cent stake in firm E, which in turn has a 21 per cent stake in firm D. Through the sum of ownership stakes along the left-hand side of the pyramid, the apex firm is entitled to cash-flow

Figure 1.1   Business group pyramid

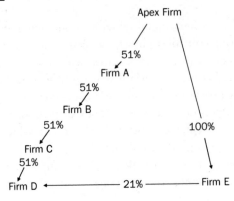

rights amounting to only 4 per cent of firm D's profits (i.e. 51% × 51% × 51% × 30% = 4%). Through the ownership chain along the right-hand side of the pyramid, the private apex firm has cash-flow rights of 21% (100% × 21% = 21%), entitling it to 25% of firm D's profits. However, due to the combined control rights of firms C and E, the apex firm is able to assemble a 51 per cent control block over firm D. The difference represents the apex firm's magnification of its control rights above its cash-flow rights. Now consider a related party transaction where the apex firm requires that firm D purchases an asset (for example, land) from firm E at $1 million above its true market value. This transaction reduces firm D's profits by $1 million and increases Firm E's profits by the same amount. The apex firm is quite happy with such a transaction because while the apex firm 'loses' $250,000 in cash flow from firm D (25 per cent of $1 million reduced profits) it gains 100 per cent increase in E's profits (E's profit increases by $1 million) providing an overall net gain of some $750,000, which is the amount of value transferred from firm D's minority shareholders.

Figure 1.2 depicts the Li Ka Shing conglomerate, which is Hong Kong's largest business group; consisting of some 25 companies, it includes some of the largest firms in Hong Kong, such as Cheung Kong and Hutcheson Whampoa. The divergence of cash-flow and control rights is illustrated through Li Ka Shing's ownership of a major utility – Hong Kong Electric. Li Ka Shing controls 34 per cent of the vote of Hong Kong Electric but has only 2.5 per cent of cash-flow rights. Li Ka Shing may use its control to extract value from the utility and transfer it

Figure 1.2 **Li Ka Shing conglomerate**

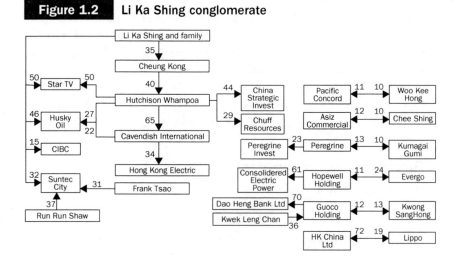

to other group firms under its control. Note that the consequences of this inter-firm transfer of funds are not the same as those observed in the diversified or conglomerate firm with common ownership, where it is standard practice to take capital from cash-cow businesses and allocate it to other businesses with better growth and profit prospects. In the case of a diversified firm, all shareholders will benefit from the efficient management of such resource reallocation. In the pyramid structure, by contrast, dominant shareholders benefit at the expense of minority shareholders.

Business groups concentrate corporate control in the hands of small elite

Critics of pyramid governance fear that a tiny elite of substantially wealthy individuals can come to control large sectors of the country's corporate sector. Studies of ownership structures in Asian business groups reveal that many are organised as pyramids (Claessens, Djankov, Fan and Lang, 1999a). As we shall see, many groups and their affiliates are ultimately owned by a single individual shareholder or his family. La Porta et al. (1999) argue that ownership stakes exceeding 50 per cent are not required for dominant owners to exercise control because many minority investors do not vote. In practice, ownership stakes ranging from 10 to 20 per cent are sufficient for control purposes. Empirical observations reveal that in many Asian economies there is a substantial concentration of corporate control in the hands of a tiny elite (Claessens et al., 2000). The second column of Table 1.1 indicates the total number of publicly listed firms in the sample of Claessen et al. (2000). The third and fourth columns show the percentage of total assets concentrated in the hands of the top five and top 15 families respectively. The last column reports the corporate assets held by the 15 most powerful family groups in each country as a percentage of 1996 GDP. Classes et al. (2000: 109) suggest that these data indicate that 'a relatively small number of families effectively control most East Asian economies'.

Business groups entrench their top management

When there is a significant deviation of control rights from cash-flow rights, dominant owners decide who will manage a firm. If poorly

Table 1.1   The concentration of assets in Asian economies

Country	Number of firms	Average number of firms per family	Top 5 families	Percentage of total value of listed corporate assets that families control (1996) Top 15 families	Assets as a percentage of GDP (1996) Top 15 families
Hong Kong	330	2.36	26.5	34.4	84.2
Indonesia	178	4.09	40.7	61.7	21.5
Malaysia	238	1.97	17.3	28.3	76.2
The Philippines	120	2.68	42.8	55.1	46.7
Singapore	221	1.26	19.5	29.9	48.3
Taiwan	141	1.17	14.5	20.1	17.0
Thailand	167	1.68	32.2	53.3	39.3
Japan	1,240	1.04	1.8	2.8	2.1

Source: Claessens, Djankov and Lang (2000b).

performing managers and corporate leaders are not replaced, the result is that many of society's most important businesses end up being run by entrenched and incompetent managers. Families are particularly prone to entrenchment because the founder entrepreneur may remain in position for many years before retiring. A dominant owner may place siblings, other relatives and friends in key executive positions throughout the businesses in the group and on retirement the founder may pass management on to a sibling. The founder may be a dynamic and talented entrepreneur, but succeeding generations may be less well-endowed with managerial skills. There is also a well-established belief that factors such as altruism, nepotism and weak risk-bearing attributes tend to harm the competitiveness and efficiency of family-owned and operated enterprises. Chandler (1990) views personally managed firms as overly concerned with wealth preservation and ill-equipped to develop the organisational capability to manage large-scale, technologically advanced industries.

Others see family firms as rife with personal rivalries and self-control problems that are not easily resolved within the context of family governance (Schulze, Lubatkin, Dino and Buchholtz, 2001). Entrenchment can provide tenure to managers who are honest but incompetent as well as to clever self-seeking insiders who use their power to extract private benefits.

Business group insiders use their complex and opaque corporate structures to exploit outside investors

Large business groups are highly visible and subject to much external scrutiny (Dewenter, Novaes and Pettway, 2001). Accordingly, Khanna and Palepu (1997) suggest that if firms behave opportunistically they will damage their valued reputations and, as such, business groups must respect property rights in all their transactions. However, business groups are often very large entities with complex structures and linkages between firms (Dewenter et al., 2001). The myriad of intra-group transactions makes it very difficult for an outside investor, equity analyst or credit rating agent to unravel and disentangle what is going on. In these circumstances, detecting opportunistic behaviour is difficult. For instance, business groups frequently bring new firms to market as they enter new industries or spin-off existing subsidiaries into freestanding firms. On the one hand, a group may spin-off a firm for many positive reasons, but the group may also wish to sell its poor and underperforming businesses while maintaining ownership of the best assets. In this view, a group may enjoy a positive reputation, but the complexity of its operations permits opportunistic behaviour. In many ways this is a variation of the first dark-side problem described above. However, the point is emphasised here because the current argument is in direct opposition to the argument that business group reputation signals quality.

Business groups are corrupt, crony, rent-seeking instruments

Scholars of Asia's industrialisation have observed that developmental states have established several policies designed to nurture the growth of infant industries. Policies such as import substitution and export-led development, which were designed to protect domestic firms from the rigours of international competition, also provided politicians and bureaucrats with significant control and discretion over resources such as licences, import quotas, subsidies, government contracts and access to local monopolies. Moreover, to give domestic firms the chance to grow, developmental states often suppressed market forces. In particular, developmental states actively and passively suppressed the development of capital markets' discriminatory taxation and cumbersome and restrictive issuance procedures that hamper market development. Passive suppression refers to the neglect of regulations governing corporate disclosure, accounting standards and protection for minority stockholders (Prowse, 1996). In these conditions, the success of a firm often depended heavily upon their 'rent-seeking' capacity to access and influence politicians and less upon managerial and technological capabilities (Kock and Guillén, 2001). Several scholars point out that in the early years of industrialisation, well-connected entrepreneurs developed widely diversified businesses based upon their capacity for rent-seeking (Yoshihara, 1988; McVey, 1992).

Once established, a small elite of patriarchs and oligarchs with substantial economic power can go on to wield significant political influence in the countries where they are based. A principal use of their political power is to resist policy changes that threaten their economic interests. Several scholars have recognised that powerful interest groups can thwart or co-opt reform processes (Shleifer and Treisman, 2000). Politics favour incumbent firms because they tend to be wealthier and more powerful than new entrants. For example, incumbents are better placed to articulate the risks posed by foreign firms than are outsiders seeking entry to a business group. If the rules governing corporate structure provide incumbents with control rights or rents they will be reluctant to relinquish their rights and may be willing to invest substantial resources in activities that preserve those rights. While close links between the state and leading entrepreneurs were thought to facilitate the goals of the developmental state, particularly in the allocation of capital to high social return projects (World Bank, 1993), attention has more recently focused upon the costs of close government-business relations (Haggard, 2001). Specifically, business groups and their allies in government and financial sectors may form a coalition to preserve existing institutions in their current relational form. In a period of structural market change, the preservation of outmoded institutions may shrink the pie, but it may be rational for incumbents to do so if they are able to maintain the size of their own pieces (Bebchuk and Roe,

1999). In this regard, political theory suggests that incumbents may capture and derail institutional innovations (Haggard, 2001) and reverse institutional developments that create competition from new entrants (Rajan and Zingales, 2001).

Business groups exercise monopoly power

Business groups typically enjoy significant economic power in the economies they dominate. These economies are often closed to foreign competition. If the threat of competition from a new entrant appears in a particular market then a business group can call upon its contacts with government or use its deep pockets to cross-subsidise its business affiliate in that market and deter the entry of a freestanding firm with fewer financial resources. Where large diversified business groups compete across numerous sectors of the economy then their multi-market contact can facilitate collusion and competitive forbearance. The monopolistic potential of large business groups is an under-researched question.

Business groups facilitate moral hazard and inefficient investment

Rent-seeking entrepreneurs who have strong ties to authorities and enter into opaque *quid pro quo* agreements with corrupt bureaucrats and politicians enjoy privileged access to resources and information. In these circumstances, central banks may lend on projects without full risk and project analysis because they know they will not be held accountable for permitting bad loans. Bankers and business managers who expect to be bailed out if projects do not succeed do not need to exercise normal precautions in their decisions. This is a moral hazard – they have no incentive to exercise judgment and prudence in capital allocation. Business group leaders have their liabilities explicitly or implicitly guaranteed by government and therefore have no incentive to exercise prudence in initiating new projects. In this manner, groups may become diversified over a wide range of businesses where they have little managerial or technical competence. Consequently, the principle of prudential lending as well as the moral hazard problems associated with government loan guarantees indicate that neither state nor commercial banks allocate long-term risk capital efficiently.

Table 1.2 summarises the bright and dark-side arguments.

Table 1.2	Bright and dark side of business groups

Value creating	Value destroying
Business groups lower transactions costs for affiliated firms	Business groups are organised as pyramids that are designed to plunder their affiliates
Business groups serve as a quasi-internal capital market for their members	Business groups concentrate corporate control in the hands of small elite
Business groups are a source of scarce human capital	Business groups entrench their top management
Business group reputation signals quality and helps acquire scarce resources in factor markets	Business group insiders use their complex and opaque corporate structures to exploit outside investors
Business groups are a mutual insurance device	Business groups are corrupt, crony, rent-seeking instruments
Business groups are effective monitors of affiliate firm performance	Business groups exercise monopoly power
Business groups are a 'catch-up' mechanism	Business groups facilitate moral hazard and inefficient investment
Powerful business groups make implied contracts with the state	

Performance measurement

The theory and practice of financial performance measurement is highly developed in mature industrial economies. Because they are readily available, measures based on accounting data are the most frequently used to determine a firm's financial health. The accounting profession has developed widely adopted standards and generally accepted accounting practices. These practices are continually updated and revised to incorporate changes in the business environment such as tax law, ethical considerations and the appearance of new business practices, such as the growing use of stock options in executive compensation packages. Recently, developments in finance have encouraged the adoption of stock market performance-based measures on the grounds that the theoretical basis for these measures reflects the firm's economic performance more accurately than historical accounting-based measures. These measures focus upon expectations of a firm's capacity to add economic and market value. Financial measures of firm performance are normally supplemented by other approaches, such as market share, reputational rankings, corporate social responsibility and other aspects of firm effectiveness. The utilisation of these diverse measures reflects the fact that stakeholders have interests in different dimensions of a firm's performance; indeed, we have recently seen the proliferation of multidimensional performance measures, such as the triple bottom line and the balanced scorecard.

Many analysts are sceptical about using the above measures to analyse business group affiliates. Appendix B briefly describes some of the difficulties in measuring the performance of business group affiliates. Concerns about the reliability of accounting data and about the assumptions underlying capital market efficiency in Asia allow for the possibility that business groups may pursue a variety of other goals. Analysts are also concerned that many empirical and comparative studies of business groups may use inappropriate and unreliable data that leave their conclusions open to doubt. As can be discerned from the above discussion of the dark and bright sides, scholars are deeply divided about the performance effects of business group affiliation. As we have documented, bright-side perspectives generally indicate that business groups are a source of value creation for their members and a source of general economic welfare in the economy. In contrast, dark-side perspectives suggest that business groups tend to destroy wealth or allocate wealth in an unjust or inefficient manner, and have a negative effect on the economic welfare in the wider economy.

Four perspectives on business group performance

Our definition of a business group focuses on two factors: diversification and ownership concentration. It is suggested that the nature of the relationship between the business group and performance will depend upon the degree of institutional development found in a particular country. Thus, where → represents the level of institutional development:

> business group (wide diversification + ownership concentration) → performance

The combination of bright and dark-side aspects of performance along with the developed/developing institutional context distinction dimensions provides a framework to identify four prevailing analyses of business

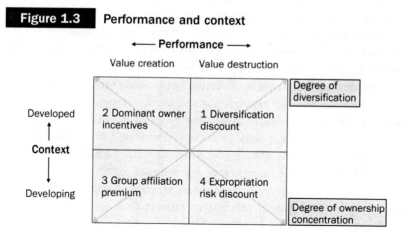

Figure 1.3   Performance and context

groups' two key features, namely their diversification and their ownership concentration. These literatures have not always focused exclusively upon business groups, especially in the context of more developed economies. Figure 1.3 identifies four main effects in each quadrant.

Cell 1 combines value destruction and the developed context. Here there is a large literature concerned with the negative effects of wide diversification, known as the 'diversification discount'. The basic idea is that the efficient capital markets diversify risk much more effectively than firms. Cell 3 addresses value creation in the emerging market context. This literature focuses on the positive qualities of group affiliation and identifies what we will describe as a 'group affiliation premium'. If we focus upon the effects of ownership concentration in the Cell 2 combination of value creation in the developed context, we can identify an agency theory literature that identifies the beneficial effect of concentrated ownership and the powerful incentives of dominant owners to monitor their managerial agents (Jensen and Meckling, 1976), which we call the 'ownership concentration premium'. Finally, in the Cell 4 combination of developing context and value destruction, there is a large and influential literature that focuses upon a concentrated owner's capacity to use ownership rights to extract value for minority shareholders, which we will refer to as the 'expropriation risk discount'. We briefly discuss each in turn.

Cell 1: The diversification discount

The diversification discount literature focuses upon product market scope rather than ownership concentration. It suggests that there is an inverted U-shaped relationship between value creation and diversification and is based upon a hypothesis pertaining to the comparative advantages of internal and external capital markets. This hypothesis posits that highly-focused firms characterised by a dominant business can increase value by diversifying into businesses related to their dominant business. The capacity for value enhancement stems from the superior ability of a firm's managers to operate an internal capital market through their capacity to audit, monitor and assess the business prospects of business units under their control (Williamson, 1975). However, the relative advantages of internal over external capital markets begin to weaken when managers attempt to apply the skills they employ in internal capital markets to businesses that are dissimilar or unrelated to their core business. Figure 1.4 suggests that the value destruction begins to occur once the firm begins to diversify past the related constrained point. However, agency theory suggests that managers may continue to expand and diversify past the point of value maximisation because it serves their private interests. The problem of over-expansion and over-diversification is particularly difficult when shareholders are highly dispersed. The potential for the diversification discount is driven by inadequate managerial oversight, known as a *type A* agency problem; this provides unmonitored managers with the opportunity to exploit shareholders. However, in the context of highly-developed capital markets, the diversification discount can be held in

Figure 1.4   The diversification discount

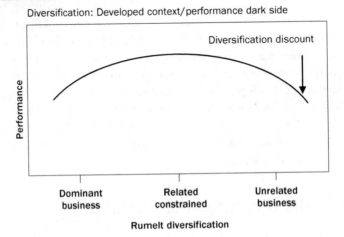

Diversification: Developed context/performance dark side

check by the presence of market agents such as institutional investors, corporate raiders, and leveraged buyout organisations; these agents may either monitor or mount hostile takeovers of businesses that have been expanded beyond an optimal point. The growing specialisation and sophistication of these capital market agents increasingly constrains managers' ability to impose type A agency costs upon shareholders. In countries such as the USA, UK, Australia and Canada, the effect of these capital market developments has been to de-institutionalise the widely-diversified conglomerate firm (Davis, Diekman and Tinsley, 1994) and most firms today organise their businesses along sharply defined lines and focus on their core competencies.

Cell 3: The group affiliation premium

The group affiliation premium is an emerging markets phenomenon; it focuses upon the advantages of broad product scope rather than ownership concentration. In emerging markets characterised by 'institutional voids' or 'missing complementary institutions' and lacking sophisticated capital markets, the trade-off between internal and external capital markets cannot be made and internal capital markets are likely to be efficient across a wider range of businesses (Khanna and Palepu, 1997). As described above, a business group may provide a range of positive assets to its affiliates including contract enforcement and access to scarce management skills, capital or technology. In this regard, continued diversification is likely to be characterised by increasing returns of scale and will probably be associated with value creation of the market premium. In these circumstances, the inverted U-shaped relation between performance and the degree of diversification does not hold. Rather, Figure 1.5 suggests a positive relationship between performance and the degree of diversification. In small economies, business groups may become very large relative to the economy as whole. In this case, the group affiliation premium may also reflect market power and the ability to extract monopoly rents.

Cell 2: Ownership concentration premium

Ownership concentration premium focuses upon the incentives of a dominant owner and the benefits of concentrated ownership of the firm. Under concentrated ownership, management and risk-bearing functions are united in the hands of a single owner or decision-making authority.

Figure 1.5 The group affiliation premium

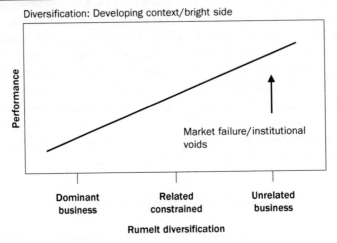

Diversification: Developing context/bright side

Concentrated ownership may take a variety of forms, such as ownership by the founding entrepreneur or his family, or the government or state authority. Concentrated ownership may also occur in specialised private equity organisations and financial institutions such as a venture capital partnership or a leveraged buyout organisation. The unification of ownership and control has several properties that may motivate a reduction in the conflict of interest found where ownership and management are separated. Because owner-managers exercise both managerial control and a direct claim on the firm's profits, they have an incentive to preserve their own resources and to use them efficiently (Alchian and Demsetz, 1972). Indeed, under certain internal and institutional conditions, concentrated ownership may produce a variety of beneficial performance outcomes. First, there is growing evidence to suggest that ownership by a founding entrepreneur who is also the firm CEO is strongly related to firm performance (Anderson and Reeb, 2003; Amit and Villalonga, 2005). Analysts suggest that founder-entrepreneurs embody certain skills, enjoy informational advantages, and adopt a long-term decision-making and investment horizon or a stewardship perspective over the enterprises they have established (Miller and Le Breton-Miller, 2005). Founding families may also view the firms as an asset to pass on to their descendants rather than a source of wealth to be consumed during their lifetimes. Hence, firm survival may become a primary concern for families rather than the maximisation of equity values. In contrast, professional managers may be self-interested and/or more preoccupied with short-term stock market constraints. The incentives of private equity organisations differ and will not be discussed here, although they possess equally compelling incentives for performance.

Several recent studies of family ownership of a public corporation in the USA suggest that these incentives are effective only within a relatively limited range of ownership. This implies that positive and negative attributes trade off against one another. With minimal equity ownership, entrepreneurs have little incentive to exert additional effort to monitor or assure the efficient use of resources. Research by Anderson and Reeb (2003) and Morck and Yeung (2003) indicates that concentrated ownership in the 10–20 per cent range appears to be associated with exceptional performance. Beyond 20 per cent ownership concentration, the positive performance effects begin to decline. Morck and Yeung conjecture that negative incentive effects, such as managerial entrenchment, begin to appear when ownership levels exceed 20 per cent. This curvilinear relationship is depicted in Figure 1.6.

In practice, the publicly-listed high-performance family firm, with a family ownership in the 10–20 per cent region and 80 per cent minority-shareholders ownership, is really a hybrid corporate form that embodies complementary incentive attributes. In particular, it is important to note that minority owners enjoy considerable and enforceable property rights. Without these rights, concentrated owners might utilise devices associated with pyramiding to expropriate minority investors. In this

Figure 1.6   **The family incentive effect**

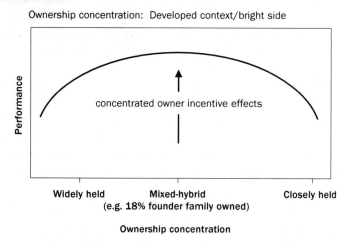

Ownership concentration: Developed context/bright side

Performance

concentrated owner incentive effects

Widely held   Mixed-hybrid   Closely held
          (e.g. **18%** founder family owned)

Ownership concentration

respect, the concentrated ownership incentive effect may depend upon the existence of sophisticated legal and stock market protection, and these institutional conditions are only associated with more developed economies.

Cell 4: Expropriation risk discount

Expropriation risk discount is an emerging market phenomenon that focuses upon the disadvantages of concentrated ownership. The focus upon the positive incentives of ownership concentration is a relatively new idea and the prevailing and established view is that ownership concentration has a mainly negative impact on performance. The performance effects of concentrated ownership, sometimes called type B agency effects, arise from the probability that concentrated large owners may use their control rights to extract private benefits at the expense of minority shareholders. Due to the illegitimate nature of minority shareholder expropriation, it is difficult to find consistent and conclusive evidence. However, Lins and Servaes (2002) provide evidence suggesting an expropriation discount in a wide range of Asian economies. Shleifer and Vishny (1997) argue that the large premiums associated with superior voting shares and other control rights, point to evidence that controlling shareholders seek to extract private benefits from their firms. In many Asian corporations there is a large divergence between control and cash-flow rights (Claessens, Djankov and Lang, 2000b). Indeed, this potential for abuse generates the motivation to provide minority investors with legal protection of their rights. Where there are few safeguards for their rights, minority shareholders rationally anticipate and expect some level of expropriation, tunnelling, propping and looting of their cash flows and will systematically discount the value of shares in firms with concentrated ownership. The effect of systematic share discounting is to depress the firm's share price and market performance. Hence Figure 1.7 suggests that performance will decline as ownership concentration increases. In underdeveloped institutional contexts, the checks and balances and regulatory constraints that are features of more advanced economies are absent. Institutional weaknesses such as the absence of minority investor protection, reliable accounting standards, and an inactive market for corporate control provide few mechanisms to permit minority shareholders to intervene and prevent prolonged value destruction. Some analysts feel that the absence of these institutions also distorts and hinders the development of capital markets and that this has

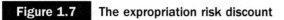

Figure 1.7 The expropriation risk discount

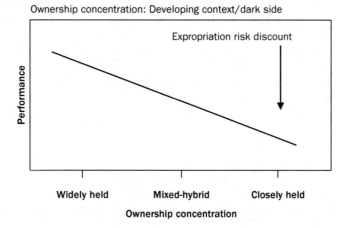

a more serious negative impact on economic development (Almeida and Wolfenzon, 2006).

Interaction of the four elements

The interaction of the four elements – performance, ownership concentration, diversification and institutional development – provides contrasting scenarios. In the context of North America and Europe, analysts have considered the diversification discount and incentive effects of concentrated ownership separately. Figure 1.8 superimposes family incentive and diversification discount on the same graph. Both effects are described by an inverted U shape, suggesting that both perspectives describe trade-offs. Initially, diversification and concentrated ownership create value but at too high a level, and both factors begin to reduce firm value. In this respect, the optimal degrees of diversification and ownership fall in an intermediate range. However, there are significant differences in corporate ownership and governance across industries and in different countries. In this respect, various hybridised corporate structures emerge to solve the particular agency problems arising from the separation of ownership and control. The widely-held, institutionally monitored firms of the UK and the USA, private equity in the form of the LBO or venture capital partnership, and the main bank systems in Germany and Japan each represent a local response to type A agency problems. In each of these structures there is

Figure 1.8 **Firms in the developed context arise as hybrid forms to cope with type A agency problems**

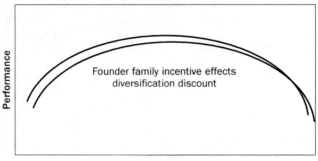

Development implies role specialisation (separation of ownership and control)
Local response develops different hybridised solution to this problem

Figure 1.9 **Business groups embody contradictory effects**

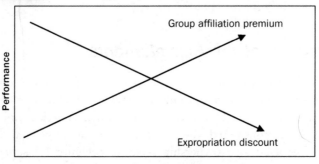

Business groups in emerging markets combine confounding effects
Much depends on local institutional solutions to the contradictions

some degree of diversification and there is also a separation of ownership and control, where professional managers are concerned with the day-to-day and strategic management of the firm, while specialised entities perform monitoring and auditing roles. Within these organisational forms, contradictory incentives and tensions are embodied in complex and specialised corporate structures.

If we perform the same exercise with the group affiliation premium and the expropriation risk discount from the emerging market context, we see a slightly different story. Here the two effects, depicted in Figure 1.9, work in opposite directions and represent contradictory effects.

Interestingly, the interaction of the two curves along the lines of ABC suggest a similar trade-off as that observed in the mature market context, albeit at an implied lower level of performance. Given the positive and negative analyses of business groups and the wide variations in their structure, ownership and product market scope, it appears that generalisations about their performance and the wider economic role they play are difficult to make.

2

Prototypes: colonial business groups in Asia before 1945

The mercantile trading groups associated with the British colonial regime and the Japanese *zaibatsu* were both key business institutions in Asia prior to 1945. The legacy of the British trading companies and *zaibatsu* is reflected in the traits of contemporary groups in Asia and in this chapter we examine their role as prototype business groups. Linked in many formal and informal ways, these diversified enterprises supplied much-emulated organisational models. Postwar governments were intent on developing their newly independent economies and encouraged entrepreneurs to exploit the numerous opportunities provided by postwar industrialisation. To do so entrepreneurs adopted the business group model in various forms.

In this chapter we examine the nineteenth-century origins of British colonial agencies[1] and Japan's *zaibatsu*, the scope of their business activities, their structure and governance, and their adaptations and subsequent decline. An examination of the full lifecycle of these prototype business groups may shed light upon the potential future of contemporary business groups. Table 2.1 identifies some of the key colonial business groups and *zaibatsu* from circa 1900–1914. After 1945, both British colonial business groups and Japanese *zaibatsu* confronted radical changes in their political environments that stimulated major changes in their structure and in the scope of their business activities. Some of these organisations went into terminal decline but others adapted and survived. Between 1945 and 1947, the US occupying authorities dismantled the *zaibatsu* but several regrouped and formed the basis of the *keirestu*, Japan's modern-day business groups. The colonial groups in Asia had a more diverse future. These nineteenth-century enterprises had begun to decline earlier in the twentieth century due to vigorous competition from local Chinese and Indian merchants, and the arrival of vertically-integrated multinational corporations. In China, the Communist Party confiscated the assets of most foreign firms between 1949 and 1952. Local owners in India and Malaysia gradually acquired the assets of colonial business groups. Other colonial business groups repatriated their assets or adopted a new geographical scope of activities. In Hong Kong, where the colonial regime persisted until 1997, local entrepreneurs acquired some colonial groups but other groups consolidated their positions and remain significant players in several commercial and financial sectors to the present day. We consider first the origins of the British colonial business groups.

The origins of colonial business groups in Asia

Table 2.1 illustrates that colonial business groups were established over a large geographic territory ranging from India to Japan, from China to

Table 2.1 Colonial business groups

Investment Group	Founded
Palmer & Co.	Calcutta, 1781
Binney & Co.	Madras, 1799
Guthrie & Co.	Singapore, 1821
Ogilvey, Gilanders	Calcutta, 1824
Boustead & Co.	Singapore, 1831
Matheson & Co.	Canton, 1832
Sassoon & Co.	Bombay, 1833
Jardine Skinner	Calcutta, 1840
McKinnon McKenzie	Calcutta, 1847
Wallace Brothers	Bombay, 1847
Ralli Bros	Calcutta, 1851
Henderson	Singapore, 1856
Finlay & Co.	Bombay, 1861
Butterfield and Swire	Shanghai, 1867
M. Samuel & Co.	Yokohama, 1878
Harrison and Crosfield	Malaya (no date)

the straits settlements of Singapore and Malaysia. Although colonial business groups were established at different points in time and traded in different commodities, they nevertheless shared several common traits, strengths and weaknesses.

The overseas colonial firm has been characterised as essentially a mercantile phenomenon variously described as an agency house (Drabble and Drake, 1981), an investment group (Chapman, 1985), a management agency (Encarnation, 1989), a freestanding company (Wilkins, 1988), an expatriate firm (Davenport-Hines and Jones, 1989), multinational traders (Jones, 1998) and business group (Jones and Wale, 1998). The profusion of terms reflects the fact that colonial business groups reinvented themselves by adapting to changing political, economic and technical circumstances; they also performed different activities at different points in time and at different stages of the region's economic and political development. Terms such as 'merchant', 'investment group' and 'agency house' suggest a limited business scope, but as Jones and Wale (1988) emphasise, the colonial firm operated within the context of a wider group of local and British-based enterprises and banks. These business groups were linked through a variety of devices including explicit contracts, equity holdings, interlocking directorships and complex social relationships, and did not operate under a unified, incorporated structure; consequently, the size and scope of the core enterprises were effectively disguised. As noted by Jones (1998: 11), 'the task of identifying investment groups is not especially easy as they were rather amorphous in character with permeable boundaries and many of them were to disappear over the course of the twentieth century'. However, the core firms at the centre of these groups were diversified and durable and were certainly much more than the financial or intermediary devices implied by the terms 'investment group' and 'agency house'.

Figure 2.1 indicates that the prototype colonial business group developed four core business activities in response to the prevailing trade and investment opportunities. These four activities were trading, financial intermediation, management agency and, latterly, franchise holding. These activities were managed within a governance structure that co-evolved along with dramatic changes in market and political conditions in the UK and Asia. By its mature phase, at the beginning of the twentieth century, the colonial business group had evolved a governance structure that is commonplace throughout Asia today. We first describe the set of environmental driving forces that shaped the colonial firms' development; second, the range of activities performed by

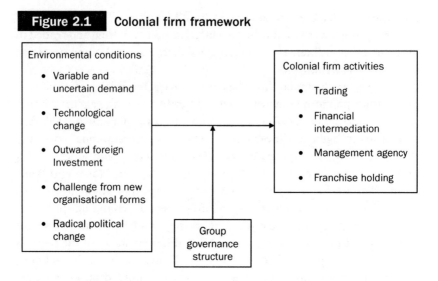

Figure 2.1 Colonial firm framework

colonial business groups are outlined; third, we describe its governance structure, and then we interpret the performance, strength and weakness of the colonial business group.

Variable and uncertain demand

The industrial revolution unfolding in Europe in the nineteenth and early twentieth century created a demand for energy, minerals and raw materials from Asia. For example, the growth in the manufacture of cotton textiles created a demand for Indian indigo, while the expansion of railways created a Thai teak logging industry to supply railway ties (Falkus, 1989). Later, the growth of the automobile industry and the development of the pneumatic tyre spurred the creation and rapid expansion of the Malayan rubber plantations (Allen and Donnithorne, 1957). A wealthy middle class stimulated the demand for Asian manufactured goods such as ceramics and silks, and for agricultural products such as spices, tea, coffee and sugar. There was also a reciprocal need to create and develop markets for European manufactured goods (Davenport-Hines and Jones, 1989). However, domestic demand for Asian commodities was highly capricious and prices were exposed to speculative bubbles. For instance, the price of Indian raw cotton was subject to a huge speculation when the British demand for cotton boomed following the outbreak of the US civil war in 1861 and the supply of US cotton to Great Britain was disrupted. When the war ended in 1865, the bubble burst, leading to a huge crisis for Indian merchants. The demand for materials was also subject to the risks posed by business cycles and from competition from substitute materials; for example, the invention of artificial dyes reduced the demand for indigo, and the invention of artificial rubber reduced the demand for natural latex (Allen and Donnithorne, 1957). Uncertainty and demand variability provided traders with a strong incentive to diversify and reduced the incentive to commit capital resources to fixed, commodity-specific assets.

Change in communication and transportation technologies

The industrial revolution was a period of enormous technological innovation; advances in communication and transportation technologies had a major impact on the opportunities and threats confronting merchant firms and also on the way they managed their business. The replacement of wooden sailing ships with steel-hulled steamships and bulk tankers and the creation of the Suez Canal vastly increased the speed and volume of European-Asian trade. In the 1870s, the activities of Asian general trading companies were undermined by the emergence of the telegraph and later the telephone because specialised commodity brokers located in Europe could deal directly with their suppliers in these distant markets. Technologies that facilitated the speed and the volume of trade reduced the working capital required to finance consignments of commodities; reduced costs benefited trading firms but also enabled many new entrepreneurs to start their own rival firms.

Outward foreign direct investment

In the period between 1870 and 1914, Britain became a major exporter of capital. Some of this investment was strictly financial in character, taking the form of bank loans to foreign governments or foreign firms. However, a significant proportion of this capital took the form of foreign direct investment in which equity investors began to seek better returns outside Britain. The spread of industrialisation and the diffusion of technical innovation created demand for mines, railways, plantations, electric and gas utilities, telecommunications infrastructure and other industrial enterprises. Direct investment differs from bank loans because investors expect to have the potential to control the use of their equity.

Prior to the creation of the multinational corporations, the 'free standing company' (Wilkins, 1988) was an important business enterprise; these companies were owned by British-based investors but locally supervised by overseas agency houses, under the so-called management agency system.

Challenge from rival organisational forms

The appearance of firms operating different organisational models posed a competitive challenge to the colonial firms' primary businesses. For example, the colonial firm's financial intermediation was undermined by the emergence and growth of multinational merchant banks in the late nineteenth century (Chapman, 1992). Multinational enterprises began to develop, especially in the USA, and these enterprises internalised many activities that colonial business groups managed by means of contractual relations. Japanese trading companies at first emulated then improved upon colonial business groups' strategies, posing a direct and formidable competitive challenge to the dominant position of the colonial firm. In addition, Indian and Chinese merchants began to adopt the agency structure to conduct business. These firms were often better connected to local business and political elites and, due to their access to family capital, enjoyed the advantage of a more stable capital structure than that provided by the partnership structure typical of the colonial firm. In some cases, merchants made radical organisational transformations in direct response to the competition by adopting a new organisational model. The case of Shell Transport and Trading is indicative and is described in Panel 2.1.

Radical political change

During periods of colonial territorial expansion in the eighteenth and nineteenth centuries, colonial business groups followed their national flag under the umbrella of British colonial rule. With origins in eighteenth-century India, British colonial business groups expanded into Malaya (Malaysia and Singapore) and the treaty ports of China. In this regard, British group expansion mirrored that of other colonial powers, and the trading houses of each major colonial power developed a distinctive sphere of influence where they were preeminent. For example, the Japanese trading houses, Matsui, Mitsubishi and Sumitomo were

---

Panel 2.1: Shell transport and trading – Victorian trader to modern multinational

In commodities for which demand was especially strong and enduring, colonial trading companies were largely shunted aside by the arrival of emerging multinationals that internalised activities previously contracted to colonial agents. The origins of the oil giant, Royal Dutch Shell, can be traced to Marcus Samuel's London-based trading company. Samuel owned an antiques business, which also imported oriental shells for use in interior design. He began importing shells from the Far East and this business laid the foundation for a successful import/export business. The scallop shell was to become Shell Transport's corporate logo. When Samuel and Marcus Samuel inherited the business from their father in 1866, they began exporting British machinery, textiles and tools to newly industrialising Japan and, from an office in Yokohama, they began importing Asian commodities to the Middle East and Europe. With the opening of the Suez Canal, the Samuels and a group of investors known as the 'tank syndicate' commissioned a fleet of oil tankers and established depots throughout the Middle East and Asia. However, Shell soon confronted vigorous competition from Rockefeller's Standard Oil, which created a vertically-integrated exploration, refining and distribution petroleum company. The Samuels' response was to form a joint venture with Royal Dutch and the Rothschilds, called the Asiatic Petroleum Company. Royal Dutch and Shell merged in 1907 to become the Royal Dutch Shell Group, which in the 1920s became a global, vertically-integrated company comparable in scale to Standard Oil. The Samuels also went on to found Samuel and Co., an important City of London merchant bank.

---

active in Korea, Taiwan and Manchuria, while Dutch traders and Dutch crown agents dominated the Dutch East Indies (Indonesia) (Allen and Donnithorne, 1957). In the wake of the Second World War, colonialism began to wane around the world and independent and sovereign states in Southeast Asia became the rule, rather than the exception. As self-government was achieved in successive countries, colonial trading houses began their retreat and initiated the process of repatriating their assets (Davenport-Hines and Jones, 1989). However, the chronology of political change varied: in India and China political change was radical and swift, in Southeast Asia the process of independence occurred during the Cold War in the context of civil conflict between nationalists, right-wing and communist parties. For example, in Malaya, the colonial administration declared a state of emergency in 1948 due to communist insurgency activities, which lasted until 1960. Malaya gained independence in 1957. In Hong Kong the colonial government persisted until 1997.

The development and diversification of the colonial firm

The prototype colonial business group in Asia followed a development path that began with trading, gradually expanding into financial intermediation, followed by the establishment of the management agency function and finally into franchise holding.

Trading

Prior to the industrial revolution, British and European trade with the rest of the world was mediated by crown-chartered trading companies who were granted trade monopolies between the homeland and a particular geographic territory. Asia was the home of the British East India Company and Dutch East India Company chartered trading companies, established in 1600 and 1602 respectively. At the end of the eighteenth century, after some two centuries of state privilege, the charter companies had lost some of their vitality and had begun to decline (Braudel, 1979). The appearance of a free-trade movement in Britain and industry's growing demand for raw materials led to the gradual relaxation of the chartered companies' monopoly. The early colonial business groups were first and foremost trading and mercantile organisations; they emerged to fill the vacuum created by the decline of the historic charter companies as trade between the UK and Asia multiplied in the wake of the unfolding industrial revolution in Britain.

Entrepreneurs who responded to this opportunity were willing to engage in two-way trade, thus facilitating the export of a vast range of agricultural commodities such as indigo, spices, coffee, tea, teak, rubber, and minerals such as tin as well as oil, while importing British manufactured goods. The two-way trade between Europe and Asia is neatly summarised by nineteenth-century entrepreneur Alexander Guthrie's description of his Singapore-based activities: 'to ship out the spices, nutmeg and pepper of the East and bring in the knives of Sheffield, the cotton goods of Lancashire and the other substantial exports of Victorian England' (Drabble and Drake, 1981: 301). Guthrie would later establish one of Singapore's eminent business groups. As one of the early movers, he was an individual with 'little capital, a keen wit and high hopes' and formed a merchant or agency house to conduct his business affairs.

The agency house first appeared in India the late eighteenth century; firms such as Forbes of Bombay, Parry's of Madras, and Palmers of Calcutta were founded between 1767 and 1798 (Tripathi, 2004) following the liberalisation of the East India Company monopoly. Many servants of the East India Company retired their positions and began to form a class of free merchants. The merchants established agency houses and began taking deposits from East India company servants and, there being no alternative exchange facility, served as a safe means of remitting funds to their families at home in Britain. Based upon the deposits made in India, a London-based agent would make payments to designated persons.

The East India Company granted licences to engage in private trade to a small number of companies. These numbers multiplied rapidly after the abolition of the East India Company's monopoly in 1813. With their contacts in London, deposits on hand locally, and knowledge of local merchant inventories and demands, agency houses began to expand their trading activities. The Indian agency house acted on behalf of a distant principal, such as a British-based ship owner or insurer; it charged a fee for securing local business for the principal and for supervising the process of trans-shipment of Indian produce. The trans-shipment style of trade married naturally to the bartering of British manufactured goods with Asian produce, for example, procuring Indian raw cotton in exchange for cotton piece goods manufactured in Lancashire. Barter minimised the need for all parties to hold large cash balances or investments in stocks. In this way, a two-way system of trade was established. The agency house would act as the agent of a British exporter and undertake to sell surplus British goods on consignment in Asia, especially English cotton and woollen goods, and would seek to procure a range of agricultural produce in demand in Britain.

An Indian agent known as a *baniya* was at the centre of the agency house operations. These agents had substantial knowledge of the character of local Indian merchants and of local supply and demand business conditions. The *baniya* was also responsible for assessing the quality and quantity of goods. On the arrival of goods, the agency house trader would break down consignments into smaller portions and advance them to local traders, often on credit. Colonial business groups based in China and the straits settlements of Malaya relied upon a *comprador*, a respected Chinese merchant to perform a similar role.

Diversification

Agency houses widened their trading-related activities to include shipping, warehousing, insurance agents, surveyors and bill brokerage. Several entered the lucrative third-country trade, especially with China. Some engaged in capital-intensive industries, which, at that time, included cotton manufacturing and, due to the growing demand for fuel, coalmining. However, the incentive to invest in fixed assets was always moderated by the need to maintain financial liquidity and thus provide the working capital for the merchants' core function of trading. London-based merchant bankers would assess the merit of their clients by the liquidity of their assets rather than by the quality of their enterprise. For a trading company, 'the cardinal commercial sin was locking up capital in risky enterprises' (Chapman, 1992: 217). Merchants who invested in fixed assets tended to purchase in easy-to-liquidate, generic assets, such as ships or commercial property that could be easily sold in the event of a liquidity crisis.

Merchants were organised as partnerships as there was no corporate law in either India or Britain at the time.[2] The partnership form was potentially unstable due to the periodic extraction of capital required when a partner retired. In addition, early Indian agency houses were dependent on the savings of company servants and wealthy Indians and these sources provided only a limited capital base. Their propensity to speculate and overtrade beyond a partnership's working capital also made agency houses prone to bankruptcy. Many agency houses remained as general traders who did not develop any particular specialisation and engaged in ventures where they had little competence. Due to their precarious capital base, many agency houses did not survive their founding partners. By 1834, all the principal agency houses in Calcutta had disappeared from the scene. Despite these high mortality rates, there was vigorous entry from new entrepreneurs willing to establish a trading business. Moreover, some firms developed a solid reputation and went on to develop new lines of business.

While many agents did not survive the system created by the first Indian agency houses, they were 'too useful to perish' (Chapman, 1985). The agency house proved highly adaptable to various lines of business and other British merchants who followed the flag of the expanding colonial regime adopted the model. Agency houses took root in the port cities of Hong Kong, Penang, Sarawak, Singapore, Shanghai and Yokohama. As agency houses sprouted up across the region, their character was shaped by the basic economic conditions, by changing technologies and the competition from indigenous entrepreneurs.

Financial intermediation

As a corollary to their trading activities, agency houses began to develop significant financial intermediation capabilities. Because agency houses had frequent recourse to barter, much trade was based upon credit. The capacity to judge the reliability and credit worthiness of a local merchant was paramount to avoiding bad debts. Merchants devised new financial instruments that developed into highly intricate systems of bills of exchange and promissory notes. At other times, merchants extended longer-term loans to affiliate firms. Competence in financial intermediation became increasingly important for merchant traders during the 1870s and 1880s. Many general trading firms failed in this period because the core trading business was undermined by the appearance of the telegraph in 1865 and later the telephone, which permitted specialised commodity brokers based in London to deal directly with suppliers in distant markets and so bypass the general trader (Chapman, 1985). Merchant banks and accepting houses also began to internationalise their activities, which also undermined the merchants' intermediation role.

In this period, the more established and successful colonial firms reinvented themselves as investment groups (Chapman, 1985) by adding investment intermediation and stock promotion to their repertoire of core activities. Colonial business groups with an intimate knowledge of local investment conditions and opportunities in the countries in which they had established their reputations were able to attract additional capital from a deeper pool of investors in Britain. Agency houses with strong links to British capital markets were set on a rich vein of investment opportunity as British equity began seeking more profitable investment opportunities than were available in Britain (Wilkins, 1988). Between 1870 and 1914, in the major metropolitan cities of the United Kingdom, thousands of freestanding companies were organised to engage in business overseas (Wilkins, 1988). Legally domiciled in Britain, freestanding companies were independent enterprises that were neither controlled by an operating enterprise nor a subsidiary of a foreign multinational. The main purpose of a freestanding company was to connect profitable overseas opportunities with British investors. The UK-based operations of freestanding companies consisted of a chairman and a board of directors, who were mandated to monitor the overseas operations and protect the rights of shareholders but little else. Chapman (1985) suggests that many of these companies' owners were little more than a brass nameplate somewhere in the City of London. Some of these ventures were fraudulent, many were in high-risk activities and others could not find suitable local management or were inadequately monitored by their British-based principals. In consequence, the mortality rate of freestanding companies was very high. However, others were substantial companies with significant assets including mines, plantations, railways, electrical and telecommunications utilities.

The better-performing freestanding firms located in Asia were those connected with established colonial groups. Wilkins (1988) argues that affiliation with an agency house constituted a governance structure or institutional apparatus for the management of specific investments and it served as an alternative to arm's length investment. In partnership with their London-based 'main' merchant bank, agency houses began to actively promote and underwrite stock issues in freestanding enterprises. As we describe below, the agency house sought to earn income from commissions and the provision of a management service rather than from dividends, so the general rule was that sufficient equity was taken to tie the affiliate to the parent. When floated companies did not generate much investor interest, the merchant retained a greater equity stake and, in this context, the merchants would operate as underwriters of new stock issues.

In the underwriting process, trading companies often became substantial holders of equity stakes in freestanding enterprises that were unrelated to trade, and hence they began a pattern of diversification that is characteristic of contemporary business groups. Jones and Wale (1998) find no systematic pattern in the equity stakes that agency houses acquired in newly floated companies. Whether trading companies reserved the best and most profitable equity issues for themselves or whether they found themselves the reluctant owners of poor-quality issues that did not sell, cannot be clearly established. What is clear is that trading companies involved in stock promotion maintained a wide range of equity stakes in these enterprises, sometimes as little as

1–2 per cent, but sometimes as majority owners. This pattern of variable equity ownership is in marked contrast to the practices of the rival Japanese *zaibatsu*, who maintained much greater ownership over their affiliates.

Debt linkages between agency houses and freestanding firms were often more important than equity because agency houses sometimes made substantial working capital loans to their affiliates and, conversely, the affiliates with surplus cash would deposit them at overseas branches (Chapman, 1985). Agency houses also borrowed large sums from UK-based banks on behalf of freestanding companies. These loans were guaranteed by the agency house in return for a commission. Because the agency house was acting as a loan guarantor, for which it charged a commission, it was essentially renting its reputation.

Figure 2.2 describes the international scope of Matheson and Co.'s international investments at the time of its incorporation in 1914. The core trading enterprise is the Hong Kong based agency house, Jardine, Matheson and Co. Its trading activities supplied access to numerous opportunities in China, such as sugar refining, cotton spinning, steam navigation and the financing of railways. Matheson and Co. was also

Figure 2.2 **Matheson and Co. circa 1914**

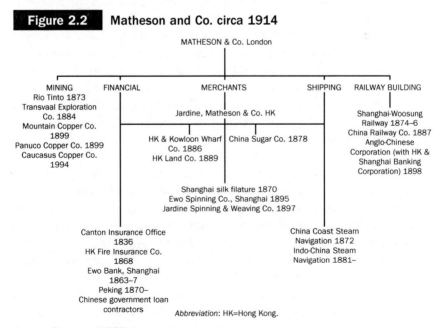

Source: Chapman (1985).

involved in the financing of mining, gold and copper exploration in Spain and Africa. The funds to finance these enterprises were channelled through the London-based partnership, which Chapman (1985) describes as an investment group.

Reputable trading companies cultivated long-term relationships with British accepting houses and merchant banks. Others developed linkages with the international banks that had begun to emerge in the second half of the nineteenth century. The credit facilities provided by domestic and overseas banks were important sources of funds and at times critical (Jones and Wale, 1998: 391). Chapman's (1985) study of the Britain's 30 largest investment groups found that families located in the City of London ultimately controlled 20 of them. The remainder were closely connected with these same families through interlocking directorships. The specialised financial intermediary function performed by groups such as Matheson is evident in Chapman's conclusion:

> There was no clear line demarcating investment groups with financial functions from merchant banks active in the promotion of public utilities and overseas shares. Indeed, the only realistic distinction seems to be between them and what might be called the English *haut bank* – Rothschilds Barings, Kleinworts, Schroders and Morgans – whose reputation depended upon their liquidity. Most of these firms were also active as issuing houses but limited their interest to safe stock, which ... often meant investments whose value had been demonstrated by investment groups. In other words the group still performed a mercantile function in a sense that they were the local experts with capital and supporting services in the countries or sectors of the world in which they specialised. (Chapman, 1985: 247)

In this regard, the affiliation of a freestanding firm with an agency house/investment group has several parallels to a venture capital partnership. Like a venture capital partnership, agency houses provide early-stage financing for the new venture but also provide monitoring and advisory functions as well as finding appropriate managerial personnel for a venture. Once a freestanding enterprise has become established, it may either be floated by one of the more prestigious merchant banks, or might be privatised and held by the founding merchant firm. For example, Burmah Oil rapidly outgrew its management agent, Finlay's of India. As one of the founder companies of the multinational, British Petroleum, Burmah's capital needs for expansion into the Middle East were too great for the agency house system. Agency houses provided their affiliated firms with a broad range of managerial services and some writers have referred to the business system of the agency house as the management agency system (Encarnation, 1989).

The growth of management agency

Chapman (1985) depicts trading companies as investment groups specialising in the early-stage financing of high-risk overseas ventures and locates the decision-making centre of the enterprise within the City of London and major metropolitan centres such as Manchester and Glasgow. Notwithstanding their geographic distance from the freestanding firms' operations, Jones and Wale (1998) argue that groups were able to develop adequate monitoring arrangements. Group head offices operated without large bureaucracies and the governance of overseas investment was the responsibility of a small board of directors consisting of six to ten members; they met weekly and often considered relatively minor items of expenditure. The board's collective ability to discharge their supervisory duties depended upon regular access to knowledge and information. Most directors had served with their companies overseas for long periods and had accumulated much regional product-specific competence. The career path to a directorship was through long service in the field abroad culminating in a senior managerial position overseas, such as branch manager. Directors each tended to become specialists and a board would include experts in the relevant commodity. It was also the practice of directors to spend several months overseas, during which they would inspect operations in detail and report back to the rest of the board. In addition, senior overseas staff back in Britain on leave would visit head office and provide directors with up-to-date information (Jones and Wale, 1998). Nevertheless, as the complexity of overseas operations increased, the decision-making capacity of the board became overloaded. Boards began to develop committee structures and groups of directors were assigned specific aspects of operations to oversee. Although control was centralised at head office, some decisions were now delegated to different levels within the group.

However, the primary difficulty for freestanding enterprises was not so much their oversight by distant principals as the difficulty of recruiting and retaining qualified local operating management and technical staff. As local agency houses were the only alternative source of expatriate managers, agencies began to turn their attention to the task of management agency and began to supply a variety of management services to freestanding firms. Management services provided by the agency houses included securing necessary materials and capital goods, shipping, insuring and selling the output, provision of working capital and the recruitment of key management and technical staff to oversee day-to-day operations. The agency function also involved assisting individual company boards in Britain in their decision making by performing secretarial tasks such as collecting, processing and transmitting information. According to Chapman (1992), the management agency system meant that a freestanding enterprise was at least nominally an independent entity with profit and loss responsibility, but in practice they functioned as subsidiaries, financially dependent upon and responsible to the management agent. The appointment of a management agent would occur simultaneously with the creation and flotation of the limited liability freestanding company. Agreements provided the freestanding company with an exclusive buying and selling agent and although the terms of such agreements were not always favourable to the company, few were ever terminated.

The idea of management agency had developed in India in the early 1840s but it was the rapid expansion of outward foreign investment that really spurred the development of the agency house function. Table 2.2 shows the expansion of the agency's role in India and Malaysia after 1914. The importance of management agency became evident in Malaysia after 1905 when the development of the motorcar precipitated worldwide growth in demand for rubber. Malaysian merchants found themselves engaged in very rapid diversification and adaptation in response to new opportunities. The Malaysian rubber boom stimulated the consolidation of small agency partnerships into large, publicly incorporated agency houses such as Bousteds, Guthrie, Harrisons and Crosfield, and Sime Derby. These large houses became much more involved in estate management and recruited staff specialising in various aspects of rubber estate management.

Freestanding plantation companies were typically too small to weather commodity price fluctuations or maintain technical and research and development staff; as a result, they became captive clients of their management agent. This dependency allowed management agencies to extract rents in the form of fixed fees for their services. One account suggests that management agencies took a basic selling commission of 1.5 per cent and a gross buying commission of 2.5 per cent on imported and local purchases, in a addition to charging an annual

Table 2.2 Post-First World War expansion of British management agencies

India	1916		1939	
Agency house	No.	Value*	No.	Value*
Tata	7	60.2	9	216.3
Birds and Heilgers	34	42.6	30	56.3
Gillanders Arbuthnot	9	40.0	16	36.5
Killick Nixon	10	38.4	13	63.7
Andrew Yule	36	28.6	51	68.0
Martin Burn	15	22.6	28	102.5
McLeod	17	17.5	17	22.5
Jardine Skinner	15	15.9	13	25.2
Macneill Barry	8	10.3	12	32.0
Shaw Wallace	17	9.0	17	11.0
Begg Dunlop	12	6.6	15	16.3
Duncan	13	5.4	25	19.2
Octavius Steel	12	4.5	23	13.2
Williamson Magor	10	4.8	14	7.0
James Finlay	3	3.1	8	17.2

Malaysia	1913		1940	
Agency	No.	Acreage†	No.	Acreage†
Barlow	31	8.3; 4.7	21	7.8; 6.0
Cumberbatch	27	3.8; 2.6	67	13.4; 11.7
Whittall	27	6.1; 3.1	29	5.6; 4.8
Harrisons & Crosfield	26	10.5; 4.4	78	39.3; 25.6
F. W. Barker	24	7.6; 2.6		
Guthrie	25	15.7; 4.7	33	30.4; 21.4
Boustead	22	8.1; 3.8	53	20.1; 15.7
Sime Darby Kennedy	12	2.0; 1.1	34	11.1; 9.5
Kennedy	9	1.9; 1.3	29‡	5.9; 4.6

* Value = capital controlled, in millions of rupees
† Acreage controlled in 10,000s acres; the first figure is the total acreage owned, the second the acreage planted
‡ Incorporating Burkill
Source: Koike (1993: 141).

secretarial fee, an annual agency fee per acre of estate management, and a handling and shipping fee per pound of produce (Drabble and Drake, 1981). Fees were modified from time to time, but for the most part the owners of the freestanding plantation company bore the all the risk. Profits might be high if commodity prices were high; however, because they controlled all the key dependencies, the agency houses dominated the relationship with freestanding firms. Indeed, Drabble and Drake (1981) suggest that management agents effectively 'digested' the rubber plantation companies without ever actually owning their assets.

Agency houses were always investigating opportunities for new lines of business. Drabble and Drake describe the situation at a leading Malaysian Agency House:

> Guthrie time and again toyed with the idea of undertaking local manufacturing, especially rubber goods, but did not act. When very liquid in 1919 the firm leant towards a less ambitious strategy of acquiring local land and godown (warehouses) on the grounds that such assets will always be readily acceptable loan collateral should money be tight in the future. (Drabble and Drake 1981: 311)

In the 1920s, the major opportunity to present itself to the agency houses was automobile distribution. Major American and European automobile manufacturers recognised that purchasing used and selling new automobiles was a viable trading proposition and one best suited to independent distribution (Chandler, 1990). Automobile manufacturers pioneered the concept of territorial franchises in which an agent would have an exclusive distribution agreement for a particular line of automobiles. The India-based agency house now known as Inchcape exemplifies the importance of automobiles franchising. Panel 2.2 describes the 200-year evolution of the Calcutta-based agency house MacKinnon and Mackenzie; today it is a multinational automobile franchise company. The significance of automobile distribution lies in the growth potential of franchise holding which permitted the continued diversification by agency houses.

Franchise holding

There are several parallels between the activities of management agency and franchise holding. Both activities involve the task of intermediation between distant principals and local actors. Both depend upon the agency's intimate knowledge of local operating and demand conditions

Panel 2.2: The transformation and development of Inchcape Group

Skills in management agency proved highly adaptive and influential as the basic competences of managerial agency are applicable across a wide range of settings. The resilience of the Inchcape Group exemplifies the adaptive qualities of the colonial agent. This organisation describes itself as 'An expert in local marketing on behalf of prestigious principals around the world'. Inchcape PLC is a British trading group headquartered in central London. It has a varied history but now specialises in car distribution. In 1990, for example, Inchcape distributed 8 per cent of Toyota's automobile production worldwide. Today, it also holds several automobile franchises including Lexus, Subaru, Ferrari/Maserati, BMW, Jaguar and Land Rover in markets such as the UK, Greece, Belgium, Australia, Hong Kong and Singapore. It supplies cars to dealers and corporate customers and has also entered the retail dealership market. In addition, it provides ancillary services such as consumer and dealer finance, insurance and leasing. Inchcape was founded in 1847 as a Calcutta-based agency house of MacKinnon and Mackenzie and Co., which also founded the Burmah Steam Navigation Co. For its first century, Inchcape's interests were concentrated in India, where it was involved in tea, coal, jute and various trading enterprises. Its pattern of diversification seems to have been driven by the need to provide shipping agency services to the British India Steam Navigation Company, which was formerly the Burmah Steam Navigation Co. (Jones, 1988).

Following India's independence, Inchcape sought to diversify and acquired assets in the UK. It also entered the Southeast Asia region through acquisition of firms such as the Anglo-Thai Corporation, Dodwell and Co., Gilman and Co. and parts of Hong Kong based Hutcheson Whampoa. Inchcape also acquired the Borneo Company and doubled the revenues of the company. Each of these firms was a major trading company in its own right; they operated in Thailand, Hong Kong and Singapore, and many held European and Japanese automobile franchises. Through these acquisitions, Inchcape entered new geographical markets in businesses it knew well or entered new businesses in territories it knew well. The firm later diversified its trading activities into East Africa, Australia and the Persian Gulf, acting as an agent for British companies such as BAT, ICI and BOAC. In its capacity as an agent, Inchcape's role was much the same as it had been in its early years. At one point in the 1980s, Inchcape marketed products for some 700 manufacturers in Asia, Latin America and the Middle East (Jones, 2000). In 1990, Inchcape derived over 50 per cent of its profits from the Far East and Southeast Asia and determined that it had ten core businesses (Jones, 2000). Inchcape experienced a major crisis in the mid-1990s; collapsing profits led to the implementation of a programme of divestment which left the firm focused on a few core businesses, mainly motor vehicle distribution. Inchcape reinvented itself several times and is now a multinational franchise holder. It is listed on the London Stock Exchange and is a constituent of the FTSE 250 Index.

and must employ soft skills to monitor and mange the delicate incentive trade-offs specified in complex franchise agreements. However, there are significant differences in principal-agent power relationships stipulated in management agency and franchise holding contracts. Under management agency there is a significant power asymmetry between strong local agents and the relatively weak arm's-length shareholders in freestanding firms. In contrast, principal-agent relationships are more equally balanced in franchise holding. The franchisor is typically the owner of proprietary assets or intellectual property and is much better organised to determine the terms of rent sharing with the agency house than an arm's-length investor. For example, under a Coke-bottling or fast food master franchise agreement, the franchisor typically sets an up-front franchise purchase fee, requires the franchisee to invest in dedicated, franchise-specific assets, and takes a percentage of revenues (Carney and Gedjlovic, 1991). The agency house, as the franchisee, earns rent from residual returns. Indeed, the structure of modern franchising reverses the fixed-fee residual returns arrangement of the management agency relationship.

In the years following 1945, several Asian states began to embark upon strategies of industrialisation, precipitating a rapid growth in the demand for capital goods, machinery and business services produced by North American, European and, increasingly, Japanese firms. Growing prosperity in the region fuelled demand for a rich variety of consumer goods. With their affinity for managing complex contracts, the agency houses diversified into numerous new lines of activity through franchise holding. Consider the case of the Hong Kong based agency house, Jardine-Matheson. In addition to its traditional trading, property, land development and financial businesses, Jardine holds the Pizza Hut franchises in Hong Kong and Australia, Taco Bell in Hawaii, and the Mercedes Benz franchises in Hong Kong, Macao and South China.

Jardine Heavy Industries holds the Caterpillar franchise in Taiwan and Schindler's elevators for all of Asia. Jardine also operates the Chubb and Securicor franchises and distributes numerous liquor and luxury brands. Through a food and drug retail subsidiary, it operates the 7-11 convenience store franchise and is the sole agent for many western branded products. Agency houses such as Swire, Inchcape and Sime-Darby hold comparable franchises. The growth of franchise holding by agency houses represents one more adaptation to the changing competitive and economic environment. Just as technology changes undermined the agency houses' pure trading activities and the appearance of international banks limited the scope of their financial intermediation activities, the development of the multinational firm threatened their function as a management agency. As firms in Europe and North America began to learn more about international competitive conditions, they began to re-internalise certain activities that had been outsourced to agency contracts. Indeed, the threat of re-internalisation is an endemic problem for colonial agents. For example, as late as the 1960s, the colonial agent Jardine-Matheson represented Vickers Aircraft in its sale of Viscount Aircraft to mainland China. However, by the early 1970s Hawker-Siddley managed to arrange the sale of Trident Aircraft to the Chinese government without the negotiating expertise of Jardine. With the consolidation of the aircraft industry, manufacturers now routinely handle the marketing function in this region internally.

Governance and structure of colonial business groups

Responding to the dynamic technological, economic and political environment of the nineteenth and early twentieth centuries, colonial agency houses diversified across a broad range of activities. They governed these diverse portfolios by developing a complex lattice of governance mechanisms to manage their relationships with capital markets, European manufacturers and Asian-based traders and customers. These relations are depicted in Figure 2.3.

Initially, agency houses adopted the partnership form of governance, with typically Dickensian sounding names like Butterfield and Swire, Jardine and Skinner, Harrisons and Crossfields. They internalised activities with high transactions costs (Jones and Wale, 1998), but in most cases agency houses avoided the costs of full internalisation by

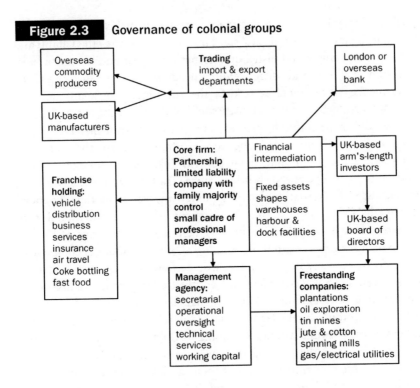

Figure 2.3 Governance of colonial groups

using governance devices such as minority equity stakes, debt contracts, cross-directorships, social relationships, and complex legal contracts. Jones and Wale suggest:

> The organisational structure of Finlays, Harrisons and Crossfield, and Borneo can be described as a business group consisting of a core trading company surrounded by a cluster of non wholly-owned firms which engaged in repeated transactions with one another. Contracts formed a very important component of the links between the parent in the affiliate but the parent was more than a market provider of the consulting distribution and financial services because there was also ties of equity and cross directorships and because the contracts were repeatedly renewed. (Jones and Wale 1998: 391)

This combination of diversification and non-hierarchical governance suggests that we should consider the colonial agency houses as prototype business groups that embody both positive and negative governance attributes.

Governance merits in colonial business groups

Lower transactions costs

Analyses that emphasise business groups' capacity to reduce transaction costs and view their reputation as a signalling device that assists in acquiring scarce resources in factor markets, describe positive attributes that are also evident in colonial business groups. These colonial business groups provided one solution to the severe problems of opportunism, information asymmetry, bounded rationality and other transactions costs attendant on international trade. The most successful groups cultivated and sustained a reputation for competence, moral probity and respect for contracts. These reputational assets provided access to London's capital markets, at that time the largest in the world, and later, to a wider pool of capital that was generated during the mature stages of the British industrial revolution. In both cases, the 'reputation for competence and honesty of the parent trading company was used to attract outside stockholders into investing in new companies' (Jones and Wale, 1998: 387). Similarly, their reputations permitted colonial business groups to operate in distant commodity markets on the basis of barter and credit, a context in which there was little legal redress for opportunistic business practice. The transactions costs advantage to colonial business groups is apparent in the simultaneous reduction in working capital requirements and increased trading volumes supported by the trust and goodwill implicit in their reputation.

Quasi-capital markets

Theories suggesting that business groups served as a quasi-internal capital market for their members are also supported by evidence that colonial business groups' financial intermediation activities constitute a form of investment group (Chapman, 1985). In this role, colonial business groups shared several characteristics with contemporary venture capital partnerships (Jones and Khanna, 2006). The central, core firms of colonial business groups retained partnership status, providing the principals with high-powered incentives to seek out and engage in profitable businesses. The leakage of capital out of the group as partners retired was a disincentive to overexpansion and forced the principals to exercise diligence in selecting industries for investment. The production and marketing of tropical commodities was highly risky because they were subject to fluctuations in price and demand and to crop and production failures. Colonial business groups that had access to capital from profit-seeking, arm's-length investors in London could acquire the resources necessary for the establishment and development of start-up enterprises. The boundaries of these business groups were permeable because new activities were spun off into separate companies in a continuing process of new firm creation. Like contemporary venture capital partnerships and business groups, colonial business groups also provided human capital resources to the enterprises they sponsored. In this regard, there is some support for the idea that business groups can be a source of scarce human capital in emerging market conditions.

Sources of human capital

Although the management agency system enabled a limited number of experienced managers to apply their professional skills in more than one field (Jones and Khanna, 2006), business groups in emerging markets know that management talent can be very scarce. Indeed, there is much evidence of incompetent management among the colonial groups and the problem of finding competent managers proved to be an enduring one. The management historian Alfred Chandler (1990) argued that pre-1945, British enterprise was characterised by a style of personal capitalism that lacked the capacity for generating the profound managerial and organisational capability necessary for international competitive advantage. For example, Chandler famously failed to find a single organisational chart for a pre-war British company. However, Jones and Wale (1998) retort that Britain is a 'high context culture' that relies upon a more tacit and informal approach to international organisation. Managerial duties, performance expectations and rules were implicit, and there was less reliance upon formal hierarchy. The control system might best be described as governance through socialisation.

International business in the nineteenth century required substantial delegation of authority to managers in the field. In the absence of direct hierarchical control, founding entrepreneurs were careful to select managerial staff that shared some basic affinities. Jones and Wale (1998) emphasise the importance of personal recommendation from members of social and religious groups that shared core values and beliefs. For example, Finlays and other Glasgow-based agencies vigorously recruited privately-educated, protestant Scots who were steeped in traditional Scottish values of moral probity and financial acumen. Most of the elite managerial cadre at Jardines was recruited in the county of

Dumfriesshire in Scotland (Jones and Wale, 1998). Because the greatest threat to a trading company was unauthorised speculative dealings, these houses sought to cultivate a managerial cadre which could be relied upon not to act opportunistically. To mitigate this risk, senior management practised 'ritual denunciation' of such activity (Jones and Wale, 1998). Chapman (1992) also stresses the importance of shared values and points to the great diversity of religious and ethnic networks that supported long-distance trade. The leading nineteenth-century 'British' trading firms were more often anchored in émigré communities of Germans, Greeks and Americans and recruited staff from within them (Chapman, 1992: 288). English and Scottish merchants were often linked through membership of small non-conformist religious congregations. The careful selection of managers, the existence of shared values and strong social bonds allowed colonial business groups' organisational structures to be more fluid and adaptive to new business opportunities.

Colonial business groups also relied heavily on incentives to motivate their senior managers in the field. Managers might be recruited with the expectation of lifetime employment but they were nevertheless appointed on three or five-year contracts which were not renewed automatically. The performance and behaviour of individual staff were discussed at board meetings and monitoring was reinforced by periodic visits. The core criteria used to appraise the performance of field management were often implicitly based on the financial performance of the branch of activity in which the staff member was involved. Success would be based upon 'the energetic pursuit of profitable business opportunities' within implied behavioural rules. Unorthodox behaviour in an expatriate community was very badly regarded (Jones and Wale, 1998). These performance criteria permitted considerable discretion and, within the implied behavioural rules, managers had autonomy to pursue new lines of activity. Chapman (1985) identifies a career path in which a combination of long and short-term incentives also reinforced the behavioural normative controls. The traditional development of the successful merchant house featured young partners investing their early careers in overseas stations and returning to a 'home' partnership as they attained entrepreneurial maturity. This arrangement 'assured a regular testing and turnover of the partners and directors' (Chapman, 1985). Viewed in this manner, colonial groups can be regarded as the generators and allocators of the scarce and valuable human capital necessary for the integration of emerging markets into the global trading system.

Governance problems in colonial business groups

Criticism of the management and governance of colonial business groups has centred on their family ownership. Indeed, dark-side perspectives view these business groups as opaque family-controlled pyramids with a structure designed to protect family wealth while externalising risks to minority arm's-length investors. On this point Chapman (1985: 243) is unequivocal when he says 'there can be no serious doubt that the investment group was primarily a device to maintain the wealth and power of the family (or families) that controlled the particular business'. The investment group system allowed the traditional, closely-knit family firm to acquire many of the advantages of the joint-stock company without losing control. The family name attracted and retained the necessary capital, while the joint-stock system contained any possible loss (Chapman, 1985). The system also offered advantages to the investor because neither the main banks nor the stock exchange were able to monitor investments in distant parts of the world. The family business group offered a relatively cheap and secure way of acquiring high rates of return from foreign investments.

While Jones and Wale (1998) acknowledge that the trading companies embodied acute principal-agency problems, they claim that 'these issues were identified and addressed'. Others are less sanguine in this regard and the means by which families extracted wealth bears consideration. We previously argued that colonial business groups that used their strong reputations to attract capital would be unlikely to promote share issues in dubious ventures. However, freestanding companies had alarming failure rates and their promoters would be motivated to retain their interest in promising ventures while shorting riskier and troubled ventures if they could do so undetected. Under conditions of high information asymmetry and complex organisational structures it is very difficult for shareholders to identify this form of opportunism.

Chapman (1992: 245) suggests that the striking feature of the investment group system is that 'it deliberately concealed the true magnitude of its operations behind a modest financial data of the parent company and this has always deceived historians'. It is also possible that deliberate concealment may have also deceived minority investors who delegated the task of monitoring to small, but well-connected boards of directors. These directors were intimately connected with financial elites in London, and their diligence in protecting the rights of minority shareholders cannot be easily ascertained. Moreover, empirical tests such as Chapman's family-wealth maintenance hypothesis are difficult to effect. Most of the surviving data on these enterprises consist of corporate biographies written by retired partners or senior executives who, not surprisingly, are reluctant to disclose findings that could tarnish the illustrious histories of these pioneering businesses (Chapman, 1992).

Nevertheless, there is some consensus that the greatest potential for opportunism by colonial business groups centred on the management agency system. Drabble and Drake (1981) suggest that the system was riddled with conflicts of interest. The agency structure severely misaligns incentives for the managing agent relative to minority investors in the freestanding firms. While minority shareholders benefit only from the profits of the firm, the managing agent enjoyed access to a series of taps through which value might be extracted from the firm, including fixed fees and fees based upon sales volume. The agent thus had an incentive to promote volume growth, to retain earnings, and to suppress the distribution of profits to shareholders. Nineteenth-century court cases provide some evidence of this kind of behaviour, but in general, the rights of minority shareholders did not enjoy much support from the English legal system. While management agents and freestanding firms were separate entities in law, there was significant ambiguity about the allocation of decision rights regarding fees and charges and, in every respect, the management agency 'clearly held the whip hand' (Drabble and Drake, 1981: 310). In the following chapters we shall address a recurrent theme: family owner-managers in opaque and vague organisational settings who appear well positioned to protect their interests at the expense of minority shareholders who possess limited or unenforceable property rights in law.

Colonial business group performance

Due to the absence of reliable data, there are few studies of colonial business groups' financial performance before 1914. Jones' (2000) study of the financial performance of eight trading companies between 1895 and 1914 shows highly variable returns on capital employed. In the war years, trading companies' returns boomed, as did those of the *zaibatsu*, and they enjoyed a generally positive performance in the 1920s. Thereafter, following the 1929 Wall Street crash, the 1930s depression, the First World War, and the Cold War, the environment for trading changed. Since the watershed of the Second World War, colonial business groups have declined in absolute economic terms and many groups have not survived. Such precipitous decline warrants explanation. Three differing accounts of decline have attracted some support: radical political change in their operating environments, inherent limitations with governance and organisational structures, and the changing pattern of competitive advantage.

The statement of absolute decline must, however, be qualified. It is evident from the earlier discussion that colonial business groups performed several value-adding activities, most importantly reducing the transactions costs of international trade, and providing funds and managerial resources for the establishment of international ventures. Some colonial groups attained great size and several also created, incubated and spun-off numerous durable, focused and competitive businesses. A few business groups, such as Swire and Jardine Matheson, have remained important under their original owners. Other colonial groups, such as Hutchinson Whampao in Hong Kong and Sime Darby, remain among the most prominent enterprises in the region, albeit operating under new ownership. Yet others have shifted the geographic scope of their activities. In addition, the chronology of decline is variable. The acquisition of British firms by local entrepreneurs in India dates from the 1920s (Tripathi, 2004). In an environment of hostility and nationalism, almost all foreign enterprise became unviable in Japan during the 1930s (Davenport-Hines and Jones, 1989). Following Malayan independence in 1957, the ownership of many colonial business groups passed into the hands of local entrepreneurs in a sequence of often hostile takeovers (Van Helten and Jones, 1989). In other parts of the region, an emergent class of overseas Chinese entrepreneurs purchased the assets of retreating colonial agents (Mackie, 1992). In a slightly later period, there was a similar drift into local ownership in Hong Kong when firms such as Wheelock Marden and Hutchinson Whampoa were acquired in the 1970s and 1980s. In China, colonial assets were nationalised within five to eight years of the communist revolutions (Osterhammel, 1987).

Radical political change

After the Second World War, colonial rule began to wane around the world. In Southeast Asia, independent and sovereign states became the rule rather than the exception. As an obvious symbol of the region's colonial past, foreign-owned colonial-era businesses were especially vulnerable to anti-colonial sentiment. Wariness of foreigners was a legacy of colonial rule and, along with the threat of ascendant communism, led the region's governments to pursue nationalist agendas. Long accustomed to being the compatriots of colonial administrators,[3] the trading houses were now operating in hostile environments in which newly-constituted indigenous governments instituted far-reaching nationalist economic programmes (Falkus, 1989; Van Helten and Jones, 1989; Mackie, 1992). As successive countries attained self-rule, colonial business groups began their retreat and initiated the process of repatriating their assets (Davenport-Hines and Jones, 1989).

Unaccustomed to operating in such environments, and with business practices rooted in the colonial order, colonial businesses were confronted with two fundamental options. They could either radically transform their business practices to the new nationalistic environment, or they could embark upon exit strategies designed to repatriate their investments in the region. Some colonial businesses chose the option of remaining and adapting, but many more chose the latter option and repatriated their assets (Allen and Donnithorne, 1957; Drabble and Drake, 1981).

The fate of the colonial firm in India exemplifies the process of post-colonial decline. Encarnation (1989: 57) describes a rapid Indianisation of colonial enterprises following 1945, which he largely attributes to the inability of cash-strapped British agency headquarters located in London and Liverpool to invest in their overseas affiliates. British agencies in India quickly mobilised local Indian capital as an alternative means of financing their local expansion and also to fund the continuing repatriation of profits to the UK-based shareholders. Indian business houses responded adroitly to the opportunity. By mid-1948, Indian business held more than 85 per cent of the equity in colonial management agencies. Historically, Indian and British capital had been intermingled to create a form of partnership. For example, Tata became associated with MacNeil, and Mukherjee and Banerjee with Martin Burn. One year after political independence, colonial British enterprise was almost entirely dependent on Indian shareholders. Converting equity ownership into managerial control was not immediate as British managers used several complex strategies to ensure continued control, but 'the insistence of Indian shareholders that ownership in British agencies be converted into control could not be denied' (Encarnation, 1989: 58). During the 1950s, Indian-managed business houses began to replace British firms as the dominant enterprises in the economy, and by 1957, the process of takeover through encroachment had run its course. A similar process of localisation of ownership and control occurred in Malaysia (Drabble and Drake, 1981; Van Helten and Jones, 1989).

Limits to groups' governance structures

Colonial business groups were intermediaries and had little inclination or competence in industries requiring capital intensity and the deployment of specialised, dedicated assets, such as those required for mining or manufacturing. Indeed, the development of the colonial-era firm is marked by an aversion to manufacturing. However, the economic goals of postcolonial independent and nationalist governments were very much focused on diversifying and industrialising their economies while reducing their dependence upon agriculture and the export of natural resources. Except as intermediaries and providers of business services, colonial business groups were not well equipped to seize the opportunities offered by the coming of industrial capitalism and the development of export-oriented manufacturing. Consequently, British colonial groups remained focused upon their traditional areas of activity and were conspicuous by their lack of participation in postwar industrialisation. Their governance and organisational systems worked well for activities based around trade and the exploitation of resources, but were less suited to financing, coordinating and developing the proprietary technological competences characterising large-scale and capital-intensive industries such as automobile manufacturing and consumer electronics. Put another way, colonial groups' core competencies were suited to a broad range of trading, intermediation agency and franchise-holding activities, but these competencies were finite; consequently, they were unlikely to be pioneers of radical new technologies or industrial processes. In hindsight, colonial business group governance systems and the core competencies they supported were well aligned to the uncertainty, information asymmetries and financial risks attendant on early transnational trade between emerging markets and dynamic industrialising economies.

The changing balance of competitive advantage

The decline of colonial groups also reflects changing trade flows and a shift in the balance of competitive advantage to local firms versus overseas firms. Colonial groups' advantage was always based on their knowledge of both the local Asian market as well as the trading conditions in Britain and Europe. The value of these advantages began to diminish in the post-1945 era. As the pace of Asian industrialisation began to accelerate after 1945, trade among Asian states became relatively more important than Asia-European trade. As we shall see below, trade within Northern Asia was soon dominated by Japanese enterprises and later, overseas Chinese merchants began to capture Southeast Asian trade. The growth of Pacific trade between Asia and North America further marginalised the colonial groups. Moreover, the intermediary's advantage is based upon information asymmetries. When buyers and sellers interact directly, the intermediary's information advantage becomes less valuable and, in addition, sellers may vertically integrate into marketing functions. Hennart and Kryda (1998) suggest that, when intermediary risks are frozen out of the transaction, trading firms may invest in manufacturing to maintain their stake in trade. However, as noted above, colonial groups were always reluctant to move decisively in this direction.

Zaibatsu

In Japanese 'zai' means money or fortune, while 'batsu' is a clique or an elite (Fukuyama, 1995). A zaibatsu is a group of diversified businesses owned exclusively by a single family or an extended family (Morikawa, 1992: xvii). The zaibatsu were the main instrument of Japan's industrialisation and transformation between 1880 and 1941; in a relatively short time, they rapidly gained economic power and accumulated massive wealth.

Before 1868, Japan had been a closed society with no contact with the industrialising nations of Europe and North America. With the restoration of the Meiji emperor in 1868, Japan embarked upon a headlong rush to modernise. From a practical perspective, we can view the zaibatsu as a mechanism for technological and economic catch-up. They provided the pools of scarce management talent and the capital that was needed to bring Japan the advanced science-based industries that were driving the second industrial revolution in the West, for example, chemicals, electrical equipment and metal fabrication.

The Japanese state sanctioned the activities and growth of the zaibatsu, but relations between business and government were not always harmonious. Indeed, the complex, intricate relationships with the state explain many of the zaibatsu's strategic decisions and organisational features during their rapid rise to maturity and their subsequent decline.

Table 2.3 provides a two-tier list of the most important *zaibatsu*. The top four were first movers; they significantly dominated the early stages of development and continue to be important today. The fortunes of the *zaibatsu* in the lower tier are more diverse. Some, such as Nomura and Assano, did not survive the economic and political turmoil of the 1930s. Others, such as Furakawa, caught up with the first movers to join the ranks of the first tier.

The family owners of *zaibatsu* exercised control through a family council and the small secretarial staff at their corporate headquarters engaged in the informal coordination and passive oversight of the diverse enterprises. The headquarters staff were not intimately involved in strategy formation or major investment decisions; rather, professional managers in the subsidiaries were granted considerable autonomy to determine their own strategies and moves into new markets. The story of the development of the *zaibatsu* is characterised by an increasing growth in the capital intensity of their enterprises and the very gradual dilution of family ownership. Indeed, at their dissolution, one could argue that the major *zaibatsu* were essentially family-owned enterprises (Fukuyama, 1995).

Table 2.3   *Zaibatsu*

The big four
Mitsubishi
Mitsui
Sumitomo
Yasuda
Second-tier zaibatsu
Asano
Fujita
Furukawa
Mori
Kawasaki
Nakajima
Nitchitsu
Nissan
Nisso
Nomura
Okura
Riken
Shibusawa

Source: http://www.experiencefestival.com/a/Zaibatsu_-_
List_of_zaibatsu/id/5605361 (accessed 3 October 2007).

Origins

Sumitomo and Furakawa originated as copper mining companies who held government-granted, exclusive mineral rights. Yasuda, Mitsubishi and Mitsui were originally political merchants who served as tax collectors for the government. Political merchants appeared in feudal-era Japan; they acted as intermediaries between government and peasants who paid land taxes to the state in the form of goods in kind, such as rice or other agricultural commodities. Trusted and well-established merchants were responsible for collecting and handling commodities, selling them in markets and sending the currency to the government coffers. Serving as the fiscal arm of the state placed the political merchants in a privileged position relative to the government, but the fiscal business was extremely risky as the government often made unpredictable demands for funds and political merchants were required to pay kickbacks to state officials. Moreover, if political patrons fell from power, the dependent enterprise also suffered a severe loss of privilege. Several powerful political merchant businesses failed for these reasons.

Nevertheless, several *zaibatsu* accumulated substantial fortunes on the basis of their political connections, and some sought to reduce their dependence on political patronage by expanding their trading business and diversifying into the new businesses. For example, Mitsui operated a dry goods store, which was a forerunner to its department stores. The move into banking was a natural step. The multitude of currencies in circulation during the early restoration period included paper money, gold coins and silver dollars. To facilitate trade, merchant houses also operated commercial currency exchange services. Based upon its experience in rice trading, Mitsui established a trading division, Mitsui Bussan, which expanded into international commodity trading with offices in Nagasaki, Shanghai, Hong Kong, London and Paris. By the 1920s, Mitsui Bussan shipped over 30 per cent of Japan's international trade.

Similarly, Yasuda was a political merchant specialising in the evaluation of gold and silver. These exchange enterprises formed the basis of Japan's first banks. Yasuda did not engage in any manufacturing businesses but diversified into various financial activities such as marine and life insurance. Mitsubishi was the most diversified *zaibatsu* in this period, with interests in copper and coal mines, agriculture and ship repair. However, all their major businesses were related to the ownership of Japan's largest shipping fleet. Mitsubishi Shipping Enterprises held the government marine mail monopoly, and during Japan's colonial expansion, Mitsubishi ships served as military transports. Mitsubishi entered the banking business to provide the trade credit services needed to support their merchant marine business. A coalmine was acquired to provide fuel for its steamships and Mitsubishi's expansion into ship repair was a natural by-product of the shipping business. The decision to enter shipbuilding resulted in the creation of a very large-scale shipyard in Nagasaki, and Mitsubishi won a share of the contracts to build battleships for the Japanese navy.

The *zaibatsu* did not play an important part in the establishment of the railways and the cotton-spinning industries, the most capital-intensive enterprises of the time. In these industries, the opened joint-stock company was the most eminent organisational form, and although the *zaibatsu* were sometimes important stockholders in these enterprises, they did not participate in the management. In the rush towards modernisation, the state established several enterprises that relied on imported machinery and highly-paid foreign engineers. These state-owned enterprises proved to be very inefficient and the government sought private sector owners to manage them. The *zaibatsu* took advantage of the opportunity offered by the state and of other privatisation programmes initiated during the 1880s. Within a very short period, the *zaibatsu* had diversified into a range of related commercial, trading, mining and manufacturing activities.

In this nascent period, capital for the development of these enterprises was generated from internal sources, including banking and trading, and through political merchant activities. Moreover, most activities were not capital-intensive. Japanese enterprises were quite large; their ownership extended to numerous members of the head family and included numerous branches. However, few family members participated in the management of the enterprise, and due to the diversity of the activities, it was soon evident that the controlling families needed the help of outside managers. The *zaibatsu* moved quickly to establish formal organisational structure and governance arrangements. The principal change was the creation of the family council, consisting of several family members, as well as an equal number of outsiders, including executives. Another important development was the establishment of a commercial code in 1893, which instituted the principle of limited liability companies in Japan. *Zaibatsu* families organised their enterprises in multiple, independent, closely held, limited liability companies.

Talented professional managers headed each of the main companies. Very soon after their foundation, the *zaibatsu* used several means to acquire a cadre of university educated managers. Mitsubishi led the way in hiring educated men. Its shipping business required multilingual managers, and many members of its upper management were foreigners. Mitsui invested heavily in training managers. Mitsui Bussan made a strategic decision to end its reliance on compradors in China and thus avoid paying commissions. Instead, it required its overseas managers in the branches to learn local languages and to engage in trading directly with principals. The acquisition of former state enterprises brought new talent to the private sector as state-owned enterprises frequently employed well-educated engineers and law graduates. Sumitomo filled management positions by recruiting retiring government bureaucrats.

The *zaibatsu*'s adoption of and extensive reliance upon professional management so soon after their establishment is a novel feature of Japanese industrial organisation. Fukuyama (1995) suggests that the practice of adopting outsider managers into the family estate was well established in traditional Japanese culture: the *banto* was an experienced and pragmatic individual who could be trusted to operate the family's business affairs. Initially, the *zaibatsu* relied upon the traditional *banto* to manage their enterprises, but the *banto* were men of narrow scope with skills derived from traditional experience and found it difficult to keep up with the hectic pace of modernisation after the Meiji restoration. Morikawa (1992) suggests that in this period, wealthy families quickly realised that reliance on traditional kinship patterns would put their business and wealth in jeopardy. Families recognised the need to bring in 'men of talent' and, above all, this meant those who possessed knowledge of the West, its business practice, technology and customs. It was believed that this knowledge could only be attained through higher education, and so bringing in highly-educated personnel was considered to be in the interests of *zaibatsu* families. Such men were in short supply and families competed to attract and retain them.

Family councils initially attempted a tighter system of control in which numerous detailed decisions were brought to counsel for discussion and approval. Families responded to the heavy flow of information by organising a secretariat to manage and formalise the headquarters-subsidiary relationship. However, closed control proved to be inflexible and slow in responding to opportunity; consequently, the system was overwhelmed by too much detail. Families responded by producing new or updated family constitutions in which the principles of family wealth preservation were spelled out. For example, the Mitsui family constitution contained ten chapters with 109 sections, specifying who had the right to participate in the joint ownership of the house assets. Family constitutions also spelled out conflict resolution mechanisms, procedures for the appointment of an arbitrator and restrictions on the family council's ability to interfere in the affairs of individual businesses. In addition, property rights over the profits of each family member were specified in precise detail. Less formally, families agreed that capable members would focus on monitoring specific enterprises. Under this system of corporate governance, the role of the family council was to monitor and informally coordinate the activities of the various enterprise units.

The *zaibatsu* were family-controlled entities, but there are important differences between the family in Japanese and Western cultures. It might be better to regard the Japanese family as a 'household' that does not necessarily correspond to a biological family. Fukuyama describes the Japanese family as:

> ...more like a trust for the assets of the household, which are used in common by family members, and the household head acting as a trustee. What is important is the continuity of the (family) through the generations ... the position of household head is usually passed from father to the eldest son, but the role of the eldest son could be played by any outsider, provided that he had undergone the appropriate legal procedures for adoption. (Fukuyama, 1995: 173)

In essence, *zaibatsu* families developed a system of governance that separated ownership and control by carefully and transparently allocating decision and property rights. This system of corporate governance provided professional managers with substantial discretion over the management of their business divisions. Figure 2.4 depicts the administrative chart of the Mitsui *zaibatsu* at the turn of the nineteenth century.

Having stabilised their governance structures, the *zaibatsu* were poised to expand their activities. The period between 1890 and 1914 was marked by steady expansion and continued diversification, funded by internally-generated earnings. The diversification patterns of some of the *zaibatsu* revealed tensions in the closed system of governance. For example, Mitsui senior managers embarked upon an industrial strategy and acquired heavy engineering and pulp and paper companies. However, the capital intensity of these industries placed great stress on family resources and management, and frequently led to conflict within the family. Mitsui's industrial enterprises were under-funded and in poor

Figure 2.4 Administrative chart of the Mitsui *zaibatsu*, 1893–1909

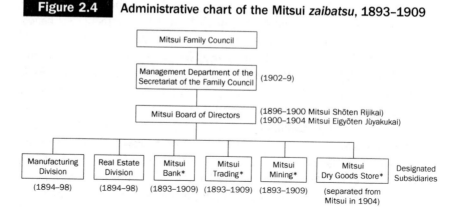

repair; their dilapidated condition was an embarrassment to the Mitsui family. After the death of the family member who designed this industrial strategy, Mitsui reverted back to a commercial strategy, which stressed banking, trading and mining. In contrast, Mitsubishi was able to advance its development of an industrial strategy particularly in the development of shipbuilding, papermaking and brewing. Mitsubishi financed the development of manufacturing enterprises through the sale of railway stock that it had fortuitously acquired. Sumitomo's holdings in copper mining were supplemented by the development of vertical integration into coalmining and production of iron. Sumitomo also developed a banking and trading business based in Korea following its colonisation by Japan. The *zaibatsu* were willing to spin-off divisions that were considered unsuccessful, that is, businesses that proved to be capital-intensive or were not self-financing. During this period of steady growth, the *zaibatsu* began to limit internal lending by the house bank to other house subsidiaries. Thereafter, the *zaibatsu* banks became independent and autonomous businesses that were expected to stand on their own feet and not depend upon loans to in-house companies to generate business.

The outbreak of the First World War provided a major growth opportunity for the *zaibatsu*. The war drastically reduced the flow of exported goods from European manufacturers into Asia. As a non-combatant nation, Japan was free to concentrate on the development of its industries. In the years between 1913 and 1919, the authorised capital of *zaibatsu* enterprises typically doubled and in some cases quadrupled. Each *zaibatsu* either established or expanded its foreign trading companies. The growth in Japan's international trade during this period also stimulated the expansion of banking and insurance. The boost in profits from wartime activities fuelled the development of heavy industries, particularly in machinery and shipbuilding.

Between the end of the First World War and the beginning of the worldwide depression that followed the Wall Street crash in 1929, Japan experienced a decade of intense economic and political instability. These unstable conditions highlighted both the strengths and weaknesses of the *zaibatsu* system of governance. The high-flying Japanese wartime economy went into an abrupt reversal following the armistice and the dramatic reduction in the demand for shipbuilding and armaments. The resumption of manufactured imports from Europe and the USA's vigorous entry into international trade reduced Japanese trading opportunities. In this period, the separation between first and second-tier *zaibatsu* became particularly marked. Many second-tier *zaibatsu* had ambitiously attempted to catch up with Mitsui and Mitsubishi with an aggressive wartime expansion of their foreign trading companies. These companies suffered in the postwar trading environment, which drained the resources of the wider group, and many *zaibatsu* declared bankruptcy. More cautious expansion by Yasuda and Sumitomo served to cement their leadership positions alongside Mitsui and Mitsubishi.

The economic instability of post-First World War Japan revealed both weaknesses and strengths in the *zaibatsu* system of governance. The staple industries that had supported the *zaibatsu*'s rapid growth, such as coalmining, copper production, trading and shipping, had now stagnated or declined. The best growth opportunities appeared in the new capital-intensive electrical, chemical and science-based industries, in which the closed, self-funding family-owned *zaibatsu* were traditionally the weaker groups. The difference between the first-tier and second-tier *zaibatsu* was the first tier's structural adjustment through the adoption of the family multi-subsidiary system. Pioneered by Mitsui, the multi-subsidiary structure was a hybridisation of the closed family system and the open, joint-stock, publicly-traded system of governance. The first step involved the incorporation of the family council and its secretariat into an unlimited partnership in which the heads of the family houses were limited partners with their share in the profits fixed by the family constitution. The assets of the partnership consisted of shares in the operating subsidiaries. The second step was more radical: it involved converting the operating subsidiaries into joint-stock companies, which provided the subsidiaries with tax benefits, access to public capital markets, and, incidentally, mitigated the growing public criticism of the *zaibatsu* as closed and secretive societies. The reorganisation further diminished families' influence over their operating businesses as the parent unlimited partnership operated somewhat like a holding company or private equity fund that can increase or decrease its participation in the ownership of operating subsidiaries based upon their market prospects or other economic criteria.

The multi-subsidiary structure of the leading *zaibatsu* mitigated the family capital constraint and facilitated a dual process of strategic centralisation and operational decentralisation that permitted them to operate at the technology frontier under highly dynamic conditions (Gerlach, 1997). The limited partnership was able to reallocate resources among divisions based upon the collective interests of the family. The family partnership possessed the financial resources, political connections and extensive network of overseas contacts required to provide access to foreign technology and product licences. Importantly, family groups retained their distribution infrastructure dating from their prewar mercantile activities. The ability to coordinate and reallocate this bundle of resources was a potent competitive advantage.

The operational decentralisation of managerial discretion to subsidiary managers was a well-established principle among *zaibatsu* companies. This managerial legacy proved to be of great value in the dynamic technology intensive industries because:

> it permitted the rapid expansion of promising technological and market areas through the localised focusing of entrepreneurial activities and strategic partnerships ... a process of creating new enterprises organisationally segregated from the head office ... a process termed satellite formation. (Gerlach, 1997: 250)

The creation of segregated and autonomous units allowed for rapid growth and/or contraction through a variety of strategies including internal organic growth acquisition of related organisations, spinning off new ventures from the core and strategic partnering with others. Spin-offs and strategic partnerships in particular, resulted in fluid organisational boundaries that possessed the flexibility necessary to operate in an uncertain technological environment and generate the benefits of a more entrepreneurial environment. The result was a simple division of labour between headquarters and satellite in which:

> the decentralised network of industrial firms taking care of the complex logistics involved in managing diverse technological and industrial activities and the head office taking on the functions of overall strategic planning and resource allocation. (Gerlach, 1997: 263)

In this regard, the term 'multi-subsidiary system' is something of a misnomer because it implies the existence of a branch that is wholly owned by a larger enterprise. The term 'satellite' is more appropriate as it is suggestive of semi-autonomous units that are only partially owned by the parent and are engaged in a variety of technological and operating alliances with firms unconnected to the parent *zaibatsu*. In this respect, the *zaibatsu* represents the nascent form of network (Fruin, 1998) or alliance capitalism (Gerlach, 1992a), which characterises post-1945 Japanese industrial organisation.

The post-First World War organisational adaptations of the *zaibatsu* enabled them to completely dominate the Japanese economy. However, the decade that followed the economic uncertainty of the 1920s was a politically disastrous period in Japan's history and ultimately led to the dismantling and dissolution of Japan's preeminent business institution. The political environment of the 1930s was marked by a growing nationalism and an intense conflict between the right-wing and left-wing political parties. This conflict resulted in the installation of an expansionary militaristic government, along with the appearance of a virulent anti-*zaibatsu* movement. In this period, the *zaibatsu* endured intensive government pressure to invest in heavy industry and step up the production of armaments. To finance the military build-up, the government also began to exact heavy taxes on *zaibatsu* profits. In competitive markets, *zaibatsu* were challenged by the appearance of the new *konzerns* such as Nissan, a class of less-diversified, vertically-integrated enterprises that actively supported Japanese military expansion in the 1930s. In response to the anti-*zaibatsu* movement, families authorised the diversion of 'vast resources to charities and community organisations' (Morikawa, 1992: 225) in an effort to appease public criticism of their economic power. It also seems plausible that families sought to extract resources from their businesses; families were often accused of purchasing US dollars to protect family wealth. This combination of forces drained the financial strength of the core enterprises.

The demise of the *zaibatsu* occurred in two successive stages. The first coincided with the outbreak of the Sino-Japanese war in 1937. To support its war effort in China, Japan reverted to the wartime command economy, and the *zaibatsu* were subject to compulsory investment in heavy industries. Between 1937 and 1945, Mitsui, Mitsubishi and Sumitomo's investments in heavy industries each increased tenfold. In 1937, heavy industry represented 22 per cent of Mitsui's paid-in capital, and by 1945 this figure had reached 57 per cent. Lacking internally-generated sources of capital to support this expansion, the families were forced to dilute their ownership in strategic business units. In a process that Morikawa (1992) calls the '*zaibatsu* conversion', both head offices and subsidiaries were converted into joint-stock enterprises. In this stage of the reorganisation, families' majority shareholder status was diluted as the state began to participate in ownership under the control of the Bank of Japan.

The second and final stage of the dissolution occurred following Japan's defeat in the Second World War. Postwar authority was vested in the general headquarters of the Supreme Commander for the Allied Powers. Dissolution consisted of the elimination of *zaibatsu* control over its subsidiaries, the liquidation of holding companies and major enterprises and the disposal of the assets of *zaibatsu* family members. Two of the largest companies, Mitsui Bussan and Mitsubishi Shoji, were immediately liquidated in a bid to address over-concentration of economic power. Finally, the assets of the wealthiest *zaibatsu* families were confiscated. Assets were seized by means of severe progressive taxes, which rose to a maximum of 90 per cent of the assets of the wealthiest. For example, ten Mitsui branch families were evaluated as having taxable assets worth some ¥350 million, of which ¥300 million was confiscated in asset taxes (Suzuki, 1997). These asset taxes, along with the dissolution of the *zaibatsu*, eliminated major individual and family shareholders in Japan's largest firms.

Comparing colonial business groups and *zaibatsu*

As prototypes of contemporary business groups in Asia, the colonial business groups and *zaibatsu* represent a study in contrasts. Francis Fukuyama (1995: 161) has described the *zaibatsu* as a 'block of granite', while as we noted above, the colonial group was 'rather amorphous in character with permeable boundaries'. The granite-like solidity of the *zaibatsu* is reflected in their household ownership structure that retained ultimate control to the end, even when the various constituent companies had adopted corporate structures with minority shareholders. The *zaibatsu* created robust constitutional governance structures that legally restricted family members' access to assets and limited their freedom to dispose of them, so assuring a stable capital base. Arguably, this financial stability facilitated the long-term development of the enterprise as a whole. *Zaibatsu* organisational structures combined financial centralisation with managerial decentralisation and, importantly, they were simultaneously industrial and mercantile entities. A family-owned bank and trading company was located at the centre of the *zaibatsu*, providing funding and assuring an international market for the outputs of the wide variety of mines and manufacturing enterprises. Operationally, the *zaibatsu* were vertically-integrated enterprises that were actively coordinated by a cadre of professional management. This combination of competitive and organisational capabilities permitted Japanese firms to overcome their 100-year late start, to catch up and ultimately surpass their Asian rivals. The resilience of this prototype business group structure is such that it survived Japan's calamitous militarisation in the 1930s, world war and foreign occupation, and then reconstituted itself in its modern *keiretsu* form.

Families were also the owners of colonial groups (Chapman, 1985). However, these families took a more instrumental view of their assets and were much more willing to extract income from the enterprise to meet family needs. The tension between the enterprise's capital requirements and family income needs is quite evident in Chandler's (1990) assessment of British personal capitalism. Lack of a stable capital base stimulated a constant concern with near-term liquidity and an unwillingness to invest in the longer-lived physical assets, which impeded their participation in industrial activities.

According to Jones (2000: 252) 'the sale of family shareholdings usually triggered a period of shareholder instability followed by acquisition or dissolution'. Linkage between the constituent firms in the group was also much more tacit; it was based on cross-directorships, shared social background and strictly contractual agreements. These more tenuous relationships permitted exceptional fluidity and responsiveness to a dynamic environment. However, these tenuous links also made the organisation a more fungible entity, rendering it more vulnerable to dismantling, dismemberment and hostile capture by new owners.

The characteristics of these two prototype business groups prefigure the emergence of the distinct forms of capitalism that developed in the UK and Japan after the war. In the UK, large-scale family ownership of the UK's largest firms was replaced by managerial capitalism, and in postwar Japan we see the emergence of what is often called 'alliance capitalism' (Gerlach, 1992a).

Notes

1. There were colonial business groups associated with other colonial powers, such as Hegermeyer (Netherlands) and Bunge and Born (Belgium) and European and North American firms that were not associated with colonial powers, such as Grace and Co. (USA) and the East Asiatic Company (Denmark).
2. The legal framework for incorporation did not occur until The British Registration Act 1844 first facilitated the widespread ownership and exchange of shares in companies. The Joint-Stock Companies Act 1856 introduced the concept of limited liability of equity owners.
3. Davenport-Hines and Jones (1989: 22) question the view that colonial business enjoyed privileged conditions in the nineteenth-century colonial environment. They suggest that the British Foreign Office and colonial administrators were not particularly energetic in supporting British financial and commercial interests in overseas markets.

3

Continuity and change in Japan's business groups

Introduction

Following the devastating military defeat in the Second World War, Japan's government focused upon rebuilding her once vibrant economy. Beginning in 1950, Japanese enterprises embarked upon a sustained 40-year period of 'vigorous equipment investment' (Morikawa, 1997). Under the guidance of the state, many Japanese firms grew to become diverse, globally-scaled organisations by building large-scale efficient factories, international sales and marketing organisations, research and development capabilities and the organisational apparatus to coordinate them. By 1990, Japanese enterprises dominated almost every industrial sector in Asia and established seemingly insurmountable competitive advantage in the world electronics and automobile industries. Many scholars attributed Japan's astonishing economic recovery to its cooperative and networked approach to industrial development. Books with titles such as *Japan as Number One: Lessons for America* (Vogel, 1979) and *MITI and the Japanese Miracle: The Growth of Industrial Policy 1925–1975* (Johnson, 1982) hailed Japan as a model worthy of emulation by mature and developing economies alike. Management consultants and academics identified a bewildering array of Japanese management practices, such as total quality management, just in time inventory, quality circles, theory Z organisation, and layered production, which were considered vital for the very survival of Western enterprise. As late as 1990, one management scholar argued that the Japanese model represented the 'New Competition' (Best, 1990) and he opened his book with a speech in which Konosuke Matsushita, the founder of the Matsushita Electric

Industrial Company, criticised the adversarial practices of Western managers. Matsushita proclaimed:

> We will win and you will lose ... you firmly believe that sound management means executives on the one side and workers on the other, on the one side men who think and on the other side men who can only work. For you management is the art of smoothly transferring the executives' ideas to the workers' hands ... We are aware that business has become terribly complex. Survival is very uncertain in an environment filled with risk, the unexpected and competition ... We know that ... only the intellects of all employees can permit the company to live with the ups and downs in the requirements of the new environment. (Best, 1990: 1)

Matsushita's thinking reflects the Japanese post-Second World War business environment that was indeed risky, unpredictable, and filled with the unexpected. Stripped of her colonies, Japan had few natural resources, there were shortages of capital and foreign exchange, the labour movement was militant and the spectre of communism haunted the region. Economically and politically vulnerable, Japan's economic planners and industrial elite saw risk and uncertainty everywhere. In this environment, the doubtful benefits of the American model of free-market capitalism did not hold much appeal. Instead of market competition, Japanese planners fashioned a 'corporate security blanket' designed to mitigate some of the worst risks of the market process. Clusters of enterprises would look out for one another in the manner of a 'convoy system', in which stronger firms would provide assistance to slow-moving enterprises. Profitable firms in the convoy paid a 'group insurance premium' in the form of lower profits with expectation that they would receive assistance should they fall upon hard times. To support this pattern, a system of dense corporate, financial and employment relations was established based upon sectoral planning, cooperation and consensual labour-management decision-making. An American management scholar described the system as 'alliance capitalism' because its key actors made mutual commitments to an enduring relationship and carried out resource allocation decisions within and across firm boundaries (Gerlach, 1992a).

After a sustained period of currency appreciation between 1985 and 1991, Japan's booming economy suffered a severe recession with the collapse of property and equity prices. During a long period of stagnation and apparent inertia, Japan's security-oriented industrial policy was questioned and doubt was cast on the merits of cooperative state-business relations. Following this decided loss of confidence in the Japanese model, books and articles with titles such as *Japanese Capitalism in Crisis* (Boyer and Yamada, 2000), the 'Twilight of the keiretsu?' (Gerlach, 1992b) and 'Mitsubishi: Fall of a keiretsu' (Bremner, Thornton and Kunni, 1999), became the norm.

Because Japan is Asia's most advanced and wealthiest economy and because large business groups still dominate a seemingly stagnant and non-dynamic corporate landscape, Japan comes closest to fulfilling the business group 'lifecycle hypothesis' (Strachan, 1976). This hypothesis suggests that a business system that is economically beneficial during a country's industrial adolescence may engender inertia in the mature and advanced stages of development. In particular, a system that is focused on guaranteeing the survival and security of its members may get into a rut, due to the creation of path dependencies. The system may be ill-suited to a mature but dynamic economy and incapable of adapting to an environment in which sustained growth depends upon innovation rather than efficiency.

In this chapter we will explore the postwar origins of Japan's cooperative capitalism, which gave birth to large inter-market or horizontal *keiretsu* and to the more focused industry-specific vertical business groups. The corporate structures and systems of governance are outlined, and the technological and competitive advantages of the systems are described. Weaknesses in aspects of this pattern of corporate organisation became apparent following a G5 meeting at New York's Plaza Hotel in 1985. The conclusion of that meeting, known as the Plaza Accord, provided for a significant appreciation of the Japanese yen against the American dollar and marked the termination of Japan's export-led industrialisation. The consequences of this policy adjustment are still being worked through and it is unclear whether the system of alliance capitalism is being dismantled or whether there is still substantial continuity in the Japanese corporate structure.

Origins and context of Japan's *keiretsu* business groups

As noted in Chapter 2, shortly after the Meiji Restoration in 1868, the Japanese state began to encourage the development of modern industries as part of a concerted attempt to catch up with the West. Until the Second World War, large enterprise was concentrated in the hands of family-owned *zaibatsu* and their affiliated *sogo-shosa*, which managed Japan's international trade. Japan's militarisation and war economy precipitated a revolutionary change in corporate governance, culminating in the separation of enterprise ownership and its control. After 1930, the military-dominated government became increasingly unhappy with the *zaibatsu* families' focus on short-term profits at the expense of building organisational capabilities (Morikawa, 1992). To build and sustain the capacity for a war economy, the state sought to dominate industrial decision-making. Under the supervision of the Bank of Japan, the state acquired stakes in the leading industrial and commercial companies and placed increased operational authority in the hands of salaried managers in the commanding heights of the economy. The *zaibatsu* had long relied upon professional managers in the operational control of their enterprises, but the complete transition to professional management control was completed following the Second World War. The owners' influence over corporate decisions was eliminated when the occupying authorities dissolved the *zaibatsu* and confiscated their assets through the imposition of a progressive tax regime. The *zaibatsu* were dissolved through the liquidation of their holding companies and several of their major enterprises. A limited number of the largest companies, including Mitsui Bussan and Mitsubishi Shoji, were immediately broken up to address concerns about the concentration of economic power. Finally, the assets of the wealthiest *zaibatsu* families were confiscated. Assets were seized by means of severely progressive taxes upon the wealthiest industrial families. Asset taxes along with the dissolution of the *zaibatsu* eliminated major individual and family shareholders in Japan's largest firms and put enterprise control in the hands of professional managers.

The initial dismantling of the *zaibatsu* owed much to the influence of a US anti-trust tradition, as the occupying authorities perceived the *zaibatsu* to be a system of anticompetitive combines. Between 1953 and 1956, however, the big three prewar *zaibatsu*, Mitsui, Mitsubishi and Sumitomo, were soon re-established. Another three, Fuyo, Sanwa and Dai Ichi Kangin, were formed in the 1960s and 1970s through the consolidation of some smaller groups. With the decentralisation of political power, significant responsibility for local economic development was delegated to major industrial cities, which attempted to establish their own corporate complexes. The presidents' council of the Fuyo complex was founded in 1966, the Sanwa complex in 1967, and when the Dia-Ichi Kangin complex was founded in 1977, the Japanese economy was already well advanced.

In the postwar period, Japan came to have the lowest levels of large family-owned enterprises among Asian economies; this pattern persists today and distinguishes Japanese corporate governance from that of the prewar *zaibatsu* and other business groups in Asia. For example, Table 3.1 shows that Japan's five largest families own only 2 per cent of the market capitalisation of the Tokyo Stock Exchange. In contrast, the largest five families in Hong Kong own some 26 per cent of the market capitalisation of the Hong Kong Stock Exchange. Arm's-length individual investors account for approximately 25 per cent of the market capitalisation in the Tokyo Stock Exchange, while stable long-term investors, such as financial institutions and group-affiliated firms, own 70–75 per cent of the market capitalisation of Japanese public funds (Gerlach, 1992a).

While much has been made of the apparent re-emergence of (some of) the prewar *zaibatsu* in the guise of modern day *keiretsu*, and the organisational continuity that this represents, it is equally important to recognise that the corporate governance of these reconstituted organisations represents a key discontinuity. The emergent *keiretsu* system provided for a new governance approach based around affiliation with a main bank and control by professional management. Managers are subject to checks and balances from managers in other *keiretsu* member firms. The difference is that, while the *zaibatsu* concentrated economic power in the hands of wealthy families, the *keiretsu* fragment power and control into the hands professional managers of operating companies, financial institutions and bureaucrats from the Ministries of

Table 3.1 Family ownership of large enterprises in Asia

Country	No. of firms	% Market cap	1 Family (%)	5 Families (%)	10 Families (%)	15 Families (%)
Hong Kong	330	72	7	26	32	34
Indonesia	178	67	17	41	58	62
Thailand	167	52	9	32	46	53
South Korea	345	51	11	30	36	38
Philippines	120	46	17	43	53	55
Taiwan	141	46	4	15	18	20
Singapore	221	45	6	20	27	30
Malaysia	238	43	7	17	25	28
Japan	1,240	4	1	2	2	3

Source: Claessens et al. (2000b).

Finance and Industry, Trade and Investment. As a result of the extensive ownership by corporations and financial institutions, 'Post war Japanese capitalism has been an *administered*, relational capitalism to an extraordinary degree' (Lincoln and Gerlach, 2004: 45). Japan's professional managers are neither subject to the rule of the founding *zaibatsu* family, nor are they appreciably accountable to the capital market constraints that attend upon professional managers whose firms depend upon equity financing. This system of governance constructed and maintained an organisational bureaucracy with the capacity to engage in a capital-intensive, vertically-cooperative and geographically-diversified business strategy. Thus, while the constituent enterprises of the postwar business groups resemble those of the prewar *zaibatsu*, their system of governance is fundamentally different.

The conditions for the reformation of Japan's business groups owe much to the intensification of the Cold War. In the early stages of occupation, the US administration set about rebuilding and reforming Japan's economy on a US blueprint based on independent firms, competition and vigorous anti-trust regulation (Djelic, 1998). US resolve to enforce an American model of anti-trust in Japan's corporate sector was, however, weakened and overtaken by US foreign policy concerns. With the outbreak of the Korean War, in which China participated on the side of North Korea, and the Russians supplied them with arms, the primary policy priorities of the USA shifted from economic reform toward checking the spread of communism. In the interests of keeping Japan firmly within the Western sphere of influence and securing its unswerving support for the US policy of containment, the US government turned a blind eye to the re-establishment of industrial groupings. Following this policy shift, officials in Japan's Ministry of Finance and International Trade and Industry (MITI) quietly encouraged the restoration of industrial groups. Due to its licensing and preferential financing powers, MITI reduced the thousands of trading companies that existed after the occupation down to around 20 large trading companies, each affiliated with the main bank of a group of smaller producers. The Ministry of Finance began to relax restrictions on manufacturing companies' cross-holdings and raised the ceiling on bank ownership of companies from 5 per cent to 10 per cent. Indeed, the USA began to support Japan's economic development and the rebuilding of Japanese industrial strength, and the US adoption of a liberal stance on Japanese exports into North American markets facilitated the success of Japan's policy of export-led development. This liberal trade policy remained in place until 1985.

As in the past, the Japanese state believed that in the postwar era, technological catch-up and building of industrial capacity could be best accomplished by large enterprises. However, the state also wanted to avoid monopolies and concentration of excessive market power. Under the aegis of MITI, Japan adopted an industrial strategy based upon managed oligopolistic competition between rival groups. Through strict controls and the close monitoring of market shares, the state prevented any firm or investment from being so large as to destabilise commodity markets. This system of managed inter-group rivalry permitted a regime of high domestic prices that allowed for high profits and sustained reinvestment in industrial capacity from retained earnings. This pricing regime was based upon high quality and relatively low export prices, and throughout the 1960s and 1970s it supported an aggressive export strategy that helped Japanese firms to establish strong positions in North American and European automobile and consumer electronics markets.

This managed approach to developing the corporate sector was supported by complementary policies in labour and financial markets and in Japan's international trade policy. These policies created an institutional architecture of coordinated and largely cooperative capitalism with a character very different from the industrial capitalism of North America.

In addition to the administered oligopoly, the architecture of Japan's post-Second World War cooperative capitalism consisted of several other core elements (Boyer and Yamada, 2000). The foremost element was the establishment of a dual labour market employment system, with a primary labour market consisting of enterprise unions, long-term employment for a core group of skilled workers and a seniority-based wage system, and a secondary labour market consisting of less-skilled, contingent employees. The creation of this labour system was motivated by a fear of large national labour federations who were thought to be ideologically inclined towards the radical politics of the communists. Japan's liberal Democratic Party needed to win the support of labour and reduce the influence of the Japan Socialist Party. The state promoted enterprise labour organisations that might be more concerned with factory-related issues. The dual labour market strategy created relatively peaceful industrial relations in Japan's leading industries and a cooperative approach to management and organisational process issues on the factory floor, an environment that was in marked contrast to the adversarial industrial relations in Europe and North America.

The second important feature of the architectural structure was the creation of a bank-led financial system. To minimise disruption to economic growth strategies, the state engaged in both active and passive suppression of non-bank sources of corporate financing. Active suppression refers to government regulations, discriminatory taxation and cumbersome and restrictive issuance procedures that hamper equity market development. Passive suppression refers to the neglect of regulations governing corporate disclosure, accounting standards and protection for minority stockholders (Prowse, 1996). In the absence of alternative sources of financing, Japanese enterprises became dependent upon bank debt and developed the relational characteristics that close and enduring lenders, borrowers and intermediaries maintain with one another (Rajan and Zingales, 1998).

A third architectural element was the state-supported acquisition of technology from foreign sources. To maintain an even playing field, the state took care to assure wide access to and rapid diffusion of available technologies to each of the main players. By imitating technologies invented elsewhere, Japan's leading firms could focus on the relentless pursuit of continuous incremental improvement and thus lower production costs and improve quality. The final architectural element was the mechanism of 'inserting Japan into the international economy'; this rested in a large part on automatic Japanese support for US foreign policy in the Pacific in exchange for running a large trade surplus with the USA and the maintenance of non-tariff trade barriers. Each of these architectural elements contributed to a context of stability and provided an environment in which adjustment was achieved by consensus. State policy and emergent corporate business practice fostered a blanket of institutions that provided Japan's risk-averse capitalists with layers of security and protection from disruptive competition.

The six major *keiretsu* were constructed through the absorption of existing enterprises, which were acquired as subsidiaries with ownership levels above 50 per cent. Additionally, internal units and divisions were spun off into independent enterprises but with continuing equity links below 50 per cent (Shimotani, 1997). The spin-offs typically outweighed the acquisitions. Several of the spin-offs were large corporate entities in their own right and they in turn possessed their own network of subsidiaries, spin-offs and subcontractors. However, the spun-off units were not restricted to large operating divisions; units such as individual factories, sales offices, research facilities and small staff sections were also spun off. Shimotani (1997) claims that the externalisation of internal units allowed the parent to transform itself into a strategic headquarters while the partially spun-off individual units could become autonomous profit centres.

In this respect, the *keiretsu* system does not appear to be fundamentally different from the large American conglomerate. Feenstra, Yang and Hamilton (1999: 79) argue that some of the differences between the corporate structure of the *keiretsu* and the American conglomerate reflect the legal provisions of each country. In the USA the Glass-Steagall Act 1933 separated banks and securities companies, so that banks could not act as both a lender and a shareholder, as occurs in Japan. Furthermore, the US Investment Company Act 1940 prevents one company from taking a managerial role in another, unless it actually owns it. Some scholars feel that Japanese banks exercise precisely this managerial and financial control over business groups, despite the fact that banks are limited in their holdings of individual companies. This does not necessarily prevent groups from exercising some financial control. The Japanese system manages to attain structural readjustment in a deliberative cooperative manner without engaging in the labour conflict and political turmoil that often attends the dismantling of industries and the surrounding communities in North America. Indeed, the Japanese system's capacity to provide labour market stability for at least one section of the workforce sustains several of its distinctive managerial and organisational features.

Similarly, Ahmadjian (2006) suggests that the structure of Japan's institutional environment determines the externalised growth trajectory of Japanese firms. She argues that firms elected to grow in this manner, rather than through vertical integration, in order to avoid the adversarial labour relations that encourage manufacturing firms to externalise as much labour as possible, and also because firms lacked the capital to grow through vertical integration. In addition, tax and accounting rules favoured loose ownership arrangements. Because small firms received better tax benefits, large firms tended to spin-off many production units into smaller legal entities. At the same time, firms were allowed to report their equity holdings in other firms at historical cost, firms were not required to report losses on the portfolios of shares in affiliates, and they could hold on to realised gains indefinitely. Japanese accounting rules did not require firms to report consolidated results, so profits and losses could be allocated among subsidiaries either to avoid taxes on profits or avoid disclosing losses, depending on which was most pressing. Ahmidjian (2006) suggests that Japanese financial reporting requirements also supported the web of shareholding ties linking firms to groups.

In the following section we survey the governance and organisation of Japan's corporate structure and examine its unique characteristics. The overall picture that emerges is a hierarchy of enterprise clusters within the six corporate complexes; numerous vertical subgroups are nested within each of these complexes and several of the subgroups intermingle and establish strong linkages with enterprises that are affiliated with other complexes. The aggregate effect of the relationships is the emergence of a heavily networked corporate structure that contains a rich blend of both competitive and cooperative strategies (Fruin, 1998).

Keiretsu corporate governance

Lincoln and Gerlach (2004: 15) define Japanese business groups as 'clusters of independently managed firms maintaining close and stable business ties, cemented by governance mechanisms such as presidents' councils, partial cross ownership, and interlocking directorates'. In an effort to capture the essence of Japanese industrial organisation, many scholars distinguish two basic forms of Japan's *keiretsu*. The first is the conglomerate or horizontal *keiretsu*, centred on a main bank or holding company such as Mitsui, Sanwa or Fuyo. The second form is the quasi-vertically-integrated 'giant companies' or *kaisha* that focus upon two or three core industries; this form includes corporations such as Toyota and Toshiba (Aoki, 1988). Shimotani (1997) further distinguishes between corporate complexes, corporate groups and subcontract systems; each is arranged hierarchically and tied together by equity, debt links, interlocking directorates, dispatched personnel and recurrent contracting relationships.

Unfortunately, categorising Japanese business groups into vertical and horizontal groups does not adequately capture the full extent of their complex structure. Enterprises vary in the degree to which they are linked by debt, equity, managerial exchanges and trading relationships and the extent to which these links are reciprocated. Sometimes firms have multiple affiliations and nominally independent firms sometimes spawn clusters or satellites in diverse businesses. Business group boundaries are fluid and their cohesiveness tends to ebb and flow, strengthen and weaken over time in response to market opportunities. Group composition is thus dynamic and organic, and firms cannot be neatly categorised as either members of a particular type of group or as independents. Cross-cutting relations link firms nominally affiliated with one group to firms within another group; consequently, relations within *keiretsu* networks tend to be more reciprocally interdependent and less obviously hierarchical than those found in other Asian business groups.

Indeed, Fukuyama (1995) characterises the formal and informal cooperative linkages in Japan's corporate sector as non-adversarial and more fundamentally consensual. Similarly, Lincoln and Gerlach (2004: 16) describe affiliates of the big six as, 'in principle, communities of equals'.

Figure 3.1 depicts some of these interactions among the big six inter-market groups. For example, Mitsui and Toyota are characterised as the classic horizontal and vertical *keiretsu*. However, while possessed of much autonomy, Toyota is historically linked with Mitsui, Nissen is linked with Fuyo, and most of Toyota's group affiliates, such as Hino and Nippon Denso, deal with Toyota's main banks, Mitsui and Tokai.

Because the extent and strength of debt, equity and trading linkages between firms vary so greatly, some affiliate firms are closely linked with their main bank and business partners and are densely and centrally situated within a particular complex or group, while more peripherally-linked affiliates endeavour to preserve their autonomy. Due to these distinctions, some scholars suggest that it is more logical to think of a 'dominant' or core group of firms at the centre of *keiretsu* networks, with other firms locked into more dependent and less powerful positions (Kim, Hoskisson and Wan, 2004). Hence, business groups in Japan are not distinct and bounded entities (Ahmadjian, 2005). As there is no clear distinction between group members and independent firms, much of the empirical research that utilises a dummy variable to denote affiliation

Figure 3.1 Interactions between major *keiretsu* and other groups

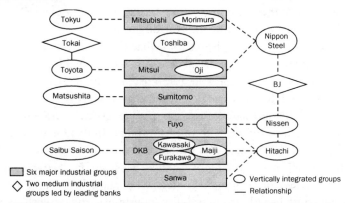

Source: WTEC Hyper-Librarian (1994) 'Some basic features and keys to the development of production systems in Japan', available at: *www.wtec.org/loyola/polymers/c7_s7.htm* (accessed 16 July 2007).

with a business group must be treated with caution. To categorise a firm as an affiliate of either the vertical or horizontal *keiretsu* oversimplifies what are in fact highly fluid overlapping, and unbounded industrial groupings.

Despite the problems of identification, most analysts agree that business groups are significant entities in Japan. Affiliates of the big six horizontal or inter-market groups dominated the postwar economy and, according to some estimates, at one point accounted for almost 75 per cent of the value of the shares in the Tokyo Stock Exchange. Figure 3.2 illustrates the sectoral structure and membership of Sanwa, a horizontal *keiretsu* and one of the big six. Sanwa exemplifies the broad market scope of a horizontal *keiretsu* across the key manufacturing and commercial sectors of Japan's economy. In the industrial composition of the big six, analysts see the deliberate and visible hand of a central planning agency that has used 'one set principle' to ensure that each major group contains a similar range of key industry segments within their boundaries (Lincoln and Gerlach, 2004).

Paradoxically, the members of the horizontal groups are legally and operationally independent and no tangible centralised control mechanism exists to bring about coordinated action between them. Although there is much evidence of coordinated action, the only instrument that resembles a centralised control mechanism is the weekly presidents' council meeting, which is attended by the presidents of each of the main enterprises affiliated with the group. For example, in 1991, Sanwa's presidents' council consisted of the presidents of 44 affiliated firms. The details of the council's deliberations are not made public, but it is understood that councils are a forum for discussing broad, common issues and that they are not price-fixing cartels, nor are they a mechanism for achieving strategic coordination.

The precise functions of groups, or 'what the groups do', is a subject of much speculation and empirical research. The prevailing view is that horizontal *keiretsu* are first and foremost a mutual group insurance scheme and an internal capital market that performs a risk pooling function, enabling affiliated firms to pursue growth strategies while mitigating pressures for short-term profitability. In this view, the role of the *keiretsu* is fundamentally different from that served by firms operating under managerial governance because the *keiretsu* system empowers a class of firm stakeholders who place little value on firm profitability but benefit from stability, continuity and growth, namely banks, partner firms and employees. Banks, whose equity holdings in individual enterprises are limited by statute, are more interested in the

Figure 3.2   Sanwa horizontal *keiretsu*

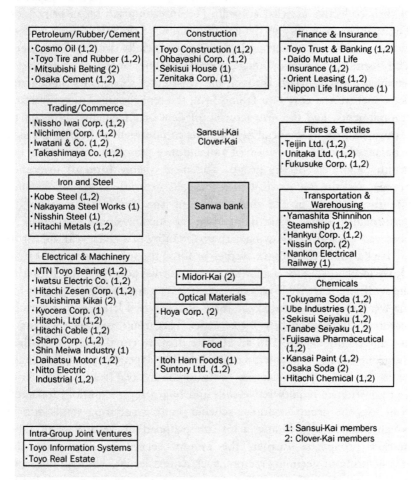

Petroleum/Rubber/Cement
· Cosmo Oil (1,2)
· Toyo Tire and Rubber (1,2)
· Mitsubishi Belting (2)
· Osaka Cement (1,2)

Construction
· Toyo Construction (1,2)
· Ohbayashi Corp. (1,2)
· Sekisui House (1)
· Zenitaka Corp. (1)

Finance & Insurance
· Toyo Trust & Banking (1,2)
· Daido Mutual Life Insurance (1,2)
· Orient Leasing (1,2)
· Nippon Life Insurance (1)

Trading/Commerce
· Nissho Iwai Corp. (1,2)
· Nichimen Corp. (1,2)
· Iwatani & Co. (1,2)
· Takashimaya Co. (1,2)

Sansui-Kai
Clover-Kai

Fibres & Textiles
· Teijin Ltd. (1,2)
· Unitaka Ltd. (1,2)
· Fukusuke Corp. (1,2)

Iron and Steel
· Kobe Steel (1,2)
· Nakayama Steel Works (1)
· Nisshin Steel (1)
· Hitachi Metals (1,2)

Sanwa bank

Transportation & Warehousing
· Yamashita Shinnihon Steamship (1,2)
· Hankyu Corp. (1,2)
· Nissin Corp. (2)
· Nankon Electrical Railway (1)

Electrical & Machinery
· NTN Toyo Bearing (1,2)
· Iwatsu Electric Co. (1,2)
· Hitachi Zesen Corp. (1,2)
· Tsukishima Kikai (2)
· Kyocera Corp. (1)
· Hitachi, Ltd (1,2)
· Hitachi Cable (1,2)
· Sharp Corp. (1,2)
· Shin Meiwa Industry (1)
· Daihatsu Motor (1,2)
· Nitto Electric Industrial (1,2)

· Midori-Kai (2)

Optical Materials
· Hoya Corp. (2)

Food
· Itoh Ham Foods (1)
· Suntory Ltd. (1,2)

Chemicals
· Tokuyama Soda (1,2)
· Ube Industries (1,2)
· Sekisui Seiyaku (1,2)
· Tanabe Seiyaku (1,2)
· Fujisawa Pharmaceutical (1,2)
· Kansai Paint (1,2)
· Osaka Soda (2)
· Hitachi Chemical (1,2)

Intra-Group Joint Ventures
· Toyo Information Systems
· Toyo Real Estate

1: Sansui-Kai members
2: Clover-Kai members

Source: 'Some basic features and keys to the development of production systems in Japan', available at: *http://www.wtec.org/loyola/polymers/fh7_17.gif* (accessed 16 July 2007).

firm's financial stability, the sale of professional services, and the continued supply of debt, rather than equity returns. Similarly, affiliated firms are commonly more interested in mutual assistance and in cementing and expanding their range of commercial ties, such as the provision of complementary assets and access to superior technology or outlets for their products. Above all, almost all the stakeholders, including those who reciprocally hold each other's shares, are interested in preserving and increasing the volume of trade within the group.

Activating this agreement for growth and stability requires that the participants share, or pool the risks and returns, the burdens and benefits of their collective activity, according to an egalitarian set of principles. The egalitarian quality of the group insurance principle is most evident in the coordinated turnaround of failing, financially distressed members. This insurance or convoy function works in times of crisis by bailing out troubled firms, typically through the dispatch of top-quality managerial personnel from a core to a failing firm, the renegotiation of contractual commitments, and the restructuring of debt arrangements sufficient to restore the firm to financial health. This commitment to helping the sick is balanced by the imposition of an insurance premium, or tax upon the healthy members of the group. The most visible form of insurance premia, and the one most often empirically determined (Gedajlovic and Shapiro, 2002), is the dampening of the profitability of high-performance firms. This dampening or income-smoothing effect is observed when firms showing high profitability in a given year appear to fall back toward the group's average profit in the subsequent year or two. Other mechanisms for achieving cross-subsidisation from the strong to the weak are less visible to external observers; for example, support for the weak may be hidden in the form of subsidised lending or it may be factored into transfer price agreements. The group insurance scheme is not universally available to all affiliate firms in equal measure. Rather, the group's commitment to an individual firm depends upon the strength of the firm's ties to the group in terms of commercial (trade and lending) and governance (equity ownership and board representation) linkages. Nor does the group insurance scheme imply a enduring status quo in which permanently failing firms are propped up regardless of their market prospects. Rather, the system serves to administer the restructuring of declining sectors, such as textiles and shipbuilding, and it facilitates the smooth reallocation of resources to sectors with better growth prospects.

The received wisdom about the function of vertical business groups is that they efficiently solve the problems of transactions costs between firms located at different points of an industry value chain. These 'hybrid' hierarchical-market networks serve to lower transactions costs, promote two-way technology transfer and stimulate investment in dedicated and co-specific assets (Dyer, 1996a). The efficiency argument is based upon the observation that multiple trading and governance linkages provide member firms with the capacity and the incentive to reciprocally monitor and discipline one another's behaviour. Such linkages increase the capacity for detecting and reducing the potential for partner opportunism (Gulati, 1998). Equally, the efficiency argument is consistent with the view that Japan's equity markets were deliberately suppressed in the immediate postwar period to permit the state to intervene directly in the planning and directing of economic and industrial reconstruction. In either account, the alliance governance system puts significant economic power in the hands of insiders and mitigates the influence of arm's-length capital markets.

The argument for transactional efficiency is more often voiced in relation to the vertical *keiretsu* (Dyer, 1996b; Dyer and Nobeoka, 2000). Incentives established between trading partners under the vertical groups alliance also favour reciprocity and the possibility of long-term multiple exchange opportunities. The expectation of long-term reciprocity allows a form of cross-temporal subsidisation to take place (Lincoln, Gerlach and Ahmadjian, 1996). For instance, stronger partners may exercise forbearance in leveraging their superior bargaining power and may even prop up faltering partners through loans, or favourable contractual provisions because they can expect that these actions will be reciprocated should the need arise. In this relationship, firms can invest in the highly productive, dedicated assets (Hill, 1993) that are advantageous in industries characterised by technical complexity (Dyer, 1996a). Long-term relationships also facilitate investment in specialised firm-specific assets that are prone to opportunism in spot-market market settings. Poor returns on one transaction can be compensated by better terms of trade in a later transaction. Because member firms are shielded from the short-term capital market demands, the effect of alliance governance is to make investments capital patient, and this allows for sustained investment in projects and programmes that have good long-term potential but show no immediate prospects of return.

The efficiency argument stumbles on the accumulating evidence that over the long term, the profitability of firms affiliated to the big six is significantly lower than that of unaligned firms (Lincoln and Gerlach, 2004). If the Japanese system of governance is so efficient, the benefits do not show in the form of increased profits.

Keiretsu organisation structure and management

Management scholars have much admired Japanese human resource and shop-floor management practices that engender high levels of employee commitment and productivity. These practices include factors such as intensive training, organisational socialisation, the commitment to lifetime employment, group work-designs, job rotation and a concern for employee wellbeing (Ouchi, 1981; Abegglen and Stalk, 1985). The normative and incentive environment of alliance governance, with its emphasis on growth and stability objectives, also contributes to these productive features of Japanese organisation. Job security encourages the workforce to invest in firm-specific learning (Whittaker, 1998) and widens the employee's zone of indifference with regards to the exercise of authority. Alliances will tend to utilise seniority-based incentive structures that reduce competitive behaviour and promote cooperation. Concomitantly, the absence of high pay-differentials may reduce an organisation's ability to motivate very high performers and those that tend toward individualism (Fukuyama, 1995). On the other hand, if management is able to institutionalise an environment that encourages identification with the firm, then it is well placed to induce strong effort-intensity and spontaneous innovation from its workforce.

In the 1980s and 1990s, a series of organisational design innovations pioneered by *keiretsu* member firms grabbed the business headlines. Productivity-enhancing techniques such as such as layered production, total quality management, statistical process control, just-in-time inventory management, and decentralised and cooperative subcontracting networks were comparable in scope and impact to American organising innovations of an earlier era (Chandler, 1962). At the heart of Japan's organisational innovation was a salaried, upper and middle management class that pioneered, perfected and deployed these capabilities. Figures 3.3 and 3.4 provide some indication of the scope and complexity of Japanese managerial hierarchies; the figures depict the corporate and organisational structures of the Hitachi vertical *keiretsu* and also plot those of the horizontal Sanwa group. The most significant aspects of these structures are the scope and functional specialisation of the operating divisions and staff functions. These complex, vertically-integrated hierarchies are often overlooked; most scholars focus their attention on the external networks of focal firms and elaborate the scale and scope of their operations in Asia. The corporate structures of family-owned and state-led business groups in other Asian countries are similarly complex and sometimes equal in their scope. However, no other groups approach the organisational complexity found in Japanese firms.

Early research on the organisational structures of Japanese firms identified high levels of bureaucracy in the form of extensive formalisation, task structuring, and the centralisation of authority

Figure 3.3 Hitachi's corporate structure

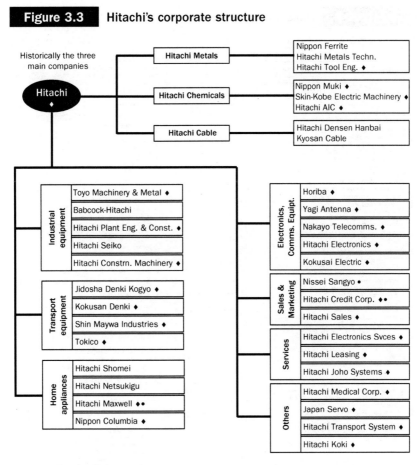

♦ Listed company
● New major companies (formally identified)

Source: Ohsono, T. (1995) *Charting Japanese Industry: A Graphical Guide to Corporate and Market Structures*, London: Cassels.

(Azuni and Macmillan, 1975). However, the prevailing view suggested that formal bureaucracy was less important than intense socialisation, shared decision-making and the attention to management development through processes such as job rotation and group evaluation (Ouchi, 1981; Aoki, 1988).

Once again, we appeal to the distinctive features of Japan's alliance governance to account for the appearance of a unique employment system and an extensive, efficient bureaucracy. Importantly, under alliance governance, senior executives typically receive a salary and profit bonuses rather than compensation linked to market performance,

Figure 3.4   Hitachi's organisational structure

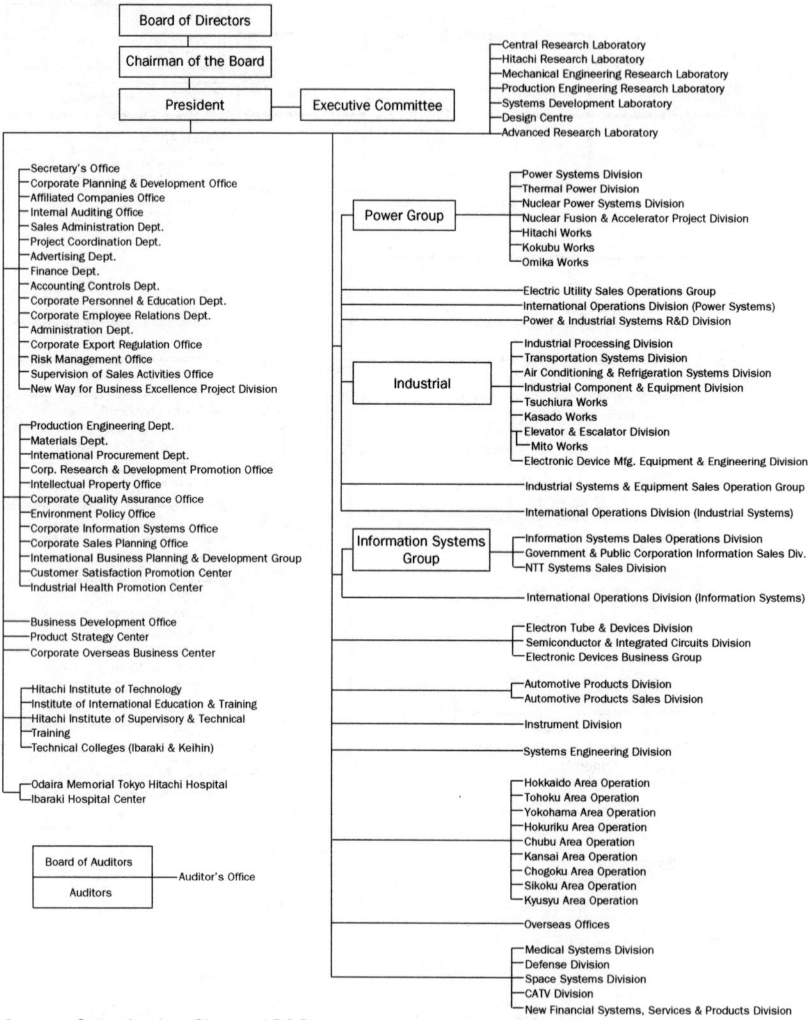

Board of Directors

Chairman of the Board

President — Executive Committee

- Central Research Laboratory
- Hitachi Research Laboratory
- Mechanical Engineering Research Laboratory
- Production Engineering Research Laboratory
- Systems Development Laboratory
- Design Centre
- Advanced Research Laboratory

- Secretary's Office
- Corporate Planning & Development Office
- Affiliated Companies Office
- Internal Auditing Office
- Sales Administration Dept.
- Project Coordination Dept.
- Advertising Dept.
- Finance Dept.
- Accounting Controls Dept.
- Corporate Personnel & Education Dept.
- Corporate Employee Relations Dept.
- Administration Dept.
- Corporate Export Regulation Office
- Risk Management Office
- Supervision of Sales Activities Office
- New Way for Business Excellence Project Division

- Production Engineering Dept.
- Materials Dept.
- International Procurement Dept.
- Corp. Research & Development Promotion Office
- Intellectual Property Office
- Corporate Quality Assurance Office
- Environment Policy Office
- Corporate Information Systems Office
- Corporate Sales Planning Office
- International Business Planning & Development Group
- Customer Satisfaction Promotion Center
- Industrial Health Promotion Center

- Business Development Office
- Product Strategy Center
- Corporate Overseas Business Center

- Hitachi Institute of Technology
- Institute of International Education & Training
- Hitachi Institute of Supervisory & Technical
- Training
- Technical Colleges (Ibaraki & Keihin)

- Odaira Memorial Tokyo Hitachi Hospital
- Ibaraki Hospital Center

Board of Auditors

Auditors — Auditor's Office

Power Group
- Power Systems Division
- Thermal Power Division
- Nuclear Power Systems Division
- Nuclear Fusion & Accelerator Project Division
- Hitachi Works
- Kokubu Works
- Omika Works

- Electric Utility Sales Operations Group
- International Operations Division (Power Systems)
- Power & Industrial Systems R&D Division

Industrial
- Industrial Processing Division
- Transportation Systems Division
- Air Conditioning & Refrigeration Systems Division
- Industrial Component & Equipment Division
- Tsuchiura Works
- Kasado Works
- Elevator & Escalator Division
- Mito Works
- Electronic Device Mfg. Equipment & Engineering Division

- Industrial Systems & Equipment Sales Operation Group

- International Operations Division (Industrial Systems)

Information Systems Group
- Information Systems Dales Operations Division
- Government & Public Corporation Information Sales Div.
- NTT Systems Sales Division

- International Operations Division (Information Systems)

- Electron Tube & Devices Division
- Semiconductor & Integrated Circuits Division
- Electronic Devices Business Group

- Automotive Products Division
- Automotive Products Sales Division

- Instrument Division

- Systems Engineering Division

- Hokkaido Area Operation
- Tohoku Area Operation
- Yokohama Area Operation
- Hokuriku Area Operation
- Chubu Area Operation
- Kansai Area Operation
- Chogoku Area Operation
- Sikoku Area Operation
- Kyusyu Area Operation

- Overseas Offices

- Medical Systems Division
- Defense Division
- Space Systems Division
- CATV Division
- New Financial Systems, Services & Products Division

Source: Organization Charts 1996.

and this tends to compress salary differentials (Kaplan, 1994). Such incentives tend to favour longevity, dependable role performance and cooperative behaviour. Salary compression can also engender self-selection processes that discourage the retention of more individualistic managers in favour of team-oriented managers. The emphasis on growth and stability enhances job security, which makes executives more likely to develop a firm-specific orientation; they are more inclined to become 'company men or women' and develop skills of a firm-specific nature. The emphasis on growth and stability objectives also enhances the job security of rank-and-file employees. The reduction in the risk of unemployment facilitates the workforce's investment in firm-specific assets (Whittaker, 1998) and widens the employee's zone of indifference with regard to the exercise of managerial authority. The extent to which management is able to institutionalise a work environment that encourages identification with the group's focal organisation will determine its ability to create a deep pool of social capital among employees and generate strong effort-intensity and spontaneous innovation from its workforce (Selznick, 1957; Rousseau, 1995).

Recently, the qualities of Japanese management-employee relations have been the subject of a more critical re-evaluation. Some scholars suggest that much of the shared decision-making is rather symbolic and ritualistic and is oriented toward the preservation of the status quo and rigid hierarchical relationships (Yoshimura and Anderson, 1999). Nevertheless, although Japanese organisations are more centralised and bureaucratic than popularly portrayed, they have created structures that embody considerable organisational capability.

To summarise, the imperatives of Japan's alliance governance, that is, its relational contracting and long-term reciprocity, influence the employees, executives and business partners in a manner that is quite distinct from managerial governance. This system bestows a unique blend of governance advantage and disadvantage. The beneficial effects of relational contracting reduce the transactions costs associated with partner opportunism and the costs of searching for and screening business partners. Moreover, such contracting provides the flexibility to exploit emergent value-creating opportunities that are foregone under more rigid contractual schemes (Ghoshal and Moran, 1996) and it stabilises relations sufficiently to support mutual investments in specialised and company-specific assets (Dyer and Singh, 1998). One might expect the reciprocal nature of the incentives under alliance capitalism governance to be advantageous to firms in capital-intensive, technologically complex industries characterised by predictable or continuous environmental changes that do not disrupt the elaborate lattice of inter-firm arrangements.

The alliance system of governance also has some predictable downsides (Carney and Gedajlovic, 2001). In particular, the incentive structures pose difficulties for firms in industries facing discontinuous change and uncertainty. In this environment, suppliers of capital to alliance firms may be ill-equipped to bear the risks involved, and stakeholders are often loath to confront the demands for restructuring (Dore, 1998). In the alliance system, the stability of relationships reduces the number of potential partners with which a firm can contract, which can cause serious difficulties when environmental conditions require the formation of new ties or the dissolution of existing partnerships (Granovetter, 1973). Hence, the expectation of fidelity will impede a firm's exit from obsolete partnerships and makes it difficult for them to adjust to market contractions or cope with technological discontinuities (Weijan, Walker and Kogut, 1994). While the self-reinforcing character of business relations can be an advantage during periods of growth, such intermeshing may stimulate a structural inertia during periods of environmental disturbance (Boyer and Yamada, 2000). Alliance governance also makes it more costly to raise capital on public equity markets because the interests of arm's-length equity investors can significantly diverge from those of suppliers who are also business partners (Fukao, 1999). There are many ways in which a supplier who is also a business partner may benefit from their association with the firm, but arm's-length suppliers of capital benefit only from the firm's profitability. For instance, shareholders' business partners may take their benefits in the form of favourable trade arrangements and externalise the cost of these benefits onto arm's-length investors. To the extent that arm's-length investors perceive this risk, it will be priced into the financial instrument and make raising capital on public markets more costly.

Performance assessment in the high *keiretsu* period

In the mid-1980s, the Japanese economy was operating at full tilt and the potential downsides of its corporate governance system were nowhere in evidence. A mid-term report card on the performance of the corporate system at that time would have been wholly favourable. Empirical evidence would have shown that the Japanese system of cooperative capitalism reduces transactions costs and promotes robust capital investment, continuous improvements in products and processes, and strong firm growth, albeit at the expense of profitability. The convoy system ensured that temporarily ailing firms could be restructured and brought back to financial health while sectors in long-term economic decline could be smoothly downsized with capital and skilled employees reallocated to growth sectors of the economy. Management guru, Michael Porter (1992), favourably compared the Japanese governance system with the short-term profit orientation prevailing in the USA. Japanese firms were provided a patient capital that provided the opportunity to adopt a longer-term orientation toward the creation and development of resources and competencies. Internationally, Japanese firms were on a foreign spending spree, acquiring high-profile assets in the USA and Europe. Managers of Western firms were enjoined to learn the lessons of Japanese corporate organisation. Indeed, such was the euphoria about the competitiveness of the Japanese industrial system that it generated an anti-Japanese backlash that focused on the concern that cooperation with Japan would compromise US interests (Reich and Mankin, 1986). There were abundant fears about the 'Japanisation' of domestic industries (Oliver and Wilkinson, 1992) and the 'hollowing out' of US industry by Japanese multinationals (Kotabe and Omura, 1989). However, the alliance capitalism that thrived under conditions of national economic reconstruction and growth had not then been tested by sustained periods of market decline and industry restructuring.

The changing international economy

In the mid-1980s, the global economic and financial order that was established at Bretton Woods in 1944 was under pressure from several sources and subject to revision. The cooling of Cold War tensions allowed Western governments to reconsider the institutions of international trade and finance. In the USA and the UK there was significant momentum behind the ideas of free trade, privatisation, liberalisation and deregulation. In Asia the spectre of communism had receded with China's adoption of economic reforms and, with Japan securely located within the Western sphere of influence, the US government felt able to address longstanding concerns about the Japan-US trade imbalances and the barriers to investment and trade. Scholars generally agree that the accord reached by the G5 countries at New York's Plaza Hotel in September 1985 signalled the beginning of a new era in Japan's economic and corporate development (Matsuura, Pollitt, Takada and Tanaka, 2003). The specific intention of the Plaza Accord was to reduce the size of the US (and European) annual trade deficit with Japan. The USA convinced the members of the G5 to achieve an orderly but significant appreciation in the value of the yen against the US dollar. The efforts of the G5 central banks were successful to an unprecedented degree. In 1985 one US dollar bought 240 yen. By 1988 one US dollar was trading at 128 yen, an appreciation that almost doubled the price of Japanese exports.

The Plaza Accord marked the beginning of a period called the *Endaka* and the end of Japan's export-oriented industrialisation as the rapidly appreciating yen stimulated Japanese producers to search for lower-cost sources of production throughout Asia. However, rather than following the Western practice of outsourcing and off-shoring production to foreign partners in low-cost locations, Japanese firms established their own subsidiaries or encouraged their domestic suppliers to follow and to co-locate with them in these countries. In this manner, internationalising Japanese firms exported their enterprise management and network management model (Martin, Mitchell and Swaminathan, 1995). Lead firms subcontracted the production of non-complex commodities to local firms and began socialising and integrating these new partners into their networks (Peng, Lee and Tan, 2001). This approach to internationalisation resulted in a boom in Japanese foreign direct investment, first in Southeast Asia and later in the USA and Europe, and created over two million jobs outside of Japan. Yet the internationalisation of Japanese production had little impact upon the system of alliance governance because ownership and control remained firmly in Japanese hands.

The Plaza Accord resulted in numerous unintended consequences that shaped the future of the *keiretsu* business groups. The continuing appreciation of the yen, or *Endaka* was to produce a more insidious effect, depressing Japanese interest rates to historically low levels that were negative in real terms. Long-term negative real interest rates set in motion an asset-price spiral in real estate and equity markets prices, creating a bubble economy. Increases in the value of equity allowed firms to reduce their dependence on bank debt and, as many firms were also cash-flow positive in this period, they could finance their expansion through retained profits; together, these factors allowed firms affiliated with business groups to loosen ties with their main bank. These circumstances also weakened the banks' capacity to discipline the market behaviour of their affiliated firms. During this period, Japanese firms were able to use the inflated currency to acquire, in a seemingly random manner, a variety of assets unrelated to the firm's core business. When the bubble economy collapsed in 1991, the severely deflating asset values instigated a decade-long depression in the financial and corporate sector. The banking sector was particularly hard-hit and degenerated into a deep crisis under the weight of nonperforming and questionable loans.

Between 1985 and 1991, the *Endaka* period revealed some of the flaws in alliance governance. The system of state oversight and main bank monitoring of enterprises had initially evolved in the harsh postwar environment, characterised by capital scarcity, economic reconstruction and a lack of foreign exchange. This system was much less effective in a more munificent and abundant environment. Flush with cash, and lacking an alternative system of checks and balances, enterprises could engage in sustained 'misdirected investment'. Moreover, the exuberance of the *Endaka* economy also disguised significant changes in the international economy.

In Korea, Taiwan and Southeast Asia, governments emulated elements of the Japanese development model; in a pattern sometimes called the 'flying geese formation'. Korean and Taiwanese firms entered industrial sectors in which Japan was losing competitiveness, for example, shipbuilding, steel and textiles, and later in electronics and automobiles (Hobday, 1995). Western firms had learned many lessons from Japan and improved their productivity and quality standards. Firms in the West had also absorbed Japanese ideas pertaining to outsourcing and had extensively disaggregated their value chains. Most importantly, US and European economies entered into a period of far-reaching liberalisation, industry restructuring and consolidation.

Liberalisation and deregulation was most far-reaching in the field of financial services. The Big Bang occurred in the UK in 1986, and a series of reforms was implemented in the USA throughout the 1980s. In 1992, the European Union's single market programme began to liberalise European financial markets and make cross-border mergers and acquisitions less costly and easier to execute. Financial sector liberalisation initiated the emergence of a new class of investors, such as private equity partnerships and leveraged buyout organisations, and stimulated the growth of institutional investors. These agents introduced new financial instruments, such as leasing, derivatives, cross-equity swaps, debt for equity swaps, foreign currency denominated bonds and currency hedging, which altered existing patterns of ownership and control.

The financial revolution soon began to affect the corporate industrial sector. Government-protected monopolies in telecommunications, water, electrical and gas utilities and the steel industries were liberalised and opened to foreign investment. In fields such as automobiles, software, information technology hardware, pharmaceuticals, mining and minerals extraction, chemicals, aerospace, defence engineering, oil and gas, steel and metals, a big-business revolution was underway; former national champions declined, there was a boom in cross-border mergers and acquisitions, and highly-focused global oligopolies emerged (Nolan, 2001). However, Japanese firms were largely excluded from these financial innovations and the attendant global consolidation of industrial sectors. The model of stable and reciprocal shareholdings thwarted mergers and acquisitions and hindered the realignment, rationalisation and consolidation occurring in numerous international industries. The new international economic order, based on the principle of liberalised trade and investment stimulated by a global big business consolidation, posed a new competitive threat to Japanese industry.

Weaker economic performance since 1991

There is accumulating evidence that the financial market performance of Japanese firms has been in relative decline since 1991. Anecdotally, Nolan (2001) notes that in 1962, Japan had just 21 firms on the Fortune 500 list of the largest international companies, fewer than either Germany or the UK. In 1993, the number of Japanese firms on the Fortune 500 had grown to 135. By 2000, many companies had dropped off the list and Japan's share of the Fortune 500 had declined to 107 firms. However, it is important note that this decline is relative. Nolan also observes that that even after the long stagnation of the 1990s, many of Japan's large businesses remained world leaders in research and development expenditure, technical capability, global brand and distribution systems (Nolan, 2001: 11). The decline in the number of large Japanese firms was less significant than their stagnant stock market performance. Some ten years after the 1991 collapse in share price, only 60 of 1,400 firms listed on the primary section of the Tokyo Stock Exchange had increased past their 1990 levels.

The prevailing view of the performance effects of *keiretsu* membership is that firms voluntarily paid an insurance premium by accepting lower profitability and lower firm risk, and in exchange, the group provided protection from hostile takeover, financial support in troubled times, preferential purchasing arrangements and favourable access to capital (Nakatani 1984; Gerlach, 1992a; Lincoln, Gerlach and Ahmadjian, 1996). The profit redistribution effect or insurance hypothesis was supposed to deliver faster and sustained economic growth for group members. However, the continuing malaise in Japan's corporate performance generated scepticism about the value of bank-led corporate governance. The focus began to turn to the negative aspects of business group affiliation. Several recent studies provide evidence that departs from the profit redistribution and insurance hypotheses, casting the *keiretsu* in less glowing terms. Main banks are viewed as imposing a variety of costs on their affiliates in a manner that captures the rents and expropriates other classes of shareholder (Weinstein and Yafeh, 1998), while powerful *keiretsu* members exploit weaker firms (Kim, Hoskisson and Wan, 2004) and utilise complex corporate structures to exploit minority investors by selling low-quality assets in equity markets (Dewenter, Novacs, and Pettway, 2001). Another study questions the extent to which *keiretsu* affiliation does in fact reduce profit variability (Gedajlovic and Shapiro, 2002).

In their study of the *keiretsu*, Weinstein and Yafeh (1998) re-examine data from the period 1977 to 1988. While it is often argued that *keiretsu* affiliates have better access to capital, their study finds that Japanese firms affiliated with bank-controlled business groups will pay higher interest rates on their liabilities than unaffiliated companies. Prior to the liberalisation of Japanese capital markets, alternative sources of capital were very limited. The main source of capital, the main banks, typically had long-term relationships with their clients and a de facto monopoly on the supply of external credit. Consequently, if client firms wanted to switch from one bank to another, they faced very high costs. Weinstein and Yafeh (1998: 640) conclude that banks use their monopoly power 'to capture most of the rents through high interest payments and through pressures on clients to use large quantities of bank financed capital inputs'. They suggest that this capacity for rent extraction explains much of the low profitability in main bank affiliated firms. Moreover, they find that these firms did not grow any faster than independent, unaffiliated firms, and that at no point in the 1960s did main bank clients outperform independents. The basic argument is that powerful but conservative banks use their influence to encourage firms to forgo risky but potentially profitable investment projects. Consistent with their own capacity for risk bearing, banks encourage the adoption of risk-averse, debt-oriented investment strategies that siphon profits and restrict investment.

In a similar vein, Kim, Hoskisson and Wan (2004) outline a power-dependence explanation that suggests the costs and benefits of *keiretsu* affiliation are not distributed equally over the whole group membership. They hypothesise that centrally located firms are more powerful and are less subject to monitoring and group discipline than peripherally located, weaker firms. However, weaker, dependent members are compelled to be more efficient and pursue profitability goals. They hypothesise that compared with independent firms, weaker *keiretsu* member firms will show a positive relationship between product diversification and profitability. In contrast, central firms possess greater power, and because they are less subject to *keiretsu* governance constraint, they can pursue diversification strategies with less emphasis on profitability. This is a theoretically interesting argument because it suggests that, far from being communities of equals, Japanese business groups should be considered as systems of domination aimed at enhancing the prestige of an entrenched elite group. This perspective stands in marked contrast to network and social theories of *keiretsu*, which emphasise cooperative explanations. Kim et al. (2004) test their hypotheses on a sample of 295 large manufacturing firms each with sales in excess of $1billion per annum in the period 1990–92, which straddles the collapse of the bubble economy. Their results provide some support for the conceptualisation of *keiretsu* as power-dependence systems as they find that less powerful firms are more focused in their diversification and more profitable than independent firms. In contrast, more powerful firms have broader, more unrelated diversification, and higher sales growth than unaffiliated firms. These results suggest that powerful firms are less monitored and can take advantage of their positions to focus upon growth benefits.

Dewenter, Novacs and Pettway (2001) examine the business group 'reputational premium' hypothesis, which suggests that large and highly visible business groups are more likely than freestanding firms to honour their contracts and resist opportunistic behaviour because, if opportunism is detected in one area, this may result in negative consequences for their reputation in other transactions. Hence, to uphold the reputation of the group as a whole, management must actively monitor and constrain opportunistic tendencies in their affiliates (Khanna and Pelapu, 1997). However, the complexity of many large business groups hinders outsiders from ascertaining firm strategies within this myriad of transactions. In the complexity perspective, the group's internal workings are not immediately transparent to arm's-length minority investors. Consequently, there is a high degree of uncertainty about the group's operations and it is difficult to effectively discern the true effect of management decisions, which limits the need to address reputational concerns and restrain actions. For example, outsiders may be unable to detect management action intended to expropriate minority investors. Hence, Dewenter et al. (2001) propose that there is a trade-off between visibility and complexity.

Dewenter et al. (2001) suggest that the potential conflict of interest between insiders and minority investors is most evident when a business group decides to spin-off one of its member firms through an initial public offer (IPO). On the one hand, IPOs can be positive events because unbundling a firm from the group raises capital for the enterprise and creates numerous investment opportunities; it also facilitates market monitoring and the establishment of the equity market values of the firm. On the other hand, IPOs can be negative events that permit a group to opportunistically divest themselves of poor quality assets. For instance, a group may temporarily inflate asset prices by taking advantage of market timing and windows of opportunity. Gerlach (1997) shows that spin-offs through IPOs are important for Japanese firms when they create satellites of firms around technological innovations. Dewenter et al. (2001) examine the trade-off between reputation maintenance and opportunism using a sample of 85 independent and 74 *keiretsu*-affiliated firms that subsequently listed on the Tokyo Stock Exchange between 1981 and 1994. Their findings suggest that *keiretsu*-linked IPOs have higher initial returns than do independent IPOs, a result consistent with the belief that complexity obscures visibility. This finding does not hold for vertical *keiretsu*, which have less complex structures. The authors conclude that the complex and opaque nature of horizontal *keiretsu* groups outweighs the potential constraining effects of high visibility and close scrutiny. The inability of outsiders to readily discern group strategies suggests that reputational concerns will not serve as an active check on group affiliates' behaviour; consequently, the potential for agency conflicts between firms in large diversified business groups and outside investors may be relevant and significant.

Finally, prior studies of performance outcomes typically conclude that group affiliates trade off profitability in exchange for risk-reduction or lower variation in profitability (Nakatani, 1984; Weinstein and Yafeh, 1998; Lincoln et al., 1996). However, contrary to the previous studies, Gedajlovic and Shapiro (2002) find that firms within *keiretsu* groups tend to have poorer performance and a greater variance than do independent firms. They speculate that there is a possible explanation for their contradictory results: most previous studies failed to control for key firm-specific factors that would have a direct and substantial impact on firm risks. They found that *keiretsu* members tend to be older and larger in size than independent firms. The effect of *keiretsu* membership on firm risk therefore cannot be correctly evaluated unless these firm-specific factors are controlled in the analysis.

Each of these studies works from a different set of assumptions about the value of *keiretsu* governance. By detailing the different strategic goals of powerful and less powerful, central and peripheral *keiretsu* members, these studies illustrate the heterogeneity of group membership and the inappropriateness of blanket conclusions about the positive or negative impact on member performance. It is worth recognising that the *keiretsu* is a group system and its members occupy a variety of roles within it. Just as the Western multidivisional firm's portfolio is comprised of cash cows, stars and question mark business units, so Japanese groups include enterprises with differing performance expectations.

Regardless of the growing ambiguity about the performance effects of group affiliation, there are numerous predictions of the imminent 'fracturing' (Drucker, 1993), 'crumbling' (Whittaker, 1998) 'decay' (Boyer and Yamada, 2000) and 'twilight' of the *keiretsu* (Gerlach, 1992b). Many who subscribe to the 'decay' hypothesis suggest that the system that functioned so well during Japan's industrial adolescence must give way to a more individualistic market-oriented system. However, in its maturity, the *keiretsu*'s adjustment to international changes is glacially slow and consistent with the long-term commitments that are integral to governance by a core firm.

Institutional change in the 1990s

In an effort to revitalise the banking, insurance and equity markets, the Japanese financial system was subject to a series of regulatory reforms beginning in 1997. Over a three-year period, there were moves to eliminate entry barriers to different financial sectors, the reintroduction of prohibited holding companies, and important reforms to accounting and financial disclosure requirements. The Ministry of Finance signalled a commitment to allow faltering financial institutions to fail; this included banks, securities companies and mortgage-lending institutions. Subsequently there have been several high-profile bank consolidations and bankruptcies. Indeed, amid allegations of corruption and the continuing inability to solve core financial problems, such as the write-off of bad loans and continuing asset inadequacy in banks, the Ministry of Finance lost much of its legitimacy. Ultimately the Ministry of Finance was broken up and its executive and supervisory functions divided among new agencies. The newly established Financial Supervisory Agency was made responsible for overseeing the financial system, while the Industrial Revitalisation Corporation was mandated to solve the continuing structural problems of financial and industrial enterprises. Working in tandem with the private sector and foreign investors, the role of the latter was to perform a 'triage' and separate companies with a realistic chance of survival from those that should be liquidated.

Efforts made to address weaknesses in equity markets included the establishment of NASDAQ Japan, and the creation of MOTHERs (Market for the High Growth and Emerging Stocks), a new section in the Tokyo Stock Exchange designed to target new ventures and technology firms. The advent of online trading and lower securities commissions was expected to create a more fertile environment for the establishment of new firms. Minority shareholders were also empowered; since 1993, modifications in the commercial code have made it easier for shareholders to litigate in cases of management misconduct. Other efforts to make management more transparent include changes in the structure and composition of boards of directors, the introduction of stock options, the appointment of an outside auditor, and reductions in the size of boards. It is worthwhile noting that reformers did not officially target the break-up of the *keiretsu* as a specific policy priority.

The architects of this raft of reforms in the financial system intended to deliver a 'Big Bang' or radical shock. Taken as a package, the amendments to the commercial code, remodelled regulatory apparatus, reduced bureaucratic restrictions, and a corresponding increase in shareholder powers and freedoms does appear to mark a shift towards greater transparency, accountability, and market-oriented standards of corporate governance as conceived by agencies such as the World Bank and International Monetary Fund. Just how much impact they will have remains to be seen. The de jure processes of corporate governance seem to be much altered but whether these reforms bring de facto adjustments in corporate governance and business practice, is an open question.

Continuity in the *keiretsu* system

Predictably, analysts are divided about the impact of increasing globalisation, technological change and institutional reform in the structure of Japan's business groups. In one view, reforms have so far been met by a substantial continuity in corporate structures and business practice. Ahmadjian and Lincoln (2001) suggest that in response to globalisation, Japanese firms have not abandoned their system of alliance governance but are regenerating their networks by shuffling and reordering transactions along the market-hybrid-hierarchy continuum. In this perspective, inter-firm relations among established and new partners have undergone a 'fine gradational stratification' (Matsuura et al., 2003: 1012), which means that the intensity of relations with some network members has increased but weakened with others. Ahmadjian

(2006) argues that even in the presence of strong environmental pressures to change, firms are reluctant to discard longstanding business relationships.

Ahmadjian (2006) analyses the equity relationships of the top 200 firms affiliated with horizontal groups in 1990 and 2000. The study finds that firms are more likely to break equity linkages with peripheral business partners with whom they trade little and have few director interlocks. However, equity ties with the main bank, with firms with director interlocks and with members of the same group are less likely to be severed. Her study also shows greater variation in the changes in dyadic trading and supply-ties among vertical groups in the auto industry between 1984 and 1996; however, the dominant theme is that severed ties occurred exclusively among suppliers that manufactured a narrow range of subcomponents, while ties among suppliers manufacturing an extensive product range were unbroken. In other words, relationships probably strengthened because many manufacturers consolidated their procurement requirements into the hands of fewer first-tier preferred suppliers.

Citing several high-profile cases, she suggests that underperforming firms are more likely to sever ties that have little continuing economic value, for example, neither Nissan nor Hitachi came to the assistance of financially-troubled Nissan Mutual Life Insurance in 1997, a firm with which they had a longstanding linkage but little continuing economic interest. In the vertical groups, second-tier and failing firms become enmeshed or consolidated into global alliances such as those of Mazda-Ford, Nissan-Renault, GM-Suzuki or Daimler Benz-Chrysler-Mitsubishi. However, the highly successful Toyota has strengthened its links to its supply chain. Similarly, horizontal groups with generally superior overall performance, such as Mitsubishi and Sumitoma, have retained their structure. Ahmadjian (2006) suggests that because high performers have not yet encountered a real crisis that could force them to break ties, they continue to preserve and find value in long-lasting established relationships. She concludes that pressures to change were most likely to disrupt more peripheral relationships but did not have much impact in groups with stronger multiple links. Firms with multiple business relationships, such as main bank ties, director interlocks or trading ties, were more likely to maintain an ownership tie. To this end, the decline in the importance of business groups has been partial and varied across groups. More autonomous and independent firms have emerged as weakly cohesive groups began to spin apart. At the same time, there is a tightening of linkages among members of surviving groups. Ahmadjian

(2006) predicts a growing bifurcation between tightly-linked members of surviving groups and a growing population of more fully autonomous firms.

Important developments in the *keiretsu* system are reflected in the gradual decline of both long-term shareholdings and cross-shareholdings, and the corresponding increase in share ownership by foreign investors, who typically hold their shares for much shorter periods of time. Between 1987 and 2000, long-term shareholding fell from 45 per cent to 33 per cent, and reciprocal cross-shareholdings fell from 18 per cent to 10 per cent. In 1990, foreign investors held just 5 per cent of total market capitalisation of domestically-listed Japanese companies; by 2000 this figure had increased to some 19 per cent. Some commentators have interpreted these figures as a change in Japan's equity markets brought about by long-term relational investors being supplanted by short-term investors seeking quick capital gains. However, Lincoln and Gerlach (2004: 324) believe these changes disguise an underlying stability and that 'the stable and patient institutional shareholders remain the norm for most large companies through the nineties'. They do acknowledge that the number of stable shareowners fell sharply in 2001 following the introduction of new accounting rules that required corporations to report assets at market instead of book value. However, once again, stable shareholdings subsequently levelled off. Moreover, while cross-ownership may have declined in some groups, it was often compensated for by increases in cross-ownership in others.

This ebb and flow in group cohesion is not new. *Keiretsu* networks have always evinced an organic and mercurial quality, shifting in response to political and market factors. Based on data from 1962 to 1997, Lincoln and Gerlach (2004) find that over the very long term, the cohesiveness of *keiretsu* linkages shows a distinct countercyclical trend, pulling together in difficult times when the need for mutual assistance is greatest, and loosening in more prosperous conditions when self-funding affiliate firms have less need for capital. In particular, debt ties tend to weaken in pre-crisis periods when stock prices and profits allow firms to meet their capital needs from markets and internally-generated funds. In post-crisis periods, high debt loads, diminished profits and weakened equity values bring about a resurgence in debt relationships. For example, the reduced dependence on bank lending began after the Plaza Accord and banks and firms pulled apart in the *Endaka* years, only to tighten after the bubble burst. In this regard, *keiretsu* affiliation reflects a fundamental tension: firms struggle to assert their autonomy but must trade this off against the desire for the protection of group membership.

Just as in any complex organisation, inter-firm trading relationships and the portfolio of joint ventures, projects and long-term contracts tend to evolve, but among *keiretsu* firms, change occurs within the framework of the *keiretsu* system. This path-dependent development is evident in their response to the re-introduction of holding companies into Japan. The Japanese commercial code was amended in 1997 to allow for the creation of holding companies, which had been prohibited since the US occupation. The holding company structure was rapidly embraced, especially by the financial sector. But unlike in the USA, where holding companies typically adapt to provide for the decentralised financial control of diverse portfolio businesses, the role played by Japanese holding companies provides for quasi-consolidation and a temporary realignment of firm linkages. In Japan, grouping firms into a holding company structure is a stepping stone or temporary expedient; contingent upon financial performance of the constituent parts, it might be either dismantled or carried further with operational integration. In the absence of a market for corporate control, the holding company structure represents a compromise solution to consolidate independent firms of similar stature while allowing firms to maintain their historical identities and seek areas to consolidate and unify their management.

Similarly, while some analysts point to the deinstitutionalisation of the Japanese employment system (Ahmadjian and Robinson, 2001), others suggest that a comparable gradational stratification may be developing among different types of employees. Japanese firms continue to operate dual labour markets but have begun to elaborate new individual and merit-based incentive systems to accommodate the growing category of highly educated and more mobile workers (Whittaker, 1998).

The overall perspective is one of substantial continuity in the business landscape. The same enterprises that appeared in the postwar period are engaged in the same longstanding relationships and still dominate the commanding heights of the economy. Wide-ranging institutional, technological and global market changes have not unleashed gales of creative destruction in Japan. As a result of numerous disruptive forces, very few new entrants have joined the ranks of Japan's leading enterprises. In the West, revolutionary changes in software, computer hardware, telecommunications and the biotechnology industry have produced an array of new competitors such as Microsoft, Cisco, Google or eBay; based upon new technological innovations, they have swept aside yesterday's champions. Contrast this corporate turnover with the remarkable stability in the population of Japan's large firms; the five leading PC makers in the 1990s all were parts of large electronics conglomerates that existed before the war. There is very little destruction but very little creativity.

How can we explain such evident continuity? Why is change so painstakingly slow? One answer lies in the inherent durability and stickiness of *keiretsu* relationships. It is worth bearing in mind that Japan's business groups were initially designed to mitigate just these kinds of disruptive forces. The implied stability of relationships under alliance governance can cause 'explosive conflicts through the addition of new ties (or subtraction of old ones)' (Zajac, 1998: 320). Faltering alliance partners are afforded an opportunity to improve their performance in the prevailing culture of Kaizen (continuous improvements). Many firms do improve within the framework of expectations. Reciprocity and norms of consultation also attenuate restructuring processes. Consequently, the regeneration of *keiretsu* networks tends to be a long, drawn-out process. However, the rebalancing and increased stratification processes described above do not signify a crumbling or fracturing of networks; rather, alliance governance is in this situation driving responses to institutional market pressures by regenerating their networks in a more open and globalised economy.

Moreover, there are forces that operate at the level of the business system as a whole. Sociologists have noted that interdependence and coherence among different subsystems in a nation's economy can make change in one part of the system difficult without corresponding changes in other areas (Boyer and Yamada, 2000). In Japan's postwar phase of rapid growth, the interdependence among corporate groups, the banking system, the employment system, linkages with the international economy, and state regulation were deeply complementary to one another. While the recent economic inertia is cause for some concern, disrupting any single element of this interactive self-reinforcing system might reduce the effectiveness of the whole, and the marginal benefits of adopting new practice in one part of the system may be more than offset by the costs of disruption in the wider system. In this view, much of the reformist zeal is mere rhetoric and the de jure amendment of the legal framework does not translate into de facto restructuring of the economy.

Underlying 'macro forces' for change

Predominant countervailing forces can also reduce the rate of change in *keiretsu* structures. External factors, such as the loss of legitimacy for neo-liberal market orthodoxy and market-based models of corporate governance following the US scandals of the early twenty-first century (Henisz, Guillen and Zelner, 2005) and the possibility that Japanese economic growth might accelerate, also moderate the legitimacy and incentives to press on with reforms.

On the other hand, there are unequivocal signs of change in the structure of the Japanese economy. The continuing crisis in the financial sector eventually brought about the consolidation of several large banks. Three major banks – Fuji, Dai Ichi Kangayo Industrial Bank of Japan – merged in 1998, and in 1999, Sakura Bank, the main bank of the Mitsui *keiretsu*, merged with the Sumintomo Bank. This effectively reduced the number of major horizontal *keiretsu* from the big six to the big four. The sale of assets to foreign investors has been most extensive in the financial sector: Japan Lease was acquired by GE Capital for $6.6 billion; Axa, the French insurance company, purchased a 70 per cent stake in Japan Group Life; and Travelers Insurance took a significant ownership in Nikko Securities. The purchase of the iconic Long Term Credit Bank by a consortium of foreign investors in 2000 was particularly significant because this bank had been at the heart of the state corporate alliance reconstruction of the postwar economy. Perhaps the greatest change stemming from the crisis in the financial sector is the banks' inability to continue bailing out financially distressed companies; banks have almost ceased lending to the corporate sector, and instead have focused on trying to assure their own survival. Several high-profile failures in the financial and corporate sector, including Hokkaidi Bank, Yamaichi Securities and the retailer Sogo, mark the passing of the old convoy system that had assured the survival of underperforming firms.

While Lincoln and Gerlach emphasise the continuity and stability of Japan's industrial architecture in the face of powerful environmental influences, they also discern five 'macro trends' that will continue to reshape its structure. They contend that these trends are non-linear, irregular and sporadic. However, a projection of their collective impact suggests that it is possible to glimpse the structure of a new Japanese economy that is significantly different from that established in the postwar era. The first of these macro trends is the 'slow and uneven dissolution of the *keiretsu*' (Lincoln and Gerlach, 2004: 373) and their replacement by a looser and more flexible mixture of 'pairings and clusters'. The thinning out of corporate structures will leave a less monolithic and less concentrated corporate structure. The second macro trend is the rejection of the convoy system as companies turn away from stable 'group insurance' arrangements. The third macro trend is the 'departure from its centre stage of the large financial and industrial firms' that had been responsible for giving birth to new enterprises through a process of spin-offs and decentralised control. To date, there is no obvious successor to this mechanism for the creation of new enterprise, and this is certainly a liability for the economy as a whole, given that the fourth macro trend is the increasing pace of technological change including the impact of the internet and the integration of communications technologies. Finally, in a process that Lincoln and Gerlach (2004: 375) describe as 'inward internationalisation', 'the barriers to foreign involvement in the Japanese economy ... are falling away'. Although Lincoln and Gerlach (2004: 377) express a deep admiration for Japanese business practice that offers important competitive advantages for its firms and equality and security for suppliers, employees and managers, they foresee Japan's network economy 'fading into history and perhaps inevitably so'.

Conclusions

Predictions that Japanese business groups are becoming obsolete and that their business relationships are likely to dissolve are overstated. That Japanese enterprises will migrate toward the arm's-length business relationships and short-term ties characteristic in the USA seems even more improbable. The financial and industrial architecture established in the post-Second World War era was primarily designed to provide Japanese enterprises with a security blanket to shield them from political and market uncertainty and allow them to focus on the overriding task of economic reconstruction. These founding institutional conditions of Japanese firms created a particular administrative heritage. The risk-reducing, core-buffering, insurance-providing convoy system offered a highly-stable environment in which leading enterprises borrowed and exploited foreign technology by systematically focusing upon upgrading, improving and perfecting existing knowledge. In so doing, they brought a single-minded discipline and gained significant economic advantages. However, this deeply embedded emphasis on the exploitation of existing knowledge has created deep path dependencies in the administrative heritage arising from it. As March (1991: 71) puts it, 'Exploitation includes such things as refinement, choice, production, efficiency, selection implementation, execution ... adaptive system engaging in exploitation to the exclusion of exploration are likely to find themselves trapped in a suboptimal stable equilibria'.

Equally, March (1991: 71) observes that 'exploration includes things captured by terms such as search, variation, risk taking, experimentation, play, flexibility, discovery, innovation' and he notes that there are risks associated with an exclusive emphasis on exploration. But excessive exploration is not a problem for Japanese enterprise. Indeed, a corporate system in which organisational procedures, decision rules, management practices and rewards systems were all geared towards exploitation, provided managers with few incentives to play, take risks or engage in innovation and invest in exploratory technology with distant payoffs.

During a long period of rapid growth, Japanese firms were hailed as a model of development worthy of emulation in mature and developing economies alike. After a long period of inertia and the fitful and uncertain restructuring, should the Japanese *keiretsu* still be regarded as an exemplary model of reform? Khanna and Yafeh (2005) are not confident that Japan's corporate groups hold many lessons for business groups that encounter problems in other emerging economies' markets. They contend that Japanese business groups are fundamentally different from groups found in other parts of the world: they are centred on banks, they are not controlled by families, they have no alternative organised mechanism of joint decision-making, and the vertical *keiretsu* are essentially operational elements.

4

State-constructed business groups: the Korean *chaebol*

Introduction

For the most part, Korea's business groups were made not born. Through government policy and the allocation of financial and material resources, the state induced and constructed a small number of large, diversified, and in some cases vertically-integrated, family-owned enterprises that have dominated the Korean economy since their foundation in the late 1950s. Korean business groups were deliberately constructed by the developing state. This is significant because the dominant hypotheses about their development and economic consequence pay scant attention to the role of the state. According to the dominant hypothesis, business groups spontaneously materialised in an institutional void to perform a variety of market mediating tasks (Khanna and Palepu, 1997). However, when the *chaebol* were established, they were state-created and regulated actors and we should expect this to have a significant bearing on their subsequent development.

The Korean state deliberately and consistently suppressed the development of market forces and institutions (Amsden, 1989). Instead, the state elaborated a system of supervisory institutions designed to lead the development of domestic industrialisation, with the express goal of catching up with archrival Japan. In this environment, the state's regulatory role was to control large enterprise that was not subject to market discipline. Because nationalist political goals have so dominated the Korean business environment, it is important to recognise whether and to what extent governments are involved in the process of liberalising and constructing market institutions.

The prevailing thesis of business group development is that the rationale for their existence will disappear as market institutions begin to appear and become stronger. In other words, if business groups are a substitute for market institutions, they will dissolve and crumble as market institutions appear. Just as business groups do not materialise in a vacuum, market institutions do not abruptly appear fully formed. In transitional and emerging economies, market-oriented infrastructure is almost always established in an incremental, piecemeal and partial manner (Henisz, Guillen and Zelner, 2005). In the process of constructing market institutions, the state often creates even greater economic uncertainty. In the context of Korea, the outcomes of partial market liberalisation are observable. First, the Korean state gradually lost its capacity to fully discipline enterprise. Second, the liberalisation process creates opportunities for the stronger or leading enterprises to strengthen and consolidate their position further. The joint effect is a more autonomous and more powerful corporate sector that has the ability to influence the pace and shape of continued liberalisation. What began as state-led industrialisation in the 1960s (Amsden, 1989) has today become a co-equal partnership between the state and large groups (Granovetter, 2005). This chapter charts the origins of Korea's largest business groups. We describe their family-dominated systems of corporate governance and their hierarchical organisational structures. We evaluate the financial and product market performance of these groups and compare their governance and structure with those of Japan's *keiretsu* business groups. We conclude with a survey of the subsequent development of the *chaebol* since the Asian financial crisis.

The origins of Korea's state-constructed business groups

Until the 1880s, Korea was a 'hermit kingdom' – a feudal society ruled by an emperor and virtually shut off from foreign influence. A colonial rivalry between Japan and Russia for territories in East Asia resulted in Korea becoming a Japanese protectorate in 1905 following Japan's defeat of Russia in the Russo-Japanese war. For the next 40 years, Korea was subject to a harsh colonial administration with punitive taxation, forced labour, seizure of crops and the eviction of tenant farmers. Japanese colonial rule was strengthened after 1931 when Japan's economy was put on a war footing. To serve its wartime economy, Japan established a modern transport and communications system across Korea and, at the end of the war, the colonial Japanese left a considerable material and technological legacy (Biggart, 1998).

However, Korea's misery did not end in 1945. As a prelude to the Cold War, the peninsula was divided into two occupation zones: the Soviet Union took over administrative control in the North and the US military forces administered the South. South Korea, officially known as the Republic of Korea (hereafter South Korea), was established in 1948. The tense and fragile division of the peninsula did not last long. A full-scale war erupted in June 1950. Chinese forces later joined with the North, and the Soviet Union supported them by supplying arms. The war ended in a stalemate in 1953 when an armistice established the current boundaries of North and South Korea.

The war also destroyed much of Korea's technological and material legacy from the colonial period (Biggart, 1998). In the immediate aftermath of the Second World War, the country's economy and society could barely sustain itself. Korean politics were deeply divided and there were conflicts between landlords and tenant farmers, and between those who had resisted Japanese occupation and those who had collaborated with it. Because the Korean army was incapable of national defence, the state was essentially dependent upon the USA for national security and internal order. The primary goal of the American administration was to keep Korea in the Western alliance. As such, it provided ample foreign aid to support the importation of basic food and consumer goods until the agricultural sector could re-establish itself. In the elections held in 1948, the USA supported the rule of the most conservative political faction, the Korean Democratic Party (KDP), but it was a strongman leader of the Nationalist Party, Syngman Rhee, a vigorous anti-communist who eventually prevailed. The KDP's most significant involvement was in safeguarding of the interests of the beleaguered landowning class. As one of its first tasks, the newly established Korean government carried out land reforms whereby Koreans with large landholdings were obliged to divest most of their land to a new class of independent family proprietors. However, members of the old landowning elite families were to reappear as politicians, bureaucrats and industrialists. Under Rhee, these elites, an oddball collection 'of patriots, notables and various circles of the intellectual stratum' (Amsden, 1989: 39), enjoyed favourable aid allocations in return for contributions to Rhee's party.

The influx of foreign aid and its allocation to politically favoured insiders spurred the development of a new entrepreneurial class and, according to Amsden (1989) its members were less conservative and more growth-oriented than the older generation of entrepreneurs in Korea's textile industry, who were the only established industrialists in

Korea at that time. Whereas entrepreneurs in the textile industry focused their energy upon redeveloping the cotton-spinning industry, those connected to Rhee were much more willing to enter a variety of enterprises. Not only did these elites benefit from an uneven distribution of foreign aid, they also enjoyed preferential access to the sales of Japanese property at below market prices. Favoured firms were also allocated hard currency to import raw materials, grain and fertiliser, which they resold on the domestic market at monopoly prices. As Amsden (1989: 40) puts it, 'the cradling of enterprise in illicit wealth was not industry-specific. These subsidised entrepreneurs were generalists devoted to moneymaking in whatever industry the opportunity arose'.

These new entrepreneurs were the forebears of the *chaebol* and the public's opinion of them was not wholly favourable. They were seen as immoral profiteers who owed their wealth to government connections and their willingness to exploit employees for the sake of corporate profits. This perception is deeply rooted and remains prevalent in Korea today. However, Amsden argues that these rather opportunistic entrepreneurs played a critical role in the development of the Korean enterprise:

> They skated over the stage of incremental growth that was characteristic of small-scale enterprise, they operated with a different logic of investment from that of traditional cotton spinning and weaving firms, and they formed crack troops to penetrate new industries ... [These entrepreneurs were] the embryo of the new social, economic, and political force. (Amsden 1989: 40)

Biggart (1988) concurs, suggesting that because Korea had no real indigenous capitalists, they were deliberately created by the Rhee regime. The entrepreneurs supported by Rhee were the only economic actors in the picture. Korea had no natural resources, and a large unskilled population with a per capita gross national product (GNP) that was less than $100. The country was engaged in continuous military conflict with its northern neighbour, it had a highly adversarial labour-relations environment and a volatile and militant student population; consequently, most foreign investors properly viewed Korea as politically unstable. It is thus unsurprising that foreign capital and multinational corporations showed very little interest in the development of the Korean economy. It was in this period that enterprises such as Hyundai, Samsung, Sanggyong, Lucky Goldstar, Hanjin first appeared, quickly developing into diversified enterprises.

Korea's early capitalism depended upon foreign aid. US foreign aid to Korea amounted to 15 per cent of average annual GNP and 80 per cent of Korea's foreign exchange for much of the 1950s. Unfortunately, very little of this aid was invested in human or physical capital. American aid workers complained of poor project management and shortages of technical and managerial skills. Student organisations and labour unions complained of corruption in the government, the military and the civil service. The malaise of the Rhee regime was terminated with a military coup in 1960 that brought General Park Ching Hee to power. Park's role-models were revolutionary modernisers such as Kemal Ataturk of Turkey, Sun Yat Sen in republican-era China and General Nasser in Egypt. Park lived a frugal existence and was determined to wipe out the excesses of corruption. Until his assassination at the hands of his own security chief in 1979, Park presided over the golden age of Korea's industrialisation. Like his predecessor Rhee, Park was anti-communist, but he formulated a developmental ideology based on importing foreign ideas, a dominant political class, and the creation of a national capitalism that would allow Korea to catch up and surpass its archrival Japan and elevate Korean society into the first ranks of industrial society.

Park believed that he required a direct connection with a progressive middle class to establish a policy framework, and an energetic group of actors that would overcome Korea's feudal past. The group chosen to serve as a new social and economic force was to be a 'select group of progressive millionaires who would be allowed to enter the center stage' (Amsden, 1989: 14). Park also recognised that economic and industrial development was needed to gain legitimacy and the support of the people. His national capitalism rested on three core foundations: the efficacy of long-range government planning, the virtues of large enterprise, and a strong state supervision to avoid monopoly and abuse of power. Maman (2002) suggests the Japanese *zaibatsu* served as a model for the formation of *chaebol*, this model of enterprise having become familiar in Korea during the period of Japanese colonial rule. In contrast with the Japanese experience, the state encouraged the formation of many groups and cultivated competition between them to avoid concentrating power in the hands of a just a few families. According to Maman (2002), Korea had a disunified elite structure; the new commercial elites were divided upon regional differences, which amplified the tendency for groups to compete with one another, whereas in Japan there was much cooperation between enterprises from different groups.

A distinguishing feature of Korean industrialisation is the deployment of a large battery of formal government institutions that were created to discipline and oversee the development of the *chaebol*. A brief survey of the reasons for the implementation of these instruments will illustrate the comprehensive manner in which the government constructed and controlled business groups. The government established the Economic Planning Board, the Ministry of Finance, and the Ministry of Trade and Industry. Many senior officials of these ministries were US-educated and technocratic in their orientation. Together, these ministries formulated a 'top-down' approach to government policy formation and were responsible for producing, implementing and monitoring a series of rolling five-year economic development plans.

In one of its first acts of state, the Park government nationalised the virtually bankrupt banking system; there being no other sources of financing, state ownership of the banking system provided de facto control of capital allocation in the country. Subsequently, all major credit decisions would be made on a discretionary basis. Amsden argues that to catalyse the process of industrialisation and begin the catch-up process, the government needed to deliberately and systematically distort prices in the economy. By 'getting prices wrong', the state actively and passively suppressed market forces and the development of market institutions. Their goal was to create profitable investment opportunities for new domestic firms, to reduce the costs of capital imports, and discourage the importation of (mainly Japanese) consumer goods. To encourage exports and protect the infant industries, the government manipulated prices by controlling interest rates and domestic and foreign currencies in a manner that promoted trade for their exports and protected against foreign competition.

To encourage firms to enter new industries, the state provided protection from foreign competition and subsidies through a licensing system that limited the number of firms allowed to enter a new-targeted sector. Non-bank financial institutions were very undeveloped and the Korean Ministry of Finance effectively controlled all forms of debt and trade credit. Access to capital was subject to state-determined priorities using a subsidy allocation principle that made diversification into new industries contingent on performance in old ones. Amsden describes:

> Repeated support by the government to a small set of big business groups was exchanged de facto for good performance ... performance is evaluated in terms of production and operations management were other than financial indicators. (Amsden, 1989: 16)

No matter how well politically connected, virtually all large-size firms were subject to the sternest discipline. To prevent monopolies and control inflation, the Ministry of Finance and the Economic Planning Board disciplined companies by means of price controls; as late as 1986, the prices of 110 commodities were under government guidance. To curb the probability of capital flight, Park followed up by a passing the 'Law for Dealing with Illicit Wealth Accumulation', which imposed severe penalties for capital exportation. While the extent of firms' compliance with this law is debatable, Amsden (1989) believes in the 1960s and 1970s, these rules provided a credible deterrent to private investors who might otherwise have used public subsidies to build personal fortunes abroad.

The state was very much the locus of initiatives taken to enter new industries; in Amsden's (1989) terms, the state was the entrepreneur. Under the auspices of the Economic Planning Board, the state exercised its capacity to collect information about trends in world markets and make decisions about which industries to enter. For example, the state was the prime mover in the decision to migrate away from light, labour-intensive manufacturing toward capital-intensive projects in chemicals, steel and other heavy industries. Because the government allocated capital, it also chose the specific firms to serve as the vehicle for industry entry. Amsden (1989) suggests that such strategic capacity was beyond the means of small backward domestic firms with little or no international experience. In late industrialising countries, the state often has a better overview of the economy than any individual entrepreneur. The importance of state initiative increases as industrialisation proceeds beyond factor cost driven industries into capital-intensive investment and scale-driven sectors, which require a more comprehensive incentive package than could be assembled by a private firm.

Moreover, in addition to selecting industries for development, choosing firms to coordinate entry and mobilising incentive packages, the government also led the process of industry restructuring, firm exit, and providing relief and bail-outs for companies in distress. One consequence of encouraging multiple entry into industries was periodic overcapacity; rival firms often competed by seeking to build large globally-efficient scale plants way ahead of real demand, which often stimulated intense price wars. The effect of overbuilding and excess capacity was periodic sectoral crises. In 1969–71, in 1979 through the early 1980s, and again in the 1990s, industrial crises caused by overcapacity led the government to step in and coordinate recovery by liquidating weaker firms and transferring their physical assets to stronger rivals through the use of tax credits and low-interest loans (Sung, 2002). In such circumstances, the state acts not only as the entrepreneur, but by adopting resource shedding and reallocation roles, it assumes the role of a corporate planner. Figure 4.1 illustrates the cycle of industrial policy.

The ostensible purpose of the government's industrial policy was to promote economic growth while simultaneously avoiding too much economic concentration. However, in its capacity as an entrepreneur and corporate strategist, the state also provided a buffering mechanism to protect firms from the vicissitudes of the international economy. Much financial and industrial policy has been aimed at promoting crisis avoidance and providing a stable and predictable environment for long-term planning and large-scale capital investment. Amsden says, 'The government used the banking sector as a buffer to absorb shocks in the real sector such as industrial restructuring and the world recession caused by the oil crisis' (Amsden and Euh, 1993: 388). In such a state-managed environment, firms are deliberately decoupled from market uncertainty, the impact of trade cycles, disruptive competition and other shocks; they are encouraged to focus single-mindedly on the tasks of growth, efficiency and improved factor productivity.

Figure 4.1   **The cycle of Korean industrial policy**

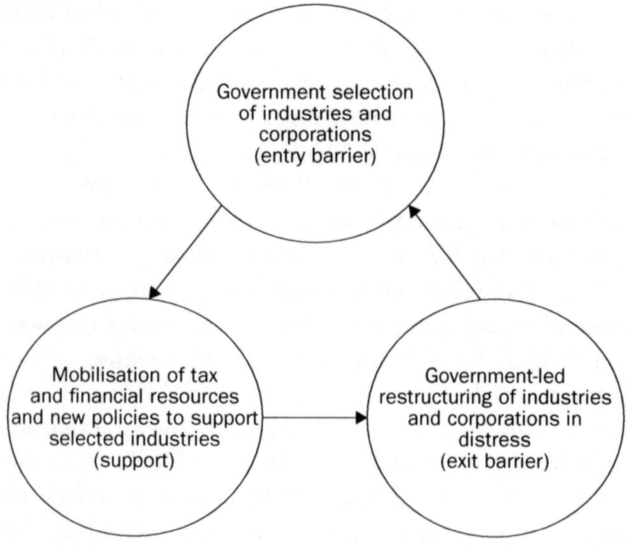

Source: Sung-Hee Jwa (2002: 18).

The Korean state's ability to lead the industrialisation process gives rise to the debate about just how the state was able to attain so much power. The 'strong state' perspective (Stubbs, 1999) suggests that geopolitical circumstances create the conditions for the uncontested exercise of authority. Korea had no history of political democracy and no legacy of institutional checks and balances on political power. In the aftermath of colonial administration, Korea's war-ravaged economy was at the mercy of the great powers. Operating on a permanent war footing, the USA initially focused its energies on establishing the apparatus of control and security. As indicated above, the major source of capital in Korea during the 1950s was US aid. However, foreign aid continued to flow into Korea throughout the 1960s and the mid-1970s due to US political interests in the region. An important ally of the USA in the Vietnamese conflict, Korea eventually sent some 300,000 soldiers to Vietnam. The USA continued to provide strong financial support; estimates suggest that Korea received over US$15 billion in foreign aid between 1961 and 1975. Only two other countries (Israel and South Vietnam) received more foreign aid in this period. The capital influx flowed into the hands of a corruption-free government who directed considerable investment into public infrastructure and supported the development of heavy industries (Stubbs, 1999).

The existence of a centralised and powerful state is also consistent with an institutional explanation of Korea's industrialisation strategy. Biggart (1998: 312) describes Korea's emergent capitalism as patrimonial: 'Power is held by a patriarch who rules over his household, which is administered by a loyal personal staff'. She argues that modern capitalist Korea is deeply rooted in Korean political tradition and exhibits several continuities with precolonial Korea. Her explanation suggests that prior to Japanese occupation, the imperial Korean state was characterised by a central monarchy that exercised control over competing regional clans of aristocratic families. All Korean subjects were treated as members of the Korean imperial household who were required to submit to the absolute authority of the emperor. The emperor's absolute authority was distinct from Japanese feudalism where the emperor's rule was limited by the defined rights and duties of the aristocratic and military classes.

Isolated and politically stable for many centuries, Korea was detached from the radical and external influences of the nineteenth century. Even during Japanese colonial rule, the large influx of a Japanese population (some 250,000 people) consisting of military, technicians, administrators, workers and their families who arrived to implement a Japanese strategy of economic exploitation had little impact upon Korean society and culture. The colonial population was to remain in social enclaves that, in Biggart's words, 'reproduced a centralised aristocratic and social order that dominated a largely peasant population' (Biggart, 1998: 313). Biggart argues that traditional Korean social organisation in which elites demand unreserved obedience to their position and enjoy unchecked authority over all spheres of their 'subjects' lives has largely continued into the postwar capitalist era.

Moreover, just as state-economy relations were governed by a patrimonial logic, Biggart (1998) suggests that the *chaebol* formed in the postwar period also inherited a similar legacy, and the organisation of households was equally patrimonial, albeit with some modern elements. Founder-owners managed their household empires as their own politico-economic spheres, with nearly unlimited jurisdiction, ruling through a personal staff organised as a secretariat. These driven entrepreneurs exhorted their employees with moral as well as economic visions that they expected their employees to embrace without question (Biggart, 1998: 316). Family households extended their power into affiliated companies that were typically run by family members and close friends. Professional managers were integrated into the upper echelons over time, but family ownership and patrimonial control continued to characterise Korean business in the 1990s. Overlaying familial ties was regional loyalty. *Chaebol* families were also associated with regions and, due to regional clan rivalries, they tended to favour employees from their home provinces in hiring and promotion. According to Biggart, these family rivalries were a throwback to the postcolonial era when aristocratic families competed for the emperor's favour.

Co-evolutionary dynamics

Researchers such as Biggart (1998) and Maman (2002), who emphasise continuities in Korean social organisation and institutional structure, may overlook the fact that relations between the state and the *chaebol* have undergone significant changes since the state initiated its push to industrialise. In contrast, a co-evolutionary perspective draws attention to the dynamics of the relationship between the state, institutions and organisations (Carney and Gedajlovic, 2002a). The co-evolutionary perspective emphasises the importance of firms' goals and strategies and pays particular attention to firms' efforts to achieve autonomy and minimise critical resource dependencies. The key insight of this perspective is the identification of the process and mechanisms that gradually undermine the state-led industrialisation model, in particular the growing power of the *chaebol* and the gradual decline in the state's capacity to discipline their behaviour.

Amsden (1989) notes that as industrialisation progressed, the task of entrepreneurship became less a monopoly of the state and became far more a joint venture between the state and big business. As the *chaebol* widened their product market scope, the size and sophistication of their planning apparatus increased. Consequently, their technical and business experience improved, and as the leading *chaebol* began to better understand the risks and returns, they began to make their own decisions about which industries to enter. Moreover, government 'allowed' the *chaebol* to make high profits to provide a continuing incentive to keep the growth engine going and develop the push into heavy, capital-intensive industries. Perhaps the symbolic marker for the beginning of this period of growing enterprise autonomy was the assassination of President Park in 1979. After Park's death, the state began to lose control of the *chaebol*. Thereafter, in what Amsden (1989: 115) describes as 'the spiralling of market power', firm 'bigness, growth and broad scope were institutionalised at the expense of efficiency, profits, and justice'.

What is remarkable about this period is the growing concentration of economic power in the *chaebol*. Numerous indicators highlight this increase. For example, in 1974 the combined sales of the top 10 *chaebol* represented approximately 15 per cent of the GNP. By 1984, just 10 years later, this figure had reached 67 per cent (Amsden, 1989: 116). In 1974, the top 20 business groups accounted for 24.6 per cent of all manufacturing shipments; by 1982 this figure had increased to 36 per cent. In 1982, 74 per cent of all commodities in the manufacturing sector were produced by a monopoly, a duopoly, or an oligopoly; only 17 per cent of manufactured commodities were produced in industries defined as competitively structured. In each case, these levels of concentration are significantly greater than those in either Japan or the USA. As a consequence of the state's industrial strategy, Korea acquired the reputation of being one of the world's most concentrated economies. In an effort to re-establish discipline, the state supported the appearance of the second wave of *chaebol* in 1970, such as Daewoo, Sunkyong, Kolan, Dooson. Despite receiving significant state patronage, few of the second-wave *chaebol* ever achieved the same scale and scope as the first movers. Amsden (1989: 131) argues that no 'countervailing forces to big business ever gathered much strength under Park'.

Moreover, as part of the big push into heavy industries, the state gradually reduced restrictions upon foreign borrowing by Korean enterprises and as a result, the *chaebol* grew increasingly reliant upon foreign debt. Indeed, with the introduction in 1960 of the Foreign Capital Inducement Act, the government effectively signalled to the international community that it would act as a lender of last resort. In retrospect, following the 1997 financial crisis, it was widely recognised that state commitments to guarantee the debt of local enterprise created an environment of moral hazard. Because firms did not need to exercise so much prudence in commercial decision-making, structural overcapacity became rampant, and subsequent failures called for massive behind-the-scenes bail-outs.

Mergers and the acquisition of weaker firms by stronger firms became endemic. Indeed, the core competence developed by the *chaebol* in this period was the skill of diversifying through repeated entry into new industries (Guillen, 2000). As Amsden (1989: 129) puts it 'the group's ability to enter new industries rapidly and cost effectively became a major economy of scope'. Once corporations were granted the freedom to borrow on their own account in international markets they were released from their state-enforced capital constraint. But financial liberalisation when combined with an absence of checks and balances within the corporation set the stage for undisciplined growth.

Throughout the 1980s and early 1990s, the government attempted to liberalise the economy in a partial and incremental manner. For example, in 1987, price controls were discontinued in some areas but maintained in others. Although Korea's commitments to the General Agreement of Tariffs and Trade included its agreement to free trade, Korea maintained a ban on selected imports, such as automobiles and consumer electronics from Japan and from Japanese factories in third-party countries. Justified by the fact that Korea ran a chronic and large trade deficit with Japan, these restrictions on Japanese imports effectively protected Korean industries from their toughest competitors (Amsden, 1997). Similarly, when the World Trade Organization (WTO) was founded in 1995, the Korean government committed to reducing its support for the construction of large-scale plants, but strengthened its patronage of technology-intensive businesses by funding research and development with preferential state credit. Everywhere the rhetoric was one of liberalisation, but the reality was otherwise (Amsden, 1997). Indeed, the Korean state has not attempted to create liberal markets but has established a patchwork of new institutions to direct growth efforts.

Extensive use of debt allowed the *chaebol* to maintain their family ownership structure, and in the mid-1980s, they were still nurtured by first-generation owners who had personally overseen huge growth. However, debt levels had by now reached dangerous heights, and the financial instability of the corporate sector began to threaten the whole economy. To reduce debt levels, the Korean state encouraged the *chaebol* to seek public listings on domestic stock markets, but limited equity ownership by foreigners, effectively thwarting the emergence of the market for corporate control. Consequently, listings floated only a minority stake in a small number of constituent firms. Predictably, stock markets have not become a source of discipline and majority ownership remains either in the direct hands of a dominant owner or indirectly concentrated in the hands of the majority owner of a pyramid-style corporation (Claessen, Djankov and Lang, 2000b; Gedajlovic and Shapiro, 2002).

To summarise the sequence of events leading to the founding and subsequent rapid growth of the *chaebol*, the Korean state began by deliberately and selectively constructing business groups to pioneer industrialisation. Second, to nurture their early growth, the state actively and passively suppressed the development of market institutions in a manner that allowed business groups to grow to a large size. Finally, when the state began to construct market institutions, it did so in the incremental and partial manner that increases, not decreases, the economic power of business groups. The consequence of this state action was to create and prolong the life of large powerful and autonomous business groups that are largely beyond the discipline of the state.

Corporate governance and organisational structure

Chaebol are diversified business groups that are typically much larger than business groups elsewhere. However, the size and business scope of the *chaebol* varies considerably. Chang and Choi (1988) distinguish three types of *chaebol*. First are the big four: LG, Daewoo, Hyundai and Samsung; these widely diversified and vertically-integrated *chaebol* have received the lion's share of attention from researchers. The second type is diversified and multidivisional, but generally not so vertically-integrated. The third type is made up of smaller groups that are neither widely diversified nor do they employ a multidivisional structure. Figure 4.2 illustrates the corporate structure of one of the top four *chaebol*, the

Figure 4.2 Hyundai company portfolio

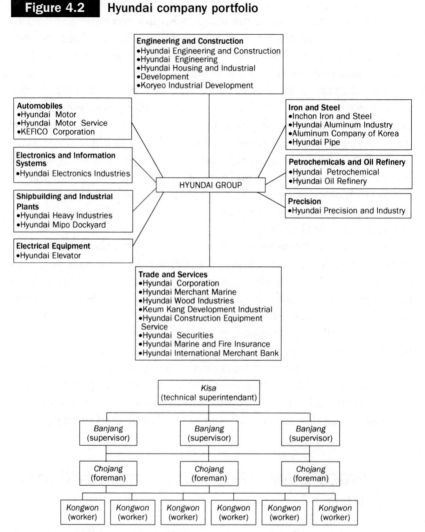

Source: Ungson Steers and Park (1997).

Hyundai group, and is typical of the scope of the larger *chaebol*. Indeed, the larger *chaebol* are much more diversified and also more vertically integrated than the Japanese *kaisha* with which they are frequently compared. *Chaebol* are also less reliant upon subcontracting (Whitley, 1992) and are less likely to enter into domestic strategic alliances (Bloom, 1994). Whitley (1999: 143) suggests that the *chaebol* are in effect managed as cohesive economic entities with a unified culture focused upon the *chaebol* owner.

The major *chaebol* have received considerable attention from researchers and their distinctive structural features are well known. In terms of corporate governance and ownership, *chaebol* are marked by family ownership, strategic control and substantial family involvement in the management of the enterprise. In their definition of *chaebol*, Steers, Shin and Ungson (1989: 34) emphasise a familial orientation: 'a business group consisting of large companies which are owned and managed by family members or relatives in many diversified business areas'. Ownership concentration in the hands of family members can be more than 50 per cent for a group's core firms. However, Claessens, Djankov and Lang (2000) note that concentrated owners can use control pyramids to exercise de facto control of an enterprise with relatively low levels of ownership. Using a 10 per cent ownership as a cut-off, they report that 68 per cent of Korea's largest firms are family controlled.

In addition to family ownership, family members' participation in management is extensive. Steers, Shin and Ungson (1989) find that in the top 20 *chaebol*, 31 per cent of senior executive officers are family members and another 29 per cent have been promoted from within the corporate ranks. Steers et al. (1989) report another study which found that 26 per cent of presidents of major companies were the founders, 19 per cent were the sons of the founders, 21 per cent of presidents were promoted from within the company and 35 per cent were recruited from outside. While this study noted that more than 50 per cent of CEOs were not family members, family members held the major and managerial positions in nearly all the companies surveyed. Other studies indicate that, while the absolute number of family members can be sometimes small, the power of these few family members is disproportionately strong (Whitley, 1992).

Steers et al. (1989) suggest that senior management in the *chaebol* can be described as a form of paternalistic leadership. Paternalism among CEOs or presidents is the quality of adopting the role of a father figure to the firm and its employees and this is often attributed to Confucian values in society. At the peak of each *chaebol* is a planning and coordination group responsible for the collection, analysis and presentation of data for decision making. The main component in the planning group is a founder chairman who assumes and exercises personal authority over every aspect of the firm's operations. This centralised and personalised authority structure facilitates negotiation and bargaining with governments and assures family oversight over strategic decisions. Steers et al. (1989) note that meetings and interactions between the group chairman and the various company CEOs emphasise the distance in authority between them. This is in contrast to the presidents' councils found in the horizontal *keiretsu*, which are at least theoretically a community of equals. Meetings of the Korean business group equivalent, the management committee, are structured to emphasise the hierarchical nature of authority in the organisation. Meetings are an opportunity for the group chairman to pose questions and issue directives to his subordinates; his elevated role is paramount throughout.

The consequence of paternalistic leadership is that non-family presidents of individual enterprises and other senior professional managers within the groups have very little power. Senior professional managers can be moved around or dismissed at the discretion of the group president. The distribution of decision-making power that emerges shows that strategic and financial decisions are concentrated in the hands of a single individual or family, while routine decision-making in operational matters is decentralised into the hands of the salaried managerial class. Moreover, the utilisation of salaried managers has been extremely parsimonious; this has tended to keep overhead expenses in check and maintained a more or less stable or even declining ratio of so-called unproductive managers. A high proportion of employees in the mid-management ranks are engineers focused upon technical tasks, suggesting an orientation toward production rather than towards sales or finance. Sales personnel typically include technical people with close ties to production (Amsden, 1989: 172). According to Ungson, Steers and Park (1997), *chaebol* have sought to develop a middle-level managerial cadre with more valuable company-specific skills. In their attempts to develop managerial resources, they have abandoned informal recruitment practices based upon nepotism and personal connections and have adopted more formalised, merit-based recruitment, selection and performance appraisal systems. Greater attention is given to formal training, and managers are circulated across functions and divisions to ensure the formation of well-rounded general managers. However, while *chaebol* attempt to develop their managerial capital, Fukuyama (1995) suggests that they are not well equipped to fully utilise it. Efforts to establish consensual decision-making processes are frustrated because managers are reluctant to express their opinion. Ungson et al. (1997) suggest that consensual decision-making systems are essentially designed to diffuse responsibility for decisions made elsewhere. Tsui-Auch and Lee (2003) suggest that *chaebol* have adopted the bureaucratic form of professional management, but remain committed to a personalistic management style.

In *chaebol* organisational structure, hierarchies are purposely tall so that differentiation between ranks is clear (Ungson et al., 1997). Reliance on staff is minimal; deputies and assistants in line positions fill advisory roles that serve narrow spans of control, further lengthening hierarchical chains of command (Chen, 1995). Managerial and operational roles are rarely formalised; job descriptions are brief, generalised role descriptions that specify broad job parameters. The absence of formal job descriptions facilitates paternalistic control and, while authority is typically centralised, responsibility for performance is often delegated (Ungson et al. 1997: 176). This authoritarian management style is also characterised by close supervision of task performance at the operational level. Plants and facilities are frequently designed to promote surveillance of work processes (Whitley, 1999). Close supervision is also allied with the prevalence of role specialisation among manual and craft workers.

A central planning office, typically known as the planning and coordination office or office of the secretary, works closely with the group chairman to develop a strategic direction for the company and is the nucleus of the management structure. The central planning office collects and analyses information and coordinates resource allocations. In addition, the office performs a monitoring function, conducting unscheduled visits to companies. The central planning office also plays a key role in personnel management by screening, hiring and assigning new college graduates and overseeing salary and bonus systems. The size of the office may vary; in some groups it consists of approximately 40 managers, while others have more than 200. The cost of maintaining the planning group is allocated across firms affiliated with the group.

In the terms of labour relations, *chaebol* management is typically less committed to promoting lifetime employment and the generation of intense employee loyalty than Japanese management. Little attention is given to training and cross-training (Whitley, 1999), and management usually relies upon extrinsic rewards to motivate employees (Chen, 1995). The main thrust of labour management is the creation of a disciplined and obedient workforce. The outcome is an industrious labour force, but one where employees lack the commitment and discretion found on Japanese shop floors (Fukuyama, 1995).

Chaebol and *keiretsu* management and structures compared

Korean economic planners were much impressed by Japanese business groups' technological and market achievements and set out to imitate aspects of Japanese organisation. Nevertheless, there are significant differences between the organisational structures of the *keiretsu* and *chaebol*. Table 4.1 summarises some of the key differences.

| Table 4.1 | Comparing *keiretsu* and *chaebol* structures and management |

	Keiretsu	Chaebol
Ownership	Cross-shareholdings and corporate bank, and widely held ownership	Cross-shareholdings and family ownership
Coordination	Informal presidents' councils	Group secretariat managed as cohesive economic entities
Decision-making style	Consensus, mutual adjustment	Centralised top-down
Corporate culture	Egalitarian culture focused upon the achievements of the enterprise	Unified culture focused upon the figure of *chaebol* owner
Finance	Main bank	State-owned bank
Network structure	Fluid boundaries, intermingling, multiple affiliation	Closed boundaries, members affiliate with one group
Insurance principal	Convoy system	State bail-outs
Employment system	Dual, lifetime employment intensive training for core employees, cooperative industrial relations	Less commitment to employees, less training, adversarial industrial relations
Unit autonomy	Importance of spin-offs with strategic control	Ownership retained under centralised management
Strategy	1) Enter market at low-end 2) Continuous improvements to penetrate middle higher-end segments 3) Go global	1) Late market entry 2) Investment in scale, cost leadership 3) Enter less contested markets

The primary difference pertains to ownership. Ownership in Japanese *keiretsu* is based upon the reciprocal cross-shareholdings held by banks, corporations and business partners in the group. In contrast, *chaebol* ownership is concentrated in the hands of a single family, often circuitously through cross-shareholdings and pyramids. Inter-firm coordination in the *keiretsu* takes place at the informal presidents' council meetings but much coordination around specific projects is decentralised in dyadic or pairwise relationships between two firms. This type of coordination does not occur in Korean business groups; in the largest *chaebol*, a group secretariat actively collects market information and makes the major financial and resource allocation decisions. The *keiretsu* decision-making style is said to be consensual based upon mutual adjustments, while the prevalent style in the *chaebol* is top-down. With regard to the group insurance principle, which is a distinguishing feature of *keiretsu*, *chaebol* typically do not perform the same kind of convoy function and they rely upon the state to undertake periodic restructuring of industrial sectors that have fallen into crisis. The *chaebol* employment system shows less commitment to employee welfare, lifetime employment and training. *Chaebol* retain a centralised management strategy and are also less likely to spin-off businesses into autonomous business units.

These contrasting organisational structures typically support different forms of product market strategy among group firms. Japanese firms' strategy entails market entry at the low end of the value chain, but their organisational structures support continuous improvement strategies that allow firms to climb up the value chain toward middle and high-end market segments. Once firms have achieved cost or value leadership they subsequently seek to become global leaders. In contrast, Korean firms have typically followed a strategy of late market entry by investing heavily in large-scale plants. They typically seek to occupy aggressive cost-leadership strategies. One Samsung vice president claims that, 'we are the world assembler of mature products and we aim to be bigger in large-scale production than anyone else' (Steers et al., 1989: 77). Using this strategy, Korean firms have been very successful in penetrating North American markets. However, Korean internationalisation strategies often begin with entry into less contested markets such as Eastern Europe and Latin America.

Social capital and innovation in Korean firms

The organisational characteristics of Korean firms have given rise to a social capital critique of their strategic and product market performance. According to Fukuyama (1995), the basis of social capital in Korean firms is relatively weak compared with Japan. Korea's different regions produce distinct local identities which sometimes serve as the basis for recruitment. Senior and middle management personnel are also recruited from Korea's most prestigious universities. Moreover, universal male conscription into the Korean army and security forces is an important source of socialisation, which has no equivalent in Japan. Fukuyama suggests that the army is the prototype of a large rational hierarchical organisation and the discipline within its ranks carries over into business life. The army was particularly important as a socialising force in the early phases of industrialisation when peasants were leaving their farms and entering the urban industrial landscape. Moreover, highly personalised, hierarchical and adversarial labour-management relationships are not conducive to generating the social capital that promotes shared decision-making and problem-solving. As a consequence, Fukuyama argues that Korean human resources have not been as fully utilised as their Japanese counterparts.

By creating a low-trust environment, Korean enterprises fail to fully exploit the benefits of large-scale and wide product market scope. Paternalistic management creates a poor fit with the demands of large-scale industry and the centralised and personalised nature of *chaebol* hierarchies, producing a continuing 'net drag on efficiency' (Fukuyama, 1995: 144). A conservative managerial emphasis upon control and discipline has mitigated productivity improvements (Young, 1995). Consequently, *chaebol*'s international production and marketing assets are weighted in unfavourable industrial positions. For example, *chaebol* production capability remains heavily dependent upon original equipment manufacturing. Their own brand positions are focused in mature and price-sensitive segments. Bloom (1994: 149) concludes that *chaebol* have become international 'in a way that denies them many of the major benefits' of being international. In the age of flexibility, Korea has built centralised inflexible hierarchies that are losing their advantage against other low-wage countries. A centralised and hierarchical management of a highly-disciplined workforce works well for relatively simple and routine processes, but this structure is increasingly ineffective in more complex technological areas. *Chaebol* have been slow to exit declining businesses and their corporate scope has become very broad.

The financial performance of the *chaebol*

Examined from a chronological perspective, studies of the financial performance of the *chaebol* begin on a positive note but become progressively negative, especially after the Asian financial crisis in 1997.

Preliminary studies on the financial performance of *chaebol* focused upon their value-creating effects, identifying positive attributes such as lower transaction costs, the utilisation of scarce human capital, and the group structure as a catch-up mechanism. Chang and Choi (1988) study 63 manufacturing firms affiliated with *chaebol* during the period 1975–84 and examine their profitability relative to a comparison group of independent firms. They find that firms affiliated with business groups that employ a multidivisional structure show superior economic performance. They attribute superior performance to the transaction cost efficiencies of a quasi-multidivisional structure that allows scarce managerial talent to be deployed over the broad range of product markets and reduces transactions costs. The profitability of group affiliation decreases in business groups that are not organised with a quasi-multidivisional structure.

Using data from a 10-year period between and 1985 and 1996, the study by Chang and Hong (2000) considers 317 business groups with over 12,000 affiliates. The authors give explicit consideration to group-level sharing of resources and assets and find that there is extensive sharing of technological skills and advertising among group-affiliated firms. The study concludes that Korean business groups generate real economies of scale and scope. The processes through which skill-sharing occurs are admirably detailed in Amsden's (1989) case studies of two leading Korean business groups. She provides detailed qualitative data describing how management know-how and project management skills are transferred across Hyundai's shipbuilding, engine and heavy machinery group, on through its motor company and then to its parts and components subsidiaries and also through several functional areas in the POSCO steel company.

Chang and Hong (2000) also test the insurance or risk-sharing hypothesis in Korean *chaebol* and find 'complex patterns of cross-subsidisation through debt guarantees, equity investments and vertical integration'. In particular, they note that debt guarantees and internal trade are used extensively to support poorly performing affiliates at the expense of profitable ones. Further, they find that cross-subsidising through risk-sharing does not appear to harm strong firms during times of economic growth, but does tend to harm the profitability of strong firms during periods of economic contraction. Using data from 1991 to 1995, Khanna and Yafeh (2005) find that the operating profit volatility of *chaebol*-affiliated firms is significantly lower than that of unaffiliated firms by some 20 per cent. They conjecture that income/profit smoothing may be achieved by adjusting intra-group exchange prices. Khanna and Yefeh (2005b) also find that group-provided insurance is particularly important during periods of economic crisis.

Khanna and Rivkin (2001) also find robust evidence of profit smoothing in Korea, although this is based on data from a later period (1991–95). The authors conclude that that there is a balance in the costs and benefits of *chaebol* affiliation. Indeed, recent studies using data from after 1990 increasingly identify the value-destroying effects of group affiliation. Based on data from on 368 business groups and 1,668 affiliates from two time periods (1985–89 and 1990–96), Chang and Hong (2002) find that the benefits of group affiliation decline over time. They also find that the beneficial effects of business-group affiliation are much smaller in the larger *chaebol* than in smaller groups. In addition, they conclude that the magnitude of the benefits of group affiliation is inversely related to the firm's degree of diversification. Chang and Hong (2002) reason that large business groups were becoming more homogeneous in the 1990s due to increasing imitation of one another's strategies of unrelated diversification. They also argue that the internal market advantage diminishes as external markets become more efficient.

Increasingly negative sentiment about business-group affiliation has prompted scholars to examine the dark side of their activities. Using a panel of 410 *chaebol* affiliates over the period 1986–96, Chang's (2003: 248) findings suggest that intra-group trade might be used to transfer profits among affiliates in a manner that is consistent with the expropriation hypothesis. Particular findings suggest that ownership by insiders is negatively associated with the reception of debt guarantees, suggesting 'that both family and affiliates reduce their ownership of affiliates with poor financial credit'. Perhaps unsurprisingly, Chang (2003) finds that high family ownership is associated with higher profitability and better long-term market value; taken at face value, this finding suggests that closer integration into the *chaebol* structure is associated with better performance. However, this is one of few studies that use controls for endogeneity, and the inclusion of this control eliminates the relationship between family ownership and positive performance. The key result of this study is the determination of reverse causality – specifically that positive firm profitability determines the degree of inside ownership but not vice versa. Put differently, families will offload their equity, including performing enterprises, and increase their positions inside underperforming firms.

With regards to the insurance hypothesis, Chang finds that families avoid direct ownership in firms with high volatility and instead use indirect ownership to control these firms. This implies that there are serious agency problems in Korean *chaebol*. The results suggest that family owners capitalise on inside information by taking higher direct and indirect equity stakes in profitable and more promising affiliates. Chang's (2003) study also recognises that family direct ownership understates the degree of control the family actually wields over affiliate firms. Through various pyramid devices, direct ownership is used to artificially inflate family owners' control rights relative to their cash-flow rights, acting as a device to extract value from minority investors.

Finally, Khanna and Yefeh (2005a) report several studies that collectively identify a syndrome of poor performance and include findings that *chaebol* affiliates have reported lower profits, misdirected investment, incurred excessive debts, and lost productive efficiency due to over-expansion and higher sales growth. What seems certain is that that the financial performance of group-affiliated firms deteriorated in the 1990s but the reasons for this decline are not clear.

Restructuring after the Asian financial crisis of 1997

Can the *chaebol*'s deteriorating performance after 1990 be attributed to the changing environmental context in which the advantages of business groups began to disappear? A variety of factors seems to be at play. Throughout the 1980s, the government had begun to liberalise the economy. We have argued that in this environment, the state's disciplinary power began to weaken and the *chaebol* took advantage of the opportunity to expand, often without any obvious rationale. Second, after the 1997 financial crisis, the government had an explicit mandate to restructure and disassemble the largest business groups and actively reduce the amount of support provided to them. Third, there has been significant entrepreneurial succession at the top of business groups. As the generation of hard-driving entrepreneurs of the 1960s and 1970s began to retire, they passed their businesses on to second-generation managers who may be less gifted. Fourthly, the structure of international competition changed during the 1990s; a cross-border mergers and acquisitions movement among larger European and North American firms consolidated several major players and created a number of global giants in industries such as automobiles, engineering, energy, pharmaceuticals, telecommunications and information technology. However, Korean firms have not been part of this global consolidation. There have been a substantial number of domestic mergers, but the resulting enterprises remain dwarfed by foreign competition. Korean firms harbour ambitions to compete in these industries, but the intensity of competition has often shifted up a notch and left some in a catch-up mode. Amsden and Euh (1993) argue that Korea's financial market liberalisations in the 1980s did not in fact establish more efficient financial markets or greater reliance on the price mechanism. Rather, these reforms introduced new forms of institutional restraint. Indeed, Chang (2006b) suggests that government actions significantly undermined the development of Korea's financial markets. Instead, reforms simply created new mechanisms to funnel cash, in the form of foreign debts and portfolio equity, into the coffers of the larger *chaebol*. The family-dominated governance structures of these groups did not provide sufficient checks and balances on the use of these funds; the result was the growing malaise of financial performance outlined in the section above. At the same time, the interpenetration of the state, banking and corporate sectors created a system of growing interdependence that threatened the stability of the system as a whole.

In Japan, the business group insurance principal reduces business risk for firms, but it has worked very differently in Korea. Specifically, the Korean insurance principal operates on the basis of loan guarantees that group enterprises grant to one another (Chang, 2003). However, loan guarantees are only a nominal form of insurance. The call on the commitment is made only if a firm actually defaults on its interest payments. In this respect, loan guarantees are an inexpensive way of securing capital to fund growth. Under this system, companies transfer risk to the government but maintain control of the benefits. In the event of a corporate failure, the government must transfer the risk to the general population. Because insurance coverage removes the incentive to act prudently, this created an environment of moral hazard in the *chaebol*. But the system is really a house of cards. Were a few firms to default, this would set off a series of debt covenants that would bring down all the others. With *chaebol* developing huge debt equity ratios of 500 per cent to some 4,000 per cent, one must question the foreign investors' judgment in making these kinds of loans. Everything rests on the assumption that the government will step in as the lender of last resort. But the process has become so endemic in society that even the government no longer has the ability to deliver on promises.

After the financial crisis, the state was unable to bail out the corporate sector. Financial weakness in the state increased the influence of international creditors, and particularly the World Bank and the International Monetary Fund (IMF), over Korean economic policy.

The IMF believed that *chaebol* were the root cause of Korea's crisis and demanded that the government enforce a far-reaching restructuring programme upon *chaebol* to reduce debts, abolish debt guarantees, sell unprofitable affiliate firms, concentrate on core businesses, and improve their corporate governance. Chang (2006b) suggests that the push for restructuring the *chaebol* is mainly an external force and the solutions favoured by the IMF, the WTO and the World Bank are not necessarily those preferred by Korean politicians and corporate owners.

The crisis created a severe contraction in the economy as well as several casualties, including the bankruptcy of Daewoo, the fourth-largest *chaebol*. Consistent with past practice, the state attempted to implement a financial restructuring programme operated by a financial supervisory board in an effort to save large numbers of poorly performing companies through debt workout programmes. According to Chang (2006b), the programmes were generally unsuccessful. Many of these companies were liquidated after two years and the programme merely extended financially troubled companies' lives rather than helping to turn them around. Another major element of the restructuring programme was a so-called 'big deal programme' aimed at solving overcapacity and bringing about mergers in strategic and capital-intensive sectors of the economy; this programme produced mixed results. The stronger *chaebol* resisted mergers because they saw few opportunities to create synergies. Most of the mergers that took place were between weak or incompatible firms. For example, the government encouraged the merger of Hyundai Electronics and LG Semiconductor, but the resulting company, Hyundai Electronics, is in severe difficulties and government has pressured banks to acquire bonds issued by this technically bankrupt company. Similarly, government attempts to impose international standards of corporate governance met with limited success and there was little progress towards establishing a competitive market for corporate control.

The government has reduced the number of banks through mergers and infused large sums of public money into keeping them solvent. The logic of these marriages was to create banks with greater economies of scale. However, Chang (2006b) suggests that 'old habits die hard', and due to the tension between restructuring and protecting employment, the state often bends in the face of large-scale job losses, and managers and politicians seek ways of continuing existing practices even though they have been proscribed. Chang sees greater hope for change in the growing shareholder activism from both foreign institutional investors and the grassroots democracy movement. Chang expects that the growing foreign ownership of the Korean corporate sector, which amounted to some 40 per cent of the total market capitalisation in 2003, will result in greater shareholder pressure for improvements in both corporate governance and shareholder value. The People's Solidarity for Participatory Democracy has successfully applied pressure on two leading companies, albeit on relatively minor issues. However, attempts to mobilise such coalitions are often met with strong resistance and they tend to produce rather limited, short-term results.

Because it takes time to fully develop financial market institutions, the surviving *chaebol* have an opportunity to prosper by utilising new approaches to resource sharing and cross-subsidisation. Chang (2006b) anticipates that *chaebol* may, in the medium term, begin to behave more like Japanese *keiretsu* by operating more loosely-coupled groups and voluntarily cooperating when there is mutual strategic advantage for both affiliates. Chang believes that the revamping of corporate governance systems will unleash the power of professional managers who have been unable to fully utilise their full managerial expertise in the past. The difficulty with this is that, because their responsibilities have been confined to operational, engineering, technical and quality-control roles, middle managers have not had the opportunity to implement their strategic and financial skills. Moreover, there is little hard evidence that family owners have really decentralised much power to middle managers.

The thrust of corporate sector reform has been to make the *chaebol* more focused in their product market and it is possible that they have conformed to an American M-form model of corporate organisation, with business focused on core competencies, separated ownership and control, and clear accountability. Kim, Hoskisson, Tihanyi and Hong (2004) point to a bifurcation in *chaebol* responses to pressures to restructure. On the one hand, the break-up of the Hyundai group and the forced liquidations, divestments and spin-offs at the heavily-indebted Hanjin and Hanwha business groups points to a more cooperative M-form structure in which business is more focused on pursuing operational synergies. On the other hand, large *chaebol* such as LG, Doosan and Kolon, have retained a holding company structure and continue to acquire enterprises in more diverse fields than before the crisis. Families retain ownership and control of these companies, suggesting that owners will be unwilling to delegate strategic control to operational managers and that they may continue to make decisions on the basis of financial criteria.

Social analysis suggests slow change

While finance and management researchers have examined the proximate causes and effects of the crisis, sociologists and development theorists have looked for social and political explanations for the dynamics of *chaebol* growth and evolution. Perhaps the most prescient of these analyses is Amsden's (1989) analysis of the industrial latecomer thesis. In this view, late-industrialising economies are characterised by the creation of the institutions of imitation, especially at the firm level. In contrast, the early-industrialising economies in Britain, Germany and the USA were innovative, and firms diversified based on skill in a very narrow technological and managerial area. The tendency has been to build core expertise and to diversify only into related fields. In late-industrialising economies the driving imperative is to catch up to the technological frontier and to accelerate their progress; frontier firms develop skills associated with imitation. Amsden suggests that in Korea, the core skill developed by domestic firms is the capacity to enter industries repeatedly via project management. Imitators have no proprietary skills and consequently, they tend to diversify opportunistically or at the bidding of government. Because their level of experience in particular industries does not enable them to develop related products or processes, firms in late-industrialising countries tend to diversify widely and this calls the sustainability of their growth into question.

Successful imitation-based strategies create an administrative heritage or path dependencies that ultimately become obstacles to continued growth. Initially, *chaebol* growth and technology acquisition strategy spread scarce managerial talent to new industries. However, the logic of linking increasingly unrelated businesses becomes more and more difficult to support. With close government ties and operating under a soft budget constraint, *chaebol* managers were not confronted with a profit-growth trade-off and had little incentive to restructure their operations. Many *chaebol* are now financially indebted and in possession of a surfeit of largely generic and tangible assets concentrated in mature overcapacity markets. Consequently, their absorptive capacity strategies, as well as new technology initiation strategies are stalled. While *chaebol* appear to possess significant organisational capabilities, new and promising businesses are starved of both internal and external capital needed for growth. Like other states in the region, Korea has recognised the importance of technological innovation, as distinct from technological imitation, but *chaebol* continue to experience difficulties in crafting incentives that would propel them into the initiating phase of the product lifecycle.

Whitley (1999) proposes that family enterprise in Korea has proved to be more enduring and less ephemeral than the family-owned business groups of Southeast Asia. The key difference is that Korean business groups were liberally assisted by the state, whereas the family business groups of Southeast Asia were confronted by more rapacious officials and politicians who demanded their cut of profits. Whitley suggests that efforts to sever and unbundle *chaebol* ownership ties are unlikely to succeed because owners are unlikely to give up control, especially if they anticipate that units will be acquired by rival groups. Moreover, groups have become strong enough to resist the conditional nature of the finance supplied by international institutions. Whitley observes that the owner-controlled *chaebol* remain quite strongly tied to the Korean economy and the state:

> Despite their growing overseas investments and the weakening of the state's control of the economy ... the highly diversified, centralised, and risk-taking nature of the *chaebol* does not appear to being greatly modified of past decade although some changes in managerial structures in practices have occurred in some of them. (Whitley, 1999: 203)

Whitley predicts that Korean enterprises are likely to adopt more favourable labour-management policies in order to remain competitive with Japan but changes in fundamental ownership relationships are unlikely to occur. He suggests that the state will need to undertake more radical actions than has yet been attempted in order to bring about change in the Korean business system.

Granovetter (2005) observes that while many *chaebol*-affiliated firms failed after the crisis, the stronger groups were able to resist pressures to change. He argues that the oldest groups were the most resilient because they possess the strongest sense of group identity. Granovetter holds that the strong emotional ties that infuse such groups not only lower transactions costs across group firms, but also produce non-economic motivations among participants for the group's survival and success. Hence, when the government attempts to break up group affiliates, equity and trading linkages may be just the tip of the iceberg. The resilience of *chaebol* is founded on a stronger basis of identity than simply equity ownership. An array of factors such as managerial career paths, employee commitments, and links with community and political leaders, provide a continuing axis of solidarity. In this respect, the *chaebol* must be seen as more than just a collection of individual firms but as a more cohesive whole. In response to the crisis, the *chaebol* remained solid because they wanted to retain their autonomy. Rather than redeploying their capital to more profitable locations, *chaebol* reallocated capital 'in such a way as to increase the leverage available from relatively small holdings', and this strategy is best described as 'a network survival strategy' (Granovetter, 2005: 446).

Conclusion

In the case of the Korean *chaebol*, the hypothesis of institutional development and business group decline is not an easy fit. Many *chaebol* enterprises have failed. This would not have occurred to the same degree in the earlier stages of industrialisation when the state performed routine bail-outs of weak firms. However, in the mature stage of industrialisation, the state was required to oversee the periodic liquidation and clearing out of underperforming and failing firms. For the most part, however, Korea's *chaebol* seem to be disregarding predictions of their imminent decline. Korea's business groups are very powerful in their home environment and remain closely linked to the state. It appears instinctive for the state to maintain a nurturing approach to the children that it created. International pressures to liberalise and deregulate the economy and reduce the state's involvement in day-to-day economic affairs have undermined the Korean model because these measures interfere with the state's ability to discipline the *chaebol*. For Granovetter (2005), the surprise ending is that the Korean economy has substantially recovered and is enjoying robust economic growth.

5

Searching for business groups in Taiwan

Business groups are much smaller and less prevalent in Taiwan than in other Asian countries. There are a few large family-owned diversified groups, including the group centred on Formosa Plastics, the Evergreen Group, and another centred on the Koo family, but business groups have not played a central role in the island's rapid and successful postwar economic development. In the early phases of development, Taiwan's largest enterprises were state-owned or 'government-led'; each enterprise focused on a single industry and followed a state-determined strategy. Some of these firms are now privatised or have become more autonomous, but the dominant feature of Taiwan's industrialisation might be described as 'planned dualism'. Taiwan's government planned and financed the direction of economic growth by supporting large-scale enterprise combined with a pro-market policy that permitted thousands of small-scale enterprises to pursue a strategy of export-led growth. Indeed, one influential study has described Taiwan's growth as government-led industrialisation (Wade, 1990).

Interestingly, Wade's comprehensive study of Taiwan's industrialisation contains only a single passing reference to business groups (Wade, 1990: 66).[1] One early study of Taiwan's 96 largest business groups in 1983 found that, in comparison with groups in Japan and Korea, Taiwanese groups were miniscule, employing only 4.6 per cent of the workforce (Hamilton and Kao, 1990). Another study suggested that business groups were loosely affiliated entities called *guanxi qiye*; composed of friends from the same town, but these groups were declining in importance in modern Taiwan (Numazaki, 1993). Studies of Taiwan's industrial and corporate structure have focused on other organisational phenomena such as networks, industrial clusters, micro-entrepreneurship, science parks and global commodity chains. Typically, researchers emphasise the institutional and cultural origins of Taiwan's predominantly small-firm industrial structure and make comparisons with Japanese and Korean giant firm structures (Hamilton and Biggart, 1988; Whitely, 1992; Orru, Biggart and Hamilton, 1997).

Reflecting the recent growth of interest in business groups, a steady stream of new research on Taiwanese business groups has appeared (Feenstra, Yang and Hamilton, 1999; Chung, 2001; Chiu, 2002; Chu, 2004; Mahmood and Mitchell, 2004; Luo and Chung, 2005; Chung, 2006; Chung and Mahmood, 2006). Several studies suggest that business groups in Taiwan have become larger and more important in the last decade. For example, Chung (2001) dates the appearance of a large cohort of Taiwanese business groups in the early 1960s following changes to the corporate tax code. Another study suggests that, between 1994 and 2002, Taiwan's largest 100 business groups have all grown significantly on measures such as group revenues, number of firms per group, and share of stock market capitalisation. By 2002, the largest 100 business groups collectively accounted for 56 per cent of total market capitalisation (Chung and Mahmood, 2006). Moreover, recent corporate legislation may further promote this growth. The enactment of the Financial Institutions Consolidation Law in 2000 and the Financial Holding Company Law in 2001 has been followed by a spate of mergers and acquisitions by banks and insurance companies, each seeking to become providers of one-stop financial services (Chung and Mahmood, 2006). This merger movement has resulted in the creation of several large financial holding companies, such as Lin Yuan, Shin Kong, China Trust, Fubon and Mega Financial Holding, that are now counted among Taiwan's largest enterprises.

While Taiwan's business groups share the ownership concentration characteristic of business groups, very few are diversified in any substantial way. Measures of firm diversification indicate that Taiwanese business groups, while participating to some degree in unrelated businesses, commit few resources to new lines of business and continue to rely heavily upon a core business for the majority of their revenues and profits (Chung and Mahmood, 2006). Indeed, many firms listed among Taiwan's top 30 business groups, such as Acer Computer, Benq, Quanta Computer, United Microelectronics and TSMC, are concentrated in a single industry with a few related product areas in information technology or electronics components (see Table 5.1). Although formally identified as business groups by the Taiwanese directory *Business Groups in Taiwan*, many of Taiwan's largest firms are in fact quite focused in their business scope and limit their operations to

Table 5.1   Taiwan's 30 largest business groups, 2002

Rank	Group name	Year of establishment	Main industry	Sales (US$ million)
1	Formosa Plastics	1954	Plastic products	20,925
2	Lin Yuan Financial Holding	2001	Financing	15,079
3	Shin Kong Financial Holding	2002	Financing	9,561
4	Lien Hwa-Mitac	1955	Electrical & electronic products	9,037
5	Kinpo	1973	Electrical & electronic products	8,789
6	Hon Hai	1973	Electrical & electronic products	8,358
7	Far Eastern	1954	Textiles	7,305
8	President	1967	Food products	7,137
9	Liton Electronic	1989	Electrical & electronic products	6,783
10	Yulon	1953	Transportation equipment	5,840
11	Evergreen	1968	Transport	5,807
12	Quanta Computer	1988	Electrical & electronic products	5,696
13	Tatung	1918	Electrical & electronic products	5,200
14	China Trust Financial Holding	2002	Financing	5,094
15	China Steel	1971	Basic metal	5,087
16	Benq	1984	Electrical & electronic products	4,878
17	TSMC	1987	Electrical & electronic products	4,704
18	United Microelectronics	1980	Electrical & electronic products	4,667
19	Ho Tai	1947	Wholesale trade	4,334
20	Acer	1979	Electrical & electronic products	4,317

Source: Chung and Mahmood (2006: 77).

the finance and IT sectors. In another context, they would be considered to be related-diversified firms.

The emergence and growth of Taiwan's business groups represents something of a paradox: contrary to the received wisdom, business groups played only a minor role in Taiwan's initial catch-up phase and early economic development. However, now that Taiwan is a relatively mature industrial economy it represents another theoretical peculiarity: at a late phase we appear to witnessing the emergence of large diversified business groups with concentrated ownership, an organisational form that is associated with earlier phases of economic development in countries such as Japan and Korea.

The context for the formation of Taiwan's business groups

Taiwan's business environment in the twentieth century was profoundly shaped by two events. The first was China's military defeat at the hands of Japan in 1895; China was forced to cede Taiwan to Japan and for some 60 years, Taiwan was subject to Japanese colonial administration. The second event took place in the wake of the Second World War; following the Communist victory in 1949, 2 million members of the Nationalist Party, or Koumingtang (KMT) fled mainland China to settle permanently in Taiwan. The Nationalists dominated politics and established a government, the KMT, which would rule for the subsequent 50 years. As Hamilton and Biggart (1988: S83) put it 'Composed largely of northern Chinese, Chang Kai-shek's forces virtually conquered and totally subordinated the linguistically distinct Taiwanese'. In the immediate postwar period, the government was preoccupied with recapturing the mainland from the Communists but contemporary political concerns now focus on the likelihood of (re-)unification with the mainland. Nevertheless, at the height of the Cold War in the 1950s and 1960s when Taiwan was establishing its industrial and commercial infrastructure, fears about relations with mainland China determined its economic and industrial policy.

As in Japan and Korea, it was convenient for the USA to have an anti-communist and pro-US supporter in the region. Taiwan received extensive US economic aid, military support and technological assistance in constructing and establishing a communications and transportation infrastructure, as well as a robust national security system. Taiwan also inherited a strong administrative tradition from Japan. These factors ensured that Taiwan was a relatively strong state with the institutional capacity to command and control the economy. In addition, the US government further supported Taiwan by agreeing to a liberal free trade regime between the two countries, which permitted Taiwan's economic planners to adopt an export oriented development strategy. The prevailing ideology of the early Nationalist era was a strong belief in the efficacy of state planning (Vogel, 1991). In the aftermath of the Second World War, a cohort of Nationalist politicians and economic technocrats, many educated in the New-Deal US and European schools, embarked upon leading domestic capitalist institutions toward national objectives and policy priorities (Wade, 1990). The government sought to control the commanding heights of the economy and specified industrial sectors that would receive special attention. However, the Nationalists did not practise detailed indicative planning nor seek to direct downstream economic activity. Rather, the government sought to plan within the context of a free economy, and such policies have allowed the emergence of family firms to shape the development of Taiwan's industrialisation (Hamilton and Biggart, 1988).

The political and business communities shared little common ground. The political elite were Nationalists from the mainland, or what Chung (2005: 465) describes as an 'émigré regime', while the business elite were domestic and their existing political ties were with a departed Japanese colonial administration. Consequently, there was little trust between the two groups. In particular, Taiwanese entrepreneurs deeply mistrusted the state (Wade, 1990). Entrepreneurs cooperated with the state when it was in their interests but not otherwise (Chu, 1994). Moreover, fear of Chinese aggression in Taiwan did little to assuage age-old uncertainties about state expropriation. Throughout the early period of industrialisation, the government remained an authoritarian one-party dictatorship that actively discouraged the growth of big business, fearing that powerful businesses might infiltrate the party and undermine its political discipline and bureaucratic loyalty (Noble, 1998: 15). In this low trust environment the state attempted to identify individual entrepreneurs with whom it could cooperate. Table 5.2 shows that many of these enterprises formed in the early 1950s had become Taiwan's largest enterprises some 20 years later.

The government was well aware of the need to establish large-scale industrial firms and did so by creating a hierarchical three-tier system of industrial organisation. Wholly state-owned enterprises were established in sectors such as banking and construction and particularly in capital-intensive industries characterised by economies of scale, such as

Table 5.2		Top 20 business groups in Taiwan, 1973		
Rank	Group name	Year of establishment	Main industry	Sales (US$ million)
1	Formosa Plastics	1954	Plastic products	397
2	Far Eastern	1954	Nonmetallic products	146
3	Tainan Spinning	1953	Textiles	143
4	Cathay	1961	Plastic products	128
5	Tatung	1918	Machinery	117
6	Yulon	1953	Transportation equipment	112
7	Hsiao's Brothers	1956	Chemical materials	102
8	Wei Chuan	1947	Food products	91
9	Shin Kong	1952	Chemical materials	85
10	Lai Ching Tien	1952	Chemical materials	75
11	Pacific Electric Wire & Cable	1950	Electrical & electronic products	71
12	China General Plastics	1955	Plastic products	64
13	Yuen Foong Yu	1950	Pulp & paper products	64
14	Sampo	1962	Electrical & electronic products	63
15	TaiYu	1954	Food products	55
16	Tuntex	1959	Textiles	55
17	Kao Hsing Chang	1951	Basic metal	54
18	Cheng He Fa	1949	Food products	49
19	All Sincere	1966	Food products	49
20	Jang Dah Fiber	1962	Chemical materials	48

Source: Chung and Mahmood (2006: 76).

shipbuilding, oil and public utilities. Downstream in sectors characterised by economies of scope, the government selectively allocated market entry rights to trusted elite entrepreneurs from prominent Taiwanese families; guided and supported by the state, these are Taiwan's so-called government-led enterprises. The price of these benefits was political cooperation and loyalty, and these firms served as an extended arm of the bureaucracy (Chu, 1994). Further, downstream in labour-intensive manufacturing sectors characterised by variable demand, the government permitted a small business and micro-enterprise sector to flourish (Shieh, 1992). In this way Taiwan developed a pluralistic and highly stratified industrial structure.

Interestingly, while the government possesses considerable institutional capacity, Taiwan's economic development was characterised by severe institutional voids in its capital markets. These capital market voids were created deliberately and their origin owes much to the government's aspiration to control the commanding heights of the economy. All Taiwan's banks were state-owned and the government carefully rationed credit by supporting only the firms and projects that it favoured. However, unlike Japan, Taiwan did not develop a main bank system of corporate governance and coordination. State-owned banks were not encouraged to take an interest in the wellbeing of their creditors and banks did not develop a strong capacity to analyse company finances nor the commercial feasibility of projects. At the same time, the government restricted other sources of external capital. Indeed, the government both actively and passively suppressed the development of public and private equity markets (Prowse, 1996). Consequently, we should recognise that institutional voids are sometimes deliberately maintained.

In the 1980s, the government recognised the need to upgrade its industrial base and changed its developmental strategy in order to develop a position in high technology. Its approach was to liberalise capital markets and to establish specialised sources of financing such as venture capital. However, the initial suppression of capital markets had persistent path-dependent effects. Equity markets were historically an unimportant source of funding in Taiwan; consequently, Taiwanese firms learned to find and utilise alternative sources of capital. Although equity markets now exist, few firms make much use of them. Shares in public companies are typically closely held by the founding family and are rarely traded. Today, Taiwan's stock market remains relatively weak and illiquid. For example, in 1995 Taiwan had only 138 certified securities analysts, whereas, in 1995, the USA counted over half a million. In addition, Taiwan's venture capital market is minimal and largely government-directed (Luo and Chung, 2005).

In the late 1980s and early 1990s, a variety of factors combined to bring about significant changes in Taiwan's institutional environment. The first factor might be called the Plaza Accord Echo. In 1987, US and European business leaders met at the Plaza Hotel in New York and agreed to a major readjustment in the value of the US dollar against the Japanese yen as a means of reducing the large US and European trade deficit with Japan. The USA also allowed the US dollar to depreciate against the value of the Taiwanese dollar, making Taiwanese products more expensive in the USA. In an effort to remain competitive and lower their costs, Taiwanese entrepreneurs began to offshore their manufacturing activities into mainland China, especially in the province of Fujian. In the same period, a number of government agencies were revamped and new initiatives were set in motion to upgrade the technical and scientific capabilities of Taiwanese manufacturing firms.

Economic changes were paralleled by liberalisation in the political environment; the growing importance of parliament and the expansion of electoral politics fragmented party politics and weakened the Nationalists' hold on power. These changes provided the business elite with new opportunities to pursue influence-buying as local politicians and emerging new parties sought patrons among the large corporations. Chu (1994: 127) describes this as 'structured corruption'. The KMT party adapted to these changes by shifting the state-directed economic policy toward a more liberal and pro-business view of the economy. During this period we see a variety of amendments to the legal code, the liberalisation of securities markets and exchange, and freedom for the private sector to enter commercial banking. Restrictions on foreign direct investment and foreign firm entry were also lifted. Key industries, previously the preserve the state, were opened to the private sector, providing scope for business groups to expand into new markets. However, despite the relaxation of economic controls, the establishment of a market infrastructure was fragmented and slow (Luo and Chung, 2005). Yu Han Chu (1994: 135) predicted that these conditions would stimulate 'the formation of enterprise groupings similar to the Keiretsu in Japan'.

Studies of Taiwan's industrialisation have attributed the country's competitiveness to organisational forms other than business groups. These forms include micro-entrepreneurship and small-firm industrial clusters (Shieh, 1992), firm participation in global commodity chains (Gerrefi, 1994), government-linked enterprises in industries characterised by economies of scale and scope (Wade 1990), and science parks (Mathews, 1997). Each of these alternative organisational forms has played an important role in Taiwan's economic development. Panel 5.1 describes the key features of each of these organisational models.

Extensive government involvement in the economy has limited the growth of very large firms in Taiwan. Compared with other East Asian countries such as Japan or Korea, few Taiwanese firms are either vertically integrated or widely diversified. The emergence of alternative organisational models has filled this gap. However, this organisational plurality has left less work for business groups to do.

Panel 5.1: Alternative organisational models in Taiwan

Micro-enterpreneurship and small-firm industrial clusters

This organisational form consists of spatially concentrated but vertically disaggregated workshop-scale enterprises, which collectively produce a diverse array of finished goods (Sabel, 1988), such as knitwear, electronics, toys and footwear. The chain of production from components manufacture to final assembly is coordinated through a system of spot market contracts in a highly flexible subcontract network. Most firms are highly specialised in one stage of production but utilise mainly generic assets to maintain flexibility and avoid dependence upon any particular contractor (Carney, 1998a). The typical single-phase workshop enterprise requires little capital investment but relies upon labour-intensive production processes, which in turn depend upon an ability to mobilise an 'industrial reserve army'. There is a continual downward circulation of technology as older machines are replaced and purchased by subcontractors lower down the production chain. When demand exceeds capacity, there is a tendency for employees to create new enterprises as former production employees seek to become their own 'bosses', a Taiwanese cultural phenomenon that Shieh (1992) calls 'Boss Island'. As an organisational form, subcontract networks and industrial clusters provide a means for coordinating multiple phases of production in an efficient, low-cost manner that makes intensive use of scarce capital resources. Taiwan's subcontract networks and industrial clusters represent an alternative coordination mechanism compared with the more formally organised *kaisha* in Japan and the more vertically-integrated production systems of Korea's *chaebol*.

Global commodity chains

This organisational form links spatially concentrated subcontract networks to global markets. Gereffi and Korzeniewicz (1994) distinguish between producer-driven and buyer-driven commodity chains. The former are common in industries such as computers and electrical machinery and are led by multinationals such as IBM and Hewlett-Packard. Lead firms possess in-house design and production facilities and, although much of their activity is outsourced, they exercise strict quality control over selected contractors. Buyer-driven chains include brand-name merchandisers such as Nike and Reebok and multi-chain retailers such as The Gap and Wal-Mart; they do not possess in-house production facilities but operate international sourcing organisations to specify designs, quantities and price points for trading and production companies. Typically located in cities such as Hong Kong, Singapore and Taipei, these second-tier companies in turn subcontract to third-party producers located in labour-abundant countries in the region. Foreign firms at the head of these chains are often unfamiliar with local production conditions and so foreign buyers typically contract with first-tier trading organisations that can handle local bureaucratic procedures and subcontract orders to smaller second-tier producers. In the 1990s, labour and land costs increased rapidly and in response Taiwanese and Hong Kong producers transferred production to South China (Hsing, 1996). The effect of this large-scale relocation of production was to lengthen the commodity chain and concentrate formerly disaggregated production clusters into large-scale, green-field factories.

Many first-tier contractors have become very large enterprises and have attempted to reduce their dependence upon lead firms by seeking to develop proprietary technologies and establish their own downstream distribution and 'branded' assets. However, celebrated exemplars of this strategy, such as Acer in Taiwan, have encountered difficulties in breaking out of their contracting role in the chain. For example, Acer still relies upon IBM for over 50 per cent of its revenue and recently withdrew from its own-brand distribution in North America. Indeed, to maintain its position as an IBM supplier, Acer has been forced to separate and spin-off its contract and 'own brand' businesses (Mak and Enright, 2001). Because lead firms continue to control the key technologies and marketing assets, first-tier contractors have remained dependent upon a continuing supply of orders, product designs and 'best practice' processes from lead firms; this has resulted in considerable technology transfer (Hobday, 1995). First-tier contractors continue to mediate access to low-cost production resources and bureaucratic permissions in third countries. As an organisational form, global commodity chains provide Taiwanese firms with access to international markets; however, they do not afford much control to domestic firms, and are perhaps a less effective alternative coordinating mechanism than the *sogo sasha* and international trading companies that are part of the *keirestu* and *chaebol*.

Government-linked enterprises

Taiwan's first postwar leader, Chiang Kaishek, did not believe that private capital alone would bring about economic development. In particular, he believed that it was necessary for the state to lead the formation of enterprises in capital-intensive industries. In some cases, such as energy, steel and shipbuilding, the state established state-owned enterprises (e.g. China Petroleum, China Steel, China Shipbuilding), in others it sought out entrepreneurs to develop and manage assets in strategic industries, such as chemicals, plastics and artificial fibres (e.g. the Formosa Group). These enterprises were expected to be commercially viable but they were also expected to create the industrial infrastructure and capacity required to supply raw materials to the hundreds of small industries that were to prove so vital to Taiwan's economic development. Government-linked enterprises (GLEs) are typically fixed asset intensive, medium-technology enterprises that are relatively easy to monitor and control. In shipbuilding, automobiles, and aviation, GLEs were unsuccessful, achieving neither financial nor technological goals. However, in other industries, such as steel, artificial fibres and electronics, GLEs were particularly successful absorbers of technology and advanced manufacturing processes (Hobday, 2000). Some analysts, such as Wade (1990), regard this industrial policy as the key factor behind Taiwan's successful industrial development. The state ensured that GLEs pursued goals that favoured national interests before return on investment. Nevertheless, GLEs have often been profitable, financially stable and have successfully established capacity. However, the cost of achieving these accomplishments has often been inefficiency and entrepreneurial weakness (Vogel, 1991; McVey, 1992). Significantly, firms have often overbuilt capacity, resulting in high levels of growth but low rates of return. While Taiwanese GLEs such as China Petroleum, China Steel, and Formosa Plastics are often giants in their local economies, very few have proved competitive outside of their protected home markets (Zutshi and Gibbons, 1998). Nevertheless, GLEs provide a mechanism for organising capital-intensive industries in a manner comparable to the more vertically-integrated *chaebol* or the alliance-like structures of the *keiretsu*.

Science parks

Despite impressive achievements in information technology, Taiwan's policymakers felt they could not hope to keep pace with the dynamic technological progress maintained in industry clusters such as Silicon Valley (Mathews, 1997). To maintain momentum, the government sought to create an institutional framework for the development of private sector technology firms that would simultaneously facilitate high-technology performance. Policymakers observed initiatives and experiments carried out in industrial districts in Italy and other parts of Europe and established intermediary organisations to create and promote the rapid diffusion of technological innovations. Rather than conducting original research or developing new products, these intermediaries specialised in promoting technology transfer. To encourage technology diffusion, the government sought to attract private sector firms to locate in adjacent science parks through the provision of tax breaks, subsidies and other financial resources. In addition, attractive housing and schools with English language education were designed to attract expatriate Chinese scientists. Locating in the science parks also lent technology firms an element of legitimacy and, with the implied backing of the state, they found it easier to raise external capital. Mathews (1997: 29) suggests that Taiwan's science parks represent government-led industrialisation in its second phase; he describes the policy as induced growth through 'an industrial ecology oriented towards the creation and sustenance of clusters of new high technology industries linked directly to the world's most advanced centres of innovation'. As an organisational form, the science park and its associated intermediary institutions provide latecomer firms with learning and resource leverage, thus improving their capacity to move closer to the technology frontier. In this respect, science parks compare with *keirestu* and *chaebol* as an alternative mechanism to facilitate technological catch-up.

Governance and structure of Taiwan's business groups

Taiwanese business groups are smaller and less vertically integrated compared with those in Korea and Japan. They are also more focused in the upstream sector, producing intermediate products that are subsequently sold to small and medium-sized firms downstream for further processing and export (Feenstra, Yang and Hamilton, 1999: 72). Taiwanese business groups do not include a main bank or financing company that might perform a capital re-allocation role or insurance role for under-performing group affiliates. Nor do Taiwanese business groups contain an overseas trading company. More than two-thirds of Taiwan's exports are produced by small and medium-sized firms that are unaffiliated to business groups (Feenstra Yang and Hamilton, 1999).

Writing in 1990 on Taiwanese business groups, Robert Wade says:

> Taiwan's business groups are much smaller in terms of sales and unemployment than their Korean and Japanese counterparts, for

example Korea's largest business group, Hyundai, had annual sales in 1983 of US$8 billion and employed 137,000 people. In contrast, Formosa Plastics, Taiwan's largest group, had annual sales of US$1.6 billion and employed 31,000 people. Business groups are also less central in the economy: only 40% of the 500 largest manufacturing firms belong to a business group and most Taiwan enterprises remain single unit operations. (Wade 1990: 66)

Nevertheless, Taiwan does have some large classic business groups. Among the best known are the groups based around the Koo family and those based around the Wang family and centred on Formosa Plastics.

The Koo family business group was founded over 100 years ago. Today, the Koo family enterprise is managed by third-generation family members and is probably Taiwan's largest business group, with assets estimated at some $25 billion. The group includes more than 90 firms, among them Taiwan Cement, Chinatrust Commercial Bank, and the United Communications Media Group, which controls the Hong Kong based CTN Chinese-language television broadcaster. The group's history epitomises the view that a business group is a powerful, politically connected familial construct, the success of which is due to the cultivation of personal relationships with insiders, market inefficiency and the acquisition of proprietary information about buyers and sellers. Group founder, Koo Hsien-jung was a prosperous Taipei merchant in 1885 when, under the Treaty of Shimoneski, China ceded Taiwan to Japan. During the colonial occupation, Koo demonstrated strong allegiance to the Japanese and developed close links with the authorities. He pursued a successful political career and in 1934, Koo became the first Taiwanese to be elected to the Japanese Parliament. His political connections facilitated the creation of a range of businesses that still form the core of the group's activities. When Hsien-jung died in 1937, his fifth son, Koo Chen-fu, inherited control of his father's business. With the arrival of the Nationalists in 1949, Koo was jailed for 19 months on charges of treason and collaboration with the Japanese. Subsequently, Chen-fu rose within the ranks of the KMT to become a long-standing member of the party's standing committee. Without ever holding office, he became one of Taiwan's most influential public figures, and is understood to have undertaken the task of leading Taiwan's informal discussions with mainland China. At the same time, Chen-fu continued to develop the family business group, establishing interests in approximately 90 companies, including the China Trust Commercial Bank, Taiwan Cement and the United Communications Media Group.

As Koo Chen-fu became increasingly preoccupied with public affairs, he gradually transferred control of business interests to Jeffrey Koo, who has sought to further diversify the group's interest internationally and into high technology sectors.

Formosa Plastics Group

While the government was able to operate capital-intensive basic and heavy industries, it was less able to lead industries with intermediate levels of technology that were characterised by economies of scope. The state recognised that the production of artificial fibres would be a necessary element in the development of a viable export-oriented textile sector and the government assisted Formosa Plastics by ensuring that it had reliable petrochemical inputs and ample sources of credit. Unlike Koo, Formosa Plastics began life as a relatively focused enterprise. Founded in 1954 as a state enterprise, the government then sought a private sector firm to take over the plant. After some difficulty, the government identified Y.C. Wang, a Taiwanese lumber dealer operating from Japan, as someone with enough entrepreneurial acumen to undertake the project and then 'persuaded' him to acquire the business (Vogel, 1991). The founder of Formosa Plastics Group (FPG) has since displayed strong commitment to keeping control of the empire within the family and each of his ten children is an executive in the family business (Weidenbaum and Hughes, 1996). Formosa Plastics was Taiwan's largest group in 1973 and remained so in 2002 (Chung and Mahmood, 2006). FPG has sought to internationalise its activities principally in the USA and in mainland China but Weidenbaum and Hughes (1996) suggest that it has encountered difficulties with this strategy. In response, FPG has turned towards a strategy of domestic diversification into many other fields, including textiles, electronics, medicine, skin care, automobile manufacturing, gasoline retail and petroleum refining. Figure 5.1 depicts The Formosa Group's corporate structure.

The KMT, Taiwan's ruling political party from 1949 to 2000, controls many of the country's largest and most important businesses. Through its Central Finance Committee (CFC), the KMT has direct ownership of or indirect investments in at least 66 companies; these assets generate funds for party activities. The foundation responsible for managing them has a full-time staff of some 4,000 employees on its payroll (Chu, 1994). The KMT's interests are organised into six holding companies focused in

Figure 5.1 Formosa Plastics Group's corporate structure

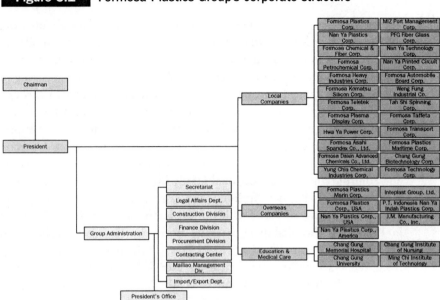

financial service areas such as insurance, leasing, retail, investment and merchant banking. In the early 1990s, the CFC began extending its business interests into new areas such as construction, property development, pollution control, engineering aerospace and telecommunications. The CFC stopped short of acquiring majority control in these business ventures. Instead, control is exerted through the dispatch and generation of executive positions for retired or high-ranking party and government officials. Chu (1994: 131) claims that CFC's sponsored joint ventures with the private sector have built up a seamless web that leads companies into collusive arrangements and large-scale irregular business practices, rendering them potentially vulnerable to government manipulation.

In addition to the state-directed groups, there are two other distinct types of Taiwanese business group: the *guanxi qiye* and *jituan qiye*. The *guanxi qiye* are loosely-affiliated entities and are sometimes called *bang*. They are the more traditional form of enterprise group in Taiwan. The *jituan qiye* resemble corporate pyramids, typically concentrating decision-making and control rights in the hands of a single entrepreneur. The *jituan qiye* are a more recent arrival on the Taiwanese corporate landscape.

The guanxi qiye

The *guanxi qiye* or *bang* originally referred to a group of merchants from the same city or locality who were engaged in the same trade, similar in some respects to a trade association. In contemporary Taiwan, the term *bang* or *guanxi qiye* is more generally applied to an informal grouping of independently owned and operated firms that are interrelated through kinship marriage, common locale, or other social ties. These groups are not authoritatively coordinated as integrated administrative entities; rather, most function more as a 'partnerships united by a common investment and mutual trust in which the critical locus of decision-making and control remains the individual family business' (Whitley, 1990: 54).

Numazki's (1993) description of the Tainan *bang*, a *guanxi qiye* from Tainan city, is one of very few historical analyses of this form. Founded in 1934 as a partnership in a textile store, the Tianan *bang* began to expand from its initial business in 1953 when the partners won a licence from the Nationalist government to establish a large spinning mill. Subsequently, between 1953 and 1982, the Tainan *bang* assisted in the creation of 20 or more large enterprises by providing the capital for their establishment and their early growth. One such firm, President Enterprise, was founded in 1967, and by 2002 it was Taiwan's eighth largest business group (*jituan*). Numazaki characterises the *guanxi qiye* as a form of network-based entrepreneurship in which the group mobilises capital, recruits personnel and provides vital information:

> Potential entrepreneurs mobilise their personal network of *guanxi* and bring a set of partners together to form a partnership and contribute certain resources to the new enterprise. The resources include not only capital, but also managerial skills and political connections, all of which are indispensable for doing business in Taiwan. (Numazaki, 1993: 394)

In this context, the *bang* operate as an interesting hybrid of the traditional Chinese rotating credit association and a contemporary venture capital partnership (VCP). Lacking the legal framework necessary for the incorporation of a formal limited liability venture capital partnership, the *bang* have crafted certain context-specific solutions to the problem of high-risk new-venture creation. Unlike a VCP, which has a legally stated date of termination, the *bang* maintain an essentially relational mode of governance. Partners with larger investments occupy monitoring positions such as chairman of the board, while secondary investors serve as directors or auditors. Yet others remain as silent partners or pure investors. All investors expect both dividends and capital accumulation from their investments.

The *bang* also differ from the VCP in the way in which firms leave the group and establish their independence. In the VCP, the partners typically oversee an initial public offering on equity markets. Given the weakness of Taiwan's equity markets, however, this option is not always feasible. Successful affiliates in the *bang* exit the group by gradually adopting a new corporate form, which gradually dilutes the partners' financial interest in the affiliate. Specifically, a growing and cash-rich member firm will evolve beyond the partnership by switching from a partnership model to the subsidiary model as a means of establishing new businesses. Eventually, the affiliate will consolidate the new ventures into a holding company in which the partners hold a highly diluted stake. These new holding companies are typically pyramid structures, but the minority shareholders are usually former partners, suggesting that these groups are less prone to expropriation by the majority owner. Hence, groups formed in this way have earned a reputation among scholars as 'trust'-based federations (Orru, Biggart and Hamilton, 1997).

Nevertheless, as they expand, the *bang* tend to become more hierarchical and differentiated, with a clear distinction between senior and junior partners. Numazaki (1993) suggests that the hierarchical structure resembles a bunch of bananas, as depicted in Figure 5.2. According to Numazaki (1993), the salient feature of this corporate structure is a partnership consisting of overlapping ownership and directorships. Each banana represents a group member, while senior owner-partners who direct the group as a whole link individual members at the stem. The partnership is hierarchical in the sense that some owners concern themselves with a more limited range of enterprises rather than being fully committed to overlapping ownership and directorship of the entire group.

By the early 1990s, the traditional *bang* had declined in importance and there are some indications that this form of cooperative organisation had been supplanted by the *jituan qiye*, a more hierarchical form of business group, characterised by ownership concentration. For example, one study of Taiwan's business groups found that common identity ties based on location and school do not improve group performance (Luo and Chung, 2005: 427). In this regard, the Luo and Chung study differs from previous work that identified the old town ties in Taiwan as central to group identity and coordination (Hamilton and Kao, 1990). Their findings suggest that the old-style *guanxi qiye* has lost some of its potency. If the *guanxi qiye* is indeed a declining form, it may be viewed as a transitional structure that was effective and adapted to the early phases of the reform

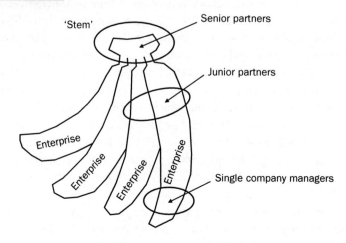

Figure 5.2 Banana-shaped *bang* in Taiwan

period. Recall that at that time, the Nationalist government suppressed the development of equity markets, controlled other sources of credit, and directed scarce resources to preferred enterprises. In this environment, small and medium-sized enterprises were left to find their own capital if they were to take advantage of the opportunities presented by rapid economic development and laissez-faire trading conditions. By the 1990s, successfully-established firms were self-financing because they were able to generate sufficient funds from their own operations and meanwhile other sources of capital were becoming available. In this perspective, the Taiwanese *guanxi qiye* appears to be a local response to capital scarcity during a period of great opportunity.

The jituan qiye

Chung (2001) argues that the period 1964–68 is crucial in the formation of Taiwan's private business groups and that elements in the institutional environment were major determinants of business group formation. According to Chung, the origins of business groups in Taiwan stem from a particular tax incentive policy. The Nationalist government believed that Taiwanese entrepreneurs were unwilling to take risks and therefore needed guidance and assistance to develop industry. Accordingly, in 1960 the KMT enacted the statute for the encouragement of investment, a statute that was critical for the formation of Taiwanese business groups. Intended to promote savings and stimulate investment and exports, the statute provided for five years of tax relief. The policy had several unintended consequences. Tax relief applied only to investments in the creation of new firms but not to the incremental expansion of existing firms. Therefore, under this regulation it was more beneficial to establish an independent new firm and to expand existing firms by adding a new branch that might go some way towards creating a new multiunit hierarchical firm. In 1964, the KMT removed these restrictions in most industries, thus providing firms with new opportunities to diversify. Between 1964 and 1968, more than half of the 150 groups in Chung's sample established a second firm. This is important as it represents the adoption of the group strategy rather than building a multidivisional firm.

However, significant changes in the institutional environments during the early 1990s appear to have had the most significant impact on the character of Taiwan's larger business groups. In particular, the deregulation of the banking sector in 1991 and the decision by some 45 of the largest 100 business groups to enter the banking sector represent a key turning point (Chung, 2006). Chu (1994) predicted that these institutional changes would bring about the appearance of large-scale business groups similar to those of Japan. Whether or not this has occurred is open to debate. Nevertheless, in the intervening decade Taiwan's business groups experienced numerous changes in the scale and scope of their activities.

Luo and Chung (2005) identify a significant trend toward unrelated diversification between 1992 and 2002 as measured by two-digit Standard Industrial Classification (SIC) codes. On average, each of the top 100 business groups entered three new industries. Luo and Chung (2005) also find a spike in restructuring between 1994 and 1996, when each of the top 100 groups exited an average of two industries. However, there is an interesting pattern in the group's commitment to those new industries. Using an entropic measure of diversification (Palepu, 1985) that considers both the number of industries in which a group operates and the relative importance of each industry in terms of revenues earned, the data show that, after 1990, the SIC count measure rises much faster than the entropic measure for the population as a whole. This pattern suggests that business groups are entering many new industries and yet make only limited resource-commitments to them. In other words, these new industries have not yet become important sources of revenue. Equally, business groups appear unwilling to exit from their existing core businesses and remain heavily dependent on them.

Taken at face value, it appears that the ownership of business groups has changed significantly. Between 1988 and 1998, ownership by individuals and families in the largest 100 groups has declined from 23 per cent to 4 per cent. However, this decline is matched by a commensurate increase in ownership by group affiliates, which suggests that individuals and families now control their affiliates through corporations rather than through individuals. Such ownership changes may accrue benefits from a taxation, estate and inheritance perspective, but they have little impact on the control and direction of the group's assets. Data compiled by Chung and Mahmood (2006: 86) suggest that government, foreign and institutional ownership of Taiwan's business groups have remained relatively constant and there is little or no increase in dispersed ownership. In other words, ownership changes in recent years appear to be nominal and control in Taiwan's 100 largest business groups remains concentrated in the hands of the few family decision makers.

Chung and Mahmood (2006) suggest that, as Taiwan's groups become larger and more diversified, they will make greater use of professional management. Luo and Chung (2005: 422) have examined the composition of senior management teams in Taiwan's largest business groups and find that, among the inner circle, 50 per cent will be family members of the key leader and about 30 per cent will have had prior social relationships. Between 1973 and 1996, the percentage of inner circle members who were total strangers to the key lead increased from about 5 per cent to 10 per cent (Chung, 2005). Following the onset of market transition in the 1990s, family representation declined by about 10 per cent in the inner circle of management (Luo and Chung, 2005). However, most of these 'outsiders' have been promoted from within after serving several years with different business units or will be confidantes of the founding family (Chung, 2003). Rarely will 'stranger managers' be appointed from an external talent market, as is routinely the case in the West. Exceptions to this pattern are usually newsworthy; for example, when Stevens Shi, founder of the Acer computer group, appointed a former IBM executive as a professional CEO, it was widely covered in the popular press and became the subject of a Harvard Business School case study. There is little evidence of a managerial revolution in major Taiwanese business groups.

In conclusion, the much-heralded changes in the governance and structure of Taiwanese business groups appear to be nominal. There has been growth in their size and scope but no fundamental change in ownership and control. Chu's prediction that Taiwan's business groups would evolve toward a Korean or Japanese *keiretsu* model has yet to be fulfilled. However, there is continuing institutional change. Legislation such as the Financial Institutions Consolidation Law (2000) and the Financial Holding Company Law (2001), which were passed following a banking crisis, continue to liberalise the financial sector of the economy. However, it is too early to assess the long-term impact of these changes.

The performance of Taiwan's business groups

This section will review evidence about the financial and market performance of Taiwan's business groups; most of this evidence pertains to very recent studies. Using both accounting and market performance measures, Chu (2004) examined the group affiliation premium hypotheses based on a sample of 340 firms affiliated to one of Taiwan's 100 largest business groups and 423 independent firms during 1997–99. These firms were all non-financial sector companies that were publicly listed on either the Taiwan Stock Exchange or on Taiwan's over-the-counter securities market. Measuring size in terms of assets and number of employees, Chu's data reveal that group affiliates are significantly larger than freestanding firms. On average, freestanding firms have 423 full-time employees, whereas group-affiliated firms are much larger, with an average of 1,200 employees. Chu's most significant finding is that independent firms, and those affiliated to one of the 30 largest business groups, significantly outperform firms affiliated to small and medium-sized business groups, i.e. those ranked as the top 31–100. In terms of the accounting performance measure, independent firms significantly outperform affiliated firms; the mean return on assets (ROA) for freestanding firms is some 8.1 per cent compared with a mean ROA of 3.55 per cent for group-affiliated firms. Among the group-affiliated firms, those affiliated to one of Taiwan's largest 30 business groups generate an average ROA of 5.39 per cent, while firms affiliated to smaller groups generate an average ROA of under 3 per cent.

With respect to the group affiliation premium hypotheses, Chu concludes that, if they are sufficiently large, Taiwan's business groups may imitate missing institutions effectively, but no business group can successfully resolve all the information and transactions cost problems associated with emerging markets. Second, given the high levels of performance displayed by freestanding firms, Chu suggests that inefficiencies in emerging markets can be solved by alternative mechanisms. In the specific context of Taiwan, we have noted an abundant variety of such mechanisms including science parks, global commodity chains and production networks. Third, the cost of group affiliation in emerging markets may be understated. This is especially pertinent when a business group is vertically integrated and the group requires affiliates to cross-subsidise one another or to engage in compulsory internal purchasing from affiliates, potentially dampening profitability. The very low levels of diversification and higher levels of vertical integration among affiliates of Taiwanese business groups suggest that compulsory internal purchasing is at play; this extensive intra-group trading requires firms to transact with less efficient group members rather than contracting in the open market for more attractive partners.

Other studies support this contention that cross-subsidisation is a tendency among Taiwanese business groups. In a multi-country study of the insurance hypotheses in business groups for the years 1990–97, Khanna and Yafeh (2005) found a significant income-smoothing effect among Taiwanese firms affiliated to business groups. The magnitude of the estimated economic impact is considerable: between 20 to 30 per cent reduction in the standard deviation of operating profitability. In contrast, Filatochev, Lien and Piesse (2005) found no significant relationship between business group affiliation and performance. Their study examined a variety of firm corporate governance effects on the accounting and financial market performance of 228 firms listed on the Taiwan Stock Exchange in 1999. Their results suggest that share ownership by institutional investors and foreign financial institutions is associated with better performance. These authors contend that a coalition of large shareholders can moderate the effects of excessive family ownership and that the internationalisation of Taiwanese capital markets may lead domestic firms to import good governance practices. However, in 1999, levels of institutional and foreign ownership were still very low.

Luo and Chung (2005) examined the accounting performance (ROA) of Taiwan's top 100 business groups every two years over a 24-year period. Unusually, rather than analysing the performance of individual firms that are affiliated to a group, the study analysed the aggregate performance of the group as whole, presumably based upon consolidated accounting data. Their main result confirms that size is of fundamental importance among Taiwanese business groups; other things being equal, groups with the largest revenues enjoy superior ROA. However, if a business group has a large number of members or affiliate firms, this has a very significant negative effect on ROA. These results suggest that more focused groups perform much better than more widely diversified groups. Luo and Chung also examine some aspects of the business group's top management team; in particular, they are interested in the performance effects of having multiple members from the same family in a group's top management team. Having two or three family members in the top management tends to have a positive impact on performance; thereafter, however, additional family members contribute less to performance – this could be described as diminishing returns to familism. Luo and Chung (2005) suggest that after a certain point, the inclusion of additional family members exacerbates the costs of information homogeneity and increases the legitimacy discount by foreign investors. That is, investors become worried if the firm appears to be too nepotistic.

The Luo and Chung (2005) study also sheds light on the temporal dynamics of transition and institutional development. Because their study covers a 24-year period, they are able to examine how business group performance was affected by the major institutional changes, which began in 1988 and continue today. Interestingly, they find that the performance of business groups in general declined after the onset of transition. However, the groups that retained a larger percentage of family members in the inner circle of the top management team performed much better than the population as a whole. Luo and Chung propose that the success of family-controlled groups can be attributed to their relative inertia. They conjecture that families are more conservative and that during a period of severe environmental uncertainty, they will stick to what they know rather than attempting to make adjustments through restructuring and new initiatives. Family businesses that made few changes outperformed groups that restructured and introduced professional managers. The relative inertia of family-dominated business groups actually enhanced their performance because they resisted incurring the short-term costs of adaptation. Whether the conservative family-dominated firms will continue to outperform other business groups, of course, remains an open question.

There is a relative lack of research on other aspects of Taiwanese business group performance. For example, there is very little evidence that business group affiliation supports the development of proprietary management or technological capability. Most research about Taiwan's rapidly improving innovative capabilities completely ignores any mention of business groups (Hobday, 1995; Mathews, 1997; Hobday, Cawson and Kim, 2001). One exception is Mahmood and Mitchell's (2004) comparative study of patenting activity in Korean and Taiwanese business groups over the period 1981–95. Mahmood and Mitchell argue that business groups in emerging markets can have a dual impact on innovation performance. On the one hand, groups facilitate innovation because they provide an institutional infrastructure for their affiliates. On the other hand, business groups may discourage innovation due to their large economic power and, by creating barriers to entry for non-group firms, they inhibit the proliferation of new ideas. Because groups have deep pockets and the capacity to cross-subsidise their affiliates, competitors can be driven out with preventive price-cutting.

Mahmood and Mitchell (2004) find support for an inverted U-shape relationship (or a trade-off) between a firm's level of patenting activity in a particular industry and the market share that business groups hold in that industry. They suggest that, if a firm has a small share of the market, it will lack both the incentive and capability to seek market leadership in an industry sector and so will not seek to develop innovative technology. Conversely, firms with very high levels of market share will seek to defend their dominant market positions through monopolistic practices or market power based strategies. They contend that innovative activity will be greatest at intermediate levels of market power when firms have an incentive to aim for industry leadership but are not so entrenched that they can utilise monopoly power. Mahmood and Mitchell find significant differences between innovative practices in Taiwan and Korea. Their results show that, in Taiwan, innovation activity peaks for firms with a 32–44 per cent of market share compared with 62–70 per cent in South Korea. In Taiwan, business group affiliates' innovative activity peaks at around 30 per cent for share compared to South Korea where it peaks at 65 per cent. That is, in Taiwan, innovation performance, as reflected in patenting activity, occurs at much lower levels of market share. Mahmood and Mitchell suggest that Korean business groups are more centrally controlled and vertically integrated than their counterparts in Taiwan, which is likely to dampen their innovative capacity. Business group affiliates in Taiwan have greater autonomy. Corporate networks of smaller specialised firms provide greater diversity among Taiwanese groups that may provide flexibility and encouragement to use innovation as a means of competing between firms in intergroup competition and may make them more willing to attempt to dislodge dominant players in the concentrated industry. Moreover,

Taiwan has a more varied innovation infrastructure with a larger segment of independent firms and government agencies that perform industry-specific innovation tasks; as such, business group affiliates encounter greater variation in competition. All these factors combine to stimulate competition at lower levels of market share.

Note

1. Wade (1990: 70) opines 'any discussion of an economy's development should give a central place to the organization of firms and industries. But since little evidence is available on this subject for Taiwan ... I say little more about it'.

Business groups in mainland China

Over the past 20 years, business groups have become China's predominant organisational form. Researchers have focused much of their attention on China's large state-induced business groups that were assembled from incumbent state-owned enterprises (SOEs) and line ministries beginning in the early 1980s (Keister, 1998, 2000; Hutchet, 1999; Mako and Zhang, 2002; Yiu, Bruton and Lu, 2005). Today, some of these firms are China's largest enterprises; they are the *Qiye Jituan* 'National Team', charged with developing technologically advanced and internationally competitive capabilities. These groups have enjoyed great state support and operate within relatively protected sectors of China's economy. They remain largely state-owned and report directly to central government. Some of these groups are known as the 'red-chips' and are listed on the Hong Kong and New York stock exchanges. Below the National Team is a large and diverse array of medium-sized business groups organised by provincial and municipal governments and the collective sector. Some of the business groups in this category have become leaders in highly competitive and less restrictive sectors of the economy. A third category is the emerging private business groups (PBGs) that are on the fringe of the economy but are of growing importance and likely to become a dynamic force. These groups are controlled and operated by a private founder-entrepreneur, family and trusted business partners. As relative newcomers on the economic scene, they have not yet received much attention from researchers. PBGs merit separate consideration because their governance and ownership relations differentiate them from their state-induced counterparts. In the latter, ownership is diffused in complex equity-ownership arrangements while operational control is exercised by executives who own little or no equity in the enterprises they manage. In contrast, governance in PBGs is characterised by pyramidal equity arrangements that concentrate ownership and control in the hands of a single entrepreneur or their family. In this respect, the governance of China's PBGs resembles the structures prevalent among overseas Chinese family business groups in Taiwan (Chung, 2001) and Southeast Asia (Carney and Gedajlovic, 2002a).

Reflecting an economic and political reform process that is both experimental and incremental, a very diverse array of business groups has emerged and these groups exhibit varied performance profiles. Their diversity also reflects the fact that China is an enormous country with a strong culture and turbulent recent political history. Interactions among a wide range of administrative bodies have also shaped the business group governance structures and performance outcomes. Significant actors include the Communist Party of China, central government executive and administrative bureaux, along with provincial and autonomous regional governments, self-governed municipalities, such as Shanghai and Guangzhou, and also governments of special administrative regions such as Hong Kong and Macau. A burgeoning private sector and numerous forms of foreign enterprise have also contributed to a complex and dynamic story in the emergence of mainland China's business groups.

The emergence of business groups in mainland China

There are at least two different accounts of the emergence of business groups in China. We shall refer to the first as the *design thesis.* This suggests that, having studied a variety of local and foreign models, the architects of China's reform experimented with a variety of organisational forms and subsequently created and promoted leading business groups. The second account, which I shall refer to as a *spontaneous emergence thesis,* suggests a more bottom-up approach in which group managers and entrepreneurs voluntarily adopted the group model in response to unfolding opportunities and the uncertainty of the transition process. The emergence of private business groups appears to be more closely aligned with the spontaneous emergence model, as the state was originally ambiguous, if not hostile towards privately-owned enterprise. The emergence of the National Team and regional business groups is perhaps best explained by a combination of the two perspectives. The mechanics of group formation reflect a range of transactions including spin-offs, start-ups, mergers and acquisitions (often made coercively), international joint ventures, state asset sales, and privatisations (Lee and Hahn, 1999).

To better appreciate the context in which the first business groups were formed in mainland China, it is worthwhile considering China's economic and industrial inheritance on the eve of its historic reforms. Since 1978, when Deng Xiaoping's 'four modernisations' policy introduced large-scale administrative reform into the economy and opened the door to international trade, China has experimented with a variety of market-oriented reforms.

Under Mao's regime, political power and economic planning were centralised but responsibility for production was decentralised to provincial authorities. Due to security concerns Mao believed every province should strive for economic self-sufficiency; this goal created a highly fragmented, autarkic economic system. In this system, production was destined for local consumption and each province developed its own industries, a situation that resulted in numerous small-scale plants and factories producing goods of low quality. For example, each province had its own agricultural machinery industry producing a wide range of tractors, harvesters and tillers in small uneconomic batches. In this regime, industrial enterprise also served an important social welfare function, sometimes called the 'iron rice bowl', in which the enterprise was responsible for ensuring employment security as well as meeting employees' housing, education and healthcare needs.

With the accession to power of Deng Xiaoping in 1977, broader social system stability became an overriding policy goal and enterprises were expected to accommodate this aim through incremental restructuring and gradual change, especially through employment practice. One of the main foundations of the new regime was the delegation of authority at all levels of the bureaucracy, a policy that strengthened the economic role of regional governments and created a host of administrative agencies, each seeking to pursue specific policy objectives. In this context, enterprises were created with distinct corporate identities and granted increasing autonomy over their internal affairs. However, enterprises were enmeshed in a 'system of dependencies' (Child, 1994) upon central and local government, and industrial bureaux.

For example, to organise a modern airline industry, the central government established a number of airlines along regional lines, such as Air China, China Southern, China Eastern, China Northern etc. However, responsibility for aircraft purchases, fuel acquisition and human resources was assigned to independent semi-commercial bureaux, while a national regulatory commission supervised access to routes and capacity and tariff setting. This division of responsibility gave rise to constant bargaining between enterprise and administrative agencies, which was open to discretion, opportunism and corruption. The early period of reform was highly politicised and the change process was circuitous. Importantly, in a wider economy, early reform left property rights over the enterprise ambiguous and ill-defined (Jefferson and Rawski, 1996). In particular, formal ownership of public, private and joint venture enterprises often bears no clear relationship to rights to use or dispose of assets or the income streams derived from them (Child, 1994).

Finding a suitable corporate form to govern and manage the myriad of state-owned or supervised enterprises was a pressing design problem for China's reformers. A major policy objective of the early reform period was to 'explore new ways of combining business autonomy with a changed role for government' (Child, 2000: 42). Confronting a need to reconcile numerous social and economic dilemmas, policy makers encouraged experiments with a large variety of organisational forms. Some experiments were imitations of foreign corporate models, others hybrid arrangements of forms compatible with socialist ideology, such as collectives and township and village enterprises (Nee, 1992; Tseo, 1996). Interestingly, the business group model was not a first choice of China's early reformers. The model initially encouraged was a horizontal association of enterprises, in which firms in the same line of business would come together to share production facilities and distribution channels while linking up with universities and research institutes for research and development support (Hahn and Lee, 2006). By the mid-1980s it was evident that horizontal associations lacked a clear and coherent organisation capable of strategic decision-making and resource allocation. Reformers also considered a model in which geographically-based state holding companies would operate under the supervision of a state economy and trade commissioner. However, this model embodied a conflict of interest because the state commission would hold dual roles as an enterprise regulator and yet retain responsibility for the enterprise's financial performance. In the concept of the business group, reformers believed that they had solved the problem of defining authority between regulation and operational management control. What remains unclear is the nature of the incentives facing senior managers of business groups and the mechanisms for intervention available to the state in the event of enterprises being mismanaged. This fundamental design problem has not yet been solved and we will return to this issue below.

Reformers also studied a variety of foreign organisation models, such as the German main bank system and the US General Electric model. However, the first indication that the state was serious about the formation of state-owned business groups is found in official State Council documents from 1986. Reformers had studied Japanese and Korean business groups but were concerned about the risks associated with 'insider governance' (Child, 1994). Despite the predictable difficulties, reformers were impressed by the evident capacity of the *keiretsu* and *chaebol* to achieve economies of scale, create high-quality industrial capacity and perform technological 'catch up' along with favourable financial performance (Keister, 1998). They believed that business groups might accomplish the same objectives for China.

Beginning in 1987, the state actively encouraged the formation of giant business groups offering a range of incentives and some coercion (Child, 1994). The response was rapid and dramatic and by the following year 1,630 state-owned business groups had been registered. By 1989, the number had reached some 7,000, and in 1995, there were over 20,000 business groups in all economic sectors. In an early study of the product-market scope of some 6,780 newly registered groups, Wu (1990) found that the largest number of these groups were conglomerate holding companies (40.6 per cent) whose diverse firms were connected by debt and equity linkages. Wu (1990) found that the second most numerous type (25 per cent) were vertically-integrated groups formed by an industrial firm together with research institutions and a number of distribution firms. According to Wu, 'horizontal integrators' are the most common group-form (15 per cent of groups); these consist of formerly independent firms from the same industry that have now consolidated under a common brand name and aim to produce to a higher-quality standard. The groups that Wu calls the 'dominant firm type' are fewer in number (8 per cent). This form consists of a large dominant firm producing strong products or brand names that operates as the 'dragon's head' of a number of member firms with related production processes. Although there are little systematic data from this period, it appears that these relatively few firms accounted for a significant proportion of China's industrial assets.

It was soon evident that the economy could not sustain so many business groups and that significant consolidation was required. In 1991, the State Council identified a batch of 57 groups described as the 'national trial groups'. These groups were given a dual socioeconomic mission: a group was to lead a particular sector into international markets and at the same time absorb a significant number of smaller firms that were performing poorly (Ma and Lu, 2005). The relative success of this experiment encouraged the State Council to select a second batch of 63 trial groups in 1997. Together these groups are formally known as National Trial Group 120 (Ma and Lu, 2005) or the 'National Team' (Nolan, 2001).

The most important members of the National Team were encouraged to seek an international stock market listing in Hong Kong where they were identified as 'red-chips'. In due course they were also permitted to seek listing in New York. One of the largest red-chips is the China International Trust and Investment Corporation (CITIC Pacific); it was established in 1990 by the Beijing State Council to generate business to international commercial opportunities. Under chairman Larry Yung, who holds an approximately 12 per cent voting stake in the enterprise, shares of CITIC Pacific rapidly attained the status of a highly-diversified conglomerate that defines its 'core' businesses as infrastructure, property development, trading and manufacturing, but also holds significant equity stakes in companies such as Cathay Pacific and Dragon Air, who in turn maintain share cross-holdings in CITIC. Other provincial governments, which sought to generate similar international linkages, soon emulated the 'CITIC' model, but many lacked entrepreneurial competence or were inadequately supervised. The high-profile failure of Guangdong Provincial Investment Group (GITIC), led to its liquidation. A subsequent performance review revealed poor project evaluation, low monitoring and multimillion-dollar theft. Central government responded by discouraging cross-shareholdings after 1997 because of perceived instability.

In the process of establishing the National Team, China's reformers encountered numerous problems and difficulties. Nolan (2001) relates what is perhaps a typical case in the creation of Aviation Industries of China (AVIC). Established in 1993 as a state holding company, AVIC comprised some 700,000 employees in 245 enterprises. Scattered throughout China, these enterprises include helicopter, military and civilian aircraft businesses, 11 aero engine manufacturers and 77 enterprises manufacturing aircraft equipment and components. AVIC's management was charged with rationalising the group's assets and transforming them into an internationally competitive aircraft company.

A large number of AVIC's enterprises were specialised in the manufacture of military aircraft, with technology and processes inherited from Soviet era cooperation. The Deng regime had promised the People's Liberation Army that military modernisation would be a high priority. However, the 1990 Gulf war had a major impact on Chinese military thinking and instilled the belief that, if China relied upon domestic technology, the country could not 'catch up' in the field of military aircraft, avionics and weapons technology. The decision to import Russian Su-27s jet fighters as the core plane of the Chinese air force effectively signalled AVIC's withdrawal as a potential military aircraft producer for the foreseeable future. Instead AVIC sought to focus upon the civilian aircraft market and selected the Shanghai Aircraft Manufacturing Company (SAMC) to lead the effort. Earlier, SAMC had unsuccessfully attempted to copy a model of the Boeing 707 aircraft; the failed programme was halted in 1985. Subsequently, SAMC entered into a joint venture to assemble McDonnell Douglas aircraft in China but this too ended in failure once Boeing acquired McDonnell Douglas and terminated production of the aircraft. By 1998 SAMC had became a subcontractor to Shanghai Bus Manufacturing Company and had abandoned any ambitions it had to become a major aircraft maker. AVIC managers encouraged SAMC and other group members to enter into a joint venture with Airbus to make a regional jet for sale initially in the Chinese market. However, Air China was unwilling to purchase the proposed plane, the AE 100, and the project was postponed. AVIC is persisting with its efforts to produce a regional jet and is currently negotiating with current market leaders Embraer and Bombardier.

AVIC was also charged with maintaining employment for a huge and relatively skilled workforce. Faced with a decline in orders for military and civilian aircraft, group management began a programme of product market diversification and established manufacturing divisions in consumer electronics, footwear, automobiles, motorcycles, textile machinery, refrigerators and air conditioners. In 1997, non-aviation products accounted for more than 80 per cent of its revenues. Following a later restructuring that broke the enterprise into two groups, AVIC 1 and 2, each with revenues of approximately US$400 million and each manufacturing a wide range of products, both groups are far from attaining the scale and focus necessary to compete in the international aircraft-manufacturing marketplace (Nolan, 2001).

In contrast to the design thesis that emphasises the strategies and objectives of reformers in the state bureaucracy, Keister (1998, 2001) gives greater weight to the adaptations made by enterprise managers in the face of an ambiguous reform process and growing market uncertainty. One of the first reforms of the Deng era was the establishment of the contract-responsibility system, which provided enterprise managers greater autonomy over internal business decisions. Formal subsidies were reduced and enterprises were permitted to retain earnings and seek alternative sources of finance. In this context the nature of uncertainty confronting managers changed significantly: for the very first time, managers were required to make fundamental decisions to determine the enterprises with which they should trade. In place of state resource allocation and production targets, managers had a contract for resources in markets characterised by incomplete information and shortages of material supplies, personnel and capital. Because factor markets were so underdeveloped, finding reliable trading partners became a key concern. Financial markets were particularly slow to develop due to continued regulation of state banks and limitations in the activities of foreign banks.

While the state had a hand in designating which enterprises belonged to which group, the state did not seek to determine trading and debt relations, in part because hundreds of ties spontaneously developed within the group (Keister, 2001). To cope with the uncertainty caused by an uneven market development, Keister argues that firms sought to enter into stable relations with business partners who could best assure access to critical resources. To identify reliable partners, managers relied upon prior social relations, especially among former bureaucrats. In this way, hundreds of ties spontaneously developed within each group (Keister, 2001). Through recurrent contracting among themselves, firms came to be associated as members of new business groups. Importantly, Keister (2001: 352) finds that regardless of the costs of alternative sources of goods and capital, and even as costs declined elsewhere, these trading relationships persisted based on prior social ties.

When an enterprise joined a group it would benefit from an increase in productivity due in part to improved access to information and assured supplies of goods and capital. Moreover, Keister suggests that the exchange ties that developed among group members in this period became enduring features of China's business landscape. Keister (2001: 337) argues that, in this regard, these business groups are similar to those found in Japan and Korea.

At the regional level a similar spontaneous emergent dynamic appears to be at work. Vogel's (1989) study of early reform era Guangdong is characterised as 'Capitalism without capitalists' and he identifies a variety of change-agents responsible for the creation of new business organisations. Vogel suggests that the local state became the entrepreneur with individuals performing three key roles, which he terms *statesman*, *scramblers* and *niche seekers*. *Statesmen* were upper-level bureaucrats who commanded respect in the party executive, championed the cause of reform, and gained the loyalty of cadres by developing a reputation for protecting and standing behind lower-level actors who were conducting experiments based on knowledge of local on-the-ground working conditions. *Scramblers* were managers who operated in the quasi-private sector. Scramblers had self-educated business skills, used their resourcefulness to start enterprises and were quick to respond

to any situation. *Niche seekers* started small businesses and household enterprises, and represented the true private sector by performing essential distribution and service activities. Vogel (1989) holds in highest esteem the statesman who understood party theory and objectives and who knew the local issues and did not over-promise results. But it was a combination of statesmen and scramblers that created new business groups and became their de facto owners and managers.

The gradual dismantling of inter-provincial barriers to competition (in sectors that were not reserved for the National Team) revealed numerous competitors in nearly every kind of product line. In what Jefferson and Rawski (1996: 62) describe as incipient competition, 'entrepreneurial leaders in hundreds of counties and thousands of production brigades were poised to take advantage of deregulation by bursting into markets they had coveted for years'. At this regional level, old elite paths have persisted; using their prestige and political influence, former state actors have accumulated significant wealth. Several factors stimulated local politicians and party members to become entrepreneurs: reforms allowed enterprises to keep part of the income generated by the business, a centralised banking system provided credits, and a promotion system for political leaders was based on their ability to develop economic activity.

Notwithstanding developments within the quasi-public sector, the rapid growth of the private sector is one of the most significant consequences of China's reform process. Although the financial size of the private sector is unclear, the growth of private sector employment has been rapid. Official statistics suggest that there are 2.3 million private firms employing some 34 million individuals, implying that the average small firm has around 15 employees. Recent surveys of China's wealthiest people suggest that a number of entrepreneurs, such as Wong Kwongyu (Gomes Appliance and Real Estate Group), Xu Rongmao (Shimao Real Estate Group), Lu Guanqui (Wanxiang Auto Parts Group) and Liu Yonghao (New Hope Animal Feed Group), have already established personal fortunes approaching US$1 billion. The largest private group in China during the 1990s, the Hope Group, traces its roots to private farming. Another example is Lenovo (formerly the Legend Group), China's largest non-state-owned business group in the high-tech area, which was founded by 11 IT scientists and engineers in 1984. Several factors indicate that private sector business groups are likely to become more important in the near future.

Foremost is the official adoption of an industrial policy of 'grasping the large and letting go the small' announced by President Jiang Zemin at the 15th Party Conference in 1997. Subsequently, the state began selling stakes in numerous financially distressed small and medium-sized SOEs (Beamish and Delios, 2005). Many recently-founded PBGs began to acquire stakes in these SOEs at very low prices amid accusations of corruption and asset striping. These privatisations were suspended briefly between 1999 and 2001 but have since resumed and will likely result in a significant transfer of state assets to the private sector. Second, stagnation in the public sector has encouraged many elites to become private entrepreneurs. Since the late 1990s, a pattern of 'elite transformation' has occurred (Ma, Yao and Xi, 2006) in which former state officials or 'professional elites' have departed from state organisations to start private enterprises. At the onset of reforms, enterprise managers, scientists and research and development staff had practically no business experience. However, their appointment as general managers of state-owned enterprises during the early stages of reform provided opportunities for elites to accumulate business knowledge, as well as political and financial contacts during the rapid growth period of the 1990s. Moreover, reduced funding and the downsizing of state organisations resulted in demotion and layoffs for many elites. These organisational changes facilitated career redirection. Third, although recent reforms have eased access to public equity markets (Green, 2004), private firms traditionally relied on self-funding and illicit channels such as rural and urban credit cooperatives in the 'popular credit market' (*minjian jiedai shichang*), which offers tontines and loans from private individuals and families. PBGs have also relied upon these and their own familial resources to raise funds and have funded group growth through retained earnings from group operations. By 2002, official statistics show that 'self-raised' finance is the largest source of funds for capital investment, greater than foreign investment, official bank lending and the state appropriations combined. Although this figure also includes earnings retained by the state sector, it seems likely that the private sector is also contributing to this growth. PBGs have also recently begun to acquire inward foreign investment from overseas Chinese entrepreneurs. Due to the absence of safeguards for external investors in private firms, much of this investment emanates from sources that have some familial connection. Finally, recent constitutional amendments recognise the right to private capital and stress the importance of private entrepreneurship in China's development. The official recognition of the private sector provides a modicum of support and is likely to further enhance growth in the private sector.

Diversification in Chinese business groups

Recent evidence suggests that Chinese business groups are more focused than their counterparts elsewhere in Asia. In a sample of some 13,000 Chinese companies, Ma et al. (2006) found very low levels of diversification. Using a Herfindahl product diversity measure, Chinese firms on average score only 0.35, which is lower than that of firms in many developed countries; for example, Japan scores 0.58 on this measure, while the USA scores 0.53. Ma and Lu (2005) suggest that firms will seek to diversify into industries such as financial services, logistics, operations, or highly related upstream and downstream sectors. To remain focused on a core industry, firms were required to attain institutional protection and legitimacy to actively resist opportunities to form joint ventures (Li, Li and Tan, 1998). Other firms diversified around a core logic; for instance, the China Everbright Group sought to establish a financial services group in banking, securities and insurance, thus emulating the related form of diversification commonly found in the West. Hahn and Lee (2006) agree that business groups in China are less diversified, noting that groups were formed to take advantage of economies of scale and to ensure better supervision of the group member firms.

However, Nolan (2001) argues that while groups were originally established as relatively focused entities, difficulties in a core business induced them to adopt the diversification strategy. Many firms were encouraged by city and regional governments to diversify into labour-intensive, assembly-based industries as a solution to labour surplus problems. Widely adopted by regional firms, this strategy has produced huge overcapacity in the production of some commodities. Other firms are diversified along the value chain via vertical integration to better secure scarce resources and to reduce transactions costs; for example, steel producers have acquired coal mines (Nolan and Yeung, 2001). Diversification has also been driven by the resistance to mergers and consolidations among relatively strong domestic firms. With the support of local politicians, charismatic and strong CEOs have been able to block acquisitions that appear to threaten local interests. In the private sector, some business groups appear to diversify in an opportunistic manner but lack long-term commitments to the industries they enter. These projects are likely to be sold after the private groups have collected their expected profits or when they cannot tolerate the temporary losses.

The net effect of all differing patterns of emergence and growth is the high probability that each of China's business groups is made up of a variety of enterprises with widely divergent investment opportunities and future profit potential. As well as underperforming firms, most groups will include cash-cow type firms in their portfolio of businesses to provide reliable revenue streams. Better-managed firms will have created new enterprises in areas with many opportunities. Underperforming enterprises should be candidates for further turnaround or liquidation. How quickly and how efficiently group managements address these adjustments will be critical and will depend upon the effectiveness of firm corporate governance, which must simultaneously provide adequate supervision and monitoring and afford managers sufficient autonomy to make strategic business decisions.

Organisational structure of mainland China's business groups

Keister (2001: 338) defines China's largest groups as 'stable structures with distinct boundaries distinguished by long-term lending and trade ties among member firms that are legally independent'. The reference to the legal independence of member firms requires qualification. China's company law requires that, if a new industry or activity is not included in the parent company's founding charter, it is required either to amend its charter or register the new activity in a new company. Amendment procedures are more costly and time-consuming than the new company registration process and firms often set up new firms as a matter of legal expedience. This is particularly true when a group seeks to enter a new provincial or city market. Local governments prefer to have more independent and taxable companies registered in their region because they generate more revenue; consequently, a wholly-owned subsidiary of a corporation, not registered as an independent company, may confront bureaucratic obstacles to its operations (Ma and Lu, 2005). In this respect, the legal independence of member firms simply reflects a legal distortion. With less cumbersome amendment procedures, firms would more frequently organise as unified hierarchical organisations.

Second, as the business group became the central government's preferred organisational form, it has attained a high degree of legitimacy. Some firms have thus adopted the legal form without taking advantage of the form's organisational attributes. The requirements to register as a business group are relatively modest. To be formally recognised by China's State Administration for Industry and Commerce, business groups are required to have a paid-in capital of 50 million RMB (US$6 million); possess at least five affiliated companies; and the total registered capital of the core and other affiliated companies should be over 100 million yuan. In addition, the parent company should have identifiable ownership ties with its affiliates, and affiliates of the group should be legally independent entities (Ma and Lu, 2005). As these requirements are easily met, many city governments and private entrepreneurs have adopted this form to hold assets with no operational linkages. Such holding or shell companies are 'empty groups' (Hahn and Lee, 2006) and they are numerous but not necessarily significant from an economic perspective.

The National Team, the large provincial and city business groups described by Keister, Nolan and others, are more significant in this regard. The organisational structure of a typical Chinese business group is depicted in Figure 6.1. Keister (1998) suggests that structural variation among groups has declined due in part to the state's attempts to influence group structure. The most significant structural variation pertains to the centralisation of authority and the autonomy of the member firms. Some business groups are managed in a highly centralised hierarchical manner, with a core firm actively involved in the strategic affairs of each

Figure 6.1 Organisational structure of the typical Chinese business group

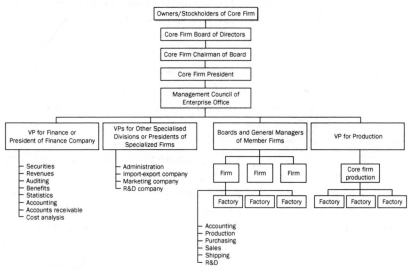

Source: Keister (1998).

member firm. Others are more decentralised, and inter-firm relationships are managed in a more cooperative manner.] Ownership ties within affiliated firms are often ambiguous and ill-defined. Keister (2001) argues that the key dimensions of group structure are prior social contacts among managers and officials, and the debt, credit and trading linkages that follow from these contacts.

With regard to Figure 6.1, [control of the core firm is nominally exercised by owners and shareholders of the core firm through a board of directors and a management council headed by the president.] Control and coordination of affiliate firm members is exercised through the structure of interlocking directorates among the boards and general management of member firms.] When a firm joins a business group, ownership of the firm is partially transferred to the group, allowing the group to be represented on the member's board of directors. Keister (1998) proposes that Chinese managers view these interlocking directorships in a positive light because they are seen as a principal means 'for sharing of rare business information and the trading favours among firms' (Keister, 1998: 412). A second important feature is the existence of an internal finance company (*caiwu gongsi*) that performs an important insider lending function. The finance company is 'a specialised firm that collected and redistributed funds within the group and also obtained funds through state banks on behalf of member firms' (Keister, 1998: 415). During the period of transition when state subsidies were being redirected and reduced and private capital markets remained significantly underdeveloped, the funds available through an internal finance company were considered to be a primary motivation to joining a business group.

However, not all business groups were granted permission by the state to form an internal finance company. For groups lacking a finance company, an alternative financial redistribution or cross-subsidisation principle becomes essential to group functioning. Keister (1998) finds that group affiliates will pay a price premium for goods and an interest rate premium for loans to do business with members of another group. In particular, firms in the coastal regions and economic trial areas have tended to have a better step-up and superior access to capital or important raw materials. Firms from these favoured regions were more likely to be senders of goods, loans and managerial personnel to firms located outside of these areas, in less developed markets. Moreover, firms in favoured regions were highly unlikely to be dependent receivers of loans, personnel or goods from firms located in less developed markets. These dependency patterns have become institutionalised as firms from less developed areas have accepted linkages because they provide security (Keister, 2001: 337). Keister's results support the contention that inequality in market access may be perpetuated by inter-firm relations developed during transition, making it increasingly difficult for firms located in poorly developed regions to improve their status, even in the long run. The pattern of cross-subsidisation implied in these transactions is that dependent firms pay an insurance premium for the secure access to capital and materials from the centrally-located core firm. The implied insurance principle differs markedly from that found among Japanese *keiretsu* member firms (Lincoln, Gerlach and Ahmidjian, 1996). In the latter case, stronger firms prop up weaker firms by smoothing profit fluctuations. In Chinese business groups, long-term relations among enterprise managers increase their reluctance to abandon lending and trade relations in established business groups. The durability of these linkages was advantageous early in the reform period but their persistence may create inefficiencies that have negative long-term consequences (Keister, 2001: 356).

Governance

The emergent governance system is the sum of shareholder linkages, debt relationships and recurrent trading linkages, and is best described as insider governance (Child, 2000). Effective control over an enterprise is exercised by insiders, managers and local state holding companies. Monitoring and intervention by external stockholders and other providers of capital is minimal. Control by insiders exposes the enterprise to the risk is of self-serving behaviour, corruption, asset stripping and profit diversion (Claessens, Djankov and Lang, 2000b). On the other hand, given limited legal protection for property rights in China, an insider-dominated governance system may be well aligned with the broader institutional environment (Dyck, 2001).

The state's policy of maintaining a significant ownership stake in numerous enterprises creates a difficult dilemma. On the one hand, the state wants enterprises to be managed efficiently; on the other, the state does not want enterprises to be operated solely for the purposes of wealth maximisation. Consequently, most enterprises have multiple objectives and enterprise managers lack clear goals and decision-making criteria. Moreover, because property rights remain undefined, decisions about cash flows derived from the use and disposal of nominally-owned state assets are subject to considerable discretion by enterprise managers. Because managers have only weak lines of accountability to entities external to the firm, there is an absence of an effective ultimate principal (Clarke, 2003). Lin (2001) suggests that the problem is one of 'agents without principals'.

Ma et al. (2006) characterise the situation as one of 'ownership voids' and conjecture that the formation of business groups is a solution to the 'absent principal' problem. Oversight by managers in the business group's core firm is a second-order form of governance, but core firm managers act as de facto owners of state-owned assets during an uncertain institutional transition. With primary instructions to create value and build strong national and internationally competitive enterprises, groups have implied priorities and possess the capacity to influence decision-making in the subsidiary enterprises affiliated to the group. Due to a shortage of qualified and experienced senior management at this stage of reform, the business group form provides an internal executive talent market. Ma et al. contend that, compared with government agencies or freestanding state-owned enterprises, managers of state-owned business groups have both the incentive and the means to monitor managers of listed companies effectively. Moreover, if the core firm group also owns a significant stake in a subsidiary, it has a strong interest in the subsidiary's welfare. Hahn and Lee (2006) support the management shortage argument. They suggest that at the provincial level, some business groups were formed by local governments with the intent of enhancing enterprise performance by using existing managerial talent across a wide array of businesses. For example, in Shandong province, the county government restructured the 29 SOEs under supervision into five business groups as a means of sharing scarce managerial talent.

A number of external factors are increasingly imposing economic discipline upon enterprise managers. The Chinese economy was once characterised by endemic shortages and hoarding but a huge production capacity has developed since the mid-1990s and virtually the entire industrial sector is now intensely competitive. Liberalisation of foreign investment along with the growth of international joint ventures has provided exposure to the new management models. A central government 'sink or swim' policy toward small and medium-sized enterprises has reduced state subsidies and imposed tighter credit restrictions, and consequently, tighter budget constraints. The combination of such factors suggests enterprise managers will be less likely to tolerate inefficiencies.

Equally, there are numerous concerns about the capacity of business groups to provide effective corporate governance over the medium to longer term. Many researchers (Huchet, 1999; Lin, 2001; Clarke, 2003) argue that the corporate governance practices of Chinese firms are seriously defective. Although competition has intensified and central government's sink or swim policy has created mounting pressure on enterprise managers, the power of competitive forces differs markedly in the protected and unprotected sectors of the economy. The large, National Team business groups are concentrated in the protected sectors of the economy where product market competition is less of a disciplinary force. Even in unprotected sectors, such as consumer electronics, household appliances, textiles and auto parts, where competition is indeed fierce, the leading business groups in this category are located in medium-sized townships outside the metropolitan areas. Their ability to create local employment has become important enough for the parent municipalities to provide local support. At this regional level, stronger firms are also required to bail out failing businesses. Politically motivated and coercive restructurings are more common on the lower echelons of the ladder; local authorities implement restructurings without regard to enterprise strategy and the development of sustainable market positions. This form of state support and coercion undermines the rationalising intent of the sink or swim policy.

In countries such as Japan and Korea where insider governance systems are prevalent among business groups, main banks often monitor and oversee business groups. It is doubtful that banks in China have the ability to play a similar role. In business groups that have been granted permission to establish their own financial companies, managers are less dependent upon bank credit and therefore a bank's ability to exercise influence on managerial decision-making is reduced. Chinese banks also appear to lack the human capital and organisational systems required for effective risk assessment. In addition, bank reform has not kept pace with developments in the industrial sector, and banks continue to be subject to political decision-making. The state is currently reducing subsidies to enterprises at the same time as banks are being encouraged to provide them with soft loans. Unsurprisingly, many loans are now non-performing and it is probable that banks will need recapitalisation to bring them back to stability. Chinese banks are reluctant to offer commercial loans to small low-prestige firms or to firms lacking debt guarantors or appreciable tangible assets. However, business group affiliates are more able to obtain loans because their core firm backing may supply debt guarantees.

The first reforms successfully cultivated a dynamic market orientation in the senior management of many enterprises. Powerful and charismatic chief executive officers closely identified with the rise of the particular enterprise have become a common phenomenon in China. Within a relatively short period, many strong CEOs, often in collusion with state authorities, have become entrenched in their positions and are now difficult to dislodge. Legally, shareholders should appoint both the chairman and CEO of an enterprise; in practice, the controlling shareholder (usually a state authority) chooses both and then notifies other shareholders accordingly.

Lin (2001) points out that that one or two board positions are made available for minority shareholders. However, the board does not act as an instrument of minority shareholders and Lin notes that there is no evidence of supervisory boards or non-executive members performing substantive oversight functions regarding senior management. Furthermore, officials who hold monitoring positions have few incentives to pursue their duties with any real vigour; heads of state line ministries and senior bureaucrats are compensated according to standardised public sector payment systems that bear no relationship to the performance of the SOEs under their control. He concludes that:

> The system of state ownership therefore comprises a cascading structure of agents who bear no residual risks yet exercise effective de facto property and control rights of assets owned by no clear and identifiable principal. Such an arrangement poses serious moral hazard problems... (Lin, 2001: 7)

Lee and Hahn (1999) propose that, due to inadequate oversight, business groups are characterised by large-scale asset diversion as managers seek to shield more valuable assets. Such diversions serve two purposes. By engaging in international joint ventures, spin-offs, acquisitions and the creation of new ventures, business groups create a series of pyramids or distant parent-child and grandparent-child subsidiaries, making effective evaluation extremely difficult. Within these non-transparent insider structures it is likely that senior managers may engage in self-serving behaviour such as taking perks or extracting rents for personal use. Alternatively, the core firm in the group may tunnel wealth away from minority investors, or from creditors to finance excessive growth and empire building: the result is very large but very inefficient businesses. In a phenomenon he describes as 'big firm fever', Granovetter (1995) suggests that because business groups attract soft capital to exercise control over ever-more distant empires, giantism and social prestige might be the ultimate goal for the firm.

In the aftermath of the 1997 financial crisis, China's lawmakers rushed to produce a raft of legal reforms designed to establish international best-practice corporate governance norms. Initiatives included restructuring state-owned enterprises, privatisation of small to medium-sized state-owned enterprises, bank reform, establishing internal controls through boards of directors and supervisory councils, a legal code for companies, principles of protection for minority stakeholders, and joining the World Trade Organization. China is confronted with the daunting task of constructing a completely new institutional infrastructure against a background of social unrest and the risk of mass unemployment. It should not be too surprising to find that international standards of corporate governance are not always vigorously pursued.

Governance in private business groups

Researchers have focused less attention on private business groups but there are some grounds for optimism about the effectiveness of their governance. PBGs merit separate consideration because their governance and ownership relations differentiate them from their state-induced counterparts. PBG governance is characterised by arrangements that concentrate ownership and control in the hands of a single entrepreneur or their family. In this respect, the governance of China's PBGs resembles that prevalent among overseas Chinese family business groups in Taiwan (Chung, 2001) and Southeast Asia (Carney and Gedajlovic, 2002a).

In terms of western corporate typologies, Chinese PBGs correspond closely to the conglomerate holding company. However, unlike their western counterparts, Chinese PBGs have not enjoyed preferential access to public equity, bank debt or inward foreign investment from foreign multinationals (Qian, 1996). Because they are reliant upon self-supplied capital, private entrepreneurs in China are less likely to engage in overinvestment, and as they face a hard budget constraint, these firms are probably the least wasteful of resources. Until recently, private firms have encountered discrimination from the state; consequently, PBGs may deliberately obscure the full extent of their activities. It is difficult to estimate how widespread this practice is, but it is believed that many private companies are set up and managed by figureheads or local bureaucrats either as a means of seeking local protectionism or to siphon off assets from state-owned enterprises. Given the novelty of the private firm and the very recent establishment of laws, taxation and bankruptcy provisions it seems that the private sector is much larger than officially recognised.

Performance

This section will review evidence available on the performance of Chinese business groups in terms of their size, their profitability, their 'insurance' principle, and their ability to facilitate technological 'catch-up'. Many business groups have exhibited rapid growth in revenues and have become China's largest enterprises. As many as eight groups were ranked in the 2003 Fortune Global 500, including State Grid Corp, CNPC, Sinopec, China Telecom, China Mobile, Sinochem, Shanghai Baosteel and Cofco. However, many of the larger business groups have remained relatively small in comparison with their international competitors (Nolan, 2001). Although Chinese business groups and Korea's *chaebol* groups have developed over a similar period of time, the Chinese groups are significantly smaller. Lee and Woo (2002) compared China's largest business groups in 1985 with Korea's largest business groups in 1986. In terms of asset values, Korea's largest 30 business groups were on average over six times larger in 1986 than the comparable top 30 Chinese business groups in 1985. Compared with the larger members of the Korean *chaebol*, Chinese business groups also have a relatively small share of the national GDP and lower levels of asset and revenue growth.

In the early stages of reform, the performance level of former state-owned enterprises varied significantly (Keister, 2000). In general, Keister finds that the greater the density of exchange relationships, the better the financial performance and productivity of the group members firms (Keister, 2000: 196). Firms with interlocking directorates, finance companies and research and development companies perform better financially and are more productive than firms in business groups lacking these qualities. Keister also finds that highly centralised, hierarchical business groups performed less well financially. Her results 'clearly indicate that firms in business groups with less authoritarian management styles performed better financially and are more productive' (Keister, 1998: 433). High levels of economic growth, continuing policy evolution, and growing competition are likely to combine in a dynamic business environment, and later studies confirm that the determinants of performance are likely to change as reforms progress.

Yiu, Bruton and Lu (2005) adopt a resource-based view on the performance of China's business groups. They hypothesise that the market-oriented resources and capabilities created by business groups are more valuable and are more likely to improve performance than the relational resources inherited from the state during the early phases of the transition process. Their data are based upon a 1998–99 survey of China's 250 largest business groups; this survey finds that the age of the business group is negatively related to its financial performance. They suggest that older business groups are more embedded in the pre-reform mentality and display greater organisational inertia than the more recently formed groups. In addition, they also find that a group's financial performance is negatively related to government ownership. Groups with a former state employee as CEO also perform poorly. In contrast, business groups that engage in more internal capability development or pursue more international diversification show significantly superior performance.

Lu and Yao (2006) examine the impact of diversification, ownership structure and control on profitability in 906 business group core firms or parent companies in 2001–02, some 10 years after Keister's study. Lu and Yao hypothesise that more diversified groups, groups with a high proportion of state ownership, and groups that have an internal finance company will achieve better performance. Using Tobin's Q and return on assets (ROA) as performance measures, Lu and Yao find a curvilinear relationship between diversification and performance. This suggests that an increase in diversification will improve performance initially, but very high levels of diversification will reduce performance levels, a result consistent with much of the literature on diversification and performance. They do not find much support for the hypothesis that state ownership is associated with better financial performance. Interestingly, and contrary to Keister's (1998) findings, Lu and Yao find that the presence of a finance company in the group has no impact on either measure of performance. They propose that, as these firms are now publicly listed, the importance of a finance company within a group begins to decline in the later stages of reform. Lu and Yao conclude that the determinants of financial performance in China's business groups is complex and that it is difficult to fully assess the impact of agency and control arrangements on performance at this time.

To find that the determinants of performance in state-owned business groups remain ambiguous should not be too surprising as managers of these enterprises continue to be subject to the discretionary power of line ministries, local party committees, local governments and state shareholders. Their involvement or interference may prove to be a double-edged sword. While some state agencies may extend a 'helping hand' by providing access to scarce resources and opportunities, others may conceal a 'grabbing hand' that expropriates value or imposes unwanted burdens on the firm (Shleifer and Vishny, 1998). Given the complex goal structures of business groups in a transitional economy, it is necessary to consider explanations of performance, including other hypotheses about the role of business groups such as the insurance and catch-up hypotheses.

With regard to the insurance hypothesis there is very little concrete evidence. Keister's (2001) study suggests that core firms provide debt and assured trade links for their affiliates in return for a transaction premium. To the extent that these relationships persist, groups would appear to embody a power-dependence dynamic in which dependent members support a powerful core firm. Alternatively, core firms may have an incentive to prop up the weaker firms during the periods in which the group is developing capabilities; this is particularly true in the regionally-based business groups that are prevalent in China's fragmented market. Some firms are seeking 'national status' and endeavour to build domestic distribution networks and acquire firms in distant parts of the country in order to create a national presence. To achieve this, firms may engage in acquisition strategies that require self-generated funds to acquire and build assets. As discussed above, formidable barriers are encountered when this strategy is adopted. Hahn and Lee's (2006: 227) asset diversion hypothesis is also consistent with the view that the core firms invest in subsidiary firms. This hypothesis suggests that enterprise managers extract funds from the core firms and invest in subsidiary businesses. It is more difficult for insiders to monitor subsidiaries and there is less risk that their assets will be extracted by the state. One study suggests that the expectation of state extraction is realistic; Cheung, Jing, Rau and Stouraitis (2007) found that business groups owned and controlled by a local government expropriate resources from minority shareholders and that the median value of the loss to these firms represents 45 per cent of the value of the related transaction.

Studies of spin-offs suggest managers can be discriminating in their investment decisions: while the core firms may support some subsidiary firms, they are anxious to dispose of other assets. Hahn and Lee (2006) suggest that about half of spin-offs are undertaken to pool capital, to expand scale, and to find a better or more flexible way of utilising assets and to enhance accountability. Another half are carried out to address the problem of surplus workers and to reduce interference from the state. This pattern suggests that the assets initially allocated to a business group are of very divergent potential. Subsequently, enterprise managers seeking to create viable enterprises may be engaged in restructuring in a rational manner, investing in businesses with potential while separating and discarding low-potential businesses.

If China's business groups are intended to facilitate the process of technological catch-up, we should expect to see firms developing capabilities through a variety of transactions. Simultaneous cross-subsidisation, spin-offs and acquisition are consistent with the acquisition of capabilities needed to operate at the technological frontier (Gerlach, 1997). However, with the exception of Nolan and his colleagues, there is little published work on how China's leading enterprises develop capabilities.

Nolan (2001) argues that China's national champions are overly diversified and confront difficulties in establishing internationally competitive strength in a single core business. National champions are embroiled in a constant battle with domestic small and medium-sized enterprises that have very low costs and protection from local authorities. The National Team continue to encounter difficulties in downsizing their new workforces. Nolan argues that the global business revolution has created large but highly focused firms in which major players have consolidated around core technologies and outsourced non-essential functions to highly-specialised global suppliers. Specialised suppliers benefit from economies of scale and scope in the products and services they supply to the core firm. Nolan points out that when Japan and Korea were engaged in technological catch-up, European and American firms tended to be vertically integrated and embedded in protected national environments. Japanese firms made innovative use of an external specialised subcontract system, creating a competitive advantage. Subsequently, large US and western firms have largely imitated these organisational innovations.

The catch-up scenario is different and more difficult in China. The supply networks available to China's national champions are weak and consequently the better domestic firms are engaged in supplying western buyers. The member firms of China's business groups are geographically scattered, imposing large transportation burdens on China's aspiring global giants. Moreover, China's business groups have generally established partnerships with weak internal suppliers who can be easily dominated but bring very little capability to the table. In addition, business groups' strategy of diversification is in marked contrast to the consolidation trend in global big business.

Similarities between Korean *chaebol*, Japanese *keiretsu* and China's business groups should not be overstated. Chinese business groups typically lack the equivalent of the Sogo Sasha, the international trading group at the centre of Japanese business groups. Importantly, there are also substantial differences in scale. China has nominated at least 160 firms to be national champions; regional governments have duplicated this pattern. As noted by Nolan, China's big groups are quite small in comparison with their international competition. In addition, unlike Japan and Korea, China has targeted a very large number of companies for government support. While the *chaebol* and *keiretsu* developed their organisational capabilities through internal or 'organic' growth, China's business groups represent a regrouping of existing state-owned assets consisting of public research institutes and manufacturing enterprises. Moreover, state authorities and main banks have closely monitored the *chaebol* and *keiretsu*. In contrast, Chinese business groups created their own financial companies, thus reducing their dependence on external finance. Furthermore, whereas the *keiretsu* were renowned for assisting distressed firms in their group, Chinese core firms seem to lack the managerial turnaround capacity to perform this function and would appear more interested in distancing themselves from underperforming affiliates.

7

Hong Kong based business groups

If the function of business groups is to solve the problems associated with institutional voids, then they should not exist in Hong Kong. The territory of Hong Kong is one of the most advanced places in the world in which to conduct business. It is an open economy and an international finance centre with a vast array of commercial and investment banks. Its communications and transportation infrastructure has long been among the most impressive in the world, while the efficiency of Hong Kong's judicial system is exemplary. In terms of the quality of its institutional governance structures, Hong Kong is in close competition with the famously virtuous places like Singapore and the Scandinavian states. The quality of the corporate governance infrastructure is also very high. On measures of the protection provided to minority shareholders, creditor rights, and accounting standards, Hong Kong is generally rated close to standards in the USA and the UK (La Porta, Lopez-de-Silanes and Shleifer, 1999). A study based upon data from the International Country Risk Guide rated 68 countries on factors such as the risk of expropriation and repudiation of contracts by government, administrative effectiveness, the quality of bureaucracy, and rule of law, found that Hong Kong rated highest on each measure (Olson, Sarna and Swamy, 2000).

However, business groups do exist in Hong Kong. Of the 650 firms listed on the Stock Exchange of Hong Kong (SEHK), some 44 per cent are affiliated to a business group (Claessens, Fan and Lang, 2002). Perhaps this is because so much of the business activity of Hong Kong's firms originates from and takes place outside of the territory in less well-developed institutional environments. Hong Kong firms are major direct investors in mainland China and other parts of Southeast Asia. Hong Kong's largest firms are also intermediaries for non-Hong Kong firms seeking to enter the Chinese mainland, and they receive major flows of portfolio and direct foreign investment from other parts of Asia,

Europe and North America. More recently, Chinese mainland firms located in Hong Kong have become important investors in Hong Kong and other parts of Asia. Indeed, Hong Kong firms are so internationalised that economic geographer, Henry Yeung (2004) suggests that Hong Kong's largest enterprises occupy a 'transnational space'. Following its return to the sovereignty of China, Hong Kong is administered as a Special Administrative Region (SAR) of the People's Republic of China under what is called 'one country, two systems'. Under this arrangement, judgments made by Hong Kong's courts are not enforceable in the mainland. Hence, the territorial reach of Hong Kong's institutional infrastructure is very limited. Hong Kong is a small place and few of its business groups confine their business activities to the region. Because two institutional systems at very different levels of development exist in close proximity, business groups located in highly-developed Hong Kong can potentially perform value-creating functions in China, which, since its opening to trade and investment in 1978, is in an earlier phase of capitalist development.

Identifying a population of Hong Kong business groups is problematic. Many firms that were originally founded in Hong Kong and are still listed on the SEHK have removed their registration from Hong Kong. As they are now registered in Caribbean states, such as Bermuda and the Cayman Islands, these firms should technically be considered as foreign enterprises. The most comprehensive typology of Hong Kong's business groups is provided by Au, Peng and Wang (2000) who identify four separate types of business group based upon their geographic origins: these are the British Hongs, Hong Kong Chinese firms, Southeast Asian firms and mainland Chinese firms. See Table 7.1 for sample firms of each type. These business groups can be summarised as follows:

- *The British Hongs:* Founded in the middle of the nineteenth century, the British Hongs dominated trade in the territory and later became the owners of Hong Kong's ports, warehouses, electric communications and transportation utilities. Following the Sino-British Joint Declaration in 1984 that established the timing of Hong Kong's return to the sovereignty of China, the Hongs have been in retreat from their positions of dominance. Many were acquired by Chinese entrepreneurs, while others relocated their principal registration to the UK or Bermuda and adopted long-term strategies to reduce their dependence upon Hong Kong.

- *Hong Kong Chinese firms:* These firms are those founded after 1948 by domestic Hong Kong Chinese entrepreneurs, often migrants from

Table 7.1 Largest Hong Kong firms grouped by geographical origin

British Hongs	Hong Kong Chinese	Southeast Asia	Mainland Chinese
HSBC Holdings	Cheung Kong	First Pacific	China Telecom
Swire	Hutceson Whampoa	CK Pokphand	Citic Pacific
Jardine	Sung Hung Kai	Sino Land	China Merchants
	Henderson Land	COSCO Pacific	
	Wharf	China Resources	
	New World		

Source: Based on Au, Peng and Wang (2000).

mainland China. Typically beginning as small export-oriented manufacturing firms, the most successful entrepreneurs accumulated significant capital during the boom-bust-boom cycle in Hong Kong's property market during the 1960s and 1970s. Successful property-based entrepreneurs used cash flows from property to acquire the assets of retreating British Hongs and to found numerous new ventures, especially as first-movers in the mainland after 1978. These entrepreneurs have constructed very large, highly-diversified conglomerates. Groups founded by these entrepreneurs now represent the dominant entrepreneurial force in Hong Kong.

- *Southeast Asian firms:* The Southeast Asian states of Singapore, Malaysia, Indonesia, Philippines and Thailand host a very large ethnic Chinese diaspora, which has formed a dominant entrepreneurial elite in each of these states since 1945. While enjoying much economic power, these entrepreneurs have often confronted political instability and discrimination in their adopted homes. To preserve their wealth, many entrepreneurs have established Hong Kong based firms as a safe haven for their capital. In addition, Hong Kong provides access to international capital and the know-how needed to facilitate inward investment to support their ventures in Southeast Asia. These business groups are principally active in sectors such as property, hotels, shipping, media and the joint-venture manufacturing initiatives that were vital in the initial industrialisation and continued growth of the ASEAN economies since the 1970s.

- *Mainland Chinese firms:* After 1978, China's central government and numerous provincial governments began to establish enterprises in

Hong Kong as a means of attracting capital, technology and management know-how, and to obtain experience in a market economy. Other enterprises were established as instruments of Chinese government policy to displace British firms from their dominant positions in strategic areas such as telecommunications and aviation. Some mainland Chinese firms are older, for example, in 1872 Chinese merchants founded China Merchants Steam Navigation as a competitor to the duopoly held by Jardine Shipping and Swire Shipping. China Merchants now owns scores of Hong Kong based enterprises. More typical of modern-day mainland-controlled firms is China Resources, which serves as a representative of China's exporters. Business groups controlled and significantly owned by mainland entities (red-chips and H-shares) now account for 20 per cent of the market capitalisation on the SEHK, a figure that is likely to grow in the future.

Chapter 6 deals with the origins and growth of mainland Chinese business groups and Chapter 9 addresses the origin and growth of Southeast Asian ethnic Chinese family business groups. In this chapter we deal with the decline of the British Hongs, with the rise of domestic Chinese capital and its structure, governance and performance.

The rise and formation of Hong Kong based business groups

In the century following its establishment as a British colony in 1842, Hong Kong was a flourishing entrepôt. It was a point of trans-shipment for imports and exports between China and North America, Europe and other parts of Asia. Britain itself was not a major trading partner, which may account in part for the UK government's adoption of an 'arm's length' approach to Hong Kong's affairs. The territory's economy was dominated by the 'Hongs', a group of colonial business groups that were discussed in Chapter 2. These business groups constructed a transportation and communications infrastructure to support Hong Kong's role as an entrepôt. The Hongs soon faced stiff competition from local traders and the number of wealthy Chinese in Hong Kong grew rapidly. Technological change reduced the Hongs' communication advantages and as early as the 1860s, they recognised that they were vulnerable to competition from small merchants. Crisswell notes that:

men like William Keswick of Jardine's decided that their future profits lay in areas outside Chinese competence ... the big Western firms would act as suppliers of capital, skills and technology to China ... the Hongs began to evolve from merchant houses dealing in commodities into management agencies concerned with shipping, insurance, utilities, engineering and banking. (Crisswell 1981: 121)

This phase of Hong Kong's history came to an abrupt end with the Japanese invasion and occupation of 1941–45, which brought the suspension of all normal activities and institutions, significant physical destruction, and the flight or death of a large proportion of the approximately 1.6 million population. When the territory was returned to British administration, it had a population of only 600,000, 80 per cent of whom were suffering from malnutrition. This wretched situation was made worse by two political developments in the early 1950s. The first was the outcome of the last stages of the civil war in China and the emergence of Communist rule under Mao. This produced a flow of refugees into the territory, quadrupling its population in just a few years. The second event was the outbreak of the Korean War and the consequent US/UN embargo on trade with China, which prevented any possible revival of Hong Kong's entrepôt function. In 1953 the territory faced a dim future with an impoverished population of some 2.4 million largely uneducated refugees, no natural resources apart from a harbour, and a very limited manufacturing base. Nonetheless, in the next 50 years Hong Kong was to accomplish an 'economic miracle'; today, its residents live in one of the world's most prosperous territories. According to IMF figures, Hong Kong enjoys the world's sixth largest GDP per capita at purchasing power parity of some $36,500, above that of Canada, Japan, Germany and Switzerland.

In prior chapters we have seen that the resource-constrained East Asian economies of Japan, Korea and Taiwan each adopted state-led economic development strategies focused upon export-oriented industrialisation and programmes designed to assist domestic firms engaging in technological catch-up. In marked contrast, authorities in Hong Kong adopted a laissez-faire position and refrained from direct involvement in promoting technology development (Yeh and Ng, 1994). It was only in the early 1990s that the state became more actively involved in the promotion of competitiveness and productivity-enhancing technologies (Carney, 1997).

In 1953, with few alternative options, the pattern of Hong Kong's resource endowments dictated that it could only make a living based upon export-oriented manufacturing that would utilise the abundant and flexible low-cost labour. The origins of Hong Kong's technical and entrepreneurial capability did not come through the dominant Hongs, who had few manufacturing capabilities, but from the inward migration of capital and skills from the Shanghai cotton spinners. These relatively large-scale industrialists had acquired organisational and technical capabilities from their Japanese competitors who had sought to capture the Chinese cotton market during China's republican period. The Shanghai Chinese cotton industrialists proved to be formidable competitors on their own ground (Wong, 1988). However, the engine driving Hong Kong's industrialisation was provided by tens of thousands of new small firms using relatively low technology and small-scale production characterised by extensive subcontracting (Carney, 1998a).

The small-scale manufacturing sector that appeared in this phase of Hong Kong's development grew very rapidly. With low barriers to entry, competition was based upon a fierce set of trade-offs pertaining to cost, time and price. In 1955, the only manufacturing sector in which large-scale activities existed to any significant extent was cotton-spinning, where there were three mills employing more than 1,000 workers. Textiles and apparel still accounted for more than 50 per cent of manufacturing employment in 1970, followed by plastic products (13 per cent) and electrical appliances and components (9 per cent).

Hong Kong's business groups did not seek to enter the automobile, chemical and heavy electrical industries, which had characterised the development of the hierarchical modern industrial corporation in the USA, UK, Germany and Japan (Chandler, 1990). Redding (1990) notes that Hong Kong's family business groups have failed to master the skills needed for entry into capital-intensive industries or businesses that require coordination of complex functional areas. In industries such as watchmaking, Hong Kong firms have remained dependent upon Japanese firms for technological innovations and for high-value components (Glasmeir, 1994). While Hong Kong's trading, banking and retailing sectors have readily absorbed information technology and adopted organisational practices that foster productivity, few manufacturing firms have developed proprietary assets or firm-specific competencies (Carney, 1998a). Indeed, Lui and Chiu (1994) suggest that the relocation of manufacturing to lower-cost sites represents evidence, not of technical upgrading but the continuation of labour-intensive low-cost production strategies. In a review of innovation in Hong Kong's manufacturing sector, Leung and Wu (1995) find little evidence of domestic research and development activity or of firms developing linkages with technology-based firms.

At the close of the 1970s, a new set of dynamics was again to shift Hong Kong's economic and institutional structures. The first was the restoration of Deng Xiaoping to a position of authority in the Chinese Communist Party. In a series of speeches after 1978, Deng began to articulate a more pragmatic approach to politics and to promote an economy based around the theme of the Four Modernisations. Economic modernisation implied a growing openness to foreign trade and investment. This gradual opening of China after some 30 years of isolation marked a watershed in Hong Kong's development. The 'open door' economic policy gave Hong Kong firms access to supplies of inexpensive labour and land at just the moment when they were becoming unavailable in Hong Kong. Throughout the 1980s, the migration of manufacturing to the mainland led to deindustrialisation in Hong Kong. Manufacturing employment in Hong Kong peaked at around 1 million workers in 1981 and then began to fall dramatically, reaching around 400,000 in 1994.

Second, in the late 1970s there was also growing concern about the erosion of the territory's ability to compete in international markets due to increasing factor costs, especially of labour, but also of land. The relocation of manufacturing led to calls in Hong Kong for the state to intervene and assist with 'the urgent need for industries to switch to higher value-added products and processes' (Yeh and Ng, 1994: 449). Perhaps due to the success of neighbouring Taiwan and Singapore, one focus of the policy debate is the development of a comparable high-technology manufacturing industry within the territory of Hong Kong. While this debate has fuelled the growth of investment in human capital, especially in the university sector, the debate about technology upgrading has more often focused upon the issue of real estate and the expressed need for science parks and technology centres (Carney and Gedajlovic, 2000).

Indeed, a major if not the prime economic driver of capital accumulation in this period was the spiralling costs of land and the opportunities in domestic and commercial property development. However, Hong Kong's property markets are not for the faint-hearted. A series of crises such as riots resulting from the Cultural Revolution in 1967, a stock market crash in 1973, concerns over the Thatcher-Deng discussions regarding Hong Kong's sovereignty in 1982, Tiananmen Square in 1989, and the Asian financial crisis in 1997, each stimulated periods of extreme turbulence and volatility in property markets. Entrepreneurs such as Lee Shau-kee (Henderson Land and Sun Hung Kai Properties), Li Ka Shing (Cheung Kong Holdings), and Cheng Yu Tung (New World Development), accurately read the direction of property price movements and would subsequently form the basis of Hong Kong's leading business groups.

The marginalisation of the Hongs and the rise of local business groups

On the eve of China's opening to the West in 1976, six British colonial business groups dominated the economy of Hong Kong: the Hong Kong Bank, Jardine, Hutchison, Swire, Kadoorie and Wheelock and Marden.

Approximately 200 companies controlled by these groups were worth 68 per cent of the stock market's capitalisation (Wong, 1996). Rivalry between the groups was sometimes strong, for example, the longstanding rivalry between Swire and Jardine. However, for the most part these groups were linked to one another through cross-directorships, equity linkages, joint ventures, or through their membership of exclusive clubs, such as the Royal Hong Kong Jockey Club. These six groups controlled the transportation and financial infrastructure of the entrepôt economy. In addition, political power and the policy process were in the hands of a small elite of mainly British administrators. Wong (1996) suggests that an elite structure of the business and policy communities exercised power through a tacit alliance consisting of overlapping membership in political bodies, boards of directors, and government advisory boards.

The 1960s and 1970s were Hong Kong's economic 'golden years' (Welsh, 1993). Despite the continuation of British administration, during this period the dominant or incumbent British-owned business groups were bypassed by the emergence of local capital. One contemporary study suggested that 'as Chinese enterprises from both within and without the colony expanded and began to show their readiness to muscle in, some of the old established Hongs suffered what appeared to be 'a collective failure of nerve' (Welsh, 1993: 495). Following periodic bouts of illiquidity, two colonial groups, Hutchison and Wharf, were acquired in hostile takeovers by Chinese entrepreneurs Li Ka Shing and Y.K.K. Pau in 1978. Interestingly, it was the sale of their equity stake in the Hong Kong banks that was pivotal in effecting this takeover.

In 1984, Y.K.K. Pau also acquired the Wheelock group. The Hong Kong Bank successfully sought to diversify internationally. It relocated its principal stock market listing to London and acquired major banks in the USA, Australia and UK, thus reducing its dependence on Hong Kong. Jardine adopted a defensive strategy; delisting from the Hong Kong Stock Exchange, it increased its cross-holdings in its Hong Kong affiliates and became a private company. Only the affiliates of the Swire group adopted a vigorous pro-China strategy. However, by 1986, the remaining independent colonial-era groups, Jardine, Swire and Hong Kong Bank, accounted for just over 21 per cent of the stock market's capitalisation (Wong, 1996).

Jardine-Matheson provides an interesting example of the difficulties faced by colonial-era firms as they sought to expand their international activities. Following the Sino-British agreement on the repatriation of Hong Kong in 1984, Jardine-Matheson signalled its intention to diversify its operations internationally. Specifically, Jardine re-incorporated in Bermuda and announced its objective to reduce its Hong Kong assets from 72 per cent to 50 per cent (Jones, 1998). However, attempts to acquire the US investment firm, Bears-Stearn, in 1989, and the UK conglomerate, Trafalgar House, both resulted in heavy losses. Ironically, in order to pay down debts resulting from these internationalisation failures, Jardine has had to significantly reduce its international holdings in Hawaii and South Africa.

Part of the difficulty faced by colonial-era business groups is that their core competence was local knowledge and reputation and these location-specific assets are not easily transferable to new regions. In addition, the loose, equity-based, cross-holding structure characteristic of colonial agents promotes neither intra-firm coordination nor the acquisition of new competencies. Attempts to internationalise are generally carried out through the acquisition of existing firms because the narrow competence base of colonial-era business groups cannot support market-seeking foreign investments. Moreover, the activities of colonial-era business groups are concentrated in service sectors requiring in-situ production and therefore efficiency-seeking relocation is not possible (Reich, 1991). As a consequence, the overseas investments of the Hongs consist mainly of passive asset holdings. In these circumstances, the Hongs may exercise de jure control over acquired assets, but can do little to add value in contexts where they possess little local knowledge and do not have an established reputation.

Perhaps due to their colonial legacy in the territory, the Hongs were not well positioned to exploit the opportunities afforded by China's opening to the world. The changing of the balance in their competitive advantage also handicapped the Hongs. At one point they constituted the principal source of technological and foreign management skills and of contacts in international markets. Increasingly, however, other sources of capital became available through the establishment of foreign banks in Hong Kong and there were improvements in the liquidity of the stock market. The return of overseas-educated personnel increased the supply of high-quality human capital and Hong Kong's investment in secondary and tertiary education increased dramatically. The growing experience of foreign multinationals in China reduced the value that Hongs could contribute through intermediation. After the handover of sovereignty in 1997, the remaining independent Hongs halted their international diversification strategies and instead focused upon making their core businesses internationally competitive.

Business groups from Hong Kong: the rise of local capital

The Hongs' domination of the Hong Kong economy could not survive the return to China's sovereignty and it was probably inevitable that local capitalists would emerge to share and eventually seize economic power. A class of Chinese entrepreneurs who were connected to and had accommodated the colonial administration already existed in Hong Kong, including such figures as Sir Kenneth Fung and Sir Robert Ho Tung. For example, Robert Ho Tung was part of a distinguished comprador family who served the Hong Kong Bank and Jardine. Compradors have been described as a bridge between the East and the West in China (Hao, 1970) and their skills were certainly an important source of local entrepreneurship. Second, as described above, following the embargo on trade with China, Shanghai entrepreneurs, especially in the field of cotton spinning, migrated to Hong Kong, where they provided an important source of entrepreneurship (Wong, 1988). However, the most significant development between 1960 and 1980 was the materialisation of a dynamic entrepreneurial class of self-made men and women who assembled large business groups that were to eclipse the incumbent Hongs in a decisive fashion. The emergence of an entrepreneurial class in Hong Kong may be viewed as a multistage process in which astute entrepreneurs accumulated vast personal wealth by rapidly and swiftly exploiting short-term opportunities and adroitly moving on to new opportunities thrown up by a dynamic political and economic environment (Weidenbaum and Hughes, 1996; Yeung, 2004).

The first stage is typically cast as a 'rags to riches' story in which penniless émigrés from mainland China worked very hard to establish manufacturing businesses in the 1950s. Many entrepreneurs fit this profile and Li Ka Shing is perhaps the paradigmatic case. In one biography he is described as 'a penniless Chaozhou boy whose only legacy from his father was a wisdom and knowledge' (Chan, 1996: 90). However, we should also note that many entrepreneurs came from fairly affluent mercantile classes. In the second stage, during the 1960s and 1970s, the major opportunity was provided by the dynamics of land and domestic property development in the new territories and by the market for commercial properties in Kowloon and on the island of Hong Kong. In this stage, the largest groups emerged and accumulated significant capital.

The third stage sees a significant internationalisation of Chinese capital. Following the opening to China and the prospect of Hong Kong's return to sovereignty in 1997, there was a two-way flow of capital. On the one hand, the major entrepreneurs began to export capital out of Hong Kong into their kinship and language group networks in Southeast Asia or to other high-growth centres such as Taipei, Singapore and Bangkok. Another trend was for entrepreneurs to purchase overseas property, especially in North America (Yeung and Olds, 2000). Some writers have characterised these investments as prudent risk diversification while others view it as the creation of the first wave of Chinese multinationals (Yeung, 2004).

While investing globally, self-made Hong Kong entrepreneurs hedged their bets and cultivated close linkages with politicians and bureaucrats from mainland China. These entrepreneurs began to invest directly in mainland opportunities and also serve as intermediaries and joint-venture partners for those seeking to establish a foothold in China. Nevertheless, it is important to establish that not all groups were quite so prolific in widening their international networks and multiplying their linkages with mainland China. Some of the groups that had made a fortune in Hong Kong's property markets, such as New World and Henderson Land, are heavily Hong Kong-centric and have failed to transcend the ethnic and geographic limitations. However, other groups have become highly cosmopolitan entrepreneurs who have developed comfortable working links with former colonial administrators,

Western bankers, Japanese and Taiwanese technologists, American management consultants, and Communist Party officials.

Hong Kong's major entrepreneurs have captured much attention, but the relatively small manufacturing businesses have followed a similar expansionary path in manufacturing Hong Kong property and investment in mainland China. These smaller, diversified enterprises promise to be a continuing source of entrepreneurial growth. Carney (1998b), examined the major investment decisions of Hong Kong's 50 largest manufacturing firms in 1994. These firms are relatively small by international manufacturing standards, with few firms having assets of more than US$1billion. Despite their relatively small size, each of these firms was typically engaged in the production of a variety of unrelated products. More surprisingly, 50 per cent of these manufacturers reported revenues from property development and almost all of them had located their manufacturing and had made investments in mainland China by 1994. Carney suggests that:

> The prevailing tendency among Hong Kong's mid-sized manufacturing firms is the adoption of a holding company format to support the pursuit of conglomerate or unrelated diversification. Once a certain size and scope of operations is reached many firms appear to break up and re-organise assets into two or more enterprises. (Carney, 1998b: 154)

Tam (1990) suggests that, due to family dynamics, such as the need to divide the family estate, Hong Kong's family firms are characterised by centripetal forces that produce a fissioning or break-up of the firm at a relatively small size. However, this pattern of growth is also consistent with the creation of a business group structure that can take advantage of opportunities in China. This pattern produces diversification at the level of the group while maintaining a focused product-market profile at the level of the enterprise.

Diversification in Hong Kong firms

Theories that emphasise lifecycle and stage dynamics suggest that Hong Kong enterprises will tend to adopt a diversified, wide-product market scope. Whitley (1992) describes the typical pattern of diversification as 'opportunistic investment' that results in diverse business portfolios lacking the coherence of a competence-based rationale. A strategic choice view of the family business group is found in Lasserre and Schutte (1995); they portray a product-market trajectory beginning with trading and moving on through manufacturing, banking and real estate, the ultimate goal being a 'golden diamond', which comprises positions in trade, industry, property and finance.

Anecdotal evidence suggests that the larger conglomerate business groups have been unsuccessful in developing stable portfolios beyond these positions and several have retreated back to the core businesses of real estate, property development, hotels and deal making. For example, Li Ka Shing diversified into telecommunications and publishing in the UK, taking stakes in firms such as Cable and Wireless, and the Pearson Group. In Canada, Li acquired Husky Oil and entered various ventures with CIBC bank. In Hong Kong, Li acquired Hong Kong Telecom and created a new firm, Pacific Century Cyber Works. These ventures have been successful in generating large profits for Hutchinson and Cheung Kong, Li's primary holding companies, but the equity stakes in these entities are quickly liquidated as Li rarely takes a role in the long-term management and development of these enterprises. A similar pattern is evident in companies such as Henderson Land.

Carney and Gedajlovic (2002b) studied 106 publicly-listed Hong Kong firms included in the Worldscope database to test the hypothesis that a firm's ownership concentration in family-controlled business groups would be positively related to product market diversification. However, their study found no support for the hypothesis. The reason is quite simple: at the enterprise level, Hong Kong firms are not particularly diversified. In a sample of 188 non-financial, publicly-listed firms in Hong Kong, Lins and Servaes (2002) found that only 29 per cent were diversified in two or more industries. They define a diversified firm as one that participates in two or more industries with a two-digit Standard Industrial Classification level, where the firm's most important industry segment accounts for less than 90 per cent of revenues. However, Lins and Servaes (2002) have also noted that 49.2 per cent of Hong Kong's publicly-listed firms are members of industrial groups. Hence, in Hong Kong's family business groups, group-level diversification occurs in another publicly-listed company, family estate or private holding company. Additionally, anecdotal data suggest that firms are more informally diversified as they engage in 'deal' syndication, or risk-sharing, project-specific ventures with friends and close business partners (Weidenbaum and Hughes, 1996).

Hong Kong business group structure and governance

In contrast to the voluminous literature on business groups in Japan, Korea and Taiwan, there are relatively few studies of Hong Kong based business groups. In one of the few descriptive studies, Wong (1996: 108) depicts Hong Kong business groups as complex, diverse, loosely connected and multi-centred. Almost all enterprises have concentrated ownership with a single dominant entrepreneur, family or corporate owner. However, determining the affiliation of an enterprise is often difficult: some firms appear to be members of more than one group, and firms sometimes change their primary affiliation in response to an active mergers and acquisitions market, syndicated deals to establish new enterprises, and partial equity exchanges. Due to the multi-centred, amorphous and dynamic nature of group affiliation and the difficulty in identifying stable business groups, there are few systematic studies available. Instead the literature on Hong Kong enterprises has focused upon its familial qualities, the critical role played by the founding entrepreneur, and the establishment of dense networked structures.

There is a large literature on the structural features and competitive strengths and weaknesses of the Chinese family firm in Hong Kong. Curiously, few of these studies have focused on the family group from a business group perspective. Historically, the Chinese family firm has been viewed as being plagued by factors such as altruism, nepotism, insularity and weak risk-bearing attributes that harm the longevity and efficiency of family enterprises and act as an obstacle to broader economic development (Whyte, 1996). Indeed, Max Weber (1992 [1930]) has famously characterised Chinese family firms as backward or pre-modern institutions beset with exclusionary values wherein loyalty to family inhibits the formation of cooperative relations with non-relatives (Fukuyama, 1995). Fukuyama argues that 'restrictive family bonds constrain the development of universal values and impersonal ties necessary for modern business organisation' (Fukuyama, 1995: 65). In the context of Hong Kong, Redding (1988: 109) concludes that Chinese family firms are governed by 'values which facilitate the initiating phase of entrepreneurship but which place barriers to the higher levels of coordination necessary for growth of the individual firm to large scale'.

The characteristic feature of the Chinese family firm's organisational structure is the concentration of decision-making and management in the hands of family members and close trusted associates (Whitley, 1992; Chen,

1995). Chan's (1982) historical perspective suggests that this structure has changed little in the modern era. Strategic issues and resource allocation decisions are rarely delegated to professional managers. Reliance on outsiders for managerial, technical and marketing skills is minimised when important issues arise. Where professional managers are employed, their roles are considered subordinate to entrepreneurial roles held by family members or trusted friends (Redding, 1990; Whitley, 1992). Even in very large business groups that possess a cadre of professional management, family owners retain strategic decision-making rights over issues such as executive appointments, capital allocations, and the discretion to make related-party transactions. For example, expatriate Scotsman, Simon Murray, one-time CEO of Li Ka Shing's Hutchison Whampoa described himself as 'the guy driving the truck, while Li's in the back telling me which way to go' (Chan, 1996: 118). Thus, although affiliated firms may be professionally managed, they remain 'family ruled' (Tsui-Auch, 2004). The family firm expects its employees to restrict their involvement to the products and services that create the company's profits (Chen, 1995). Family firms make little use of formal organisational structure, rules or written procedures (Chen, 1995). Nor do they typically create indirect or direct service functions such as personnel offices or market research. Whitley (1992) says that ethnic Chinese family firms exhibit much lower degrees of role-specialisation and work-standardisation than comparable UK or Japanese firms. Simple organisational structure is partly explained by small size, but as Kao (1993) notes, even larger enterprises maintain 'immature organisational patterns'.

Much analysis has focused upon the segmenting tendencies (Wong, 1985), fissioning and centripetal forces (Tam, 1990) that cause Hong Kong family firms to fracture and dissolve when the founder retires. This tendency is variously attributed to the absence of primogeniture, a succession pattern in which the first-born inherits the family estate, or to the inability of succeeding generations to retain their autonomy and manage their own business. Such familial patterns are believed to constrain enterprise growth and size and thus prevent family firms from establishing large-scale and broad-scope enterprises.

Despite the evident prevalence of small-scale family enterprises and the tendencies for firm-fragmentation, the emergence of large family-controlled businesses in Hong Kong suggests that some Chinese firms have managed to transcend their enterprise-size constraints through the adoption of a business group structure. The creation of larger-scale and more internationally-diversified enterprise groups has resulted in a change in the way scholars view family firms.

First, analysts have recognised that Chinese family enterprises are embedded in tight networks based on kinship, language and social relations and that the legal boundaries of the firm do not properly delineate its true scope. Indeed, some scholars suggest that using the model of the firm to study the activities of Asia's network form is a fundamental mistake (Biggart and Hamilton, 1992). The network structures of Hong Kong's family business groups consist of numerous business units, and both formal and informal joint ventures are tied together in a circuitous web of cross-holdings, but ultimately, they are held in a focal private company and controlled by an entrepreneur or family (Redding, 1990; Weidenbaum and Hughes, 1996). In their approach to business contracting, entrepreneurs adopt a discriminating contracting pattern of relational and arm's-length styles. For example, some writers point out that entrepreneurs engage in informal relational contracting with trusted partners in transactions related to joint ventures, creating deals, extending credit or transferring a business (Weidenbaum and Hughes, 1996). However, entrepreneurs adopt a more arm's-length style of contracting for routine transactions involving standard short-term contracts (Carney, 2005).

The personalised governance structure of family business groups actually facilitates the creation of complex network structures. Because owner-managers retain full decision rights over their enterprises, they have full discretion to engage in 'risky deals' and to commit their firm's assets on a handshake. Unlike professional managers, owners are relatively free to exercise a 'capacity to trust' (Redding, 1990) and cultivate *guanxi* (Xin and Pearce, 1996). In other words, the owners of family firms may access and use social capital as a key resource.

The networks of established ethnic Chinese family business groups are sometimes characterised as tribal, closed or impenetrable (Weidenbaum and Hughes, 1996). However, as we have noted, the social and economic networks of many of Hong Kong's new entrepreneurial class appear cosmopolitan and open; as well as family members, they include western bankers and capitalists and mainland communists (Yeung, 2004). The open nature of Hong Kong's business groups and their networks reflects the fact that decision-making power is so concentrated in the hands of the founder-entrepreneur and family that they are free to establish highly rational, value-maximising partnerships or more idiosyncratic deals with old friends and business partners.

Analysis of Hong Kong's family business groups' boards of directors suggests that owners will be proactive in appointing mainland directors to their boards, and that, similarly, Hong Kong red-chips will show preference to representatives from Hong Kong's Chinese business groups. This reflects new patterns of interdependence between the two (Au, Peng and Wang, 2000).

The preceding discussion suggests that the governance and structural characteristics of personally owned and managed firms have both advantages and disadvantages relative to professionally managed firms with widely dispersed ownership. On the one hand, linking ownership and control creates a powerful incentive for owner-managers to manage their operations efficiently and profitably. On the other hand, such tight control also allows majority owners to adopt inefficient practices that reflect their particular values and interests. Similarly, their preference for conglomerate holding companies and network linkages that produce a portfolio of alliances also has an impact on the kinds of competitive advantages that Hong Kong business groups will be able to sustain.

There is a considerable literature that proposes that the structure of Hong Kong's family business groups stems from their speculative orientation; they are frequently cast as 'deal structurers' rather than 'builders' who prefer short-term rents to long-term development of proprietary capabilities (Chu and MacMurray, 1993). Tachiki (1997) observes that family firms are most at ease with deal-driven investments, which are managed on a project-by-project basis. Projects commonly have a higher priority than formal business divisions, and entrepreneurs prefer to observe the development of an investment before formally committing to it (Tachiki, 1997). Chen (1995) proposes that the competitive advantage of the family business groups is rooted in their deal-making skills, and notes that a mentality of 'fast-in' and 'fast-out' permeates the deal-making approach of family business groups. Similarly, Lasserre and Schutte (1995) argue that Hong Kong's successful entrepreneurs owe much to the systematic exploitation of market imperfections that arise from either temporary scarcity or from the entrepreneur's access to privileged contacts (*guanxi*) and non-publicly available information. Many of these opportunities are self-limiting or otherwise ephemeral, and once rival firms locate the niche, assets are liquidated and diverted to another opportunity.

Carney and Gedajlovic (2002b) suggest that this deal-making approach will manifest as asset churning. Redding (1990) suggests that Hong Kong firms with concentrated ownership and personal control make little use of financial control mechanisms and lack the means of detecting and monitoring the effects of strategic adjustments. Indeed, many analysts cite the adoption of simple organisational structures and the paucity of professional managers as reasons why family business groups are ill-prepared to effect turnaround strategies. In contrast, firms controlled by salaried managers will be more likely to attempt to effect a turnaround of underperforming assets. The expected difference between 'churning' and 'turnaround' strategies should be reflected in higher observed levels of asset disposal in firms with coupled ownership and control – one should also expect to find a correlation between a project's need for capital investment and relatively high levels of asset disposal. Carney and Gedajlovic (2002b) tested the hypothesis that insider ownership of firms in Hong Kong is positively related to the disposal of fixed assets; however, their hypothesis was not supported. Hong Kong firms with a tighter coupling ownership and control are no more likely to dispose of fixed assets than other Hong Kong businesses. The absence of a relationship between asset disposals and inside ownership suggests that family business groups' deal-making activities may be focused on projects requiring investments in liquid rather than fixed assets or that firms may use off-balance-sheet accounting mechanisms and related-party transactions (Cheung, Rau and Stouraitis, 2006).

Performance

An examination of the value-enhancing and value-destroying hypotheses is handicapped by the relative absence of large sample studies of Hong Kong business groups. The following conclusions must therefore be treated with caution. Nevertheless, using anecdotal, direct and indirect data from several studies, it is possible to piece together a general but incomplete picture of business group performance.

First, like many Asian economies, a large majority of Hong Kong's firms are closely held by a single dominant family shareholder. Of 330 publicly-traded Hong Kong firms in 1996, 66.7 per cent were family-controlled, where control is defined as owning at least 20 per cent of equity (Claessens, Djankov and Lang, 2000b). Moreover, there is a positive correlation between the age of the firm and the control exercised by a dominant owner, in other words, as firms age they do not become more widely held, rather, the control of the dominant owner increases. What is most distinctive about Hong Kong's corporate sector is the concentration of wealth in the hands of a few families. In 1996, the 10 largest business families owned over 32 per cent of listed assets, and the top 15 business families owned assets worth 84 per cent of Hong Kong's 1996 GDP, the highest among all Asia's economies. By comparison, the wealth of the 15 richest US families in 1998 was 2.9 per cent of GDP.

While this level of wealth concentration may be interpreted as the superb performance of an entrepreneurial elite, Claessens et al. (2000b) suggest that wealth concentration is consistent with crony capitalism as a small number of families effectively control the economy. They speculate that rather than their superior business acumen, these families use their elite status to extract preferential treatment from senior government officials. Claessens et al. (2000b: 109) also suggest that this concentration of control might retard society's institutional development as 'a concentrated control structure of the whole corporate sector could lead to the suppression of minority rights and hold back the institutional development of legal and regulatory channels to enforce these rights'. However, it is difficult to see how this argument squares with Hong Kong's sophisticated and well-developed legal and regulatory structure.

Claessens et al. (2000b) find that, among Hong Kong firms, the average separation of cash-flow rights and control rights is at intermediate levels for the population of Asian firms. Hence there is a fairly strong probability that concentrated owners with an excess of control over cash-flow rights will have the capacity to expropriate minority shareholders. Such studies assume that excessive control over cash-flow rights is associated with the likelihood of minority shareholder expropriation and, ex ante, these firms can be expected to trade at lower market valuations.

In another multi-country study, Claessens, Djankov, Fan and Lang (2002) find that increases in the market valuations of Hong Kong enterprises correspond to increases in the cash-flow ownership by the largest shareholder. This result is consistent with the literature on the positive effects associated with concentrated ownership. Equally, the same study also found that increases in the control rights of the largest shareholder are accompanied by declines in firm value. This negative relationship is especially strong where there is a large wedge between ownership and control rights; in Hong Kong, it is also associated with statistically significant lower valuations (Claessens et al., 2002). In a companion study, Claessens, Djankov, Fan and Lang (1999a) find statistically significant results of shareholder expropriation among Hong Kong firms.

The strongest direct evidence for minority shareholder expropriation by Hong Kong firms is found in a study of the market valuation impact of the announcement of some 375 related-party transactions made by publicly-listed Hong Kong firms between 1998 and 2000 (Cheung, Rau and Stouraitis, 2006). This study distinguishes between transactions that are likely to result in expropriation (tunnelling), transactions that are likely to benefit listed firms (propping), and transactions that may be driven by a strategic rationale. The results of the study suggest that transactions likely to result in expropriation are the most common form and that the announcement of such transactions results in significantly negative, market-adjusted abnormal returns of approximately –10 per cent after 10 days and –20 per cent in the succeeding 12-month period. Moreover, abnormal returns are negatively related to concentrated ownership by the main shareholder; in other words, firms with the most concentrated ownership experienced the largest value losses. Cheung et al. conclude that:

> Overall firms announcing connected transactions that might be likely to result in expropriation lose between a third and quarter of the market value over the announcement and post announcement period suggesting substantial expropriation of minority shareholders. (Cheung et al., 2006: 365)

These authors also find that the probability of undertaking related-party transactions is higher for firms whose ultimate ownership is located in mainland China. The authors claim that:

> the relationship between expropriation and the location of the firm's ultimate parent provides direct evidence of the impact of the legal system in allowing firms to undertake actions that benefit the controlling shareholder at the expense of minority shareholders. (Cheung et al., 2006: 346)

What is perhaps puzzling about these data is that minority investors continue to invest in firms with a governance structure that appears to represent a high probability of expropriation. According to the work of Claessens et al. (1999, 2002), minority investors should severely discount the value of such equities in anticipation of the risk of expropriation. However, Claessens' conclusions are contradicted by Cheung and his co-authors who find no evidence of an ownership concentration discount among Hong Kong firms. The absence of such a discount is due in part to the fact that there is little variation in the governance structures of Hong Kong firms: all will typically have very high levels of ownership concentration combined with other high-risk expropriation factors, such as pyramid ownership, cross-shareholdings, and deviations in cash flow and control rights. Because Hong Kong firms possess governance structures with similar characteristics, firms engaging in expropriation through the use of related-party transactions do not appear to differ from other Hong Kong firms with respect to these factors. In other words, before the fact, investors cannot determine the firms that are more likely to expropriate. There is one exception: H-share and red-chip companies controlled by mainland China are significantly more likely to undertake related-party transactions and such firms are not subject to the enforceable judgments of Hong Kong-based courts.

In short, minority investors should be wary of investing in Hong Kong firms affiliated to business groups. The best protection seems to be to invest in firms in which owners retain high cash-flow rights. Notwithstanding the sophisticated institutional infrastructure designed to protect minority investors, minority investors would do well to heed the maxim 'caveat emptor', a policy consistent with Hong Kong's laissez-faire economic policy. Unlike Japan, Korea and Taiwan, the state did not impose an onerous social or developmental mission upon its largest enterprises who were at liberty to pursue their own self-chosen goals. That Hong Kong's family business groups focus upon the task of making money for themselves should not come as a surprise. The basic governance typology outlined in the introduction to this book proposes that family governance structures are designed primarily to generate and preserve family wealth. Maximising the interests of minority investors is not a dominant priority in such governance systems. It is little surprise then that the heavy flows of foreign portfolio investment prior to 1997 did not deliver foreign investors the kinds of returns they could expect from North American or UK equity markets. A more secure source of investment is in foreign managerial governed firms who team up with Hong Kong's business groups in joint ventures or strategic alliances. In such contractual agreements, both sides of the partnership are generally in a position to enforce their agreements.

In their discussion of the risk-sharing hypothesis, Khanna and Yafeh (2005: 301) cite the following anecdotal comment made in the wake of the recent Asian financial crisis by Li Ka Shing, the dominant owner of the Hutchinson Whampoa and Cheong Kong groups: 'Our diversification has provided us with varied sources of income and has shielded us from the worst of the financial crisis'. However, there is no systematic evidence that Hong Kong business groups serve as a mutual insurance device. For example, Cheung et al. (2006) find a great deal of expropriation or tunnelling but little evidence of propping via related-party transactions. Perhaps one reason for the absence of propping is the presence of a more active mergers and acquisitions market. If a group can liquidate an underperforming firm there is little incentive to rescue a troubled firm. However, few, if any, scholars have tested the mutual insurance hypothesis.

With regard to the catch-up mechanism hypotheses, it is evident that business groups play an important role in the economic development of the territory. However, with respect to technological capabilities, there is no compelling evidence that Hong Kong business groups have performed a role comparable with that played by their counterparts in Japan, Korea and Taiwan. Nevertheless, it is apparent that Hong Kong's business groups were instrumental in generating a significant high value-added economy. The economy has proved robust and flexible; the pre-Second World War entrepôt economy was transformed into a dynamic industrialised economy by the 1950s. Since the 1970s, the economy has de-industrialised to become a service-based logistical centre (Carney and Davies, 1999). Perhaps most importantly, Hong Kong's business groups were among the first-movers into China's open door and were instrumental in establishing the Shenzhen-Zhuhai-Guangdong industrial megapolis through the introduction of management and marketing skills, capital, and world-class manufacturing processes and technology into this region.

8

Business groups in India

Introduction

Family business groups are the foundation of the Indian economy, accounting for most of the GDP and nearly the whole of the industrial economy (Ward, 2000). Indian family business groups are known as business houses, a term that emphasises their household and extended family qualities – a defining feature of this form of business group. Khanna and Palepu (2000a: 867) define Indian business groups as 'collections of publicly traded firms in a wide variety of industries with significant amounts of common control, usually by a family'. Similarly, 'group firms are often linked together through the ownership of equity shares. In most cases the controlling shareholder is a family' (Bertrand, Mehta and Mullainathan, 2002: 16). However, India's family business groups do not conform to Fukuyama's notorious characterisation of family capitalism as a 'loose tray of sand' (Fukuyama, 1995), a characterisation which depicts atomistic family businesses as mistrustful of state institutions and jealously guarding their own interests at the expense of the wider society. Rather, studies of India's business groups emphasise their embeddedness in a wider set of community relations. Due in part to India's diverse cultural and ethnic composition Encarnation (1989: 45) claims that business houses are connected through a multiplicity of relationships among group members: '[I]n each of these houses, strong social ties of family, caste, religion, language, ethnicity and region reinforced financial and organisational linkages among affiliated enterprises'.

Many analysts divide India's post-independence economic development into two distinct phases. In the immediate post-independence phase (1947–91), the state adopted a highly statist orientation and planned to modernise a postcolonial agricultural economy into a self-reliant industrial state by means of centralised government bureaucracy operating in accordance with five-year economic plans. This approach resulted in economic stagnation, and after 1991 the state changed course and gradually implemented a policy of economic liberalisation and re-opened to foreign participation. In this new era, business groups have adopted a variety of new strategies to cope with a more competitive open economy.

Nevertheless, India is a very large country with great regional inequalities and deep urban and rural divide. The creation of a market-based economy is a slow and uneven process. Many regions and industries have not fully participated in India's economic miracle. Just as in China, where we find a rapidly developing coastal region and a less developed interior, so with India we can expect to find areas of significant development coexisting with areas of deprivation and underdevelopment. Nor should we expect to find a uniform institutional development across the country. We may see the appearance of clusters of highly-developed, world-class enterprises with ready access to a managerial and scientific talent, ample financial resources, and efficient physical infrastructure in certain states and cities. At the same time, we should also expect to find less-developed sectors with little access to capital and human resources, and hampered by poor physical infrastructure. In less competitive industries we are likely to see continued government intervention to guide the process of structural adjustment and to protect firms, employment and dependent communities. In less-developed sectors of the economy we might reasonably expect a continuing role for business group activity.

The origin of business groups in India

Prior to the Second World War, a variety of British trading and management organisations called management agents, agency houses, investment groups and expatriate firms were important in the Indian economy. Jones and Wale (1998) propose that these organisations were prototype business groups that coexisted alongside domestically-owned family merchant business groups. The latter were often linked with ethnically homogeneous merchant communities such as Gujaratis, Marawris (Birla) and Parsis (Tata). Characteristic of colonial economies, foreign investment was concentrated in the plantation industries; for example, 85 per cent of the area planted with tea was foreign-owned (Chibber and Majumdar, 1999). Prototype business groups that developed a reputation for reliability and honoring their contracts thrived in an environment replete with uncertainty and the risk of expropriation. Indeed, Khanna and Palepu's (1997) influential *Harvard Business Review* article, 'Why focused strategies may be wrong emerging markets', provides the logic for the emergence of business in uncertain and underdeveloped institutional conditions, casting India in the role of the archetypal emerging market. In this article, Khanna and Palepu compare and juxtapose the advanced institutional infrastructure of the USA and Japan with India's underdeveloped and missing institutions. Their analysis provides a long list of market imperfections and institutional failings including underdeveloped capital markets, illiquid state-owned banks only weakly monitored by government officials, inflexible and highly-regulated labour markets, scarcity of management talent, little managerial training, few business schools, the absence of executive search firms, an excess of government regulation and red tape, misguided attempts to supervise and direct economic growth, and a cumbersome inefficient legal system.

Following the Second World War, British agency houses were short of capital as there were limits on capital exports from the UK. British shareholders wanted dividends and to repatriate capital; meanwhile, British agency houses were willing sellers and Indian business groups were willing buyers, as such there were continuing sales of British-owned assets to Indian entrepreneurs. In 1938, there were 61 business groups controlled by the British; but by 1962 fewer than 25 business group remained in British hands. Prominent British colonial agency groups, such as Martin Burn, Bird Heileger, Jardine and Henderson, and McNeil and Barry, went into steep decline. The management agency system was subsequently abolished; however, the new Indian owners decided to retain important elements of business group structure as it continued to be well aligned with emergent institutional conditions.

After independence, the government pursued a policy of national self-reliance and supported domestic enterprise over foreign multinationals (Encarnation, 1989). During the 1950s, Indian-owned and managed business houses began to acquire the assets of exiting British firms. By 1957, the process of acquisition and the assertion of control had run its course. Indian-owned and managed business houses were to emerge as the dominant enterprises in the economy. Between 1950 and 1991, the Indian government became increasingly interventionist in managing the economy. In the early 1950s, as part of a second five-year plan, the government committed to a 'socialist pattern of society' and set about nationalising many sectors of private industry. Nevertheless, the family business house remained an important element of the industrial landscape.

Bureaucratic state capitalism

The policy of self-reliance produced inward-looking economic development and planning processes that might be best described as bureaucratic state capitalism. Following independence, an industrial policy regime was created by numerous acts of parliament between 1951 an 1973, giving state institutions substantial powers to direct private enterprise. Such was the extent of these powers that nearly every decision an entrepreneur or manager could make was governed by a rule, regulation and statute. Moreover, bureaucrats at various levels of government had substantial discretion in interpreting the rules. Before an entrepreneur could perform any productive activity, they would be required to run a circuitous gauntlet of obstacles to obtain the necessary permissions. The industrial regime became know as the 'licence-permit-quota raj'. One analyst describes the regime in the following terms:

> few outside India can appreciate in full measure the extent and nature of India's controls … Indian planners and bureaucrats sought to regulate both domestic entry and export competition, to eliminate product diversification beyond what was licensed, to penalize unauthorized expansion of capacity, to allocate and prevent the reallocation of imported inputs, and indeed to define and eliminate virtually all aspects of investments and production through a maze of kafkaesque controls. This all encompassing bureaucratic intrusiveness and omnipotence had no rational economic or social logic... (Bhagwati, 1993, cited in Chibber and Majumdar, 1999: 228)

The industrial policy environment was characterised by two tiers. The macro policy environment was comprised of larger overriding policy goals, such as self-reliance, state intervention and socialist economic policy, about which there was much consensus in the government. The micro policy environments focused on regulations pertaining to particular industries and firms. Whereas business groups could have no impact over macro policy, they found it much easier to influence micro policies on issues particular to their interests.

While the licence-permit-quota raj was highly restrictive and apparently hostile to business interests, the highly protectionist regime it created proved very attractive to entrepreneurs who had established themselves. Indeed, India's bureaucratic state capitalism worked favourably for business groups as the state protected domestic firms from foreign competition and established infrastructure industries that provided them with cheap inputs, especially subsidised loans. Eventually, the state monopolised financial institutions and became the sole source of external credit and finance. As the industrial policy regime required permissions for nearly every commercial decision, entrepreneurs established special government relation offices, called 'industrial embassies' where they cultivated social capital with elected officials and civil servants to advance their own interests through the complex bureaucracy. The industrial embassies of the major business groups each devised their own strategies to maximise the chances of success. For example, the Tata group submitted fewer applications for licences and quotas but applied all its power to gain their acceptance. In contrast, Birla inundated government regulators with numerous applications for licences, many of which were rejected. Encarnation suggests that there were economies of scale to political strategy:

> To secure government licenses and equally important to block competitors from obtaining such licenses both required some exercise of political skills. So the larger business houses maintained specialized industrial embassies in New Delhi. Often run by former civil servants or military officers ... in contrast those enterprises with fewer financial and managerial resources and located far from the capital found it more difficult to conduct lengthy and repeated negotiations requiring reams of data and correspondence with a dozen or more regulatory agencies in the central government... (Encarnation 1989: 134)

The two largest business houses illustrate the extent of economies of scale in industrial lobbying. Together, Tata and Birla attained 10 per cent of all applications approved by the government during a 10-year period between 1956 and 1966. Attaining licences was often used as a strategic deterrent to new entry. Many firms did not utilise their production licences or build the industrial capacity for which they had been granted permission.

Unlike the developmental states of Japan and Korea, which closely monitored the performance of the beneficiaries of state credit by measuring their performance on criteria such as technology development and export achievements, the Indian state rarely concerned itself with the outcome of the licensing process. Once applicants had secured their licences, government officials rarely made inspections to guarantee compliance with the terms of the original agreements. Indeed, while business houses engaged in strategies to achieve their licences and permits, top ministers and senior bureaucrats generously reciprocated, actively competing for the work of progressing the applications of specific business houses. In these conditions, rent-seeking activity became the normal course of action and some houses were better able to play the game better than others.

Indeed, by the mid-1960s it became evident that the licence granting and state capital allocation process had been fully captured by a small number of large business houses, producing a concentration of economic power that was to prefigure similar outcomes in other state-led economic regimes in Asia in the 1980s and 1990s. At this point, the Indian government became concerned about the extent of industrial concentration in the hands of the top four family-owned business houses and began to investigate their restrictive practices. The government's response was to pass the Monopolies and Restrictive Trade Practices Act (MRTP) in 1969, a significant piece of legislation that stimulated further diversification by business houses. The MRTP severely limited large companies' ability to expand their production lines. To continue growing, firms sought to diversify outside of their major areas of business through the establishment of new businesses. Just as the strict enforcement of the 1890 Sherman Anti-Trust Act by President Roosevelt and Chief Justice Taft in the USA precipitated the growth of conglomerate enterprises (Davis, Diekman and Tinsley, 1994) so did the MRTP stimulate a new wave of conglomerate diversification among Indian business houses, especially into industries deemed important to the Indian government.

Rather than restricting the power of large business houses, the MRTP seems to further promote their growth as diversified business houses became increasingly organised into pyramids to circumvent MRTP restrictions. According to Encarnation (1989), independent firms were typically less successful in the labyrinthine licence-granting process under MRTP legislation and responded to the MRTP by seeking to invest abroad. However, many business houses showed little proclivity to invest outside of the Indian market, as Encarnation puts it:

> direct investments abroad remain notably absent from the portfolios of three of India's ten largest conglomerates with the important exception of Birla ... Indian business houses did not have the regulatory incentive or technology to invest aggressively overseas. (Encarnation, 1989: 148)

The 1969 MRTP legislation, accompanied by other legislation including corporate income taxes that were raised to nearly 100 per cent, marks a high point in anti-private business legislation. However, this nadir of aggressive and protectionist bureaucratic state capitalism hindered external trade, inward investment, and retarded the development of financial markets. These conditions only served to cement the position of family business groups, which came to dominate the economy. Moreover, regressive tax policies fortified the household character of business groups. Extremely high levels of income tax created strong incentives for family members to join and remain in company positions to protect their standard of living by using tax-deductible company resources for housing and personal expenses (Ward, 2000: 274).

The political environment of India shifted considerably in the mid-1970s. Prior to that the Congress Party had controlled both federal and state governments did not face any serious threats to its rule. Such political stability facilitated firm rent-seeking and political deal-making. Since the Janata Party took control of the federal government in 1977, the political situation became more fragmented and unstable. Now that politicians' tenure is less secure, it is less likely that they will be able to pay back political favours, which makes rent-seeking more difficult (Kang, 2002). India's industrial policy was gradually liberalised throughout the 1980s, with the de-licensing of specific industries in 1983.

Through the early 1980s, political leaders made strong statements against capitalist enterprises but continued to support established enterprises with protectionist policies. In turn, business houses were careful to the frame their demands in terms that were acceptable to political leaders. Business was not in a position to much influence the macro-environment and was forced to take direction from the government. However, this strategy of state-led capitalism was in no way comparable with that found in Japan or in Korea during the period 1950–80. While the state influenced the rules of the game by controlling finance and mediated access to foreign technology, the state's overriding goals of self-reliance did not produce sustained economic performance in the form of export-oriented growth or capital accumulation. Instead the licence-permits-quota raj created numerous impediments to productive investment and economic activity. In contrast with Japan, Taiwan and Korea, which had successfully cultivated domestic competitive industries, the Indian state overestimated its capacity to influence economic activity and overextended itself by failing to selectively focus on clear economic goals or achievable tasks. That strategy became unsustainable and imposed heavy burdens on a stagnant economy. By the mid-1980s, both state and business recognised the need for rationalisation and liberalisation in the industry regime.

Liberalisation

In 1991, the government begun a major economic transition, with policies designed to reverse a 30-year era of bureaucratic state capitalism. The stimulus behind this policy shift was a balance of payments crisis. In 1991, prime minister Narshima Rao, and finance minister Manmohan Singh, initiated a series of liberalising measures. In a statement on industrial policy to parliament, the government pledged greater transparency and more uniform application of rules. Except for a shortlist of industries related to security and strategic concerns, industrial licensing restrictions were abolished and rules restricting enterprise diversification were relaxed. Other licensing restrictions on the location of industries and import of capital goods were eased. The mountain of paperwork required to open a new business or expand an existing one was curtailed and processes streamlined. To raise resources, public sector enterprises were to be partially privatised. Industries reserved for the public sector were now sharply circumscribed. Restrictions on foreign capital were also eased. Automatic approval would be given for foreign direct investment of up to 51 per cent foreign equity in high-priority industries. The government sought to become more proactive in attracting foreign investment. A programme with incentives to attract substantial foreign investment and access high technology was created. An agency was established to negotiate with a number of large multinational firms and attract direct foreign investment in select areas. The MRTP Act was amended to focus the commission on regulating monopolistic, restrictive and unfair trade practices.

In this context, government business relationships improved and the environment of suspicions of mutual mistrust began to fade. Importantly, the government did not attempt to dismantle the powerful business houses or impose any new restrictions on their activities. In theory, business groups would be required to adapt to new institutional conditions or risk fading away.

Despite the commitment towards liberalisation, the industrial policy process remains politicised. Not all business houses have uniformly embraced the policy of liberalisation. Many firms have benefited from state handouts and protection from foreign competition for so long that many are not entirely prepared for continued liberalisation. Several have expressed reservations about continued deregulation and extended liberalisation. To avoid economic dislocations and the traumatic effects of a 'big bang' approach to liberalisation, the government has implemented restructuring policies selectively and partially. For example, while there has been a relaxation of restrictions on foreign investments, much foreign capital is located in export zones and selected high-technology industries. The complexities of Indian coalition politics inevitably accommodates entrenched interests and affects the implementation of liberalising policies. Moreover, the licence raj had its own inertia and is difficult to change. This system is deeply institutionalised in the national psyche. Over the years, there has been a build-up of vested interests who have benefited from the labyrinthine system of industrial regulation. Nevertheless, there appears to be the political will to push the reforms ahead. Indeed, while India is still far from the ideal of an open market economy, significant progress toward the market end of the spectrum has been made in recent years.

Corporate governance and organisation structure

From a legal perspective, corporate governance laws are quite strong. India has a common law heritage and well-developed legal system. In practice, however, corruption is common, laws are not always enforced, and the legal system can be inefficient. Prior to 1991, the concept of corporate governance was not well understood. While the government dominated the provision of finance to the private sector in the belief that this would lead to industrial development, it did not pay much attention to the monitoring of these loans. Indeed, the dominant tendency was to continue pouring money into an underperforming enterprise in the vain hope that it would work its way out of trouble. In turn, banks were not monitored by the state and there were numerous constraints on the ability of minority shareholders to monitor their investment. The Indian Companies Act of 1956 had restricted the acquisition and transfer of shares and effectively prohibited the creation of a market for corporate control. With share ownership concentrated in the hands of entrepreneurs and their extended families, there was no practical way of new management ever taking over a poorly-managed firm. Protected from competition, inefficient and unprofitable firms could remain in a state of inertia for long periods. The closure of a plant was to be avoided at all costs (Fisman and Khanna, 2004).

Firms affiliated to Indian business groups are legally separate entities. Indian business groups are collections of private and publicly traded firms in a wide variety of industries with a significant amount of common ownership and control (Khanna and Palepu, 2000a). There is no group-specific main bank that coordinates group firm activities. Instead coordination between member firms is orchestrated through common board members and through the involvement of the family at the head of each group. However, some of the very largest and most diversified groups have also installed formal systems of coordination and control among group companies (Khanna and Palepu, 2000a).

The central feature of Indian corporate governance is the centrality of the family. Indian family norms have typically had a strong impact upon the management of the firm. Family members typically have respected elders and married within small social and religious communities. The family units often contain several generations living together within the same household. Historically, social custom dictated that businesses were passed along to the eldest son. A common way of coping with conflict was to provide each son with responsibility for managing his own business. The often inevitable impact of this practice was conflict, rivalry, and the division and dissolution of an established business house, a fissioning phenomenon that is also reported to be typical of Chinese family business groups (Wong, 1985). In India, Ward (2000) characterises the process as the 'partitioning of fiefdoms' and attributes the process to performance and management skills differences among brothers. Ward suggests that conflict is endemic in this system; for example, a more a frugal and capable brother can subsequently gain control and acquire the assets of the underperforming businesses of his fraternal rivals. High-profile conflicts are often intense and followed closely in the popular press. However, others have reported that family relationships are mutually supportive and family businesses may operate as mutual insurance schemes where family firms come to each other's aid and help one another in times of crisis (Douma, George and Kabir, 2003).

Professional management could be brought into the firm, but owners typically recruit individuals with similar values. Owners could be highly paternalistic toward their employees. Indeed, a paternalistic management culture is typical attribute. In a 1965 case study of Tata Business Group affiliate Air India, Corbett describes the group's managerial philosophy of 'enlightened paternalism':

> Air India provides housing for families and its employees and is building flats for more of them … it provides subsidized canteens, holiday homes, an elaborate subsidized sports program in which the executives make a point of taking part along with the ordinary employees. The corporation's personnel department arranges

financial help for employees when funeral expenses are needed or when the expenses of a daughter's wedding puts the employee into financial difficulties. The corporation provides scholarships for the employees' sons and daughters. Air India also provides loans to employees who wish to build or otherwise acquire houses of their own. The corporation, like the whole Tata group of companies also contributes to employee benefit plans and charities. (Corbett, 1965: 306)

Corbett concedes that Tata's enlightened paternalism is more advanced than the prevailing practices in the Indian industrial environment. However, he argues that enlightened paternalism is a rational strategy for professional management in India's developing economy due to the existence of extreme poverty and absence of alternative career opportunities. In exchange for its paternalism, management may expect unquestioning loyalty from its management cadre.

In some parts of Indian society, these traditions of familism and paternalism have changed rapidly in the last 20 years. The 1991 reforms also affected family life through changes in the tax regime, such as reductions in income, capital gains, estate and inheritance taxes. The creation and rapid growth of an information technology sector has created a new generation of independent entrepreneurs who have accumulated substantial wealth and now represent new cultural role models for prospective entrepreneurs and professional managers. Several other factors have appeared that might be expected to create the conditions for the emergence of approaches to corporate governance. To establish an institutional infrastructure that would support the functioning of market exchange, there is a raft of new market-oriented economic reforms. The Securities and Exchange Board of India Act 1992 established a regulation agency with a mandate to improve the functioning of Indian capital markets. A mergers and acquisitions code was introduced and restrictions to the entry of foreign investors are gradually being eliminated.

In a case study of the software industry leader Infosys, which has emerged as an exemplar of good corporate governance in India, Khanna and Palepu (2004) argue that that the globally competitive market for technological talent is driving this company to adopt best practice governance norms. Because of intensive competition for talented individuals, it is more difficult for some employers to maintain their paternalistic and non-transparent governance. Instead of being servants of the well-established business houses, the most qualified talent can choose foreign employers or the more meritocratic, equitable and open local firms. However, contrary to their expectations Khanna and Palepu (2004) do not find that Infosys's peers have moved much toward the adoption of 'best practice' corporate governance practices. For instance, they note that Tata Consulting Services, another leading software company and close affiliate of the Tata Group of companies, has not adopted corporate governance practices comparable to Infosys. They speculate that large business houses do not necessarily need to compete in the market for external talent because they already possess a large volume of internal talent in addition to the mechanisms to develop talent internally. Likewise, business groups have less incentive to adopt comparable practices as they are more able to meet their requirements internally. Moreover, Khanna and Palepu (2004) find that few new entrant and freestanding software houses have made much progress in the direction of good corporate governance. Equally contrary to expectations, firms competing for top-quality talent in sectors of India's new intellectual property based economy – such as the pharmaceutical industry – have also not fully adopted best practice. Khanna and Palepu conclude that the external and shareholder-centred model of corporate governance, such as that adopted by Infosys, has not spilled over into the mainstream of Indian corporate governance.

It may be unrealistic to expect market-oriented reforms to have an immediate impact on corporate governance practices among Indian firms. A typical problem in emerging markets is that the rules are put on the books but not enforced. For example, although a mergers and acquisitions code has been established, the Indian Securities Exchange board found that it lacked adequate power to enforce regulations on mergers. The emergence of the market for corporate control continues to be hampered by the absence of information and the existence of high transactions costs. There is still very little competition among financial institutions, and transparency and disclosure rules are still not well understood or sufficiently stringent. In terms of the adoption of corporate governance best practice, corporate governance indices generally place Indian corporations around the middle (Khanna and Palepu, 2004); nonetheless, numerous problems remain.

There is also the probability of resistance by politicians and those potentially harmed by changes in corporate governance practice, and US shareholder-centred models of corporate governance may not yet be desirable or applicable in India's emerging market. Many stakeholders, such as employees and pension holders, do not have any means to protect themselves against the impact of an aggressive shareholder wealth maximisation orientation. To the extent that shareholders can expropriate profits while externalising the costs onto other stakeholders, it is unlikely that policy elites will be willing to adopt an industrial regime that may produce undesirable redistributive outcomes such as increasing income inequality and high unemployment. Rapid restructuring in developing economies lacking robust social infrastructure and welfare arrangements may bring greater social and political instability. As in China, Indian firms are often seen as indispensable providers of social welfare, in the form of job security for employees, to large segments of the population. To abandon this capacity in the absence of an alternative viable state-mediated social welfare system is politically and socially risky, and it seems unlikely that a pure form of shareholder-oriented capitalism will be adopted in the foreseeable future.

The performance of business groups and their affiliates

One legacy of the long period of protectionism in the Indian economy is the large variation in productivity and efficiency of firms (Khandwalla, 2002). Prior to 1991, firms were rarely allowed to go out of business, regardless of their financial performance. In the reform era, efficiency and productivity improvements are occurring only gradually in many sectors and we can anticipate a long period of restructuring as more inefficient firms are either acquired, restructured or slowly fade away. Many small family firms demonstrate a remarkable resilience and are likely to find new market niches that are sheltered from global competition. Large-scale closures that would result in large-scale unemployment and social dislocation will be politically unacceptable. In this context of continuing economic development, evidence about whether affiliation to a business group improves or hurts firm performance cannot be decided conclusively.

One major study of the performance impact of affiliation is based upon a sample 272 business groups and 1,300 firms listed on the Bombay Stock Exchange, of which 655 were group-affiliated firms (Khanna and Palepu, 2000a). Based upon data from a single year (1993) the authors assessed accounting (RoA) and market-based (Tobin's Q) measures of performance. Their main finding is that as a whole, firms affiliated to diversified groups do not underperform compared with non-affiliated firms. However, Khanna and Palepu report that firms affiliated to the most highly-diversified groups outperform their unaffiliated counterparts. Their findings suggest that there is a curvilinear relationship between the performance of group-affiliated firms and the degree of diversification of the group. Specifically, firms belonging to groups with the least amount of diversification perform no differently from firms that are not affiliated to business groups. However, firms affiliated to the groups that have an intermediate level of diversification perform significantly more poorly than the mean for unaffiliated groups. Other less significant data also suggest that there are performance benefits for firms associated with larger groups. Khanna and Palepu interpret these results as indicating that the most diversified business groups do indeed add value to their affiliates by replicating the functions of institutions missing in this emerging market. However, in the context of India, this 'missing institutions' or intermediation role is governed by a scale economies effect. As Khanna and Palepu put it:

> large business groups have the scale and the scope to justify the fixed costs needed to create the internal structures and processes for performing the intermediating function. Moreover, it may be that is only the largest and most diversified groups that derive benefits from their political connections in an economy where government interference in the economy remains pervasive. Importantly, the governance structure adopted by large business groups serve to offset the costs of diversification. Because firms are organised as a collection of independent companies with their own financial accounts this restricts their ability to use internal capital markets to prop up inefficient operations. (Khanna and Palepu 2000a: 888)

Other results in this study show that relative to unaffiliated firms and firms affiliated to smaller and less diversified groups, affiliates of the most diversified Indian groups also enjoy better access to international capital, are more likely to issue Global Depository Receipts, more likely to be followed by international equity analysts, and more likely to engage in international joint ventures and gain access to foreign technology. In contrast, small and medium-sized business groups operating at intermediate levels of diversification seemingly lack the management skills, internal processes, and political connections to generate benefits from diversification. Indeed, due to weak capital market control, these groups are likely to suffer from severe agency problems, such as owner expropriation. Consequently, a large majority of firms affiliated to Indian business groups may be prone to underperformance. In this regard very large and diverse groups may represent a special case.

Fisman and Khanna (2004) argue that Indian business groups may also play a key developmental role across states and regions that are at very different levels of institutional and economic development. Some Indian states have inadequate essential public services, such as poor roads, telecommunications and electrical power. Several states also have a poorly educated workforce and an absence of social services and healthcare. Such services may be considered public goods, the provision of which is the responsibility of the state. In some cases, however, the government monopoly responsible for providing public goods may be inefficient or lack the resources to provide adequate services. In these areas it is extremely difficult to attract high-quality managers, technicians and related workers.

Furthermore, there is a lack of ancillary industries that provide essential inputs and business services. Industrial development is seriously retarded in such areas because it is unattractive for standalone firms to locate in them. One alternative is for companies to supply inputs for their own private use. In the case of infrastructure provisions, business groups may be able to take advantage of economies of scale by locating a number of group-affiliated plants and sharing the costs of infrastructure services (Fisman and Khanna, 2004). In these cases, Indian business groups may have the potential to provide the necessary infrastructure that a freestanding firm cannot. Fisman and Khanna (2004) propose that the firms best able to deal with infrastructure shortages will be more likely to locate in a region with a weak industrial base and poor infrastructure because it provides them with access to low-cost factors of production such as land, labour and locally-available raw materials. In these conditions, large firms that can absorb a high degree of fixed costs in infrastructure investments and spread these expenses over a large volume of assets have an economic advantage. Therefore, it is likely that only the very largest business groups are able to take advantage of the scale efficiencies of these assets.

This kind of resource-sharing is observed in varying degrees throughout India and is most obvious in the self-contained industrial cities constructed by India's largest groups. Fisman and Khanna cite the examples of Jamshedpur and Tatanagar, affiliated to the Tata group, Pirojshanagar (Gdorej Group) and Birlagram (Birla group). In each case, the business group provides basic services such as power generation, roads, schools and employee housing for the joint use of its co-located companies. Fishman and Khanna tested the hypotheses more generally on a sample of some 1,193 plant location decisions by 957 Indian firms. The study found a negative relationship between the percentage of group-affiliated firms in a state and that state's developmental level, as measured by an index of factors including energy production, telephone lines per capita, percentage of surfaced roads, public provision of education and health per capita. According to Fishman and Khanna group-affiliated firms are on average more likely to locate in less developed regions. Quantitatively, faced with a choice between locating a new plant in an averagely developed state or an underdeveloped state, a firm affiliated to a business group is 10 per cent more likely than a standalone firm to locate in the undeveloped state (Fisman and Khanna, 2004: 616). The authors conclude that too often researchers focus on the negative rent-seeking aspects of business groups and may underestimate their importance in catalysing economic development in the most poorly-developed regions, They also note that foreign-owned firms are unambiguously more likely to locate in more developed regions of India.

While Khanna, Fisman and Paelpu have sought to find a positive element in India's business groups, the weight of research focuses upon the negative aspects of their performance. Singh, Nejadmalayeri and Mathur (2007) examine the relationship between group affiliation, diversification and financial performance of 889 Indian firms between 1998 and 2000. The study finds that diversified firms perform significantly worse than focused firms and that there exists a significant negative relation between the degree of diversification and firm performance. The study indicates that the negative impact of diversification on performance for firms affiliated to domestic business groups is due to cost inefficiencies. The authors argue that their results are consistent with the idea that the elimination of market imperfections and the reduction in rent-seeking opportunities have hurt the profitability of well-established larger business houses.

Using an innovative methodology designed to test how groups respond to environmental shocks to their profits, Bertrand, Mehta and Mullainathan (2002) find that owners of Indian business groups engage in significant expropriation of minority shareholders. Firms high in the pyramid that hold minority interests in firms lower down extract an average of about 25 per cent of annual profits through the use of tunnelling mechanisms. In particular, owners appear to extract cash through non-operating losses and gains rather than directly expropriating profits. Importantly, cash flows only from low to high cash-flow rights firms but not vice versa. This is indicative of minority shareholder wealth expropriation rather than cross-subsidisation or risk sharing. These results suggest that affiliates of Indian business groups do not seek to help one another out in times of distress, a result that contradicts the hypothesis that the heads of Indian businesses will tend to assist fellow brothers and kinsmen in other troubled businesses. Nor do Bertrand et al. (2002) find that Indian business groups serve as internal capital markets, as their methodology controls for intragroup borrowing. Given the significant volume of minority shareholder expropriation, Bertrand and her colleagues question why rational investors buy into these firms in the first place. One answer is that lack of information, such as corporate ownership details, makes it difficult for shareholders to 'figure out with any reliability which group firms are high and which are low cash flow right firms' (Bertrand et al., 2002: 146). The impact of transaction costs and information asymmetries creates obstacles to the functioning of effective capital markets.

Douma et al. (2003) test the profit redistribution (risk sharing) hypothesis in Indian business groups. They argue for a redistributive position, suggesting that stronger firms will support weaker firms through profit redistribution. In this respect we may see extensive tunnelling but not from high-performance firms with low control rights to firms with high control rights, Rather, they argue that because affiliation is based upon kinship and family ownership, a parent firm will come to the aid of firms controlled by sons and kin. However, Douma et al. (2003) argue that the benefits of business group membership will decline over time as the costs of affiliation will rise. They anticipate that on balance the negative effects of group affiliation outweigh the benefits in the Indian context due to freeing up of capital markets and liberalisation of import and export policies. Specifically they test three hypotheses: (1) other things being equal, group-affiliated firms will be less profitable than unaffiliated firms, (2) affiliated firms with a lower prior profitability will benefit from profit redistribution, while firms with higher profitability will suffer, and (3): in group-affiliated firms, the degree of profit distribution is influenced by the size of the group of the extent of family control of these groups. Douma et al. examine accounting performance (ROA) of 844 firms listed on the Bombay Stock Exchange from 1998 to 2000. Fifty-six per cent were independent firms and the remaining 44 per cent were group-affiliated firms. Their major finding is that group-affiliated firms perform significantly less well than independent firms, with a return on assets some 3–5 per cent lower for affiliated firms, and a Tobin's Q of around 22–26 per cent lower.

While studies of group affiliation in the early 1990s find no significant effects or mixed effects (e.g. Khanna and Palepu, 2000a), a negative effect is identified, suggesting that improvements in capital markets functioning are beginning to be noticeable by the year 2000. Secondly, Khanna and Palepu (2000a) find that group membership tends to have a smoothing effect on the performance of individual firms. That is, the variability of profits, measured by the standard deviation of ROA and Tobin's Q, is lower among group firms and relative to non-group firms. Moreover, the larger the business group, the greater the extent of profit redistribution. They interpret this finding as evidence of solidarity among family members.

A recurring theme of research on Indian business groups is that firms owned and controlled by domestic interests will be outperformed by firms that have some degree of foreign ownership. Adopting a property rights perspective, Chibber and Majumdar (1999) find that significant foreign ownership will significantly improve a firm's return sales and return on assets. This finding is unambiguous at foreign control levels above 51 per cent. The authors suggest that if foreign investors do not possess the capacity to actively influence and control decision-making they will lack the incentive or capacity to actively improve the management firms. However, when foreign firms have de facto control, they are more likely to actively intervene in the management and decision-making process in the Indian firms. In a study of Indian firms' ownership structure and performance, Douma, George and Kabir (2006) find evidence that concentrated domestic ownership significantly harms firm performance. However, they also find that concentrated domestic ownership harms firms that are members of business groups. The authors argue that traditional family business groups exert their influence on the affairs of affiliated firms to extort the benefits of control. However, they find that foreign corporate ownership or ownership by foreign financial institutions positively affects market-based measures of firm performance. An interesting picture emerges when Douma et al. describe how differences between foreign financial institutions and foreign corporate owners can affect performance. In particular, foreign corporate ownership has a significant impact on return on assets but not on market returns, while foreign financial institutional ownership affects a firm's market performance measures but not accounting measures. Douma et al. suggest that foreign corporations can provide an integrated package of capital management and technology that cannot be easily assembled as separate resource bundles, which may make a material difference to a firm's performance. On the other hand, foreign financial institutions have little capacity to actively intervene in management decision processes or otherwise impact performance. Instead, foreign financial institutions may simply monitor, track and select investments in the best-performing Indian firms.

Chacar and Vissa (2005) find that compared with freestanding Indian firms and firms in more advanced economies, business groups in India facilitate the persistence of underperformance due to differences in the intensity of competition. Using comparative data from 1989 to 1999 taken from more than 4,000 manufacturing firms in India and the USA, Chacar and Vissa (2005) report that firms affiliated to business groups tend to have longer periods of poor performance compared with independent firms. One potential reason offered is that business group members may support these poorly-performing affiliates to avoid being associated with failure or exit. Their study tests what they describe as the convergence hypothesis, namely that superior performance should decline towards the industry average because high-performing firms will attract imitators who will erode high returns through competition. At the same time, the convergence hypothesis also suggests that underperforming firms should redirect resources to more profitable business opportunities or, alternatively, managers of underperforming firms might be replaced by new managers who seek to turn around the company's fortunes. Hence, we should expect poorly-performing firms to improve and tend toward the industry average.

In contrast, the persistence hypothesis suggests that both inferior and superior performance persists over time due to friction in competitive processes. Superior performance may persist due to barriers to entry or barriers to imitation, which may produce a sustainable source of competitive advantage. Poor performance may also persist if the barriers to entry and exit are established and maintained by the government, for example by providing subsidies. Alternatively, in the absence of a market for corporate control, company managers may become entrenched and continue to implement weak strategies. Chacar and Vissa (2005) argue that it is in emerging economies where we expect to find less competition, as potential new entrants cannot get capital or powerful interests use government contacts to protect their franchises. As such, they expect that superior firm performance will persist longer in emerging markets than in mature and developed economies.

In the absence of strong property rights it can be relatively easy to imitate successful firms because there is little action for intellectual property such as patents. Thus, there may be no difference in the persistence of superior firm performance between emerging and developed economies. However, underperformance tends to persist in emerging economies because firms find that they cannot exit from industries, and well-connected firms enjoy preferential access to government subsidies, which may serve to prop up underperforming firms. Because there is no market for corporate control and very few mergers and acquisitions, it is very difficult to displace poor managers. Social and cultural reasons may also facilitate continuing underperformance; for example, if there is social stigma associated with failure then entrepreneurs may continue to operate their businesses for non-economic reasons. Another view suggests that emerging market firms affiliated to a business group could gain preferential access to the group's valuable central resources such as reputation managerial talent or capital that could enable a speedy recovery from poor performance.

Chacar and Vissa's (2005) results show that that firms affiliated to foreign firms have a higher persistence of superior returns. Importantly, they also find that the there is no significant difference in the persistence of superior performance in India relative to the USA. That is, competition erodes superior performance in both economies at a similar rate. Compared with US-based firms, Indian firms have a statistically higher persistence of negative performance, suggesting there is less pressure to improve underperformance in India. Chacar and Vissa (2005) also analyse the impact of business group formation on Indian firms. On average, they find that unaffiliated firms improve their underperformance more quickly than group-affiliated firms, possibly because affiliated firms have less pressure to improve and may rely on support or 'propping' by the business group. In addition, the persistence of superior performance does not last longer for firms affiliated to business groups relative to unaffiliated firms. Chacar and Vissa also find no performance premium for affiliated firms. In contrast, they do find superior performance persistence for the subsidiaries of foreign-owned firms.

Chacar and Vissa (2005: 943) conclude that their results are at odds with theories about the ability of business groups to fill institutional voids. In India, business groups appear to prop up the walking wounded but show no signs of providing valuable resources to affiliate firms that might help them improve their performance. They suggest that the only evidence of a positive business group effect among business groups is either anecdotal or is based upon studies using unrepresentative samples, typically of elite firms in an economy.

Chacar and Vissa suggest a number of explanations for their statistical results on Indian business groups. First, groups may have once filled institutional voids in some countries, but the institutional conditions leading to their rise may be disappearing at different rates or may have disappeared already. This may indeed be true but it ignores the possibility that business groups are deliberately keeping uneconomic firms afloat in order to maintain employment and minimise or moderate the effects of economic transformation and the attendant social dislocation. In this regard continued relationships with political elites are necessary to establish implicit social contracts in which firms agree to provide certain social benefits, such as inflated payrolls, in exchange for implied protection.

The second explanation is that group managers may in fact be pursuing a variety of corporate goals, possibly sacrificing short-term profitability for other goals such as repaying political favours, building market share, or developing the organisational capability to compete in an international marketplace (Elango and Pattnaik, 2007). While Japan, China, Korea and Taiwan each built internationally competitive businesses under an explicit state strategy of government-led industrialisation, firms in the India have not had the benefit of a developmental industrial policy and to develop international-level capabilities they have had to adopt alternative strategies.

The third explanation is in line with the suggestion that that the benefits of membership differ between member firms. As suggested by the literature on tunnelling, family control of the business group may be employed to expropriate minority shareholders' rights so that the benefits of group membership accrue to the central and most powerful firms within the group to the detriment of others.

In practice, both the capabilities development and expropriation perspectives may be both true. Given the incentives and opportunities offered by the reform era, Indian business groups may be responding in a measured manner, responding to their environment by simultaneously building market-oriented competitive positions while seeking to protect incomes and family wealth in a period of intense uncertainty. In the recent past, firms have faced aggressive redistribution and fiscal policies designed to extract wealth from the private sector. While there appears to be commitment to ongoing economic liberalisation, India's entrepreneurs may have learned to be cautious and hedge their positions. The lack of transparency and expropriation observed in business groups can thus be viewed as a defensive response in an environment of continuing uncertainty.

9

Ethnic Chinese business groups in Southeast Asia: social capital and institutional persistence

Business groups owned and controlled by ethnic Chinese entrepreneurs in the Southeast Asian states of Thailand, Malaysia, Indonesia and the Philippines share several structural features with their counterparts in Hong Kong and Taiwan. However, while ethnic Chinese are part of the majority population in Hong Kong and Taiwan, they are a visible minority in Southeast Asian societies and their demographic status has been a significant factor in the development of entrepreneurs. In particular, the Chinese minority has not always enjoyed the full protection of the state and at times has met with official discrimination, regulatory restrictions and other prohibitions. In Malaysia and Indonesia, ethnic Chinese have encountered official cultural repression and sporadic violence. At the beginning of the twentieth century, the Thai monarchy considered its Chinese minority to be 'enemies of the people' (Tejapira, 1997: 77) and the state sought to solve its 'Chinese problem' through assimilation policies. Wealthy Chinese currently living in the Philippines are still the subject of kidnappings and victims of organised crime that often goes uninvestigated by the police (Chua, 2003). The situation has been equally difficult in other parts of Southeast Asia. Ethnic Chinese communities were expelled from Burma in 1950s and from Vietnam in the 1970s and 1980s.

The rigour of the institutional context as experienced by ethnic Chinese entrepreneurs in Southeast Asia has stimulated several adaptations to the business models and practices of ethnic Chinese business groups. This distinguishes them from groups operating in Hong Kong and Taiwan and therefore warrants a separate treatment. Southeast Asia is a culturally diverse region consisting of predominantly Muslim (Malaysia, Indonesia), Buddhist (Thailand), Sinic (Singapore) and Christian (the Philippines) societies. Sinic culture is prevalent throughout the region due to a broad and continuing movement of Chinese diaspora into the region but it is far from dominant. Notwithstanding cultural variation, over a 30-year period following the Second World War, a small number of pyramidal business groups, each owned and controlled by a single ethnic Chinese entrepreneur or family, have emerged to dominate the economic landscape in each state.

Many ethnic Chinese entrepreneurs have overcome the chronic difficulties of their environment to gain significant economic power in the countries in which they are based. While ethnic Chinese are a minority in most Southeast Asian states,[1] they control a disproportionate share of private sector assets and own a large proportion each country's leading businesses. For example, in the Philippines, Chinese Filipinos control as much as 60 per cent of the private economy but comprise just 1 per cent of the population (see Table 9.1).

The statistics in Table 9.1 suggest that ethnic Chinese entrepreneurs in Southeast Asia may constitute the paradigmatic case of a market-dominant minority (Chua, 2003) or an ethnically homogeneous commercial elite (Davis, Trebilcock and Heys, 2001). Market-dominant minorities emerge in 'low trust societies' (Fukuyama, 1995) characterised by low levels of civic culture and weak institutional structures. In these circumstances, the norms of mutual support and trust among elites or subgroups can engender superior economic performance. Such groups

Table 9.1	Ethnic Chinese entrepreneurs' enterprise ownership in Southeast Asia		

Country	Population (millions)	Ethnic Chinese population (%)	Ethnic Chinese ownership of private sector assets (%)	Number of largest firms controlled by ethnic Chinese (%)
Indonesia	182	2.8	70	80
Malaysia	60	33.0	65	44
Philippines	61	1.5	40	33
Thailand	56	11.0	90	N/A
Brunei	374,577	15.0		
Singapore	4,553,009	76.8		

Sources: Hodder (1996); Limlingan (1986); Weidenbaum and Hughes (1996).

also enjoy elevated levels of social capital and this may accrue economic benefits to group members. Not all subgroups share such norms but those that do typically enjoy economic advantages over those that lack them. Economic benefits, such as reliable contract enforcement and lower transaction costs, provide a framework for executing intermediate-term and non-simultaneous transactions; in a marketplace without reliable enforcement mechanisms, such transactions are normally vulnerable to opportunism (Davis et al., 2001). The advantages enjoyed by these subgroups also promote faster rates of capital accumulation and wealth generation.

Ethnic Chinese family business groups (FBGs) are typically identified with their founder and/or his successors. The group is not usually centred upon a bank or a single core firm; rather these groups are pyramidal, with control tracing back to a single entrepreneur or family. In some cases, these pyramids are controlled from relatively small asset bases and owners practise leverage to control much larger empires (Morck, Wolfenzon and Yeung 2005). Owners typically adopt an instrumental orientation toward the constituent firms within the group and they are willing to sell and spin-off assets that no longer serve the family's interests. There is an extensive reliance on joint ventures, shared equity, project financing and deals. Because membership of a Southeast Asian group is fluid, surveys of the region's industrial and commercial structure typically select the entrepreneur and his holdings as the unit of analysis. See, for example, Yoshihara's (1988: 152–82) appendix entitled 'Major indigenous capitalists', Mackie's (1992) 'Major Chinese conglomerates in Thailand, Indonesia and Malaysia', and Brown's (2000: 290–2) 'dramatis personae'. In each of these inventories, the constituent enterprises are identified by the name of the founding entrepreneur; the name of the enterprise is of secondary importance. This is a 'tycoon' or personal form of capitalism (Chandler, 1990) in which the firm is always subordinated to the interests of the family fortune. Some analysts consider it an 'ersatz' or ephemeral form of capitalism (Yoshihara, 1988).

The account of this market-dominated minority's rise and their accumulation of significant wealth is a co-evolutionary story (Carney and Gedajlovic, 2002a). Their minority status and the attendant environmental hazards have shaped the character of ethnic Chinese business groups throughout Southeast Asia; but in turn, that environment has been shaped by the Chinese minority's overwhelming domination of the economy and the concentration of wealth and economic power in their hands. This domination now limits the range of institutional reform the state may realistically hope to enact. Hence, the institutional environment in many Southeast Asian states is both the cause and consequence of the large family-controlled business groups established by ethnic Chinese entrepreneurs in the Cold War period. We begin by describing the initial conditions that shaped the character of the region's business groups.

Origins and context

Ethnic Chinese migration to Southeast Asia long predates the European colonial era. Immigration peaked in the late nineteenth and early twentieth centuries, as a result of both problems in China and the expansion of a colonial plantation and mining economy in Southeast Asia. A precise definition of who constitutes the ethnic Chinese merchant class in Southeast Asia has long challenged scholars of the region (e.g. Sommers-Heidues, 1974; Wu and Wu, 1980; Suryadinata, 1989; Hodder, 1996). However, most agree that the Chinese in Southeast Asia are not a homogeneous group but are stratified along various dimensions. For example, among Chinese immigrants to Indonesia, scholars typically differentiate between the long-established *peranakan*, and the more recently arrived *totok*, who typically are ascribed a lower social status. More generally, Chinese communities are differentiated according to their province of origin, and their dialect such as Hokkien, Hainan, Hakka and Hokchia. Moreover, communities are further differentiated along ancestral clan and family lines. These concentric circles of association form a thick and layered social wall that surrounds and protects the basic family unit and also provides relationships through which business transactions are mediated. Moreover, these communities have produced a diaspora extending across Asia and into China. In rather vivid terms, Backman says:

> They didn't so much as pour into any one location, but fanned out across Asia. One clansman from a particular village in China would migrate to, say, Bangkok, and another would settle in Singapore. The way the Chinese settled across Asia ensured that they had a ready-made international network of connections within which they could trade and raise capital. (Backman, 1999: 195)

Several writers emphasise the theme that close-knit and regionally dispersed networks offer 'safe havens of capital' (Wu and Wu, 1980: 94), as well as channels for mobilising assets and sharing information about business opportunities (Kao, 1993).

Prior to the colonial period, ethnic Chinese occupied several economic roles including trading, money lending, mining and rice milling. With the establishment of the colonial economy, a variety of new intermediary roles were created. The colonial administration encouraged Chinese entrepreneurs to gravitate toward occupations in retailing and tax farming (tax collection), or to act as compradors, middlemen who would liaise between the colonial merchant class and indigenous commodity producers (Wu and Wu, 1980). Within the colonial order, ethnic Chinese entrepreneurs developed contacts with indigenous elites and developed commercial and manufacturing expertise.

Colonial-era economic relations were suddenly and permanently dislocated after 1941 when Japanese military administration was established throughout Southeast Asia. Military administration was severe, but the wartime economy of shortages offered opportunities for trade and smuggling. Penalties for economic crimes were extremely severe yet several entrepreneurs created fortunes in this era. Indeed, under Japanese administration, Chinese entrepreneurs were propelled into key trading and financial roles (Purcell, 1965; Twang, 1998). In the subsequent postwar period, Chinese entrepreneurship was to emerge as the region's most significant economic force (Wu and Wu, 1980).

The immediate aftermath of the Second World War was a period of intense economic, political and social upheaval in Asia. Colonial administration had crumbled in Southeast Asia and did not regain a firm foothold. As colonialism began to wane, independent and sovereign states were established in Southeast Asia. As self-rule was achieved in successive countries, the Cold War and the rise of Asian communism emerged as the main threats to newly-established independent countries and undoubtedly played an important role in the setting of nationalistic economic agendas across the region (Stubbs, 1999). The top priority of post-Second World War governments in the region was national security.

In the context of a Western Cold War containment policy, many governmental policies of Southeast Asian nations were driven by the need to fight civil wars, restore internal order and to repel the threat of communism. Consequently, governments focused upon strengthening the coercive instruments of the state by channelling resources into the military, police and intelligence services (Stubbs, 1999). In both Indonesia and Thailand, senior government officials were drawn predominantly from the military. Although bureaucrats were recruited from a more heterogeneous range of backgrounds, few knew much about business (McVey, 1992). Southeast Asian economic agendas were limited to managing strategic industries and rebuilding basic infrastructure. Strategic industries were managed by establishing state-owned enterprises and infrastructure was created with the assistance of foreign aid. Almost without exception, states in the region adopted highly nationalistic economic agendas featuring import substitution and export-oriented development policies (Stubbs, 1999).

Another legacy of colonial rule was wariness of foreigners, especially of Chinese minorities, who were now associated with communism and suspected of being agents of communist infiltrators. The uncertain loyalties of Chinese communities engendered the suspicions of local authorities. The governments and populations of newly established nations such as Indonesia and Malaysia were wary of the minorities within their borders, whose loyalties they considered unsure at best. In Thailand, attempts at Chinese assimilation were adopted and economic activities limited. As a result of their migrant status, the Chinese in Southeast Asia faced more or less explicit discriminative measures, and occasionally mob violence and attacks on their property (Mackie, 1992). Officials in military governments sought to extract discretionary taxes, contributions, donations and fees from individuals and groups believed to be wealthy. In an effort to protect themselves from extortion, Chinese entrepreneurs attempted to establish patrimonial linkages with prominently placed officials. The specific challenges faced by Chinese minorities were different in each Southeast Asian country; they ranged from a heightened risk of asset confiscation and selective discrimination to regulatory restrictions on language and other cultural prohibitions. Ethnic Chinese generally confronted a 'relentless restriction' on their commercial, political and social activities. As migrants from a frequently turbulent mainland China, many of the entrepreneurs who were to establish FBGs held deeply embodied 'life-raft values' (Kao, 1993: 27) that stemmed from generations of economic and political uncertainty (Redding, 1990). The popular discrimination and bureaucratic harassment that these entrepreneurs faced in their new homes reinforced their belief that they faced a hostile environment and profoundly influenced both their world view and their business practices (Brown, 1995).

Although the postwar business environment of Southeast Asia often appeared threatening and hostile, it also presented an abundance of opportunity. The colonial-era resource and trading companies began the process of repatriating their assets and were willing sellers to equally motivated Chinese buyers (Davenport-Hines and Jones, 1989). The exit of Japanese trading companies occurred even more abruptly when their assets were confiscated at the end of the Second World War (Yoshihara, 1988). One consequence of colonial exit was the creation of a vacuum of entrepreneurial expertise; Chinese entrepreneurs were willing and able to fill this void. While Southeast Asia had no equivalent of the Marshall Plan, the USA was open to supporting the military regimes of the region and willingly accepted their exports. Initially, local states sought to develop industries by establishing import substitution programmes, which put great discretionary power in the hands of state officials and politicians (McVey, 1992). Such bureaucratic discretion allowed Chinese entrepreneurs to cultivate personal connections and/or *guanxi* in order to secure lucrative production franchises and other licences (Mackie, 1992). Nationalist policies intended to cultivate indigenous entrepreneurship in Malaysia and Indonesia generally failed as the recipients of government licences often sold them on to Chinese buyers.

Observing the success of export-oriented development in Korea and Taiwan, governments in the region began to emulate these policies and attempted to attract foreign capital. Chinese entrepreneurs were able to use their Second World War era contacts to acquire technology and management know-how from Japanese firms in exchange for mediating the re-entry of revitalised Japanese firms into Southeast Asian markets (Yoshihara, 1988). Later, the Plaza Accord of 1985 increased the value of the Japanese yen and precipitated a wave of labour and resource-seeking investment into the Southeast Asian region and again put Chinese entrepreneurs into close contact with Japanese firms. Due to their large size, visibility and widely-advertised connections with the politicians and state bureaucrats, Chinese entrepreneurs also served as a major conduit for a flood of portfolio investment during the emerging market fever of 1992 and 1997. The entrance of such portfolio capital facilitated the entry of Chinese entrepreneurs into capital-intensive areas such as financing, property development and manufacturing.

Corporate governance

In response to this environment replete with both opportunity and hostility, Chinese entrepreneurs developed common business models and practices that have since become their hallmarks. The core challenges faced by Chinese entrepreneurs were twofold. First, they needed to develop business models that would allow them to take advantage of the remarkable opportunities afforded by the exit of colonial firms and the nationalistic economic policies designed to promote regional economic development from within (Mackie, 1992). Simultaneously, Chinese entrepreneurs had to cope with the discrimination and open hostility they faced as an ethnic minority and a growing economic power in their adopted homes.

In a mature economy, a firm can be conceptualised as a complex value chain or wealth-creation device, in which its residual value is considered to be the property of equity investors; however, a firm operating in a weak and hostile institutional environment becomes a more dualistic entity. Lacking the security of enforceable property rights and subject to the risk of bureaucratic extraction, the family business unit necessarily becomes something more than a value-creation device. In the absence of secure alternatives, the family firm also serves as a wealth-protection device; using various informal and often non-transparent means, the firm may be required to transfer wealth across generations and geographical space.

The most essential characteristic of FBGs is the fact that they are family-owned and managed operations; 'wealth conservation and consolidation' (Wong, 1985) is their overriding strategic goal. As argued by Fukuyama (1995), in the absence of institutional trust, or faith in government, family firms and kin-based networks such as the FBGs arise as a basic defence mechanism against a potentially predatory state. It is unsurprising to observe that such firms will choose strategic goals related to creating and preserving familial wealth as opposed to organisation building and value maximisation, the prevalent goals in professionally-managed firms (Redding, 1990). To the families who control these business groups, the constituent units of their groups are mainly goal-attainment devices; thus, firms become disposable if they no longer serve family interests. This highly-instrumental orientation toward the firms they own and manage explains in large part the business practices associated with FBGs, such as the propensity for deal-making, the acquisition of fungible assets, rapid asset turnover, and unrelated diversification. The operating structures of FBGs are characterised by multiple small-scale operating units tied together in a web of cross-holdings; the linkages may be circuitous but ultimately the group is controlled by the family (Redding, 1990).

Studies of risk-bearing in family firms support similar conclusions about their strategic goals. These studies begin with the assumption that the family firm's assets account for a significant proportion of that family's wealth. This concentration of assets creates a significant risk that can be reduced by extracting capital from the business and allocating it to secure, less risky investments. Fama and Jensen (1983) observe that families are inherently risk-averse in their strategic behaviour because their personal wealth is closely tied to the firm's fortunes. Such an analysis is consistent with studies that have found FBGs to be generally risk-averse (Kao, 1993) and that they favour investments in generic rather than specialised assets (Redding, 1990). The concentration of personal and family wealth in owner-managed firms normally creates a preference for income and for wealth preservation over other dimensions of enterprise performance such as growth and innovation (Wong, 1985; Morck, Strangeland and Yeung, 1998).

Organisational structure and management process

Risk aversion is manifest in a preference for noncomplex technical processes, projects with near-term payback horizons and simple organisational structures. Management is exercised through a senior owner-manager who typically assumes the presidency of the core firm in parallel with holding other senior posts in the major affiliated firms whose presidential posts are occupied by kin or close long-serving business partners. Typically, the top management team will be small with limited numbers of non-kin professional managers; the latter are often excluded from strategic decision-making processes (Redding, 1990; Kao, 1993). Where professional managers are employed in senior positions, their roles are considered subordinate to the entrepreneurial roles held by family members or trusted friends (Redding, 1990; Whitley, 1992). Redding also notes that groups avoid organisational complexity and tend to subdivide business units to maintain financial simplicity. This solution allows entrepreneurs to 'carry the paper and pencil in the head' (Redding, 1990: 181).

However, Brown (1995) argues that the financial accounts of Chinese FBGs are typically a 'morass' due to an inability to separate family and firm assets. As a result of the widespread practice of guaranteeing loans and credit to constituent firms and business partners, business groups are beset with off-balance-sheet liabilities that are impossible to determine even with extensive due diligence. Brown argues that:

> the financial structure, which might have held the structure together more firmly, did not play a large part in pulling the parts together into a cooperation. The purposes of the accounting system were to track sales and purchases and to prevent fraud. (Brown, 1995: 2)

Figures 9.1 and 9.2 illustrate the corporate and organisational structure of a medium-sized Thai family business group. The majority of the group's revenues and assets are concentrated in steel distribution and real estate businesses (Tanlamai, 1996). However, as illustrated in Figure 9.1, the corporate structure emphasises many of the firm's diverse technology

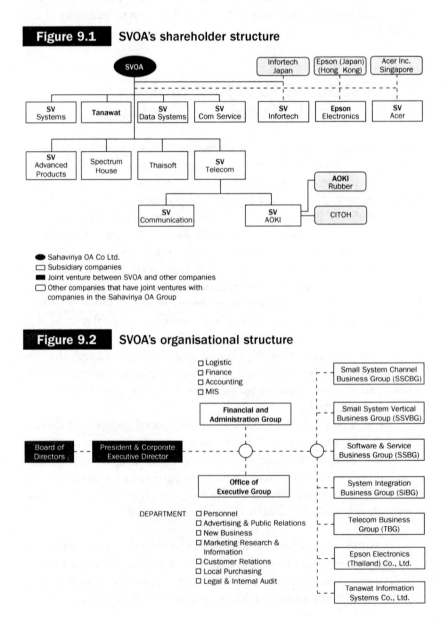

Figure 9.1 SVOA's shareholder structure

Figure 9.2 SVOA's organisational structure

affiliates and subsidiaries. Its subsidiaries and involvement in numerous joint ventures is indicative of a highly-flexible deal or project-based structure that allows financial assets to be easily shifted between separate legal entities (Carney and Gedajlovic, 2002b). Sahaviriya's organisational structure, depicted in Figure 9.2, describes a simple product structure consisting of two support offices, an office of the executive and a financial and administrative group.

The structuring of the larger group's assets across smaller units with individual legal identities is a mechanism for asset mobilisation. It also reduces the enterprise's visibility, which can be a crucial defence mechanism when operating in hostile environments (Hodder, 1996). Moreover, this structure provides for a means of achieving monitoring and feedback on unit performance when subsidiary managers are not trusted or when the organisation's capacity to perform a thorough internal auditing function is inadequate (Carney, 1998b).

Managerial processes are infused with paternalistic leadership values (Westwood, 1997); the consequences to the organisational structure include high centralisation, low formalisation and non-complex structural processes. The human resource implications of such structures are significant. Immediate and extended family and trusted quasi-family employees may be expected to be highly committed and motivated members of the management team (Whitley, 1999). On the other hand, the commitment of those employees lacking close relationships with the patriarchy is tenuous. Non-trusted employees in the organisation may be subject to a functional handicap because 'didactic leadership emasculates subordinates by depriving them of the information necessary to have a clear idea of what is going on in the organisation' (Westwood, 1997: 469). Consequently, these firms encounter difficulties attracting and retaining management talent, and employee turnover tends to be very high with exit decisions precipitated by marginal salary differences.

In Southeast Asian family firms, such characteristics are often attributed to cultural (Westwood, 1997), institutional (Hamilton and Biggart, 1988) and national business system characteristics (Whitley, 1992). However, the simple organisational structures and management processes adopted by FBGs may represent an efficient response to the imperatives of latecomer industrialisation. In the catch-up phase of industrialisation, much of the imported technology was routine, mature and highly codified. Owner-managers did not require a large support staff or elaborate technostructure to assimilate these technologies (Mintzberg, 1979). Export-oriented development required product-market strategies based upon prices and low costs. In these circumstances, owner-managers could utilise centralised organisational structures without any economic penalty. In mature commodity markets characterised by rapid price movements, firms lacking the management capacity to sell directly into overseas markets did not develop extensive planning, control and marketing infrastructures nor seek to differentiate their products through innovation. Moreover, even if FBGs had attempted to attract and retain them, management talent was in short supply.

Relationship management

Perhaps the most important feature of the region's business groups is the cultivation of long-lasting relationships with a variety of political and economic stakeholders. Through these relationships entrepreneurs accumulated knowledge and developed valuable capabilities such as the skills required to access resources, perceive opportunities and correctly interpret latent threats posed by their environments. Competitive advantage in these hazardous trading environments may rest on various forms of social capital such as social solidarity (Granovetter, 1994), network resources (Gulati, 1998), contact capabilities (Guillen, 2000), political resources (Frynas, Mellahi and Pigman, 2006) or *guanxi* (Xin and Pearce, 1996). As discussed above, Chinese communities with links to family, clan or linguistic groups that may be geographically dispersed, are surrounded by a thick and layered social wall that offers protection against threats, such as channels for capital flight, and in times of opportunity, these links provide access to sources of capital. These relationships also provide a source for recruiting trusted senior executives and channels for identifying overseas business opportunities. Indeed, it is the strength of these in-group relationships that have led to characterisations of ethnic Chinese as closed and 'tribal'. It is sometimes suggested that the non-transparent nature of FBGs' corporate structures and their owner-managers' preference for transacting within a closed kin or ethnic network cause FBGs to display a 'tribe-like' quality that is ill-suited to global competition (Chang, 1995).

However, FBGs have also transcended the ethnic networks and established diverse, cosmopolitan networks that belie the tribal image. Historically, Chinese entrepreneurs acted as compradors (go-betweens) for colonial firms and domestic interests in the region (Davenport-Hines and Jones, 1987). When many states adopted import-substitution based industrialisation strategies, Chinese entrepreneurs initiated linkages with Japanese firms to transfer technology to the region (Yoshihara, 1988). Members of business groups also forged a variety of linkages with prominent politicians and bureaucrats (McVey, 1992) and at the same time, in response to statutory restrictions on their businesses, established numerous inter-ethnic ventures in countries such as Malaysia and Indonesia (Twang, 1998; Menkhoff and Gerke, 2002). Moreover, due to their large size, their visibility and their contacts with prominent politicians, entrepreneurs succeeded in attracting foreign portfolio investments and established relationships with the international financial community. Indeed, more than any other type of network in the region, FBGs were anchored in multiple 'axes of solidarity' (Granovetter, 1994) that, in addition to kin and ethnicity ties, include corporate, community and political affiliations.

The subordination of business interests to the interests of the family and the influence of the hostile post-Second World War environments suggest several interrelated explanations that account for minority entrepreneurs' adoption of the business group structure. First, a business group structure provides a means for the family to simultaneously diversify and protect its wealth. As the FBGs are largely based upon both the primacy of family interests and the distrust of outsiders, diversification through ownership of legally independent business units provides a means of wealth diversification without the need to relinquish control to outside investors. Given the political uncertainty and economic opportunity of the turbulent Cold War era, a business group structure represented a rational response to an uncodified institutional context beset with the risk of asset expropriation, undefined property rights, cronyism, underdeveloped capital markets, and a shortage of managerial expertise. These structures allowed entrepreneurs to exploit new business opportunities and to cope with their hostile environments while limiting their family's exposure to risk.

Moreover, a second advantage of the business group structure is that it allows for the dispersal of family assets across multiple small-scale enterprises and limits the size and visibility of the firm in the majority population. Indeed, business group members may seek to obscure their corporate identity as a precaution against exciting antipathy in the majority population. For example, Salim was the largest Indonesian business group for much of the 1980s and the 1990s. Dieleman (2007) identifies some 330 companies affiliated to Salim. Interestingly, only one-fifth of these companies bear the Salim family name. Seeking to maintain a low profile is a reasonable precaution and a rational means of managing the risk of discrimination and asset expropriation they have faced in countries such as Indonesia, Malaysia and Thailand (Mackie, 1992; McVey, 1992).

Third, fear and mistrust of outsiders resulted in a managerial capacity constraint (Carney, 1998b). As FBGs grew into large-scale economic enterprises, they had to determine how to manage and control their empires in the face of the growing need for outside managers. FBGs addressed this problem by structuring the family business in terms of discrete small-scale business units; if outside managers were required, they could be evaluated and monitored through the financial results of their business units. This structure permitted strategically-placed family members to exercise effective control over their far-reaching portfolio of diverse operating units. An added advantage of these operating structures was that the impact of hired managers on familial wealth could be minimised; no outsider could hold a position that would allow them to challenge the interests of the family or become indispensable to the FBGs (Wong, 1985; Redding 1990). As such, the use of conglomerate holding company structures consisting of multiple small business units allowed these firms to avoid many potential managerial agency problems.

To summarise, in the initial conditions of post-Second World War insecurity and the subsequent period of industrialisation, Asian FBGs exhibited strategic behaviour aimed at generating and preserving family wealth. The conglomerate diversification strategies they pursed were often based on opportunities facilitated by connections with politicians and officials. They raised capital in their local communities and from state-controlled banks and later from their networks in the international financial community. International investments were often driven by capital flight considerations and based upon a competence at relational contracting. FBG entrepreneurs created simple, lean, personally-directed organisational structures as a cost-effective vehicle for implementing their strategies. Widely practised across the region, such strategies provided the entrepreneurial drive behind the export-led era of East and Southeast Asian industrialisation. Indeed, it is the great success of these strategies that constitutes the lasting administrative heritage of the FBG as an organisational form.

At the time of their emergence, FBGs were clearly a product of their operating environments. However, FBGs did not passively accept the constraints imposed by their environments. Indeed, it is apparent that the structures and practices of FBGs represented rational, goal-seeking behaviour by agents who were aware of their interests and were capable of organising to achieve their goals. Their linkages with prominent officials and politicians have been characterised as symbols of crony capitalism and have attracted much attention from analysts (Fisman, 2001). Because the value of such linkages stems from gaining privileged access to limited resources such as scarce capital, government contracts and monopolies, they are necessarily limited to a small group of entrepreneurs. Case studies (e.g. Dieleman and Sachs, 2006) suggest that entrepreneurs fortunate enough to establish linkages with strongman politicians such as Marcos in the Philippines, Suharto in Indonesia, and Matathir in Malaysia were able to establish very large business groups on the basis of these linkages. Only a relatively small elite has benefited from this type of linkage.

Institutional change and persistence

In her 1992 essay, 'The materialisation of the Southeast Asian entrepreneur', Ruth McVey argues with some confidence that business environments in Southeast Asia underwent a radical transformation during the Cold War era: the state, which had once been an incubus, or nightmare, was now an incubator for business. Politicians and officials who were previously parasites on business were now its promoters. Chinese entrepreneurs who had been considered pariahs were now revered as paragons. In this new environment, Southeast Asia is more integrated into the world market system and subject to a wider set of non-local influences. The Japanese economic crisis of 1992 and the regional financial crisis of 1997 marked the advent of a mature, slower-growth phase of development for many of the region's economies. As most Asian firms are now integrated into the international economy, their development is increasingly shaped by factors external to the region.

When the Asian financial crisis engulfed Southeast Asia in 1997, the International Monetary Fund (IMF) made the granting of financial support conditional upon institutional reform and the curtailment of protectionist policies favouring friends and family members. Many analysts implicated FBGs as a root cause of the crisis (Johnson, Boone, Breach and Friedman, 2000). Due to the practice of issuing a loan guarantees based on relationships rather than on sound risk analysis, weak firms had accumulated massive liabilities. Corporate governance systems that were designed to protect and consolidate family wealth were unable to adequately control and respond to the rigorous accountability standards associated with portfolio equity. Family domination of the enterprise, the absence of managerial hierarchies and bureaucratic systems of checks and balances made the Chinese family firm inherently unstable (Brown, 2000). The prevalence of such firms produced a veritable organisational monoculture that in turn destabilised the economic system as a whole.

With the exception of Malaysia, which adopted a set of regressive non-market policies (Rajan and Zingales, 2001), Southeast Asian governments became committed to the creation of market-oriented reforms. The subsequent establishment and strengthening of credit rating agencies, the promulgation codes of corporate governance, improved accounting standards, an openness to foreign private equity and venture capital firms, and the establishment of executive recruitment agencies and an automated equity trading system all resulted in the partial closure of certain institutional voids. States also established financial and corporate sector restructuring agencies to bring about reform, which, in some cases, included dismantling large business groups. The efforts of these restructuring agencies were often frustrated due to severe asset valuation problems; in addition, many groups were structured in a web of separate legal entities, including equity joint ventures and partnerships with domestic and foreign investors. Most governments were reluctant to expropriate the assets of these companies for fear of alienating the foreign investors on whom they now depended. More importantly, governments came to realise that many of the large business groups were too large to fail, and perhaps because no indigenous capitalist class had emerged to take their place, Chinese entrepreneurs were needed more than ever to rebuild collapsed economies.

In the wake of the 1997 financial crisis, FBGs have adapted to changing circumstances. Importantly, many controlling entrepreneurs and their families have managed to maintain significant autonomy over the restructuring of their assets and the composition of their external networks. In renewing their networks, FBGs display an enduring capacity to generate new relationships while severing older links that have become redundant. This relational capacity facilitates the rapid creation of new and increasingly diverse network linkages. Thus, while the partners may change, the dance remains the same. Entrepreneurs in local firms are able to engage in relational contracting both within and beyond their supposedly preferred ethnic networks as indicated by their relationships with politicians, bureaucrats and foreign firms. Equally, FBGs appear to be comfortable with the more arm's-length contracting preferred by managerial governed firms. Moreover, compared with the slow adjustment to change in Japan's *keiretsu* networks, which share similar relational contracting styles, the pace of group renewal appears much swifter in FBGs as owner-entrepreneurs appear able to exit from linkages with little recourse to their partners. The personalised governance system of family firms endows owner-managers with the authority necessary to commit the firm's assets to transactions. Because such commitments are personal, they may be more binding than formal or arm's-length ties.

This personalised, 'tycoon-style' social capital is a distinguishing feature of family governance and appears to have persisted in the post-crisis era. However, FBGs social capital inheres in the entrepreneur rather than the organisation and therefore its scope is more constrained than the social capital that derives from organisational sources. This distinction has a bearing upon FBGs' internationalisation strategies. Their capacity for relational contracting offers a competitive advantage in markets with numerous institutional voids but affords less advantage in more developed institutional contexts (Lovett, Simons and Kali, 1999). Consequently, FBGs are likely to gravitate to locations where their attributes offer an advantage. Thus, although China and Southeast Asian countries continue to become more integrated into the global economy, FBGs tend to remain embedded in the local regional context where their governance structures offer a competitive advantage.

The performance of ethnic Chinese family business groups in Southeast Asia

The practical effects of institutional underdevelopment in conjunction with social and political threats to their property suggest that family businesses will perform a greater number of economic tasks in an emerging market. In a mature economy, the firm can be conceptualised as a complex value chain, or wealth creation device, in which residual value is considered to be a property of equity investors. Investors in mature economies can easily reallocate and safely preserve their wealth through alternative financial instruments such as bonds and equities, pension and trust funds, venture capital and private equity funds. In addition to lacking robust protection of property rights, emerging markets lack alternative financial instruments specialising in wealth reallocation and preservation; consequently, the family business unit necessarily becomes something more than a value creation device.

Through the use of informal and often non-transparent means, the family business unit serves as an instrument of wealth protection. In this respect, the family firm has dual financial goals that are subject to frequent trade-offs between entrepreneurial wealth-generating initiatives and more defensive wealth-preservation activities. The performance of ethnic Chinese family businesses in Southeast Asia should be understood in the light of this dilemma.

Initial performance assessments cast ethnic Chinese businesses in Southeast Asia in overwhelmingly negative terms, describing them as 'pariahs' (McVey, 1992), 'ersatz capitalists' (Yoshihara, 1988) and 'rent seekers' (Morck and Yeung, 2004). Later scholarship, coinciding with Southeast Asia's economic boom 1990s, recast ethnic Chinese family businesses as the entrepreneurial engine in the region's economic development. In this view, Chinese family business networks and conglomerate structures were characterised as a novel and innovative organisational form that was a dynamic alternative to the sclerotic bureaucratic firms in the mature economies (Whitley, 1992; Whyte, 1996; Orru, Biggart and Hamilton, 1997). A popular literature appeared, lionising Southeast Asia's new business elite (Seagrave, 1995; Hiscock, 1997; Haley, Haley and Chin, 1998). In the wake of the Asian financial crisis, ethnic Chinese family businesses were again cast as the villains of the piece, and a critical analysis that focused on concentrated ownership, cronyism and weak governance structures resurfaced (Rajan and Zingales, 1998; Claessens, Djankov and Lang, 2000a). Recently, a new stream of analysis has focused upon the 'global reach' (Yeung, 2004) of Chinese family businesses, describing them as 'dragon multinationals' (Mathews, 2006). This tendency either to glorify or vilify obscures a basic strategic tension implicit in all family business, but these tensions have been magnified in the context of Southeast Asia's hothouse capitalist development. Like any other economic institution, family business has both advantages and disadvantages, which is evident in many empirical studies of Southeast Asian business groups.[2]

Several studies have examined aspects of Southeast Asian business group structure and performance; viewed collectively, their conclusions are ambiguous and indeterminate. In a study of 1,200 firms in Indonesia, Malaysia, the Philippines and Thailand, Claessens, Djankov, Fan and Lang (2002) use financial data from 1996 in an attempt to unravel value-creating and value-destroying effects of ownership concentration. They find that firm value, measured as the market to book ratio of assets, increases with the cash-flow ownership of the largest shareholder, a finding that is consistent with a positive value-enhancing incentive effect.

However, they also find that firm value falls as control rights of the largest shareholder exceed their cash-flow ownership, which is consistent with a value-destroying entrenchment effect. These effects are statistically significant in Indonesia, Malaysia and Thailand. Claessens et al. (2002) conclude that this combination of incentive and entrenchment effects can lead to unclear net effects of ownership concentration in firm value.

In a study of the effects of vertical integration and diversification strategies and performance in East Asian firms, Claessens, Djankov, Fan and Lang (2002) provide evidence of a diversification premium in lower-middle income countries (Indonesia, the Philippines and Thailand), which is indicative of support for the value-enhancing effect of internal capital markets when capital markets are undeveloped. In these settings, Claessens et al. (2002) find that mean excess value, an industry-adjusted measure of firm performance, increases with firm participation in at least two industries. However, in lower-income countries, participation in more than two industries produces a negative effect, and in middle-income countries (which in their sample includes Malaysia), the results are negative after participation in three or four industry segments. This suggests that diversification does not necessarily lead to lower market valuations in these emerging markets.

Interestingly, Claessens et al. (2002) find that vertical integration is associated with low performance in East Asian economies except in Japan. They speculate that vertical integration is a more difficult strategy to implement successfully as it requires greater learning and coordination capacity. Investments in vertical and complementary assets are of critical importance because they are required to commercialise and distribute products on global markets. Hobday (1994) suggests that East Asian firms have successfully caught up in a variety of manufacturing technologies but have not yet acquired upstream and downstream competences. Claessens et al. (2002) suggest that related diversification is an easier strategy to implement and that in these economies, it is associated with better performance.

In a direct test of the positive effects of group affiliation on the profitability of some 1,700 manufacturing firms in Indonesia, the Philippines and Thailand, Khanna and Rivkin (2001) found a positive and significant group affiliation effect among Indonesian firms and a negative but insignificant group affiliation effect in the Philippines. In Thailand their results suggest balance in the costs and benefits of group affiliation, leaving no net profit impact. More significantly, Khanna and Rivkin (2001) also tested a variant of the mutual insurance or profit-smoothing hypothesis. Specifically, Khanna and Rivkin tested the hypothesis that levels of firm profitability within a particular group will be more similar to one another than to levels of profitability outside of the group. Their results show very strong and robust evidence of a profit similarity in 12 of the 14 countries examined in this study, including Indonesia, the Philippines and Thailand. In a related study, Khanna and Yefeh (2005) examined a different sample of firms in 12 emerging markets. They found that firms affiliated with Philippine business groups exhibit superior performance in the form of high profitability and low risk (intra-group profit-smoothing) relative to unaffiliated firms. In contrast, in Indonesia and Thailand, they find that business group affiliation is associated with low profitability but low risk (intra-group profit-smoothing) suggesting that groups primarily perform a risk-reduction function.

Bertrand, Johnson, Samphantharak and Schoar (2004) studied 70 Thai FBGs using data from 1996 and 2001 and found that groups owned and managed by large families tend to have lower performance and tend to be financially unstable due to high debt levels. Bertrand et al. (2004) also find that large families are associated with larger groups but not with larger assets, which suggests that large family groups tend to divide their assets into a larger number of smaller firms to accommodate the direct involvement of all family members. Larger groups are also associated with more fragmented internal capital markets and more tunnelling along the pyramidal structure. Moreover, all of these effects are especially pronounced in groups in which the founders are no longer active and ultimate control has been passed on to an heir. Bertrand et al. (2004) ask 'Why don't families separate ownership and control rights more effectively by placing management and control in the hands of professionals but retaining ownership control within the family?' Such an arrangement would allow family members to worry about the division of cash-flow streams without distorting the efficiency of the business decisions within firms. Bertrand et al. conjecture that in countries like Thailand, limited enforcement of contracts and weak institutional governance create difficulties in separating ownership and control over cash-flow rights and owners may believe that these rights can only be guaranteed in conjunction with direct management control over their assets. These findings are consistent with those of scholars who contend that Chinese FBGs are prone to fragmentation, fissioning and rivalry when family control passes on to the second generation (Wong, 1985; Tam, 1990; Fukuyama, 1995). Consequently, as the number of family members involved increases, the deterioration of family-run group performance may be due in part to infighting for access to group resources as control becomes more diluted among different family members. This suggests that family competition for resources, especially from powerful heirs, may subject family businesses to internal as well as external pressures for expropriation. These pressures undermine the stability of the enterprise, and along with fragmenting tendencies that undermine scale and scope efficiencies, they deprive firms of adequate management.

Advocates of the industrial latecomer hypothesis contend that Chinese FBGs played a key role in helping Southeast Asia to catch up with more technologically advanced states. Most scholars agree that owners of business groups used their relational capabilities to acquire technology and low-cost manufacturing know-how from Japanese, US and European firms during the 1970s (Hobday, 1994) and to establish new telecommunications and media infrastructure in the 1990s. Equally, other analysts believe that this approach to technology acquisition is not self-sustaining and that Chinese entrepreneurs have shown an indifference to organisational learning and the development of competencies specific to the proprietary firm. Brown asserts that:

> The financial freedom before the crisis enabled Chinese businesses to indulge in economically unconnected pursuits without facing financial difficulties or competition … Chinese companies sought markets through technology but still neglected innovation. Enough information was taken in to meet immediate expansionary needs but Chinese capitalists consistently failed to engage in the long-term technological learning necessary to develop a strong basis in technology based industries. (Brown, 2000: 167)

Brown further argues that, in partnerships, Chinese capital is often subservient to foreign capital, as foreign entrepreneurs retain control of the core technologies while exploiting the political connections of their Chinese partner. The position of Chinese entrepreneurs is weakened in a more democratic environment because their assets consist of precarious connections to a rotating political class. In these relationships, Chinese entrepreneurs are a vulnerable entrepreneurial class that remains unable to establish a dynamic technological capability. Consequently, in most sectors of the economy, technological development remains unevenly distributed with the coexistence of advanced capital-intensive technology sectors linked into international markets along with traditional and labour-intensive technologies. The outcome of these dynamics is a co-evolutionary stalemate in which Chinese family firms are a powerful entrepreneurial class able to retard institutional developments that threaten their interests, but simultaneously, they are unable to adjust to continuing changes in the world economy. This seemingly paradoxical strength and weakness stems from an administrative heritage formed in the factor cost and investment-driven stages of economic development, when technology was primarily based upon imitation and acquired from foreign sources. In this stage, Chinese family firms learned to rely upon internal financing and relational bank credit, and this capital structure has created deep path dependencies for them. These firms are unlikely sources of innovation as they tend to use their positive cash flow to diversify their family's risk exposure rather than reinvesting it in order to build technology and organisational competencies.

As Southeast Asian economies confront regional competition from India and China, their competitive advantage must increasingly come from initiation rather than imitation, that is, from the creation and commercialisation of proprietary assets. In this innovation-driven stage of development, a more diverse set of financing methods is required to support the needs of firms that will innovate rather than imitate technologies invented elsewhere. In the Southeast Asian financing system, in which family-owned business groups are a core feature, the bias toward investment in physical and tangible assets, such as property and factories, signifies an important inefficiency. One corollary of this bias is that the Southeast Asian financial systems may deprive new entrants of the capital needed to create intangible assets, such as research, patents, copyrights and organisational innovations that promote learning. In the catch-up phase, this financial system bias yielded successful results by fostering the creation of a physical infrastructure and a low-cost, high-quality manufacturing sector. However, movement up the value-added chain requires the development of a more diverse financial sector, and the bias favouring physical assets, which worked so well in the take-off stage of industrialisation, may now have run its course. Left unchanged, it is poised to produce ever-diminishing returns (Carney and Gedjlovic, 2000).

The existence of adequate capital market institutions that can efficiently assess the potential value of their projects is key to the growth and development of firms that rely upon intangible assets and are dependent upon external sources of funding. The provision of external finance to small and innovative firms is a universal problem because the risks associated with innovation are high and, concomitantly, firm survival rates are low. Banks are ill-equipped to supply finance to such firms. Yet a high rate of new firm formation is critical to an innovation-driven economy (Porter, 1990). The timely provision of external funding is especially important to opportunity-rich, cash-poor small firms in high-growth sectors because such firms are rarely self-financing. Without adequate soft market infrastructure, Southeast Asian economies may systematically undervalue and fail to support the growth of indigenous firms whose assets are intangible; consequently, these economies may risk becoming stuck at the low value-added stage in international division of labour. In terms of the foregoing analysis, the Southeast Asian market may be characterised as possessing a strong physical infrastructure but a weak soft infrastructure. The pursuit of initiatives such as Malaysia's Cyberjaya and its multimedia corridor reflect this emphasis on establishing a physical infrastructure at the expense of institutional reforms that would provide an environment favourable to authentic entrepreneurial development.

In one view, indigenous high-technology firms characterised by the separation of ownership and control are comparatively new in the region and are the victims of an institutional lag (McVey, 1992). That is, a diverse range of financial institutions that could support the growth of such firms do not exist because they were not needed in previous stages of industrialisation. However, in more globalised and competitive market conditions, these institutions are required to foster a new stage of development. The analysis of this chapter suggests that this may not occur. Even as individual family fortunes rise and fall, it seems likely that privately-owned family firms will continue to dominate the economy. So long as there is the potential for political and social discrimination against minority family businesses, the advantages of private and non-transparent governance favoured by the family firm will persist. Minority owners will perceive the cloak of privacy surrounding the financial interests of family business groups as a prerequisite to the preservation of capital and for conducting transactions. If Southeast Asia's ethnic Chinese family business owners continue to perceive their environments as latently hostile, it is unlikely that entrepreneurs will give up their well-established business model. In this context, the value of advice from the international business community concerning the desirability of adopting professional management, transparent governance, and public share ownership seems limited. Critics of pyramid structures and non-transparent corporate structures, such as the World Bank and the IMF, seek to diffuse models of corporate governance developed in a context of high-quality institutions and a greater official tolerance for diversity; however, their advice might have more impact if they were more sympathetic to the precarious social and political entrepreneurial class whose organisational adaptations reflect a legacy of adversity.

Notes

1. Singapore is an exception; ethnic Chinese are a majority in this city-state.
2. Many empirical studies of Southeast Asian business groups do not distinguish between ownership by ethnic Chinese, state and indigenous entrepreneur groups. However, because ethnic Chinese own such a large percentage of business groups in each of these regions, these data shed some light upon their performance.

10

The development of Asia's business groups

In the preceding chapters we have chartered the origins of the business groups in a variety of settings, described their governance and organisational structures, and surveyed their financial and market performance. We have also attempted to review patterns of business group development as industrialisation proceeds. Similar surveys have reached different conclusions about the continued development of business groups. Granovetter (2005: 445) says, 'business groups have typically defied predictions of their imminent demise, surviving both conscious attempts by political authorities to break them up and the impact of financial crises'. Morck, Wolfenzon and Yeung (2005: 711) believe business groups have the capacity to entrench their positions; nevertheless, they conclude that 'sometimes, highly concentrated corporate control does not induce economic entrenchment. Strong institutions develop and diffuse capitalism takes hold. This apparent indeterminancy in the coevolution of institutions and corporate control is an important puzzle'. Khanna and Yafeh (2007:364) ask 'can groups ever die peacefully? We are not sure ... Because business groups do not fully realise the full costs of their presence ... presumably they will not dissolve on their own'. In his survey of the impact of the Asian crisis on business groups, Chang (2006a) agrees that they were significantly harmed by the crisis and the subsequent attempts to enhance institutions and dismantle groups. Chang does not expect business groups to disband overnight but he does anticipate that Asia's corporations will eventually converge to resemble the more focused and international firms found in North America. In this view, the forces driving convergence are intensified international competition and the development of domestic market institutions that also resemble North American institutions. In this respect, Chang implicitly favours the hypothesis that the logic for business groups will disappear as market institutions are established.

This view has become a dominant hypothesis, informing academic research on business groups.

The dominant hypothesis of business group development

In the preceding chapters, the implied hypothesis about business group development is a two-stage 'institutional void' model, which proposes that business groups first emerge to solve institutional and market failures. By internalising market failures, business groups facilitate economic development through the creation of industrial capacity and a supporting infrastructure. In this perspective, business groups form because it is profitable to do so. In conditions of institutional voids and market imperfections, affiliation to a business group provides a firm with a competitive advantage relative to a freestanding firm and so assures the ascendancy of the business group model in Asian economies.

In the second, succeeding, stage of development, governments begin to pursue market-oriented policies that seek to establish a 'soft market infrastructure' that will support a more complex, specialised and advanced industrial structure. As the state oversees the development of market institutions that plug institutional voids, the rationale for business group existence and the basis of their competitive advantage begins to erode. Several scholars believe that, as the institution-building project proceeds, business groups will gradually disappear. The creation of market institutions is expected to stimulate the entry and successful performance of freestanding firms possessing different competitive advantages. In competition with freestanding firms supported by market institutions, the costs of business group affiliation begin to exceed the benefits. The business group structure will become increasingly inefficient and business groups will either fail or restructure by spinning off their affiliates to become more focused entities concentrating upon their core competencies.

One difficulty with the institutional void hypotheses is that there is no convincing explanation for the origins of business groups. The implied assumption is that business groups endogenously or spontaneously form to seize the opportunities created by institutional voids. However, this assumption does not reflect the circumstances in which Asian business groups initially emerged. In many nation states, business groups did not emerge, but were deliberately constructed with the assistance of an active and entrepreneurial state. In contemporary China, central and provincial governments assembled business groups from a population of existing state-owned business groups. In Korea, a modernising president selected 'a few millionaires' and pushed them into the centre stage of economic development (Amsden, 1989). In Taiwan, the government established a tax regime that favoured the formation of business groups and penalised firms that grew organically (Chung, 2001). Similarly in Indonesia, Malaysia, the Philippines, Singapore and Thailand, single-party states and strongman leaders with long and uninterrupted periods in power have directly constructed or encouraged the development of large diversified business groups to pursue their nationalist economic agendas.

Moreover, far from cultivating market institutions, in the initial stages of development the vast majority of Asian states have actively and intentionally suppressed market institutions so as to exert and maintain power over the economy (Prowse, 1996). Furthermore, states have often used their extensive control of credit and market access to determine which firms will profit and by how much. Similarly, the impact of business group affiliation on a firm's performance is far from clear. Although states have liberalised their grasp on the economy, there is no evidence that business groups have begun to systematically refocus and restructure. The picture is far too complex to make any unequivocal claims. Khanna and Yefeh (2007: 366) believe that 'any blanket characterization of business groups as either paragons or parasites would be unwarranted, both because of the nature of the existing evidence and because of the continued existence of unanswered puzzles'.

Our survey of Asia's business groups has uncovered substantially different developmental paths that do not fit comfortably into a two-stage development model. However, other hypotheses have been developed in the context of Asia and other developing regions of the world. In the following section we explicate three alternative hypotheses of business group development and performance outcomes. Each emphasises slightly different roles for the leading actors and each sheds light on some aspects of group development.

Three alternative hypotheses of business group development

Table 10.1 outlines the key elements of the institutional void hypothesis of business group development. Also listed are three other hypotheses,

Table 10.1 Four hypotheses of business group development

Hypothesis	Key actors	Origins and growth	Decline	Performance
Institutional voids	Firms	Spontaneous emergence	Institutions appear, rationale for business groups disappears	First, affiliation improves profits; later, costs exceed benefits
Rational choice-lifecycle	Firms	Firms choose to affiliate	Inertia/ decadence	First, profits based on efficiency; later, profits based on power
State-led industrialisation	State firms	State creates business groups, firms learn	As firms approach technology frontier they restructure and focus	First, state determines profits; later, profit based on competitiveness
Crony capitalism	Politicians and entrepreneurs	Deals	Business groups persist	Non-transparent, firms hide profits

which may be described as the rational-choice lifecycle, state-led industrialisation and crony capitalism.

Rational choice-lifecycle

The rational choice lifecycle hypothesis model originates from some of the earliest studies of business groups (Strachan, 1976; Leff, 1978) and may be considered the antecedent of the institutional void hypothesis. However, these earlier models were less sanguine about the behaviour of mature business groups and the consequences for economic development and welfare. In the rational choice-lifecycle hypothesis, the entrepreneur is the key actor and will select the most profitable of the competing organisational forms. In this perspective, business groups may appear when independent entrepreneurs choose to affiliate themselves to a particular group. Alternatively, a group may emerge as a single entrepreneur diversifies through partial acquisitions and/or spins off other firms as semi-autonomous entities. Both Leff (1978) and Strachan (1976) propose that business groups will be particularly important in emerging market conditions and propose the possibility of a group lifecycle.

In the early phase of the lifecycle, a group forms voluntarily in order to provide financial services to its members, especially the financial services connected to securing credit and making investments. Strachan also suggests that the group insurance principle is an especially important motive for forming or joining groups in emerging markets because government policy and economic development cause uncertainty for the firm.

Strachan provides a succinct summation of the developmental logic of the lifecycle model:

> In the formative years, the group is climbing to a position of power. Its growth will almost always depend upon its being situated in the number of fast-growing, profitable industries. The groups ... achieve an initial critical mass from firms who have successfully adapted new technology to old activities or who are leaders in developing new industries. Having reached a position of relatively great size the job of maintaining historic growth rates becomes increasingly difficult. About this time an alternative business strategy opens as the concentration of power within the group makes the elimination of competition and the use of political power an increasingly feasible road to profits ... I suspect that in their mature years business groups follow a strategy built more on power than on performance. (Strachan, 1976: 98)

According to Strachan's hypothesis, the hard-driving entrepreneur successfully establishes a group but is transformed by his or her success and begets 'a decadent elite' (Strachan, 1976). The entrepreneur's successors seek to entrench their power and resort to politics to protect their wealth, a phenomenon that Morck, Strangeland and Yeung (1998) describe as the Canadian disease. As illustrated in Figure 10.1, entrepreneurs initially embody the positive attributes of the business group form, which brings great success. Yet success is fleeting and self-limiting: to maintain their position, groups increasingly betray the negative attributes of business groups. In contrast to the institutional void perspective, business groups do not disappear or fail in the second stage of development nor do their profits decline, instead business groups remain strong and frustrate continued economic development by inhibiting the entry of new firms into the economy.

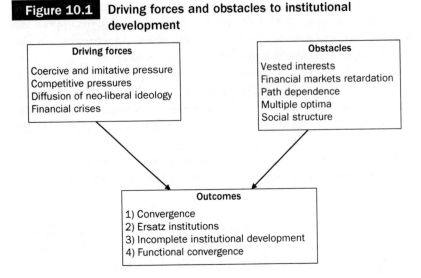

Figure 10.1 Driving forces and obstacles to institutional development

Driving forces

Coercive and imitative pressure
Competitive pressures
Diffusion of neo-liberal ideology
Financial crises

Obstacles

Vested interests
Financial markets retardation
Path dependence
Multiple optima
Social structure

Outcomes

1) Convergence
2) Ersatz institutions
3) Incomplete institutional development
4) Functional convergence

State-led industrialisation in late-developing countries

While the rational choice hypothesis puts the entrepreneur and the family at the centre of the analysis, there is little room for the state. The state is viewed mainly as a potential threat to business that must be actively managed. In contrast, political-economy scholars bring in the state to share the stage, with entrepreneurs in the leading roles. Indeed, in the state-led industrialisation model, the state is cast as the most important character: the state is the entrepreneur. Because the state is viewed as having more information and more power than the private sector, it takes the lead in driving economic development. The state also decides the timing and manner of entry into certain industries, selecting particular firms to perform the market entry activity (Amsden, 1989; Keister, 2000). The 'strong developmental state' can override vested interests, such as landowners, the military and organised labour, and direct economic resources toward establishing industrial capacity on its own terms. In this perspective, business groups may be actively assembled or cultivated under the guidance of the state, and provided with resources and policies that favour capital accumulation and the acquisition of technology.

The state-led industrialisation thesis views domestic entrepreneurs as 'industrial latecomers', who lack the resources to catch up with technological leaders from advanced economies. This introduces another actor into the state-led industrialisation hypothesis: the foreign firm, which possesses the advanced technological and managerial capabilities that the latecomer state would like to acquire. Under a free-trade regime, foreign firms could enter and dominate a local economy because they have overpowering technological skills relative to domestic entrepreneurs. To provide an opportunity for domestic entrepreneurs to imitate, learn and catch up with firms from advanced economies, the state must deliberately manipulate property rights in favour of local players. Through a regime of licensing and permissions, the state establishes a protected trading environment that allows domestic entrepreneurs sufficient time and protection to catch up with more advanced firms. The state also manages domestic markets by setting the competitive 'rules of the game'. For example, the state allocates opportunities to entrepreneurs and sets prices for inputs; it also determines the number of competitors and which foreign firms may participate. If a favoured entrepreneur becomes complacent or is perceived as inefficient, the state may encourage new firms to enter a sector. By controlling the competition and resource levers, the state directly or indirectly determines the enterprise's profits.

As industrial strategy is largely determined by the state, the role of the business group is to 'implement' the industrial capacity building process (Amsden, 1989; Hobday, 1995). The entrepreneur's task is to be a pupil, and by acquiring technological learning, perform a catch-up function and more generally assist the movement of a country's domestic economy towards the technological frontier. The core task of the firm is to imitate technology and organisational processes invented and created elsewhere. At the same time, firms must become skilful at efficiently executing projects and running plants. During the learning or catch-up phase, business groups compete for allocation of state resources and must perfect their project management skills and demonstrate production efficiency (Amsden, 1989; Kock and Guillén, 2001).

To effect its entry strategy, the state typically selects the assembly or manufacturing stages of labour-intensive industries in which it holds a comparative advantage, such as garment making or textiles. Later, the state may emphasise capital-intensive industries by providing capital that is beyond the means of most domestic entrepreneurs. Because firms in latecomer economies, at least initially, do not possess proprietary skills (Amsden, 1989; Kock and Guillén, 2001), they become generalists, whose skills enable them to operate in a variety of protected industrial sectors. This may also result in economies of scope, which provide a basis for firm growth.

A firm's financial performance may be improved by the quality of the entrepreneur's contacts with officials inside the government, or its 'contact capabilities' (Koch and Guillén, 2001). However, contact capabilities are skills associated with an individual, and because they are not embedded deeply within the organisation, they rarely form the basis for international competitiveness. To maintain growth, the entrepreneur must establish contacts with foreign firms that have appropriate capabilities they are willing to share with a local firm (Kock and Guillén, 2001).

Large firm size is often accompanied by the problem of control loss (Williamson, 1975) and to avoid this, the group must devise some mechanism for establishing autonomy among firms that have matured sufficiently to stand on their own feet. Gerlach (1997) contends that repeated entry needs to be associated with and complemented by decentralisation and repeated spin-offs to keep the group within a manageable scope as it approaches the threshold of technology frontier.

According to the state-led industrialisation hypothesis, a new phase of development begins once a country achieves a significant level of economic development and income for its citizens. Confronted by growing factor costs, the state revises its industrial strategy. At this stage of advancement the economy is typically complex and the state now encounters difficulties making effective entrepreneurial decisions and allocating resources. Importantly, it becomes increasingly necessary for the locus of decision-making to be decentralised to a wider group of actors. Recognising the need to travel up the value-added chain, the state seeks to establish an institutional infrastructure that supports innovation, such as science parks, venture capital and NASDAQ-style equity markets, and provides tax incentives for research and development (Hobday, 1995; Mathews, 1999).

Greater demands are made upon entrepreneurs and managers of firms at this more advanced stage of economic development. In place of the generic skills of imitation, industry entry and production efficiency, firms are enjoined to develop proprietary organisational and technological capabilities. The firms are expected to move from a strategy of imitation towards a strategy of innovation, and from dependent pupil to active originator. Firms must develop the skills to enter either the initiating phase of the industry product lifecycle or enter the infant industries. To do so, firms must progress beyond their generic skills and assets and develop more specialised and related capabilities. The product market focus will shift from that of conglomeration and wide diversification toward a more focused, coherent strategy driven by core competences. Skills are no longer embedded in a single individual but diffused within the middle tiers of the organisation among engineers, marketing and research and development specialists. These significant changes in strategic emphasis lead to significant structural readjustments on the part of the business group, which evolves towards a formally integrated and centralised M-form organisation. This organisation-based set of capabilities implies that the firm is better placed to cope with competition from more advanced firms.

Improvements in firms' organisational and technological capabilities combined with enhancements in the quality of the innovation infrastructure may set the economy on a virtuous circle of incremental, continuous improvement. The trade barriers that were initially erected to protect weak domestic firms may now be incrementally dismantled, gradually introducing domestic firms to the stimulus of international competition.

In this perspective, the competitive or selection environment gradually becomes more market-based and firms prosper or fail based upon their ability to compete in the international marketplace, not upon their connections to politicians. Business groups are placed between a pincer movement of growing foreign and domestic competition from focused firms with superior specialist capabilities on the one hand and a more developed institutional and soft market infrastructure, which undermines the logic of business groups' competitive advantage. At this late stage of catch-up, domestic firms' profitability is dependent upon their international competitiveness. Business groups that remain widely diversified become the targets of restructuring and takeover by stronger domestic or foreign rivals.

Crony capitalism-business group persistence hypothesis

The implicit assumption of the state-led industrialisation hypothesis is that the state is a strong actor capable of resisting demands for favourable treatment from special interest groups. Rather than being corrupt, politicians and officials display a relatively technocratic orientation. They are intent on pursuing nationalist agendas aimed at improving the security and economic wellbeing of the country as a whole. However, not all Asian states have enjoyed such enlightened leadership. Politicians and officials have not always been disinterested nation-building technocrats and many have sought to extract a private and personal stake from the opportunities provided by industrialisation.

In a closed economy with significant state intervention, politicians and officials reserve the right to allocate resources on a discretionary basis. The discretionary authority of state officials creates opportunities for entrepreneurs who are skilled at exploiting their network connections or *guanxi* to cultivate reciprocity with resource gatekeepers (Xin and Pearce, 1996). The practice of striking bargains with corrupt political leaders to gain access to state mediated credits and local monopolies has also been described as 'rent-seeking' (Morck and Yeung, 2004) or 'crony capitalism' (Kang, 2002). In what Fukuyama (1995) calls 'low trust societies', the state may be ideologically hostile toward the business community or some subsection of it. Low-trust societies sometimes have a long history of social and ethnic conflict or state predation on business. In these circumstances, entrepreneurs confront a heightened risk of asset confiscation, rent expropriation, corruption, discrimination, regulatory restriction and other risks that engender defensive behaviour in its entrepreneurs. To protect their interests, entrepreneurs may construct a thick social wall to separate reliable insiders from untrustworthy outsiders (Fukuyama, 1995). Such exclusionary behaviour is an understandable response to conflict or state predation, but it can also impede the development of the more open and universalistic values that are needed to support the diffusion of liberal market institutions. If the state has been historically poor in delivering collective goods, such as security and justice, then secret societies, cliques and criminal organisations may emerge to provide basic levels of security, but such organisations will retard the later stages of institutional development.

To pursue the opportunities provided by discretion or mitigate the threat posed by expropriation, entrepreneurs seek to gain the patronage of a high-level politician or official. These relationships, which MacIntyre (1994) describes as patrimonial or clientelist, typically place the entrepreneur in a subordinate position relative to the patron. An exchange of resources is an essential element in these relationships and this can be either the sharing of the spoils of patronage or of payments for security and protection money. However, relationships are often unstable, as their value will depreciate rapidly if the patron falls out of power. Moreover, the entrepreneur must also keep the demands of a patron in check while preserving the relationship. Entrepreneurs understate their wealth by creating non-transparent and complex business structures, or pyramids to disguise resources. Such structures also provide for 'capital flight' and shield resources in the event that relations turn sour. As the true economic picture is deliberately hidden, these conditions make it very difficult to determine the profitability of business groups. Patrimonial and crony relationships are often characterised as trust-based but more often the reality is much more precarious as a lack of trust begets a lack of trust. In this way, crony capitalism generates an inertial dynamic as entrepreneurs, politicians and state officials mistrust one another, creating a rent-seeking society (Morck and Yeung, 2004).

When patrimonial relationships among politicians and entrepreneurs are endemic in society, there is likely to be a continuing politicisation of the economy. Societies remain crisis-prone with the potential for political discontinuity, instability and dramatic reversals in their development. Because contextual threats remain latent, uncertainty and risk may be viewed as long-term phenomena and the firm may regard the 'transitional/emergent phase' as permanent. If entrepreneurs accumulate skills that allow them to perceive, interpret and manage active and latent threats, this may serve as a long-term and valuable capability. If officials and politicians find it difficult to give up their interventionist ways and do not allow competitive market forces to operate, the selection environment will remain politicised and competitive environments will stagnate at low levels of firm capability.

In this perspective, there is nothing inevitable about the decline of business groups based upon patrimony linkages with the state. If risk, uncertainty, hostility and cronyism are persistent environmental factors, firms whose capabilities are based upon managing these qualities may remain dominant features of the industrial landscape. Family firms, especially those originating in business-friendly, ethnic-minority communities, may enjoy a considerable advantage over professionally-managed companies. Indeed, family firms can use their flexibility and the longevity of their leadership to build and exploit two forms of social capital: bonding capital, which is inherited from membership in the minority community and provides better bases for business transactions than underdeveloped institutions; and bridging capital, the mutually beneficial links to government and market elites that mediate access to opportunities and scarce resources.

The future of Asian business groups

It is far from clear that any single hypothesis fully explains the developmental trajectory of any Asian state. In some settings no single theory is satisfactory. In two large Asian economies, China and India, there are significant differences in the timing of the appearance of business groups. In India, cohorts of business groups were formed in very different historical conditions. Several groups were formed by indigenous entrepreneurs during the period of British colonial rule. Another cohort was formed in the chaotic post-independence period when departing colonial firms transferred their assets to Indian ownership. Yet another cohort was formed during the highly protectionist period of the 'licence raj' in the 1960s and 1970s. In China, the larger, government-assembled, state-owned business groups were located in Northeast China where the Communist Party was historically strong. In the south of the country, private and family-owned business groups were formed with the injection of capital from overseas Chinese communities based in Taiwan, Hong Kong and Southeast Asia. Within both these very large economies there are widely divergent patterns of economic development, such as between rural and urban communities in India and between China's interior and coastal regions.

Nevertheless, there are some common patterns in the developmental process:

- The state played an important interventionist role in the early stages of development and has, with varying degrees of success and discipline, fostered the development of domestically-owned business groups as the national instruments of industrialisation.

- Due either to their transactional efficiency or to their preferred connections in government, a small number of large business groups have accumulated a significant concentration of economic power within the host economy.

- Having gained substantial economic power, business groups have succeeded in reducing their dependence upon state resources and increasing their autonomy from state control.

- Subsequent attempts by the state to liberalise the economy and construct market institutions have occurred in the context of a powerful domestically-based industrial elite.

Future changes to these economic and institutional environments will determine whether or not business groups survive and continue to evolve and if so, to what extent and at what speed. Figure 10.1 indicates that there are both driving forces and obstacles to the continued development of market-based institutions in Asian economies. The interaction between driving forces and obstacles will influence institutional development and outcomes.

Forces driving institutional development

Coercive and imitative pressures

Important and powerful forces for change in institutional structures may emanate from beyond the local national system. Such forces may be characterised as coercive, normative or ideational, and competitive. Coercion stems from the ability of powerful states and international organisations to shape the rules of the international game and enforce compliance by weaker states. Normative ideational forces arise from the emergence of ideas, ideologies, and beliefs in desirable institutions. Djelic and Quack (2003) have described the similar impact of transnational influences that emanate from world society and disseminate organising trends, fashions and fads that result from new scientific knowledge, discoveries or changing material conditions. New ideas and beliefs diffuse through processes of voluntary adoption and imitation in receiver societies. At a higher level of abstraction, the upheaval in the international geopolitical order stemming from conflict, crises and adjustments to the decline of communism in the region has generated a series of exogenous shocks to local states' local systems (Carney and Gedajlovic, 2002a). Coercive and imitative pressures may interact in a variety of ways and we may identify at least two concrete expressions of pressures on the Asian states to adopt market-oriented institutions: the diffusion of a neo-liberal ideology and the periodic eruption of financial crises. Peng (2003) suggests that national systems react incrementally and as a result, incumbents and new entrants adopt elements from one another in a manner that produces hybrid institutions consisting of international and locally constructed elements.

Competitive adoption

Competitive pressures stem from the receiver society's need for resources or from changes in the aspirations of local actors. If states determine that they wish to develop industry sectors or improve their trade, they begin to compete to attract resources from external entities. Asian states have long recognised that technological and management know-how is embedded in the proprietary processes of multinational enterprises. Hence, states are in direct competition with one another to attract foreign direct investment. Countries competing in the same market have chosen to adopt similar policies in order to maintain competitive parity. For example, states such as Hong Kong, Singapore and Malaysia have each attempted to attain the status of 'regional financial centre' and have proposed a raft of policies to attract foreign capital.

The diffusion of neo-liberal ideology

Over the past two decades there has been a gradual turning away from state intervention in the economy and a move towards the adoption of a neo-liberal ideology of free markets. For the most part, Asian states have avoided the worst excesses of the 'shock therapy' liberalisation strategies that were implemented in Latin American and Eastern Bloc countries in the 1970s and 1980s. However, several emerging Asian economies and former communist states have gradually and incrementally adopted a package of economic policies aimed at reducing the scope of government intervention in the economy. This policy package includes fiscal and macroeconomic liberalisation of trade, capital outflows and foreign investment restrictions, and the liberalisation of the banking and financial sectors. In industries such as electrical utilities and telecommunications, the policy package includes factors such as the privatisation of state enterprises; the formal separation of regulation and provision of service; the de-politicisation of regulatory authority; and deregulation and the opening of the retail market to multiple service providers (Henisz, Guillen and Zelner, 2005). Although neo-liberalism is today the dominant economic policy paradigm, it has not emerged simultaneously in all states and nor has it been adopted to the same degree everywhere. For example, privatisation frequently occurs without deregulation or the de-politicisation of the bureaucracy.

Liberalisation and financial crisis

Some scholars and policymakers believe that liberalisation renders economies vulnerable to market destabilisation and financial crisis. For example, in North America, the deregulation of utility and telecommunication markets produced the Enron and Worldcom corporate scandals. In Asia, the liberalisation of foreign capital flows without the corresponding creation of an effective regulatory authority, played a large part in the lead up to Asian financial crisis (Stiglitz, 2002). In addition to the costly effects of disruption to the economy, financial crises legitimise the adoption of financial sector and corporate reforms and also make states vulnerable to the coercive influence of international institutions. The IMF, the World Bank and other multilateral developmental agencies granted loans and debt relief packages to emerging markets but this assistance was conditional upon governments committing to carrying out extensive constitutional reforms according to the principle of liberal market economics. Low-income and indebted countries are particularly vulnerable to the coercive influences of international institutions.

Obstacles to the development of market institutions

The forces driving institutional change are met with numerous obstacles and inertial forces that retard the development of high-quality institutions.

Vested interests

Newly powerful business groups may be expected to resist reform efforts because they threaten their rents. Liberal market institutions also threaten the power base of incumbent firms that have grown powerful during the period of state-led industrialisation. As noted above, incumbent business groups have sunk costs and investments into relational assets that are well adapted to existing environments. If the environment were to change radically, business groups could not quickly unlearn their routines and would see the value of their assets reduced. For example, in economies where capital is mainly mediated through banks, funds tend to be more readily available to business groups with extensive social capital, providing these firms with an important competitive advantage over new entrants (Khanna and Pelepu, 1997). Another key resource of well-placed groups is their capacity to mediate access to domestic resources and foreign multinationals (Guillen, 2000). However, the move toward greater transparency or toward equity-market capital allocation will reduce the value of relational assets.

Because the business elite is relatively small, the coordination of political action is uncomplicated and dominant firms may set the rules and agendas for others, such as new entrants and challenger firms. The latter can better assure their survival by finding ways to fit into the dominant scheme. Consequently, business groups and their allies in government and financial sectors may form a blocking coalition that preserves existing institutions in their current non-market form. In a period of structural market change, the preservation of outmoded institutions may shrink the pie, but this may be a rational strategy if incumbents are able to maintain the size of their own pieces (Bebchuk and Roe, 1999). Political theory suggests that this may motivate incumbents to capture and derail institutional innovations (Haggard, 2001) and reverse institutional developments that create competition from new entrants (Rajan and Zingales, 2001).

Internal capital markets retard development of external capital markets

According to Almeida and Wolfenzon (2006), the allocated efficiency of the external capital market is retarded by business groups that have become very large relative to the economy. Claessens, Djankov and Lang (2002) have demonstrated very high levels of concentration in Asian economies. Business groups rely upon internal capital markets to allocate resources, and in this regard they may be relatively efficient. However, business groups cannot easily invest outside of the group. Due to 'limited pledge ability', or the high transactions costs of investing in projects outside the group, they will frequently prefer to invest in relatively mediocre projects within the group despite the potential for higher returns in projects outside the group. Consequently, business groups suffocate the development of external capital markets by retaining investment decisions to firms within the group. Almeida and Wolfenzon (2006) suggest that internal capital markets are beneficial at very low levels of financial development and business groups may improve allocated efficiency because the external market works so poorly that it is practically impossible for firms to raise capital. In this situation, internal capital market reallocation from low productivity to mediocre productivity projects is better than no reallocation at all. At very high levels of investor protection and financial market development, the conglomerate's internal reallocation advantage typically disappears as it is possible for firms with high-productivity projects to credibly attract capital from external sources. Almeida and Wolfenzon (2006) theorise that the negative effects of business group conglomeration on external capital markets are most pronounced at intermediate levels of financial market development because the costs associated with the external capital market's residual underdevelopment make it fragile to the negative externalities imposed by business groups. The capacity for high-productivity firms to raise additional capital is sensitive to the capital supply versus the degree of conglomeration; in this intermediate stage, the efficiency of external capital allocation decreases with increased conglomeration.

Path dependencies and complementarities

Much of the literature on institutional development focuses upon path-dependencies, suggesting that once an economy has adopted a state-led developmental path, it becomes difficult to change to another path. More generally, Hollingsworth (1997: 265) claims that 'there are serious limitations on the extent to which a society may mimic the forms of economic governance and performance in others societies'. Path dependencies arise because the initial development regime selected engenders numerous complementary and interdependent institutions and administrative practices in the host society; emerging regulatory agencies, governmental and business organisations will conform to the character of the regime. Complementary institutions, their decision rules and the behavioural norms they exhibit may be so deeply embedded that they become invisible or 'taken for granted' by actors in the system. Nobel Prize winning economist Douglas North (1990) refers to this interdependence of organisation, administrative practice, decision rules and norms as an institutional matrix. North has observed that institutional matrices can experience 'lock-in' and reform is difficult because so many players are linked; thus, change in one field cannot be effected without change in another and so on. Consequently, planned, systematic administrative reform will tend to be the exception rather than the rule. In most cases, reform will be slow and incremental and seemingly unrelated to a change in the architects' original goals.

Network externalities

Network externalities also engender resistance to reform. Because the routines and assets of incumbent firms tend to be complementary with those of other incumbent firms in the local environment, they will find it profitable to maintain their routines. For example, if firms' trading routines and cognitive biases are based upon relational contracting, they will tend to find it more efficient to transact with firms possessing similar cognitive biases. If a firm were to unilaterally adopt a more transparent and arms-length approach in an economy dominated by relational firms, it would face difficulties in finding similar firms to trade with and would face increased costs when transacting with firms characterised by differing routines. The presence of significant transactional externalities and complementarities creates inertia; established ways of doing business cannot be shifted unless many firms simultaneously adopt new routines.

Multiple optima

The notion of multiple optima suggests that differences in the efficiency levels of alternative institutional modes may be small. Literature on the various forms of capitalism suggests, at least among advanced economies, liberal market economies and coordinated market economies, that although their institutional environments are characterised by important differences, each may be equally effective in terms of generating income and productive efficiencies for members (Hall and Soskice, 2001). The idea of multiple optima also applies at the level of the firm. Given the choice between two institutions, the individual firm may be relatively indifferent. For example, the benefits of market-based financial institutions may reduce the average cost of capital for a closely-held firm. However, given that the risks and difficulties of changing from a closely-held to a widely-held firm would impose significant transitional costs, maintaining the status quo and living with higher capital costs may be more efficient (Bebchuk and Roe, 1999).

Liberalisation and deregulation create uncertainty

Powerful states and international organisations exert pressure for liberal reforms and this is a potent force for change. Nevertheless, countries vary considerably in their efforts to adopt liberal reforms. Very few countries are either capable of or willing to adopt the full package in one stage. Instead, states more often adopt a staged or phased transition toward neo-liberal policies. Indeed, Henisz et al. (2005: 892) find that the diffusion of market-oriented reforms is typically a partial phenomenon. In particular, they find that international pressures for reform will increase the likelihood of privatisation and regulatory separation but they also show that neither regulatory de-politicisation nor the liberalisation of competition is likely to increase. It is relatively easy to liberalise industrial sectors and remove restrictions on formerly prohibited activities, but it is more difficult to establish fully-functioning market institutions. Paradoxically, reform and liberalisation initially create even more uncertainty. Early-stage transitions toward market institutions occur in a context of considerable institutional gaps and a transition period is always characterised by uncertainty. These conditions promote the emergence of business groups, or if they already exist, uncertainty strengthens their advantages in the economy. In China, the policy of gradual regulatory reform was instrumental in the formation of business groups (Keister, 2000). In Taiwan, sweeping liberalisation and deregulation of the financial sector and several industrial sectors led to the strengthening of formerly weak and fragmented business groups (Luo and Chung, 2005). Partial and incremental liberalisation in Korea also led to a strengthening of the larger business groups (Amsden and Euh, 1993). Initial reforms in Indonesia followed the oil price increases of the 1980s and saw the growth of a small group of extremely powerful business groups. In these settings, privatisation of state enterprises and the relaxing of restrictions in capital flows provide incumbent insiders with considerable market power. Hence, at least in the early stages of the creation of market institutions, it seems that business groups become more important in the economy rather than less important.

Outcomes

Convergence

The institutional void hypothesis suggests that business groups will fade away following the development of market institutions – this is consistent with a global convergence outcome. Strategy and institutional theorists have been interested in the idea of convergence. Strategy scholars have argued that factors such as competition and technology will drive rival firms to adopt similar corporate structures (Ohmae, 1985). Theodore Levitt's statement on the case for convergence is perhaps the most unambiguous:

> The global company will shape the vectors of technology and globalization into its great strategic fecundity. It will systematically push these vectors towards their own convergence, offering everyone simultaneously high quality, more or less standardized products at optimally low prices, thereby achieving for itself vastly expanded markets and profits. Companies that do not adapt to the new global realities will become victims of those that do. (Levitt, 1983)

In contrast, institutional theorists see global convergence driven by bureaucratic rationalising forces or an 'iron cage' that progressively spreads common standards, norms and beliefs (Meyer, 1994). Others see convergence in corporate governance stemming from the more diffuse forces of world society (Drori, Jang and Meyer, 2006). However, a more prevalent view is that convergence is limited by the continuing importance of local factors (Guillen, 2000). In this view, forces driving institutional convergence interact with resistant obstacles and produce divergent change trajectories. In their theory on the effects of globalisation in transitional economies and emerging markets, Djelic and Quack (2003) suggest that the appearance of market institutions is a result of a 'double process of institutionalisation and de-institutionalisation'. The process is portrayed as a clash of ideology and practice involving several global challenger institutions, homogenising pressures and incumbent local institutions. This collision of powerful structural forces generates micro-interactions in which a succession and combination of incremental trickle-up and trickle-down processes may culminate in one of several outcomes. The interaction of driving forces and obstacles may produce at least three other alternative and hybridised outcomes including reversals, symbolic or ersatz institutional change, and functional convergence.

Reversals

If external sources exert excessive coercive pressure to adopt market institutions, this, in combination with recurrent crises and uncertainty attributed to market institutions, may engender excessively reactionary responses in host economies, especially if too many stakeholders lose valued positions over too short a period. Moreover, if the beneficial effects of reform appear to be concentrated in the hands of a small business elite, visible minorities, or a particular ethnic group (as appears to be the case in some Southeast Asian states) then market institutions may be perceived to aggravate income inequality and the lack of justice, especially if the state is slow to build mass welfare institutions or social safety nets for vulnerable members of society. If pro-market reform is associated with political reform aimed at establishing liberal democracy, free elections and mass participation in politics, the conditions favour the election of populist political parties and politicians who may scapegoat or vilify wealthy minorities or foreign business interests (Chua, 2003). These conditions produce a combustible political environment that is open to instability and reaction.

Few theories of institutional change contemplate the possibility of 'great reversals' in the direction of institutional development (Rajan and Zingales, 2001); the assumption is that the bureaucratisation and/or marketisation of society will continue to grow. A great reversal represents the repudiation of liberal market institutions and their displacement by norms and values derived from alternative concepts of rationality. The Islamic Revolution and overthrow of the 'modernising' Shah of Iran represents a dramatic example of a reversal in the direction of institutional development (Carney and Farashahi, 2006). Social and political upheavals may disrupt efforts to imitate liberal market institutions and replace rational-legal institutions with those based upon traditional authority patterns. For example, after years of seeking to establish Malaysia as an international financial centre, Prime Minister Mahathir's handling of foreign capital and his resistance to IMF restructuring procedures during the 1997 Asian financial crisis was indicative of a reversal in the direction of institutional development. Institutional reversals will typically reinforce the position of business groups in the economy.

Ersatz institutional reform

Ersatz institutional reform occurs when regulatory and supervisory agencies are established but are under-resourced or vested with little executive authority, or when legislation is put on the books but not enforced. Ersatz reform is symbolic. Governments may either fail to understand what is required to make market institutions work or they fail to invest in the institutional capacity needed to breathe life into the formal rules. Ersatz institutional reform may bring legitimacy to the host government as potential trading partners receive the signal that the host state is engaged in attempting to reform its economy. Yet beneath the veneer of compliance and the adoption of seemingly pro-liberal market institutions, there is active and latent resistance. For example, Khanna, Kogan and Palepu (2006) find robust evidence of de jure similarity in corporate governance systems but find virtually no evidence of de facto similarity. In other words, 'best practice' institutional rules are widely diffused across many societies but are not being implemented. Khanna et al. (2006) claim their findings are consistent with the view that complementarities result in different national systems but also consistent with the view that globalisation is not strong enough to overcome powerful vested interests. Enforcement of market rules may initially be limited by an inadequate complementary institutional capacity, for example, the lack of a competent and impartial judiciary. Ersatz institutional reform exhibits an inertial self-reinforcing dynamic. Through their political strategies and control pyramids, incumbent business groups may strengthen their position. Because they so dominate the economy, business groups' internal capital markets weaken the development of external capital markets and new entrants are thwarted. The absence of external capital markets also inhibits the development of a market for corporate control, allowing existing firms to further entrench economic power in the hands of a few first-mover business groups.

Functional convergence

Legal scholars such as Gilson (2000) distinguish between formal and functional convergence. When different states adopt similar institutions this is referred to as formal convergence. Advocates of the functional convergence perspective believe that different institutional arrangements are equally capable of performing the same governance task and producing similar outcomes. For example, most scholars agree that it is dysfunctional for economies to entrench weak management in major corporations. In North America, the market for corporate control can terminate weak top management. In Japan, the market for corporate control is much weaker due to the system of cross-shareholdings. However, Kaplan (1994) finds that Japanese firms achieve executive turnover in underperforming firms through other means. Institutional reform based upon functional convergence may be better fitted to the idiosyncrasies of historical situations. Functional convergence recognises that attempts to improve corporate governance may be more fruitful if reformers work within the traditions of existing institutions rather than attempting to fashion completely new institutions.

Appendix A:
A selection of business group definitions

The following is a non-exhaustive list of definitions of business groups selected from the literature. They are ordered chronologically, followed by several country-specific definitions.

'[The] long-term association of a great diversity of firms and the men who own and manage these firms' (Strachan, 1976: 2).

Strachan also suggests that three characteristics distinguish business groups from other types of associations: (1) the great diversity of enterprises in a group; (2) pluralism: the groups consist of a coalition of several wealthy businessmen and families; and (3) an atmosphere of loyalty and trust 'normally associated with family or kinship groups. A group member's relation to other group members is characterized by a higher standard of fair dealings and disclosure than that which generally is found in arm's length commerce' (Strachan, 1976: 2–3).

'In the typical conglomerate ... a common parent owns the subsidiaries but generally few operational or personal ties exist among the sister subsidiaries. On the other hand, within business groups ... there are generally personal and operational ties among all the firms' (Strachan, 1976: 20).

'The group can be conceptualised as an organisation structure for appropriating quasi-rents which accrue to scarce and imperfectly marketed inputs. Some of these inputs such as capital might be marketed more efficiently but in the conditions of the less developed countries they are not. Some of these inputs are inherently difficult to market efficiently for example honest and trustworthy competence on the part of higher-level managers' (Leff, 1978: 666).

'The group can perhaps best be understood as an institutional innovation for internalising the returns which accrue from interactivity operations in the imperfect market conditions of the less developed countries. What has happened in effect is that the groups have appropriated as against the quasirents of the output which leaving Stine envisaged would otherwise be forgone due to factor markets and insufficient entrepreneurship … the group constitutes a pattern of industrial organisation which permits structure rather than gifted individuals to perform the key interactivity function of entrepreneurship' (Leff, 1978: 669).

'A group of companies that does business in different markets under a common administrative or financial control … its members are … linked by relations of interpersonal trust on the basis of a similar personal, ethnic or commercial background' (Leff, 1978: 673) .

'The group pattern of industrial organization is readily understood as a microeconomic response to well-known conditions of market failure in the less developed countries, especially imperfect markets in capital and intermediate products' (Leff, 1978: 666).

'Only the formation of a central administrative or corporate office can permit the [business] group as a whole to become more than the sum of its parts' (Chandler, 1982: 4).

'Business groups, if they are to become efficient, must eventually move toward the multidivisional form … [Thus, the] most important single event in the history of an industrial group is when those who guide its destinies shift from attempting to achieve market control through contractual cooperation to achieve it through administrative efficiency' (Chandler, 1982: 23).

'Business houses … [are highlighted by]…a multiplicity of relationship among group members … [I]n each of these houses, strong social ties of family, caste, religion, language, ethnicity and region reinforced financial and organizational linkages among affiliated enterprises' (Encarnation, 1989: 45).

'What is a business group? … As a rule that business groups are composed of a set of legally independent firms which may or may not have economic or fiscal relationships among themselves and which normally have no overarching accounting or management system that coordinate the activity of member firms. In some cases, all the firms in the group are at least partially owned by a core firm, sometimes a holding company, a bank or a key manufacturing firm. At other times an individual or small group of individuals sometimes, a family owns or controls all the firms in the group' (Hamilton, Zeile and Kim, 1990: 107).

'A collection of firms bound together in some formal and/or informal ways' (Granovetter, 1994: 454).

'I want to include under the heading of "business groups" sets of firms that are integrated neither completely nor barely at all; many such groups operate in the middle range of coalitions and federations – forms that some business historians such as Alfred Chandler (1977, 1990) have treated as transitional and unstable, at least in capital intensive industries, where, in his accounts, they must give way to the greater efficiency of large, integrated firms. It is in this middle range of organization among firms that I believe a theoretical treatment is most needed and least available' (Granovetter, 1995: 95–100).

'Business groups formed by interlocking directorates, cross shareholdings, family ties or other means is a kind of semi organization serving a resource allocation function somewhere in between the perfect market in the self-contained organization' (Wong, 1996: 88).

'An organizational form characterized by diversification across a wide range of businesses, partial financial interlocks among them, and, in many cases, familial control' (Ghemawat and Khanna, 1998: 35).

'A set of firms which though legally independent, are bound together by a constellation of formal and informal ties and are accustomed to taking coordinated action' (Khanna and Rivkin, 2001: 47).

'A collection of formally independent firms under single common administrative and financial control, that are owned and controlled by certain families' (Chang and Hong, 2002: 266).

'A corporate organization where a large number of firms are linked through stock pyramids and cross-ownership' (Claessens, Fan and Lang, 2002: 1).

'A diverse set of businesses, often initiated by a single family, and bound together by equity cross-ownership and common board membership' (Fisman and Khanna, 2004: 609).

'A collection of legally independent firms that are bound by economic (such as ownership, financial, and commercial) and social (such as family, kinship, and friendship) ties' (Yiu, Bruton and Lu, 2005).

'Business groups are sets of legally separate firms bound together in persistent formal and/or informal ways. The level of binding is intermediate between and should be contrasted to two extremes that are not business groups: sets of firms linked merely by short term strategic alliances and those legally consolidated into a single entity' (Granovetter, 2005: 428).

'Diversified business groups have two key characteristics: they are diversified across distinct markets, and they include a large number of member firms in a formal group. The most salient features of group networks involve a group governance system under girded by varying and ever-changing mixes of director interlocks, mutual equity ownership, debt relationships, trade relationships, personal exchangers, political ties with state actors, and social ties among key players' (Abegaz, 2005: 378).

'Business groups pursue related diversification under centralised control' (Chang, 2006a: 1).

Country-specific definitions

'The definition of group membership is country-specific, i.e., there is no unified approach to recording group affiliation. In Korea, for example, we use data provided by the Korean Fair Trade Commission, which defines group-affiliated firms as those which are owned at least 30% by other firms in the same group. In contrast, the definition of Indonesian and Thai business groups is based on whether the controlling family is the largest shareholder in the firm, irrespective of the actual level of holding. For Chile, we define business groups based on the lists provided by the Superintendencia' (Claessens, Djankov and Klapper, 2000c).

China: 'Business groups are coalitions of firms from multiple industries that interact the over long periods of time and are distinguished by elaborate interfirm networks of lending, trade, ownership, and social relations. The organizational structure of the business group resembles a conglomerate, but relatively exclusive internal relations make the group highly stable and resistant to reorganisation' (Keister, 2001: 336).

China: 'Business groups are coalitions of firms bound together by varying degrees of legal and social collection, that transact in several markets under the control of the dominant, or core, firm' (Keister, 1998: 405).

India: 'Group firms in India are often linked together through the ownership of equity shares. In most cases the controlling shareholder is a family' (Bertrand, Mehta and Mullainathan, 2002).

Japan: 'Japanese business groups are best defined as clusters of firms linked through overlapping ties of shareholding, debt, interlocking directors, and dispatch of personnel at other levels, shared history, membership in groupwide clubs and councils, and often shared brands' (Ahmadjian, 2006: 30).

Indonesia: 'The Indonesian business group is virtually interchangeable with "conglomerate". Indonesian business groups are comprised of strategically and technologically unrelated companies. Regardless of how diversified they are most Indonesian business groups are controlled and managed by their founders and the founders' families and long-time friends' (Hanani, 2006: 179).

Turkey: 'A business group is defined as having group members operating in more than two industries where each industry is assigned a two digit SIC code' (Gunduz and Tatoglu, 2003: 50).

Appendix B:
The problem of business groups performance measurement

Accounting data distortions

In some emerging markets, generally accepted accounting practices have not been developed. If firm reporting requirements exist, they are often minimal or weakly enforced. In addition, factors such as inflation and currency instability make stable asset evaluations difficult. In these circumstances, distortions and deliberate accounting manipulations seem likely as firms report financial data in a manner that suits their own interests. Without independent verification it is difficult to know which firms are manipulating data and which are reporting reliably.

Capital market inefficiency

The validity of capital market measures of performance depends on strong assumptions about market efficiency, which in turn depend on the wide availability of reliable information. Access to reliable information depends upon the existence and enforcement of disclosure requirements and rules governing issues such as conflict of interest, protection of minority shareholders, bankruptcy procedures and the authority and power of the securities market regulator. If information is not widely available and rules and regulations not enforced, stock prices are unlikely to reflect the firm's true, fundamental value. In these circumstances, the assumption that the market operates efficiently becomes problematic. Indeed, some business groups have been designed to suppress the impact of capital market forces on firm behaviour.

Business groups may pursue non-financial goals

In the absence of meaningful or reliable financial or accounting measures, two metrics that are more readily available may hold a special appeal as indicators of performance. These are the absolute size of the group's revenues, and the rate of revenue growth over time. Increasing the size of the firm may be viewed as a legitimate goal because in many contexts, the large firm size is valued for its own sake (Granovetter, 1994). Economists have also noted that the size of an enterprise is frequently positively related to factors such as senior management compensation, perks and social status. In other cases, the state may not require firms to maximise financial performance but expects them to focus on other issues such as building industrial capacity or maintaining employment levels.

Performance related to external factors

The successful performance of a business group may be attributable to factors unrelated to group affiliation. Many Asian governments have adopted specific policies designed to favour business group formation. In these circumstances economic and commercial success may be due to factors such as provision subsidies, soft loans from government, protection from competition, or exclusive access to government-created monopolies and contracts.

Incentives to manipulate performance data

Dishonest bureaucrats and state officials often possess the authority to levy fees and discretionary taxes in emerging markets. Successful firms can be targeted and coerced into making special contributions to state funds. These practices provide owners with additional incentives to disguise profits and evade tax liabilities and, consequently, the true financial performance of the firm may be hidden.

Incentives for owners to extract revenues

Negative business group practices such as looting of affiliates, transfer pricing, related party transactions and tunnelling will systematically understate the performance of funds located in the lower echelons of a group pyramid. If the ultimate holding company at the peak of a pyramid is a private firm that is not required to report financial results, then we may be unable to form a true picture of the group or affiliate performance. The true performance of the publicly-listed firms in the pyramid will be understated by practices such as tunnelling and expropriation.

Cross-subsidisation and insurance effects

The positive practices of business groups, such as the development and support of new enterprises through cross-subsidisation and the continuing protection of underperforming firms via insurance transfers, will make underperforming firms appear to do well while comparatively strong firms will appear to be weaker. If practices that distort the true financial performance of a firm are prevalent among business group affiliates, academic studies that seek to estimate the effect of business group membership upon a firm's financial performance may be systematically misleading. Several additional factors can also limit the conclusions and reliability of academic studies of business group performance. These factors are selection bias, endogeneity and difficulties in determining business group membership.

Selection bias

Many studies rely upon data provided by data collection organisations such as Datastream International and Worldscope. Typically these organisations collect accounting information for only the largest and most prominent firms in Asian economies and therefore their data may not be wholly representative of business group performance in a particular economy.

Endogeneity

The implied assumption of many studies is that joining a business group will provide a firm with resources and benefits that will improve its performance. Endogeneity refers to the possibility of a reverse causality, specifically, that high-performing firms are retained or acquired for affiliation to business groups, while underperformers are spun-off. In a context characterised by a lack of transparency, information asymmetries and the inability to detect opportunism, it is possible that opaque and financially complex business groups may more readily spin-off their underperforming business affiliates units (Dewenter, 2000). It is also believed that politically connected insiders may enjoy privileged access to information that can be used to acquire independent businesses with good prospects on favourable terms. Endogeneity is unlikely to be a problem when business group affiliation is stable with firms remaining loyal to a group for long periods. Endogeneity may be a more important factor in groups in which stakes in firms are frequently bought and sold, or during periods of restructuring, such as occurred in Korea following in the Asian financial crisis.

Measuring group affiliation

Many empirical studies of business groups make simple binary distinctions between group and non-group affiliation. However, binary measures are unlikely to be sufficiently rich to capture the power-dependent relationships found among members of the business group. Conceptual studies suggest that group affiliation is more complex; it is characterised by multiple linkage mechanisms and some firms may be core members while others remain largely peripheral to the group's affairs.

Bibliography

Abegglen, J. and Stalk, G. (1985) *Kaisha: the Japanese Corporation*, New York: Basic Books.

Abegaz, B. (2005) 'The diversified business group as an innovative organizational model for large state-enterprise reform in China and Vietnam', *International Journal of Entrepreneurship and Innovation Management* 5: 379–99.

Ahmadjian, C. (2006) 'Japanese business groups: continuity in the face of change', in S.-J. Chang (ed.) *Business Groups in East Asia: Financial Crisis, Restructuring, and New Growth*, Oxford: Oxford University Press, pp. 29–51.

Ahmadjian, C. and Lincoln, J. R. (2001) 'Keiretsu, governance and learning: Case studies from the Japanese automotive industry', *Organization Science* 12: 683–701.

Ahmadjian, C. and Robinson, P. (2001) 'Safety in numbers: Downsizing and the deinstitutionalization of permanent employment in Japan', *Administrative Science Quarterly* 46: 622–58.

Alchian, A. A. and Demsetz, H. (1972) 'Production, information costs, and economic organization', *American Economic Review* 62: 777–95.

Allen, C. G. and Donnithorne, A. (1957) *Western Enterprise in Indonesia and Malaya*, London: Allen and Unwin.

Almeida, H. and Wolfenzon, D. (2006) 'Should business groups be dismantled? The equilibrium costs of efficient internal capital markets', *Journal of Financial Economics* 79: 99–144.

Amit, R. and Villalonga, B. (2004) 'How do family ownership, control, and management affect firm value?' *Journal of Financial Economics*, 80: 385–417.

Amsden, A. (1989) *Asia's Next Giant: South Korea and Late Industrialization*, New York: Oxford University Press.

Amsden, A. H. (1997) *South Korea: Enterprising Groups and Entrepreneurial Government*, Cambridge: Cambridge University Press.

Amsden, A. H. and Euh, Y.-D. (1993) 'South Korea's 1980s financial reforms: Good-bye financial repression (maybe), hello new institutional restraints', *World Development* 21: 379–90.

Anderson, R. C. and Reeb, D. M. (2003) 'Founding family ownership and firm performance: Evidence from the S&P 500', *Journal of Finance* 58: 1301–28.

Aoki, M. (1984) *The Co-operative Game Theory of the Firm*, Cambridge: Cambridge University Press.

Aoki, M. (1988) *Information, Incentives, and Bargaining in the Japanese Economy*, New York: Cambridge University Press.

Au, K., Peng, M. W. and Wang, D. (2000) 'Interlocking directorates, firm strategies, and performance in Hong Kong: towards a research agenda', *Asia Pacific Journal of Management* 17: 29–47.

Azuni, K. and Macmillan, C. J. (1975) 'Culture and organization structure: a comparison of Japanese and British organization structure'. *International Studies of Management and Organization* 5: 35–47.

Backman, M. (1999) *Asian Eclipse: Exposing the Darkside of Business in Asia*, Singapore: Wiley.

Beamish, P. and Delios, A. (2005) 'Selling China: looking back and looking forward', *Management and Organization Review* 1: 309–13.

Bebchuk, L. A. and Roe, M. J. (1999) *A Theory of Path Dependence in Corporate Governance and Ownership*, New York: Columbia Law School Center for Law and Economics.

Bertrand, M., Mehta, P. and Mullainathan, S. (2002) 'Ferreting out tunneling: an application to Indian business groups', *Quarterly Journal of Economics* 117: 121–48.

Bertrand, M., Johnson, S., Samphantharak, K. and Schoar, A. (2004) 'Mixing family with business: a study of Thai business groups and the families behind them', working paper, MIT Sloan School of Management.

Best, M. (1990) *The New Industrial Competition: Institutions of Industrial Restructuring*, Cambridge, MA: Harvard University Press.

Biggart, N. W. (1998) 'Deep finance: The organizational bases of South Korea's financial collapse', *Journal of Management Inquiry* 7: 311–20.

Biggart, N. W. and Hamilton, G. G. (1992) 'On the limits of a firm-based theory to explain business networks: The Western bias of neoclassical economics', in N. Nohria and R. G. Eccles (eds) *Networks and Organizations: Structure, Form and Action*, Boston, MA: Harvard Business School Press, pp. 471–90.

Bloom, M. D. H. (1994) 'Globalization and the Korean electronics industry; A Chandlerian perspective', in H. Schutte (ed.) *The Global Competitiveness of the Asian Firm*, New York: St. Martin's Press, pp. 138–52.

Boisot, M. and Child, J. (1996) 'From fiefs to clans and network capitalism: Explaining China's emerging economic order', *Administrative Science Quarterly* 41: 600–29.

Boyer, R. and Yamada, T. (2000) *Japanese Capitalism in Crisis: A Regulationist Interpretation*, London and New York: Routledge.

Braudel, F. (1979) *Civilization and Capitalism 15th–18th Century: The Wheels of Commerce*, London: Harper and Row.

Bremner, B., Thornton, E. and Kunii, I. M. (1999) 'Mitsubishi: fall of a keiretsu', available at: *http://www.businessweek.com/1999/99_11/b3620009.htm* (accessed 26 January 2008).

Brown, R. A. (1995) 'Introduction: Chinese business in an institutional and historical perspective', in R. A. Brown (ed.) *Chinese Business Enterprise in Asia*, London: Routledge, pp. 1–26.

Brown, R. A. (2000) *Chinese Big Business and the Wealth of Asian Nations*, Basingstoke and New York: Palgrave.

Carney, M. (1997) 'State development strategies for small enterprises: the roll of structural service agencies', *International Journal of Innovation Management* 1: 151–72.

Carney, M. (1998a) 'The competitiveness of networked production: the role of asset specificity and trust', *Journal of Management Studies* 35: 457–480.

Carney, M. (1998b) 'A management capacity constraint? Barriers to the development of the Chinese family business', *Asia-Pacific Journal of Management* 15: 1–25.

Carney, M. (2005) 'Corporate governance and competitive advantage in family-controlled firms', *Entrepreneurship: Theory and Practice* 29: 249–65.

Carney, M. and Davies, H. (1999) 'From entrepot to entrepot via merchant manufacturing: adaptive mechanisms, organizational capabilities and the structure of the Hong Kong economy', *Asia Pacific Business Review* 6: 13–32.

Carney, M. and Farashahi, M. (2006) 'Transnational institutions in developing countries: the case of Iranian civil aviation', *Organization Studies* 27: 53–77.

Carney, M. and Gedajlovic, E. (1991) 'Vertical integration in franchise systems: agency theory and resource explanations', *Strategic Management Journal* 12: 607–29.

Carney, M. and Gedajlovic, E. (2000) 'East Asian financial systems and the transition from investment-driven to innovation-driven economic development', *International Journal of Innovation Management* 4: 253–76.

Carney, M. and Gedajlovic, E. (2001) 'Corporate governance and firm capabilities: a comparison of managerial, alliance, and personal capitalisms', *Asia Pacific Journal of Management* 18: 337–56.

Carney, M. and Gedajlovic, E. (2002a) 'The co-evolution of institutional environments and organizational strategies: the rise of family business groups in the ASEAN region', *Organization Studies* 23: 1–31.

Carney, M. and Gedajlovic, E. (2002b) 'The coupling of ownership and control and the allocation of financial resources: evidence from Hong Kong', *Journal of Management Studies* 39: 123–46.

Chacar, A. and Vissa, B. (2005) 'Are emerging economies less efficient? Performance persistence and the impact of business group affiliation', *Strategic Management Journal* 26: 933–946.

Chan, W. K. K. (1982) 'The organizational structure of the traditional Chinese firm and its modern reform', *Business History Review* 46: 218–35.

Chan, W. K. K. (1996) 'Personal styles, cultural values and management: The Sincere and Wing On companies in Shanghai and Hong Kong, 1900–1941', *Business History Review* 70: 141–66.

Chandler, A. D. (1962) *Strategy and Structure: Chapters in the History of American Enterprise*, Cambridge, MA: MIT Press.

Chandler, A. D. (1982) 'The M-Form: industrial groups, American style', *European Economic Review* 19: 3–23.

Chandler, A. D. (1990) *Scale and Scope: The Dynamics of Industrial Competition*, Cambridge, MA: Harvard University Press.

Chang, M. H. (1995) 'Greater China and the Chinese global tribe', *Asian Survey* 35: 955–67.

Chang, S. J. (2003) 'Ownership structure, expropriation, and performance of group-affiliated companies in Korea', *Academy of Management Journal* 46: 238–53.

Chang, S.-J. (2006a) 'Introduction: business groups in Asia', in S.-J. Chang (ed.) *Business Groups in Asia: Financial Crisis, Restructuring, and New Firm Growth*, New York: Oxford University Press, pp. 1–28.

Chang, S.-J. (2006b) 'Business groups in East Asia: Post-crisis restructuring and new growth', *Asia Pacific Journal of Management* 23: 407–18.

Chang, S. J. and Choi, U. (1988) 'Strategy structure and performance of Korean business group', *The Journal of Industrial Economics* 37: 141–58.

Chang, S. J. and Hong, J. (2000) 'Economic performance of group-affiliated companies in Korea: Intragroup resource sharing and internal business transactions', *Academy of Management Journal* 43: 429–48.

Chang, S. J. and Hong, J. (2002) 'How much does the business group matter in Korea?' *Strategic Management Journal* 23: 265–74.

Chapman, S. D. (1985) 'British based investment groups before 1914', *Economic History Review, 2nd Series* 15: 230–51.

Chapman, S. D. (1992) *Merchant Enterprise in Britain: From the Industrial Revolution to World War I*, Cambridge: Cambridge University Press.

Chen, M. (1995) *Asian Management Systems: Chinese, Japanese and Korean Styles of Business*, London: Routledge.

Cheung, Y.-L., Rau, P. R. and Stouraitis, A. (2006) 'Tunneling, propping, and expropriation: evidence from connected party transactions in Hong Kong', *Journal of Financial Economics* 82: 343–86.

Cheung, S. Y.-L., Jing, L., Rau, P. R. and Stouraitis, A. (2007) *How does the Grabbing Hand Grab? Tunneling Assets from Chinese Listed Companies to the State*, Hong Kong: City University of Hong Kong, Department of Economics and Finance.

Chibber, P. and Majumdar, S. (1999) 'Foreign ownership and profitability: property rights, control, and the performance of firms in Indian industry', *The Journal of Law and Economics* 42: 209–38.

Child, J. (1994) *Management in China During the Age of Reform*, Cambridge: Cambridge University Press.

Child, J. (2000) 'Management and organization in China: Key trends and issues', in J. T. Li, A. S. Tsui and E. Weldon (eds) *Management and Organizations in the Chinese Context*, Basingstoke: Macmillan, pp. 33–62.

Chiu, Y. H. (2002) 'The impact of conglomerate firm diversification on corporate performance: An empirical study in Taiwan', *International Journal of Management* 19: 231–7.

Chu, T. C. and MacMurray, T. (1993) 'The road ahead for Asia's leading conglomerates', *McKinsey Quarterly* 3: 117–26.

Chu, W. (2004) 'Are group-affiliated firms really more profitable than nonaffiliated?', *Small Business Economics* 22: 391–405.

Chu, Y. (1994) *The Re-alignment of Business-Government Relations and Regime Transition in Taiwan*, Ithaca, NY: Cornell University Press.

Chua, A. (2003) *World on Fire: How Exporting Free Market Democracy Breeds Ethnic Hatred and Global Instability*, New York: Doubleday.

Chung, C. N. (2001) 'Markets, culture and institutions: the emergence of large business groups in Taiwan, 1950–1970', *Journal of Management Studies* 38: 719–45.

Chung, C. N. (2003) 'Managerial structure of business groups in Taiwan: the inner circle system and its social organisation', *The Developing Economies* 41: 37–64.

Chung, C. N. (2005) 'Beyond guanxi: network contingencies in Taiwanese business groups', *Organization Studies* 27: 461–89.

Chung, C. N. and Mahmood, I. (2006) ,Taiwan business groups: steady growth in institutional transition', in S. J. Chang (ed.) *Business Groups in East Asia: Financial Crisis, Restructuring and New Growth*, New York: Oxford University Press, pp. 70–93.

Chung, H.-M. (2006) 'Managerial ties, control and deregulation: An investigation of business groups entering the deregulated banking industry in Taiwan', *Asia Pacific Journal of Management* 23: 505–20.

Claessens, S., Djankov, S., Fan, J. and Lang, L. (1999a) 'Expropriation of minority shareholders: Evidence from East Asia', World Bank policy research working paper no. 2088, available at: *http://papers.ssrn.com/sol3/papers.cfm?abstract_id=620647* (accessed 26 January 2008).

Claessens, S., Djankov, S., Fan, J. P. H. and Lang, L. H. P. (1999b) 'Corporate diversification in East Asia: The role of ultimate ownership and group affiliation', World Bank policy research working paper no. 2089, available at: *http://papers.ssrn.com/sol3/papers.cfm?abstract_id=615021* (accessed 26 January 2008).

Claessens, S., Djankov, S. and Klapper, L. (2000) 'The role and functioning of business groups in East Asia and Chile', World Bank discussion paper, available at: *http://siteresources.worldbank.org/DEC/Resources/ABANTE.pdf* (accessed 26 January 2008).

Claessens, S., Djankov, S. and Lang, L. H. P. (2000a) 'East Asian corporations: heroes or villains?', World Bank discussion paper no. 409, available at: *http://www1.fee.uva.nl/fm/PAPERS/Claessens/chapters/heroes.htm* (accessed 26 January 2008).

Claessens, S., Djankov, S. and Lang, L. H. P. (2000b) 'The separation of ownership and control in East Asian corporations', *Journal of Financial Economics* 58: 81–112.

Claessens, S., Fan, J. P. H. and Lang, L. H. P. (2002) 'The benefits and costs of group affiliation', World Institute for Development Economics Research working paper, available at: *http://papers.ssrn.com/sol3/papers.cfm?abstract_id=316163* (accessed 26 January 2008).

Claessens, S., Djankov, S., Fan, J. H. and Lang, L. H. P. (2002) 'Disentangling the incentive and entrenchment effects of large shareholdings', *Journal of Finance* 57: 2741–71.

Clarke, D. (2003) 'Corporate governance in China: an overview', *China Economic Review* 14: 494–507.

Corbett, D. (1965) *Politics and the Airlines*, Toronto: University of Toronto Press.

Crisswell, C. (1981) *The Taipans: Hong Kong's Merchant Princes*, Hong Kong: Oxford University Press.

Cuervo-Cazurra, A. (2006) 'Business groups and their types', *Asia Pacific Journal of Management* 23: 419–39.

Davenport-Hines, R. and Jones, G. (eds) (1989) *British Business in Asia Since 1860*, New York: Cambridge University Press.

Davis, G. F., Diekman, K. and Tinsley, C. H. (1994) 'The decline and fall of the conglomerate firm in the 1980s: the deinstitutionalization of an organizational form', *American Sociological Review* 59: 547–70.

Davis, K., Trebilcock, M. J. and Heys, B. (2001) 'Ethnically homogenous commercial elites in developing countries', *Law and Politics in International Business* 32: 331–61.

Dewenter, K., Novaes, W. and Pettway, R (2001) 'Visibility versus complexity in business groups evidence from Japanese keiretsu', *Journal of Business* 74: 79–100.

Dieleman, M. (2007) *How Chinese are Entrepreneurial Strategies of Ethnic Chinese Business Groups in Southeast Asia? A Multifaceted Analysis of the Salim Group of Indonesia*, Leiden: Leiden University.

Dieleman, M. and Sachs, W. (2006) 'Oscillating between a relationship-based and a market-based model: The Salim Group', *Asia Pacific Journal of Management* 23: 521–36.

Djelic, M.-L. (1998) *Exporting the American model: the postwar transformation of European business.* New York: Oxford University Press.

Djelic, M.-L. and Quack, S. (2003) 'Globalization as a double process of institutional change and institution building', in M.-L. Djelic and S. Quack (eds) *Globalization and Institutions: Redefining the Rules of the Economic Game*, Cheltenham: Edward Elgar, pp. 302–33.

Dore, R. (1998) 'Asian crisis and the future of the Japanese model', *Cambridge Journal of Economics* 22: 773–87.

Douma, S., George, R., and Kabir, R (2003) 'Underperformance and profit redistribution in business groups', paper presented at the Business Economics Seminar, Antwerp, February.

Douma, S., George, R. and Kabir, R. (2006) 'Foreign and domestic ownership, business groups, and firm performance: evidence from a large emerging market', *Strategic Management Journal* 27: 637–57.

Drabble, J. H. and Drake, P. J. (1981) 'The British agency houses in Malaysia: survival in a changing world', *Journal of South East Asian Studies* 12: 297–328.

Drori, G. S., Jang, Y. S. and Meyer, J. W. (2006) 'Sources of rationalized governance: cross-national longitudinal analyses, 1985–2002', *Administrative Science Quarterly* 51: 205–29.

Drucker, P. (1993) 'The end of Japan, inc: an economic monolith fractures', *Foreign Affairs* 10: 10–16.

Dyck, A. (2001) 'Privatization and corporate governance: principles, evidence and future challenges', *World Bank Research Observer* 16: 59–84.

Dyer, J. H. (1996a) 'Specialized supplier networks as a source of competitive advantage: Evidence from the auto industry', *Strategic Management Journal* 17: 271–91.

Dyer, J. H. (1996b) 'Does governance matter? Keiretsu alliances and asset specificity as sources of Japanese competitive advantage', *Organization Science* 7: 649–66.

Dyer, J. H. and Nobeoka, K. (2000) 'Creating and managing a high-performance knowledge-sharing network: The Toyota case', *Strategic Management Journal* 21: 345–67.

Dyer, J. H. and Singh, H. (1998) 'The relational view: Cooperative strategy and sources of interorganizational competitive advantage', *Academy of Management Review* 23: 660–79.

Elango, B. and Pattnaik, C. (2007) 'Building capabilities for international operations through networks: a study of Indian firms', *Journal of International Business Studies*, 38: 541–55.

Encarnation, D. J. (1989) *Dislodging Multinationals: India's Strategy in Comparative Perspective*, Ithaca, NY and London: Cornell University Press.

Falkus, M. (1989) 'Early British business in Thailand', in R. Davenport-Hines and G. Jones (eds) *British Business in Asia Since 1860*, New York: Cambridge University Press, pp. 117–56.

Fama, E. F. and Jensen, M. C. (1983) 'Separation of ownership and control', *Journal of Law and Economics* 26: 301–26.

Feenstra, R. C., Yang, T.-H. and Hamilton, G. G. (1999) 'Business groups and product variety in trade: Evidence from South Korea, Taiwan and Japan', *Journal of International Economics* 48: 71–100.

Filatotchev, I., Lien, Y.-C. and Piesse, J. (2005) 'Corporate governance and performance in publicly listed, family-controlled firms: evidence from Taiwan', *Asia Pacific Journal of Management* 22: 257–83.

Fisman, R. (2001) 'Estimating the value of political connections', *American Economic Review* 91: 1095–102.

Fisman, R. and Khanna, T. (2004) 'Facilitating development: the role of business groups', *World Development* 32: 609–28.

Friedman, E., Johnson, S. and Mitton, T. (2003) 'Propping and tunneling', *Journal of Comparative Economics* 31: 732–50.

Fruin, W. M. (1998) *Networks, Markets and the Pacific Rim*, New York: Oxford University Press.

Frynas, J. G., Mellahi, K. and Pigman, G. A. (2006) 'First mover advantages in international business and firm-specific political resources', *Strategic Management Journal* 27: 321–45.

Fukao, M. (1999) *Japanese Financial Instability and Weakness in the Corporate Governance Structure*, Paris: OECD.

Fukuyama, F. (1995) *Trust: The Social Virtues and the Creation of Prosperity*, New York: Free Press.

Gedajlovic, E. and Shapiro, D. (2002) 'Ownership structure and firm profitability in Japan', *Academy of Management Journal* 45: 565–75.

Gereffi, G. (1994) 'The organization of buyer-driven global commodity chains: How US retailers shape overseas production networks', in G. Gereffi and M. Korzeniewicz (eds) *Commodity Chains and Global Capitalism*, Westport, CT: Praeger, pp. 95–122.

Gerlach, M. L. (1992a) *Alliance Capitalism: The Social Organization of Japanese Business*, Berkeley, CA: University of California Press.

Gerlach, M. L. (1992b) 'Twilight of the keiretsu? A critical assessment', *Journal of Japanese Studies* 18: 79–118.

Gerlach, M. L. (1997) 'The organizational logic of business groups: evidence from the zaibatsu', in T. Shiba and M. Shimotani (eds) *Beyond The Firm: Business Groups in International and Historical Perspective*, Oxford University Press, pp. 245–73.

Ghemawat, P. and Khanna, T. (1998) 'The nature of diversified business groups; A research design and two case studies', *Journal of Industrial Economics* 46: 35–61.

Ghoshal, S. and Moran, P. (1996) 'Bad for practice: A critique of the transaction cost theory', *Academy of Management Review* 21: 13–47.

Gilson, R. (2000) *Globalizing Corporate Governance: Convergence of Form or Function*, New York: Columbia Law School Center for Law and Economics.

Glasmeir, A. (1994) 'Flexibility and adjustment: the Hong Kong watch industry and global change', *Growth & Change* 25: 223–46.

Granovetter, M. (1973) 'The strength of weak ties', *American Journal of Sociology* 78: 1360–80.

Granovetter, M. (1994) 'Business groups', in N. J. Smelser and R. Swedburg (eds) *The Handbook of Economic Sociology*, Princeton, NJ: Princeton University Press, pp. 453–75.

Granovetter, M. (1995) 'Coase revisited: business groups in the modern economy', *Industrial and Corporate Change* 4: 93–130.

Granovetter, M. (2005) 'Business groups and social organization', in N. J. Smelser and R. Swedburg (eds) *The Handbook of Economic Sociology* (2nd edn), Princeton, NJ: Princeton University Press, pp. 429–50.

Green, S. (2004) *The Development of China's Stock Market, 1984–2002: Equity Politics and Market Institutions*, London: RoutledgeCurzon.

Guillen, M. F. (2000) 'Business groups in emerging economies: a resource based view', *Academy of Management Journal* 43: 362–80.

Gulati, R. (1998) 'Alliances and networks', *Strategic Management Journal* 19: 293–319.

Gunduz, L. and Tatoglu E. (2003) 'A comparison of financial characteristics of group affiliated and independent firms in Turkey, *European Business Review* 15: 48–54.

Haggard, S. (2001) 'Politics, institutions and globalization: The aftermath of the Asian financial crisis', *American Asian Review* 19: 71–98.

Hahn, D. and Lee, K. (2006) 'Chinese business groups: their origins and development', in S. J. Chang (ed.) *Business Groups in East Asia: Financial Crisis, Restructuring, and New Growth*, Oxford: Oxford University Press, pp. 207–31.

Haley, U., Haley, G. and Chin, T. (1998) *New Asian Emperors: The Overseas Chinese, Their Strategies and Competitive Advantages*, London: Butterworth Heinemann.

Hall, P. A. and Soskice, D. (2001) *Varieties of Capitalism: The Institutional Foundations of Comparative Advantage*, New York: Oxford University Press.

Hamilton, G. G. and Biggart, N. W. (1988) 'Market, culture and authority: a comparative analysis of management in the Far East', *American Journal of Sociology* 94: S52–S94.

Hamilton, G. G. and Kao, C.-S. (1990) 'The institutional foundations of Chinese business: the family firm in Taiwan', *Comparative Social Research* 12: 135–51.

Hamilton, G. G., Zeile, W. and Kim, W.-J. (1990) 'The network structures in East Asian economies', in S. Clegg and G. Redding (eds) *Capitalism in Contrasting Cultures*, Berlin: de Gruyter, pp. 105–29.

Hanani, A. (2006) 'Indonesian business groups: The crisis in progress', in S.-J. Chang (ed.) *Business Groups in East Asia: Financial Crisis, Restructuring, and New Growth*, New York: Oxford University Press, pp. 179–206.

Hao, Y. (1970) *The Comprador in Nineteenth Century China: Bridge Between East and West*, Boston, MA: Harvard University Press.

Henisz, W., Zelner, B. and Guillen, M. (2005) 'The worldwide diffusion market oriented infrastructure reform 1977–1999', *American Sociological Review* 70: 871–97.

Hennart, J. and Kryda, G. (1998) 'Why do traders invest in manufacturing?' in G. Jones (ed.) *The Multinational Traders*, London: Routledge, pp. 212–27.

Hill, C. W. L. (1993) 'National institutional structures, transaction cost economizing and competitive advantage: the case of Japan', *Organization Science* 6: 119–31.

Hiscock, G. (1997) *Asia's New Wealth Club Who's Really Who in Twenty-first Century Business: The Top 100 Billionaires in Asia*, London: Nicholas Brealey Publishing.

Hobday, M. (1994) 'Technological learning in Singapore: a test case of leapfrogging', *Journal of Developmental Studies* 30: 851–8.

Hobday, M. (1995) 'East Asian latecomer firms: learning the technology of electronics', *World Development* 23: 1171–93.

Hobday, M. (2000) *East vs South East Asian Innovation Systems: Comparing OEM and TNC-led Growth in Electronics*, Cambridge: Cambridge University Press.

Hobday, M., Cawson, A. and Kim, S. R. (2001) 'Governance of technology in the electronics industries of East and Southeast Asia', *Technovation* 21: 209–26.

Hodder, R. (1996) *Merchant Princes of the East: Cultural Delusions, Economic Success and the Overseas Chinese in Southeast Asia*, New York: Wiley.

Hollingsworth, J. R. (1997) 'Continuities and changes in social systems of production: The cases of Japan, Germany and the United States', in R. Boyer, and J. R. Hollingsworth (eds) *Contemporary Capitalism: The Embeddedness of Institutions*, Cambridge, MA: Cambridge University Press, pp. 260–82.

Hsing, Y. (1996) 'Blood thicker than water: interpersonal relations and Taiwanese investment in southern China', *Environment and Planning A* 28: 2241–61.

Huchet, J.-F. (1999) 'Concentration and the emergence of corporate groups in Chinese industry', *China Perspectives* 23: 5–17.

Jefferson, G. H. and Rawski, T. G. (1996) *The Paradox of China's Industrial Reform*, Toronto: University of Toronto Press.

Jensen, M. C. and Meckling, W. H. (1976) 'Theory of the firm: managerial behavior, agency costs and ownership structure', *Journal of Financial Economics* 3: 305–60.

Johnson, C. A. (1982) *MITI and the Japanese Miracle: The Growth of Industrial Policy, 1925–1975*, Stanford, CA: Stanford University Press.

Johnson, S., Boone, P., Breach, A. and Friedman, E. (2000) 'Corporate governance in the Asian financial crisis', *Journal of Financial Economics* 58: 141–86.

Jones, G. (2000) *Merchants to Multinationals: British Trading Companies in the Nineteenth and Twentieth Centuries*, Oxford: Oxford University Press.

Jones, S. (1988) 'Inchcape plc', *International Directory of Company Histories*, London: St James Press, pp. 521–4.

Jones, G. (1998) 'Trading companies in theory and in history', in G. Jones (ed.) *Multinational Traders*, London: Routledge, pp. 1–16.

Jones, G. and Khanna, T. (2006) 'Bringing history (back) into international business', *Journal of International Business Studies* 37: 453–68.

Jones, G. and Wale, J. (1998) 'Merchants as business groups: British trading companies in Asia before 1945', *Business History Review* 72: 367–408.

Kang, D. C. (2002) 'Transaction costs and crony capitalism in East Asia', Tuck School of Business working paper no. 02–11, 2002.

Kao, J. (1993) 'The worldwide web of Chinese business', *Harvard Business Review* 71: 24–36.

Kaplan, S. (1994) 'Top executive rewards and firm performance: a comparison of Japan and the US', *Journal of Political Economy* 102: 510–47.

Keister, L. A. (1998) 'Engineering growth: business groups structure and firm performance in China's transition economy', *American Journal of Sociology* 104: 404–40.

Keister, L. A. (2000) *Business Groups: The Structure and Impact of Interfirm Relations During Economic Development*, New York: Oxford University Press.

Keister, L. A. (2001) 'Exchange structures in transition: lending and trade relations in Chinese business groups', *American Sociological Review* 66: 336–60.

Khandwalla. P. N (2002) 'Effective organisational response by corporates to India's liberalisation and globalisation', *Asia Pacific Journal of Management* 19: 423–48.

Khanna, T. and Palepu, K. (1997) 'Why focused strategies may be wrong for emerging markets', *Harvard Business Review* 75: 41–51.

Khanna, T. and Palepu, K. (1999) 'The right way to restructure conglomerates in emerging markets', *Harvard Business Review* 77(July–August): 125–34.

Khanna, T. and Palepu, K. (2000a) 'Is group affiliation profitable in emerging markets? An analysis of diversified Indian business groups', *Journal of Finance* 55: 867–91.

Khanna, T. and Palepu, K. (2000b) 'The future of business groups in emerging markets: long run evidence from Chile', *Academy of Management Journal* 43: 268–85.

Khanna, T. and Palepu, K. (2004) Globalization and convergence in corporate governance: evidence from Infosys and the Indian software industry, *Journal of International Business Studies* 35: 485–507.

Khanna, T. and Rivkin, J. (2001) 'Estimating the performance effects of business groups in emerging markets', *Strategic Management Journal* 22: 45–74.

Khanna, T. and Yafeh, Y. (2005) 'Business groups and risk sharing around the world', *Journal of Business* 78: 301–40.

Khanna, T. and Yafeh, Y. (2007) 'Business groups in emerging markets: paragons or parasites?' *Journal of Economic Literature* 45: 331–72.

Khanna, T., Kogan, E. and Palepu, K. (2006) 'Globalization and similarities in corporate governance: a cross-country analysis', *Review of Economics and Statistics* 88: 69–90.

Kim, H., Hoskisson, R., Tihanyi, L. and Hong, J. (2004) 'The evolution and restructuring of diversified business groups in emerging markets: the lessons from chaebols in Korea', *Asia Pacific Journal of Management* 21: 25–48.

Kim, H., Hoskisson, R. E. and Wan, W. P. (2004) 'Power dependence, diversification strategy, and performance in keiretsu member firms', *Strategic Management Journal* 25: 613–36.

Kock, C. J. and Guillén, M. F. (2001) 'Strategy and structure in developing countries: Business groups as an evolutionary response to opportunities for unrelated diversification', *Industrial and Corporate Change* 10: 77–113.

Koike, K. (1993) 'Introduction: business groups in developing economies', *Journal of Developing Economies* 31: 363–78.

Kotabe, M. and Omura, G. S. (1989) 'Sourcing strategies of European and Japanese multinationals: A comparison', *Journal of International Business Studies* 20: 113–30.

La Porta, R., Lopez-de-Silanes, F. and Shleifer, A. (1999) 'Corporate ownership around the world', *Journal of Finance* 54: 471–519.

Lasserre, P. and Schutte, H. (1995) *Strategies for Asia-Pacific*, London: Macmillan.

Lazonick, W. and O'Sullivan, M. (2002) *Corporate Governance and Sustainable Prosperity*, Basingstoke: Palgrave.

Lee, K. and Hahn, D. (1999) 'Market competition, plan constraints, and asset diversion in the enterprise groups in China', Institute of Economic Research, Seoul National University, working paper no. 20, available at: *http://ideas.repec.org/p/snu/ioerwp/no20.html* (accessed 26 January 2008).

Lee, K. and Woo, W. (2002) 'Business groups in China: compared with Korean chaebols', in R. Hooley and J. Yoo (eds) *The Post-Financial Crisis Challenges for Asian Industrialization*, New York: Elsevier Science, pp. 721–47.

Leff, N. H. (1978) 'Industrial organization and entrepreneurship in the developing countries: The economic groups', *Economic Development and Cultural Change* 26: 661–75.

Leung, C. K. and Wu, C. T. (1995) 'Innovation environment, R&D linkages and technology development in Hong Kong', *Regional Studies* 29: 533–46.

Levitt, T. (1983) 'The globalization of markets', *Harvard Business Review* 61: 92–102.

Li, S., Li, M. and Tan, M. (1998) 'Understanding diversification in a transition economy: A theoretical exploration', *Journal of Applied Management Studies* 7: 77–94.

Limlingan, V. S. (1986) *The Overseas Chinese in ASEAN: Business Strategies and Management Practices*, Manila: Vita Development Corp.

Lin, C. (2001) 'Corporatisation and corporate governance in China's economic transition', *Economics of Planning* 34: 5–35.

Lincoln, J. R. and Gerlach, M. L. (2004) *Japan's Network Economy: Structure, Persistence, and Change*, Cambridge: Cambridge University Press.

Lincoln, J. R., Gerlach, M. L. and Ahmadjian, C. L. (1996) 'Keiretsu networks and corporate performance in Japan', *American Sociological Review* 61: 67–88.

Lins, K. V. and Servaes, H. (2002) 'Is corporate diversification beneficial in emerging markets?' *Financial Management* 31: 5–31.

Lovett, S., Simmons, L. C. and Kali, R. (1999) 'Guanxi versus the market: ethics and efficiency', *Journal of International Business Studies* 30: 231–48.

Lu, Y. and Yao, J. (2006) 'Impact of state ownership and control mechanisms on the performance of group affiliated companies in China', *Asia Pacific Journal of Management* 23: 485–504.

Lui, T. L. and Chui, S. A. (1994) 'A tale of two industries: the restructuring of Hong Kong's garment-making and electronic industries', *Environment and Planning* 26: 53–70.

Luo, X. and Chung, C. N. (2005) 'Keeping it all in the family: the role of particularistic relationships in business group performance during institutional transition', *Administrative Science Quarterly* 50: 404–39.

Ma, X. and Lu, J. (2005) 'The critical role of business groups in China', *Ivey Business Journal* 69: 1–12.

Ma, X., Yao, X. and Xi, Y. (2006) 'Business group affiliation and performance in the transition economy: a focus on the ownership voids', *Asia-Pacific Journal of Management* 23: 467–84.

MacIntyre, A. (1994) *Business and Government in Industrializing Asia*, Ithaca, NY: Cornell University Press.

Mackie, J. (1992) 'Changing patterns of big business in Southeast Asia', in R. McVey (ed.) *Southeast Asian Capitalism*, New York: Cornell University, pp. 161–90.

MacNeil, I. (1974) 'The many futures of contract', *Southern California Law Review* 47: 691–896.

Mahmood, I. and Mitchell, W. (2004) 'Two faces: effects of business groups on innovation in emerging economies', *Management Science* 50: 1348–65.

Mak, V. and Enright, M. J. (2001) *Acer in 2001: The Reorganization*, Hong Kong: Center for Asian Business Case, University of Hong Kong.

Mackie, J. (1992) 'Changing patterns of big business in Southeast Asia', in R. McVey (ed.) *Southeast Asian Capitalism*, New York: Cornell University Southeast Asia Program, pp. 161–90.

Mako, W. and Zhang, C. (2002) 'Exercising ownership rights in state-owned enterprise groups: what China can learn from international experience', World Bank background paper, available at: *http://www.worldbank.org.cn/English/content/ownership_en.pdf* (accessed 26 January 2008).

Maman, D. (2002) 'The emergence of business groups: Israel and South Korea compared', *Organization Studies* 23: 737–58.

March, J. G. (1991) 'Exploration and exploitation in organizational learning', *Organization Science*, 2: 71–87.

Martin, X., Mitchell, W. and Swaminathan, A. (1995) 'Recreating and extending Japanese automobile buyer-supplier links in North America', *Strategic Management Journal* 16: 589–619.

Mathews, J. A. (1997) 'A Silicon Valley of the East: Creating Taiwan's semiconductor industry', *California Management Review*, 39: 26–54.

Mathews, J. A. (1999) 'A Silicon Island of the East: creating a semiconductor industry in Singapore', *California Management Review* 41: 55–78.

Mathews, J. A. (2006) 'Dragon multinationals: New players in 21st century globalization', *Asia Pacific Journal of Management* 23: 5–27.

Matsuura, K., Pollitt, M., Takada, R. and Tanaka, S. (2003) 'Institutional restructuring in the Japanese economy since 1985', *Journal of Economic Issues* 37: 999–1022.

McVey, R. (1992) 'The materialisation of the Southeast Asian entrepreneur', in R. McVey (ed.) *Southeast Asian Capitalism*, New York: Cornell University, pp. 7–34.

Menkhoff, T. and Gerke, S. (2002) 'Asia's transformation and the role of the ethnic Chinese', in T. Menkhoff and S. Gerke (eds) *Chinese Entrepreneurship and Asian Business Network*, London: RoutledgeCurzon, pp. 3–19.

Meyer, J. W. (1994) 'Rationalized environments', in W. R. Scott and J. W. Meyer (eds) *Institutional Environments and Organizations: Structural Complexity and Individualism*, Thousand Oaks, CA: Sage Publications, pp. 28–54.

Miller, D. and Le Breton-Miller, I. (2005) *Managing for the Long Run: Lessons in Competitive Advantage from Great Family Business*, Boston, MA: Harvard Business School Press.

Mintzberg, H. (1979) *The Structuring of Organizations*, Englewood Cliffs, NJ: Prentice Hall.

Morck, R. and Yeung, B. (2003) 'Agency problems in large family business groups', *Entrepreneurship Theory and Practice* 27: 367–83.

Morck, R. and Yeung, B. (2004) 'Family control and the rent seeking society', *Entrepreneurship Theory and Practice* 28: 391–409.

Morck, R. K., Strangeland, D. A. and Yeung, B. (1998) *Inherited Wealth, Corporate Control and Economic Growth: The Canadian Disease*, Cambridge, MA: National Bureau of Economic Research.

Morck, R. K., Wolfenzon, D. and Yeung, B. (2005) 'Corporate governance, economic entrenchment, and growth', *Journal of Economic Literature* 43: 655–720.

Morikawa, H. (1992) *Zaibatsu: The Rise and Fall of Family Enterprise groups in Japan*, Tokyo: Tokyo University Press.

Morikawa, H. (1997) 'Japan: Increasing organizational capabilities of large industrial enterprises, 1880–1980s', in A. D. Chandler and F. Amatori and T. Hikinio (eds) *Big Business and the Wealth of Nations*, New York, New York University Press, pp. 307–35.

Nakatani, I. (1984) 'The economic role of financial corporate grouping' in M. Aoki (ed.) *The Economic Analysis of the Japanese Firm*, Amsterdam: North Holland, pp. 227–58.

Nee, V. (1992) 'Organizational dynamics of market transition: hybrid forms, property rights, and mixed economy in China', *Administrative Science Quarterly* 37: 1–27.

Noble, G. W. (1998) *Collective Action in East Asia: How Ruling Parties Shape Industrial Policy*, Ithaca, NY: Cornell University Press.

Nolan, P. (2001) *China and the Global Economy*, Basingstoke: Palgrave.

Nolan, P. and Yeung, G. (2001) 'Large firms and catch-up in a transitional economy: the case of Shougang Group in China', *Economics of Planning* 34: 159–78.

North, D. C. (1990) *Institutions, Institutional Change and Economic Performance*, Cambridge: Cambridge University Press.

Numazaki, I. (1993) 'Tainanbang: The rise and growth of a banana-bunch-shaped business group in Taiwan', *Journal of Developing Economies* 31: 485–511.

Ohmae, K. (1985) *Triad Power: The Coming Shape of Global Competition*, New York: Free Press.

Ohsono, T. (1995) *Charting Japanese industry: A Graphical Guide to Corporate and Market Structures*, London: Cassel.

Oliver, N. and Wilkinson, B. (1992) *The Japanization of British Industry*, Cambridge, MA: Blackwell.

Olson, M., Sarna, N. and Swamy, A. V. (2000) 'Governance and growth: a simple hypothesis explaining cross-country differences in productivity growth', *Public Choice*, 102: 341–64.

Orru, M., Biggart, N. W. and Hamilton, G. G. (1997) *The Economic Organization of East Asian Capitalism*, Thousand Oaks, CA: Sage.

Osterhammel, J. (1987) 'British Business in China, 1860–1950s', in R. Davenport-Hines and G. Jones (eds) *British Business in Asia Since 1860*, New York: Cambridge University Press, pp. 189–216.

Ouchi, W. G. (1980) 'Markets, bureaucracies and clans', *Administrative Science Quarterly* 25: 129–41.

Ouchi, W. G. (1981) *Theory Z: How American Business Can Meet the Japanese Challenge*, Reading, MA: Addison Wesley.

Palepu, K. (1985). 'Diversification strategy, profit performance and the entropy measure'. *Strategic Management Journal* 3: 239–55.

Peng, M. W. (2003) 'Institutional transitions and strategic choices', *Academy of Management Review* 28: 275–85.

Peng, M.W, Lee, S.-H. and Tan, J. (2001) The keiretsu in Asia: implications for multilevel theories of competitive advantage, *Journal of International Management* 7: 253–76.

Perotti, E. C. and Gelfer, S. (2001) 'Red barons or robber barons? Governance and investment in Russian financial-industrial groups', *European Economic Review* 9: 1601–17.

Porter, M. E. (1990) *The Competitive Advantage of Nations*, New York: Free Press.

Porter, M. E. (1992) 'Capital disadvantage: America's failing capital investment system', in M. E. Porter (ed.) *On Competition*, Boston, MA: Harvard Business Review Book, pp. 431–67.

Poukliakova, S., Estrin, S. and Shapiro, D. (2006) *The Performance Effects of Business Groups in Russia*, Vancouver, BC: CIBC Centre for Corporate Governance & Risk Management, Simon Fraser University.

Prowse, S. D. (1996) 'Corporate finance in international perspective: legal and regulatory influences on financial system development', *Federal Reserve Bank of Dallas Economic Review*, Third Quarter: 2–16.

Purcell, V. (1965) *The Chinese in Southeast Asia*, London: Oxford University Press.

Qian, Y. (1996) 'Enterprise reform in China: agency problems and political control', *Economics of Transition* 4: 422–47.

Rajan, R. G. and Zingales, L. (1998) 'Which capitalism? Lessons from the East Asian crisis', *Journal of Applied Corporate Finance* 11: 40–8.

Rajan, R. G. and Zingales, L. (2001) 'The great reversals: The politics of financial development in the 20th century', University of Chicago working paper, available at: *http://www.nber.org/papers/W8178.pdf* (accessed 26 January 2007).

Redding, S. (1988) 'The role of the entrepreneur in the new Asian capitalism', in P. L. Berger and M. H. Hsin-Huang (eds) in *Search of an East Asian Development Model*, Oxford: Transaction Books, pp. 99–114.

Redding, S. G. (1990) *The Spirit of Chinese Capitalism*, New York: De Gruyter.

Reich, R. (1991) *The Work of Nations*, New York: Vantage.

Reich, R. and Mankin, E. (1986) 'Joint ventures with Japan give away our future', *Harvard Business Review*, 67: 78–86.

Rousseau, D. M. (1995) *Psychological Contracts in Organizations: Understanding Written and Unwritten Agreements*, Thousand Oaks, CA: Sage.

Rumelt, R. (1974) *Strategy Structure and Economic Performance*, Cambridge, MA: Harvard University Press.

Sabel, C. (1988) *The Resurgence of Regional Economies*, Oxford: Oxford University Press.

Scharfstein, D. S. and Stein, J. C. (2000) 'The dark side of internal capital markets: Divisional rent-seeking and inefficient investment', *Journal of Finance* 55: 2537–64.

Schulze, W. S., Lubatkin, M. H., Dino, R. N. and Buchholtz, A. K. (2001) 'Agency relationships in family firms: theory and evidence', *Organization Science* 12: 99–116.

Seagrave, S. (1995) *Lords of the Rim: The Invisible Empire of the Overseas Chinese*, London: Bantam.

Selznick, P. (1957) *Leadership in Administration: A Sociological Interpretation*, New York: Harper and Row.

Shieh, G.-S. (1992) *'Boss' Island: The Subcontracting Network and Micro-Entrepreneurship in Taiwan's Development*, New York: P. Lang.

Shimotani, M. (1997) 'The history and structure of business groups in Japan', in T. Shiba and M. Shimotani (eds) *Beyond The Firm: Business Groups in International and Historical Perspective*, Oxford University Press, pp. 5–30.

Shleifer, A. and Triesman, D. (2000) *Without a Map: Political Tactics and Economic Reform in Russia*, Cambridge MA: MIT Press.

Shleifer, A. and Vishny, R. W. (1997) 'A survey of corporate governance', *Journal of Finance* 52: 737–83.

Shleifer, A. and Vishny, R. W. (1998) *The Grabbing Hand: Government Pathologies and their Cures*, Cambridge, MA: Harvard University Press.

Singh, M., Nejadmalayeri, A. and Mathur, I. (2007) 'Performance impact of business group affiliation: An analysis of the diversification-performance link in a developing economy', *Journal of Business Research* 60: 339–47.

Sommers-Heidues, M. F. (1974) *Southeast Asia's Chinese Minorities*, Hawthorn, VIC: Longman Australia.

Steers, R. M., Shin, Y. K. and Ungson, G. (1989) *The Chaebol: Korea's New Industrial Might*, New York: Ballinger.

Stiglitz, J. (2002) *Globalization and its Discontents*, New York: Norton.

Strachan, H. W. (1976) *Family and Other Business Groups in Economic Development: The Case of Nicaragua*, New York: Praeger.

Stubbs, R. (1999) 'War and economic development: export oriented industrialization in East and Southeast Asia', *Comparative Politics* 31: 337–55.

Sung, H. J. (2002) *The Evolution of Large Corporations in Korea: A New Institutional Economics Perspective of the Chaebol*, Northampton, MA, Cheltenham: Edward Elgar.

Suryadinata, L. (1989) *The Ethnic Chinese in the Asian States*, Singapore: Institute of Southeast Asian Studies.

Suzuki, K. (1997) 'From zaibatsu to corporate complexes', in T. Shiba and M. Shimotani (eds) *Beyond The Firm: Business Groups in International and Historical Perspective*, Oxford: Oxford University Press, pp. 59–87.

Tachiki, D. S. (1997) 'Striking up strategic alliances: The foreign direct investment of NIEs and ASEAN transnational corporation', paper presented at the conference on the Asian Multinational Corporation and Business-Government Relations, 27–28 February, Singapore.

Tam, S. (1990) 'Centrifugal versus centripetal growth processes; Contrasting ideal types for conceptualizing the development patterns of Chinese and Japanese firms', in S. Clegg and R. S. Gordon (eds) *Capitalism in Contrasting Cultures*, New York: de Gruyter, pp. 153–83.

Tanlamai, U. (1996) 'Sahaviriya OA group of companies', in L. M. R. Calingo (ed.) *Strategic Management in the Asian Context: A Casebook in Business Policy and Strategy*, Singapore, New York, Chichester, Brisbane, Toronto: John Wiley and Sons, pp. 307–33.

Tejapira, K. (1997) 'Imagined uncommunity: The Lookjin middle class and Thai official nationalism', in D. Chirot, and A. Reid (eds) *Essential Outsiders, Chinese and Jews in the Modern Transformation of Southeast Asia and Central Europe*, Seattle, WA: University of Washington Press, pp. 75–98.

Tripathi, D. (2004) *The Oxford History of Indian Business*, New York: Oxford University Press.

Tseo, G. K. Y. (1996) 'Chinese economic restructuring: enterprise development through employee ownership', *Economic and Industrial Democracy* 17: 243–79.

Tsui-Auch, L. S. (2004) 'The professionally managed family-ruled enterprise: ethnic Chinese business in Singapore', *Journal of Management Studies* 41: 693–723.

Tsui-Auch, S. and Lee, Y.-J. (2003) 'The state matters: management models of Singaporean Chinese and Korean business groups', *Organization Studies* 21: 379–90.

Twang, P. Y. (1998) *The Chinese Business Elite in Indonesia and the Transition to Independence 1940–1950*, Kuala Lumpur: Oxford University Press.

Ungson, G., Steers, R. M. and Park, S. H. (1997) *Korean Enterprise: The Quest for Globalization*, Boston, MA: Harvard Business School Press.

Van Helten, J. J. and Jones, G. (1989) *British Business in Singapore and Malaysia since the 1870s*, New York: Cambridge University Press.

Vogel, E. F. (1979) *Japan as Number One: Lessons for America*, Cambridge, MA: Harvard University Press.

Vogel, E. F(1989) *One Step Ahead in China: Guangdong Under Reform*. Cambridge, MA: Harvard University Press.

Vogel, E. F. (1991) *The Four Little Dragons: The Spread of Industrialization in East Asia*, Cambridge, MA: Harvard University Press.

Wade, R. (1990) *Governing the Market: Economic Theory and the Role of Government in East Asian Industrialisation*, Princeton, NJ: Princeton University Press.

Ward, J. L. (2000) 'Reflections on Indian family groups', *Family Business Review* 13: 271–78.

Weber, M. (1992) [1930] *The Protestant Ethic and the Spirit of Capitalism*, translated by Talcott Parsons, London: Routledge.

Weidenbaum, M. and Hughes, S. (1996) *The Bamboo Network: How Expatriate Chinese Entrepreneurs Are Creating a New Economic Superpower in Asia*, New York: Free Press.

Weijan, S., Walker, G. and Kogut, B. (1994) 'Interfirm cooperation and startup innovation in the biotechnology industry', *Strategic Management Journal* 15: 387–95.

Weinstein, D. E. and Yafeh, Y. (1998) 'On the costs of a bank-centered financial system: evidence from the changing main bank relations in Japan', *Journal of Finance* 53: 635–72.

Welsh, F. (1993) *A Borrowed Place: The History of Hong Kong*, New York: Kodansha America.

Westwood, R. (1997) 'Harmony and patriarchy: the cultural basis for paternalistic headship among the overseas Chinese', *Organization Studies* 18: 445–80.

Whitley, R. D. (1990) 'Eastern Asian enterprise structure and the comparative analysis forms of business organization', *Organization Studies* 11: 47–74.

Whitley, R. D. (1992) *Business Systems in East Asia: Firms, Markets and Societies*, London: Sage.

Whitley, R. D. (1999) *Divergent Capitalisms: The Social Structuring and Change of Business Systems*, Oxford: Oxford University Press.

Whittaker, D. H. (1998) 'Labour unions and industrial relations in Japan: crumbling pillar or forging a "third way"', *Industrial Relations Journal* 29: 280–93.

Whyte, M. K. (1996) 'The Chinese family and economic development: obstacle or engine?', *Economic Development and Cultural Change* 45: 1–30.

Wilkins, M. (1988) 'The freestanding company, 1870–1914 an important type of British foreign direct investment', *Economic History Review* 16: 259–82.

Williamson, O. E. (1975) *Markets and Hierarchies: Analysis and Antitrust Implications*, New York: Free Press.

Williamson, O. E. (1985) *The Economic Institutions of Capitalism: Firms, Markets, Relational Contracting*, New York: Free Press.

Wong, G. (1996) 'Business groups in a dynamic environment: Hong Kong 1976–1986', in G. G. Hamilton (ed.) *Asian Business Networks*, Berlin: Walter De Gruyter, pp. 87–112.

Wong, S.-L. (1985) 'The Chinese family firm: A model', *British Journal of Sociology* 36: 58–72.

Wong, S. L. (1988) *Emigrant Entrepreneurs: Shanghai Industrialists in Hong Kong*, Hong Kong: Oxford University Press.

World Bank (1993) *The East Asian Miracle: Economic Growth and Public Policy*, Oxford: Oxford University Press.

Wu, C. (1990) 'Enterprise groups in China's industry', *Asia Pacific Journal of Management* 7: 123–36.

Wu, Y. L. and Wu, C. H. (1980) *Economic Development in Southeast Asia: The Chinese Dimension.* Stanford CA: Hoover Institution Press.

Xin, K. and Pearce, J. (1996) 'Guanxi: good connections as substitutes for institutional support', *Academy of Management Journal* 39: 1641–58.

Yeh, A. G. and Ng, M. K. (1994) 'The changing role of the state in high-tech industrial development: the experience of Hong Kong', *Environment and Planning* C, 12: 449–72.

Yeung, H. W.-C. (2004) *Chinese Capitalism in a Global Era: Towards Hybrid Capitalism*, London; New York: Routledge.

Yeung, H. W.-C. and Olds, K. (2000) *Globalization of Chinese Business Firms*, New York: St. Martin's Press.

Yiu, D., Bruton, G. D. and Lu, Y. (2005) 'Understanding business group performance in an emerging economy: acquiring resources and capabilities in order to prosper', *Journal of Management Studies* 42: 183–206.

Yoshihara, K. (1988) *The Rise of Ersatz Capitalism in South-East Asia*, Oxford: Oxford University Press.

Yoshimura, N. and Anderson, P. (1999) *Inside the Kaisha: Demystifying Japanese Business Behaviour*, Boston, MA: Harvard Business School Press.

Young, A. (1995) 'The tyranny of numbers: confronting the statistical realities of the East Asian growth experience', *Quarterly Journal of Economics* 110: 641–80.

Zajac, E. J. (1998) 'Commentary on alliances and networks by R. Gulati', *Strategic Management Journal* 19: 319–21.

Zutshi, R. K. and Gibbons, P. T. (1998) 'The internationalization process of Singapore government-linked companies: A contextual view', *Asia Pacific Journal of Management* 15: 219–47.

Index

Lightning Source UK Ltd.
Milton Keynes UK
12 December 2010

164219UK00001B/37/P